Changed for Good

Changed for Good

A Feminist History of the
Broadway Musical

STACY WOLF

OXFORD
UNIVERSITY PRESS

OXFORD
UNIVERSITY PRESS

Oxford University Press, Inc., publishes works that further
Oxford University's objective of excellence
in research, scholarship, and education.

Oxford   New York
Auckland   Cape Town   Dar es Salaam   Hong Kong   Karachi
Kuala Lumpur   Madrid   Melbourne   Mexico City   Nairobi
New Delhi   Shanghai   Taipei   Toronto

With offices in
Argentina   Austria   Brazil   Chile   Czech Republic   France   Greece
Guatemala   Hungary   Italy   Japan   Poland   Portugal   Singapore
South Korea   Switzerland   Thailand   Turkey   Ukraine   Vietnam

Published by Oxford University Press, Inc.
198 Madison Avenue, New York, NY 10016

www.oup.com

Oxford is a registered trademark of Oxford University Press

Library of Congress Cataloging-in-Publication Data
Wolf, Stacy Ellen.
Changed for good : a feminist history of the Broadway musical / Stacy Wolf.
p.   cm.
Includes bibliographical references and index.
ISBN 978-0-19-537823-8 — ISBN 978-0-19-537824-5 (pbk.)
1. Musicals—New York (State)—New York—History and criticism. I. Title.
ML2054.W64   2002
782.1′4082097471—dc22   2010036263

9 8 7 6 5 4 3 2 1

Printed in the United States of America
on acid-free paper

In memory of my father,
Larry M. Wolf,
who introduced me to
Broadway musical theatre

CONTENTS

ACKNOWLEDGMENTS

This book has spanned my life and positions at two different universities in two different parts of the country, and I have many people to thank in both places (and others).

I thank the University of Texas at Austin and Dean Doug Dempster for a Dean's Fellowship, which allowed me to begin the manuscript in earnest. I was blessed with astonishing feminist colleagues in the Performance as Public Practice Program at UT: Charlotte Canning, Ann Daly, Jill Dolan, Lynn Miller, Omi Jones, and Deborah Paredez, who was a terrific reader and interlocutor as well as a great colleague and friend.

At Princeton, I want to thank David Dobkin, Dean of the Faculty, and Paul Muldoon, Director of the Lewis Center for the Arts, for granting me a research leave so that I could finish the book soon after my arrival at Princeton. I am grateful for my new colleagues who have been extraordinarily supportive and generous: in the Program in Theater, Michael Cadden, Bob Sandberg, and Tim Vasen; in the Program in Dance, Susan Marshall and Rebecca Lazier; in Music, Wendy Heller and Marty Elliott; in "performance studies" in English, Daphne Brooks, Anne Cheng, Alex Vasquez, and Tamsen Wolff, as well as English Department Chair Claudia Johnson. I want to thank Toni Turano, Associate Dean of the Faculty, for her help, and the wonderful Princeton staff—Carmelita Becnel, Dan Benevento, Janine Braude, Cathy Cann, Fanny Chouinard, Paul Csogi, Marguerite D'Aprile-Smith, Ellen Goellner, Victoria Haddad, Kelly Huschke Barratt, Kevin Mensch, Crystal Henderson-Napoli, Maria Papadakis, Rick Pilaro, Marcia Rosh, Kristy Seymour, Cathy Sterner, Hope VanCleaf, Sandy Voelcker, Evan Younger, Darryl Waskow, and especially the indispensable Joe Fonseca—for their daily support.

Tracy Davis first invited me to talk about *Wicked* at Northwestern, and that lecture became the seed for the book. I thank her for her encouragement and support. Others who invited me to present work at various stages were Elizabeth Crist (University of Texas at Austin, Musicology Symposium); Sue-Ellen Case, Gary Gardner, Ray Knapp, and Mitchell Morris (University of California, Los Angeles); Donnalee Dox (Texas A & M); Marilee Lindemann (University of Maryland, College Park); Leah Lowe (Connecticut College); Joseph Roach and Emily Coates (Yale University, World Performance Project); Karen Shimakawa and Barbara Sellers-Young (University of California, Davis); Michal Kolbialka and Sonja Kuftinec (University of Minnesota); Henry Bial, Michele Leon, and Iris Fischer-Smith (University of Kansas); Anita Gonzalez (PSI in Mainz); Bill Worthen (University of Michigan); Stuart Hecht (Jews and World Performance Conference); Lisa Moore (University of Texas at Austin); Marie Griffith (Princeton Women's Studies); Janis Runkle (Princeton Health Services); and Doug Reside and Laura MacDonald (Song, Stage, & Screen IV). The questions and comments I received from engaged audiences at each of these talks helped me immeasurably.

I also thank journal editors who published earlier versions of chapters: Ann Cvetkovich, Jill Dolan, Alex Doty, Ric Knowles, David Román, Catherine Schuler, and Patty White, as well as the many anonymous peer reviewers who read and commented on drafts.

I am grateful to many extraordinary students, both graduate and undergraduate, who helped me with research, technology, ideas, and unbridled enthusiasm along the way, including Chase Bringardner, Claire Canavan, Clare Croft, Zachary Dorsey, Michelle Dvoskin, Amber Feldman, Jordan Haynie, Kristin Leahy, Jamie Lippman, Shelley Manis, Erica Nagel, Dee Michel, George Reddick, Holley Replogle-Wong, Adam Roberts, Susanne Shawyer, Meg Sullivan, and Christin Essin. Adrienne Brown and Eric Glover at Princeton were invaluable research assistants during my final-stage research.

I appreciate the librarians and archivists who guided me through the process: Beth Kerr at the Fine Arts Library at UT-Austin, Helen Adair at the Harry Ransom Center at UT-Austin, and Kevin Winkler, Jeremy Megraw, and Tom Lisanti at the New York Public Library.

I've had the amazing good fortune to meet musical theatre artists whose generous reflections on the artistic process have inspired me and expanded my thinking: Thomas Kail, James Lapine, John Rando, Stephen Schwartz, Jeffrey Seller, and John Weidman. I also owe huge thanks to Michael Cole for all of his help.

My dear friends and colleagues in "musical theatre land" have been bouncing these ideas around with me for years, and their work and intellectual generosity has profoundly influenced me. I thank Steven Adler, James Bueller, Liza Gennaro, Barbara Grossman, Mary Jo Lodge, Mitchell Morris, Becca Rugg, Carol Oja, and Jessica Sternfeld, as well as those who read and responded to chapter drafts: Jonathan Burston, Andrea Levine, Ann Pellegrini, Korey Rothman, Susan B. Russell, and Liz Wollman. David Román has been a helpful, supportive, critical reader since day one. David Savran read the whole manuscript and offered comments that completely altered its shape. Ray Knapp has been a crucial sounding board, guide, advisor, provocateur, coeditor, and friend. Ahuva Braverman is the icing on the cake. I am grateful that I got to know and work with the late Bruce Kirle, who would have fixed all of the mistakes that I'm sure remain.

I feel so lucky to have colleagues and friends (in addition to those named above) in Madison, D.C., Austin, New York, and Princeton who have heard way too much about musical theatre: Emily Bartels, Janis Bergman-Carton, Evan Carton, Dorothy Chansky, Ann Ciccolella, Laurie Beth Clark, Madge Darlington, Eve Ellis, Frank Guridy, John Kucich, Mary Kearney, Michael Kackman, Lisa Moore, Annette Niemtzow, Claudia Voyles, Gretchen Phillips, Michael Peterson, Dianne Sadoff, Tara Smith, Timea Szell, and Judith Weisenfeld. Sarah Myers, Karen Engle, and Betsy Armstrong were supportive and smart on weekly runs. Andrea Levine and Gayle Wald are always there no matter what.

My family is simply amazing, and I thank them more than I can say: Saralee and Ellis, Alice, Allie and Jay, Josh and Vanina, Jacob and Daniel. Special thanks to my nieces Liliana and Noë for helping me with the title. The Dolan crew was lovely throughout, especially at 6 Kingfisher—thanks to Cyma and Jerry, David, Randee, Rachael and Morgann, Ann, Bert, Ally, and Ben.

Working with OUP is an author's dream. Norm Hirschy has been the most fabulous editor imaginable—encouraging, supportive, and unbelievably smart and savvy. I thank him for his intelligence, generosity, and tact. Michael O'Connor and Joellyn Ausanka oversaw the production process with good humor and impressive skill.

Jill Dolan deserves more labels and more thanks than I can even muster: my partner in life, theatregoing (I'm Feminist Spectator 2 on http://www.feministspectator.blogspot.com/), travel, colleague, editor, therapist, cheerleader, reader, editor, and more. She is an inspiration to me as a scholar, teacher, administrator, writer, and my role model as a person of remarkable integrity, modesty, and generosity.

Earlier versions of chapters have been published as:

"*Wicked*'s Women and Other Queer Conventions in the 21st Century Broadway Musical." *Theatre Journal* 60.1 (2008): 1–21.

"*Wicked* Divas, Musical Theater, and Internet Girl Fans." *Camera Obscura: Feminism, Culture, and Media Studies* 65 (2007): 39–71.

"'We'll Always Be Bosom Buddies': Female Duets and the Queering of Broadway Musical Theatre." *GLQ: A Journal of Lesbian and Gay Studies* 12.3 (2006): 351–76.

"'Something Better than This': *Sweet Charity* and the Feminist Utopia of Broadway Musicals." *Modern Drama* 47.2 (2004): 309–32.

Changed for Good

Introduction: "Defying Gravity"

At the end of act 1 of *Wicked*, Stephen Schwartz and Winnie Holzman's 2003 blockbuster hit, Elphaba, the misunderstood, green-skinned witch-heroine, separates from her dear friend and co-conspirator, Glinda, to pursue her passion as an activist and truth seeker. In the climactic number, which begins with the two girls planning to fly off together and then realizing that they have different dreams to follow, Elphaba hoists her broom, and as she shrieks, "It's meeeee!" she flies up and up and up (161).[1] As the actor rises toward the theatre's catwalk, huge shafts of blue and green light appear, extending prismatically and seeming to emanate from her limbs, as if she herself is the source of light. Her arms wide open, broom in hand, and eyes lit with excitement, Elphaba sings the last verse of the song an octave higher than the song began, "So if you care to find me/Look to the western sky," and sails onto the final chorus, "I'm flying high/Defying gravity!" (161). When she gets to the last section, she speaks, forcing breath into the words, "And nobody in all of Oz/ No Wizard that there is or was," and then opens up to sing, "is ever gonna bring me down!" (161). She sings the word "me" on the highest belted note with a flourish, and concludes with "down" on a slightly lower note, as she looks up and out, above the balcony seats in the Gershwin Theatre and to a future that, in the second act of the musical, will lead to her unmasking the wizard, faking her own death, and self-imposing her exile from Oz. As the song comes to its explosive end, the citizens of Oz, the ensemble, and Glinda below her gaze up in amazement and awe. Elphaba holds the note loud and long in this expression of ecstatic determination. The stage goes black and the audience goes wild.

The spectacular and thrilling act 1 finale of the Broadway musical that inspired and that frames this book enacts the moment when the *The Wizard of Oz*'s Wicked Witch of the West becomes a star. Transformed from Margaret Hamilton in the MGM-produced cultural imaginary, the twenty-first-century witch, as played by Tony Award–winning Idina Menzel in the original Broadway

3

cast, wears the same black hat, the same glowing green skin. As she levitates to twenty feet above the stage floor, and most crucially, belts a loud and long "me," Elphaba tells the audience that this show is hers.

The show *is* hers, which is what this book is about. *Changed for Good* examines women in the Broadway musical, from Anita in *West Side Story* to Nina in *In the Heights*, from Adelaide in *Guys and Dolls* to Lucille in *Parade*. It demonstrates women's centrality in the form as friends, sisters, girlfriends, and wives, as journalists, mission workers, students, and maids, and as singers and dancers. It asks, How have Broadway musicals, typically considered too commercial and too mainstream, contributed to a feminist performance history? *Changed for Good* answers this question by exploring who those characters are—ingénues, divas, and wisecrackers; what the women who perform them do on the Broadway musical stage—sing, dance, propel the plot, make jokes, form relationships, galvanize the audience; how their musicals *converse* with women's changing roles in U.S. society since 1950; and how they *change* the form of the musical itself.[2]

When Elphaba nails her final note in "Defying Gravity" and the lights go down, the performance contributes to Broadway musical theatre's archive of belted act 1 finales of female self-assertion, which includes, for example, Fanny Brice's "Don't Rain on My Parade" from *Funny Girl*, Dolly Levi's "Before the Parade Passes By" from *Hello, Dolly!*, Effie's "And I Am Telling You" from *Dreamgirls*, and what might be the most terrifying and enthralling display of confidence on the Broadway musical stage, Mama Rose's "Everything's Coming Up Roses" from *Gypsy*. While each of these songs in its first incarnation was a unique, never-heard-before combination of notes and words, the act-1-finale-of-female-self-assertion is a conventional song type, repeated and reproduced in countless musicals.

The conventionality of "Defying Gravity" compromises its purpose, meaning, and effect not at all; in fact, quite the opposite: conventions tell the audience what a number means in a specific place in the show. Feminist musicologist Susan McClary writes that "a great deal of wisdom resides in conventions: nothing less than the premises of an age, the cultural arrangements that enable communication, coexistence, and self-awareness."[3] "Defying Gravity" can only come at the end of act 1 after the audience has gotten to know Elphaba a bit and witnessed the forces that conspire against her, which she must defy. Moreover, the number's placement at the end of the act leaves the audience in suspense: what will happen to Elphaba in act 2 when she inevitably does come down? Given that nearly everyone knows *The Wizard of Oz*, the basis for *Wicked*'s story, they wonder what will happen to this feisty witch-girl. Furthermore,

"Defying Gravity" can't come later in the show because the plot must thicken and then resolve. Act 2 would be too late for Elphaba to express something so primal about herself, and if "Defying Gravity" was the musical's climactic eleven o'clock number, then the focus would be entirely on Elphaba and not on the pair of women, which is Wicked's larger purpose.

The pair, whose relationship the musical traces as each also forges her own identity and purpose in Oz's political geography, avow their emotional partnership in Wicked's eleven o'clock number, "For Good." While Glinda stands below the flying Elphaba in "Defying Gravity" at the end of act 1, near the end of the musical, they stand face to face, the big book of spells between them, and Elphaba passes the tome of knowledge and power to her partner and friend. The duet from which this book takes its title also has a conventional function: to musicalize the women's unbreakable bond. They sing, "Who can say if I've been changed for the better? . . . Because I knew you/I have been changed for good" (176). This book examines how the musical's conventions contribute to the whole.

In addition to its conventional place and purpose in the musical, "Defying Gravity" is built from the stuff in musical theatre's toolbox. Not merely a song, the number is the constellation of intricately arranged and mutually dependent artistic components. What is heard—the melody, harmony, orchestration (an "active string fugue" to create a "swirling effect of levitation," says orchestrator William Brohn[4]), and lyrics—however irresistible, memorable, and important, makes up a fraction of the total experience. Set, costume (an enormous black cape that rises and expands from the stage floor), lighting design (plus stage smoke to enhance and add texture to the lights), casting and the actor's unique embodiment of the role, choreography, and direction (how the whole scene is put together) all coalesce in the moment that is performance. One purpose of this book is to demonstrate a methodology for taking apart the total experience to understand how the pieces of a richly multivalent performance make meaning.

The ultimate success of the number depends on the audience, both their give and take with the actors—live theatre's essence—and their willingness to buy a ticket, an increasingly expensive choice in the twenty-first century. This book understands Broadway musical theatre to be a social event and a commercial product always and necessarily in conversation with its context.[5] In the commercial theatre of Broadway, whether a show runs for a month, a year, or a decade depends solely on ticket sales.[6] Word of mouth, fansites, blogs, and t-shirts and other souvenirs enhance mammoth marketing machines that urge tourists and locals to buy a theatre ticket for a Broadway musical.[7] Wicked initially garnered negative reviews—Ben Brantley of the New York Times called it "bloated" and a

"Technicolorized sermon of a musical"[8]—but audiences' affection for the show created enough buzz that it made back its record-breaking fourteen million dollar production cost in a record-breaking fourteen months. In the year 2003, nostalgia for *The Wizard of Oz* and old-fashioned American individualism remade into a twenty-first-century, can-do story of girl power placed *Wicked's* spectacular design and infectious music beyond critics' influence. *Wicked's* blockbuster success—the musical continues to sell out as of this writing in December 2010—is all the more remarkable because the musical is about two women and their relationship. As chapter 6 demonstrates, *Wicked* uses the tools and conventions of traditional musical theatre—the musicals of Rodgers and Hammerstein from the 1940s and 1950s, from *Oklahoma!* to *The Sound of Music*—to craft a feminist and queer musical.

Why Gender?

Wicked's concomitant celebration of women and its astonishing commercial success are at once surprising and expected—surprising because the mainstream press characterizes the twenty-first century as postfeminist, and expected because musical theatre has always been the terrain of women and girls, from its vibrant female characters to its passionate female fans. But it's not only that musical theatre bears the mark of women onstage and off, but that gender—the performed, embodied, and envoiced difference between women and men—is foundational to the very genre of musical theatre. Gender is a constitutive element of Broadway musical theatre, fundamental to the musical's architecture, and as vital a building block as music, lyrics, orchestration, spoken text, choreography and dance, lights, sets, costumes, and props. *Changed for Good* looks at and listens to the different ways that women actors and female characters interact with all aspects of the performance, from singing together in duets to dancing alone center stage, from participating in a community's formation to becoming a cog in the theatrical machinery.

Gender inflects and shapes every aspect of the musical. As soon as an actor steps foot onto the stage, the audience sees the actor's gender and interprets that character accordingly. The character of Curly in Rodgers and Hammerstein's *Oklahoma!* (1943) isn't just a happy person singing about the beautiful morning; he's a man, he's a cowboy. Dressed—that is, costumed—in jeans and boots, he walks bowlegged and with jaunty but charming arrogance. In Curly's first encounter with Aunt Eller, she isn't simply a person churning butter; she is an old woman alone on the stage doing so when the curtain rises. How he flirts with her when he enters the scene, and every gesture, line spoken, and expression exchanged, is about gender.

By the same token, as soon as the audience hears a voice, they identify it as male or female through culturally recognizable timbre, pitch, or vocal quality.[9] Aunt Eller and the audience hear gender when Curly's lush baritone intones offstage, "I got a beautiful feelin'/Ev'rythin's goin' my way" (11), anticipating the entrance and appearance that confirms the voice's masculine qualities.[10] A few musical theatre jokes depend on the audience misrecognizing gender in the voice. Mary Sunshine, the female reporter in Kander and Ebb's vaudevillian satire *Chicago* (1975, revived 1996), is played by a man, identified in the program only by a first initial. She sings "A Little Bit of Good," a silly saccharine ditty that recommends, "It only takes the taking time/With one another/ For under every mean veneer/Is someone warm and dear" (36, 37) in a musical where all of the characters are manipulative liars.[11] At the curtain call, he removes the wig, revealing himself drag queen-style, and his deception enhances the musical's cynical portrayal of the court and legal system. More typically, though, voices in musicals express character accurately: sopranos are often ingénues and altos usually strong and forceful women.

While cross-gender performance intensifies the distinction between the character and the actor, the fact that musicals communicate in multiple modes—speech, music, dance, design—means that gender is not only an aspect of characterization. What a character is like, the character type, matters, but her actions, what the actor does, matters, too. Musicologist Carolyn Abbate argues that in opera, although some female roles are narrow, demeaning, passive, or long-suffering and convey weakness, the performer sings with incredible strength. "Listening to the female singing voice is a more complicated phenomenon," she writes. "Visually, the character singing is the passive object of our gaze. But aurally, she is resonant; her musical speech drowns out everything in range." A singer, she continues, "more than any other musical performer ... stands before us having wrested the composing voice away from the librettist and composer who wrote the score."[12] Sally Banes, in *Dancing Women*, applies this schema to canonical ballets, rereading them from a feminist perspective to highlight the performers' physical strength. The score or text in dance "provides the skeleton on which the musculature of the individual performer's interpretation is built."[13] She adds, "Indeed, the plot and the performance can come into direct conflict, as when dancers stress nuances of gesture or posture that seem to underline or render ironic the narrative flow."[14] Musical theatre's simultaneous use of singing and dance can stress this performative power even more. Chapter 2, for example, demonstrates how 1960s musicals' narratives punish women for trying to be independent even as the musical celebrates the actor through lavishly expressive solo numbers. Women in megamusicals in the 1980s, such as *Miss Saigon* or *The Phantom of the Opera*, sing for much of the show, so the actor has a lot to do, but she plays a narrow and demeaning stereotype, and the spectacular scenography diminishes the actor's body. In this way, performance is crucial. Reading a scene on the page or a song in the score can differ markedly from the effect in performance. Finally, the meaning of gender in performance, how gender has been used and what it signifies in musicals, has changed over the course of musical theatre's history, from the 1950s on.

Heterosexual Romance and U.S. Symbologies

Gender makes meaning for individual characters but also in relation to other characters and their genders. When many people think of musical theatre, they think of a love story or romance or "boy meets girl, boy loses girl, boy gets girl." Conventional musical theatre form—the telling of a story through speech, song, and dance—is linked to content: a love story and developing romance. This heteronormative narrative is so deeply embedded in musical theatre's historical trajectory that few commentators even note it as a convention rather than a fact or requirement. The great musical director, orchestrator, conductor, and author Lehman Engel wrote in 1971, for example, "It should be clear that—to date—no musical without principal romantic involvement has worked. Romance is the fuel that ignited the music and lyrics."[15] (And Engel means heterosexual romance, of course.) Audiences "believe" the formation of a couple in musical theatre, if unconsciously, because the romance develops through the order of songs; musical theatre's heteronormative conventions lodged long ago in the U.S. cultural unconscious. Even musicals that buck the trend of the heterosexual couple's formation, like the famously cynical and antiromantic musicals of Stephen Sondheim, including *Company* (discussed in chapter 3) and *Follies*, muse on love and heterosexual relationships.

Because of the form's intimate connection to U.S. history, gender in the Broadway musical does more than identify the character or legitimate relationships. "Femininity" and "masculinity" are invariably tied to other traits or tropes, working symbolically and metaphorically and taking on larger associations; that is, of the binary oppositions of culture and nature in *The Sound of Music*, honesty and deception in *The Music Man*, bigotry and enlightenment in

South Pacific, for example. In this way, heterosexual romance stands in for larger struggles in U.S. society that are symbolically resolved in marriage. In addition, the specific issues that are sources of struggle and debate have changed in U.S. society since the 1950s, and the musical theatre, too, has changed, continually revising its representation of gender and of heterosexual romance to navigate social ills and conflicts.

Broadway Musical Theatre's Histories

Starting in the mid-1940s, the critical judgment of a musical depended on how well the show's elements were formally integrated.[16] When the script and the music became "integrated," theatre history asserts that the form found its highest achievement; that is, when the story unified all of the parts, which were seamlessly connected, with speech moving imperceptibly into music (think the beginning of "Adelaide's Lament" in *Guys and Dolls*), drama moving invisibly into a musical number (think Eliza's garbled speech transforming into perfect pronunciation with the line "the rain in Spain stays mainly in the plain" (140) and moving directly into song in *My Fair Lady*),[17] and everyday stage blocking moving naturally into dance (think the Jets' opening choreography in *West Side Story*).[18] Rodgers and Hammerstein's *Oklahoma!* generally marks the brave beginning of the new genre of the book musical in musical theatre history with its cast of nonstars, its everyday setting, its music richly evocative of the prairie just before Oklahoma became a state in 1907, its lyrics that sound like the characters were inventing the words as they sang them, and dances that made sense in the story. (However surprising and groundbreaking *Oklahoma!* was, though, many of the accolades piled on the musical were actually generated by the creators themselves, Rodgers and Hammerstein and the Theatre Guild, which produced the show. Press releases blurred into reviews, which morphed into theatre history.)[19] During and after the era of Rodgers and Hammerstein, the value of "integration" was hegemonic, and musical theatre artists aimed for an interdependence between the speech and song. As Leonard Bernstein wrote in 1959, "The whole growth of our musical comedy can be seen through the growth of integration, [which] demands that a song come out of the situation in the story and make sense with the given characters."[20]

One of Rodgers and Hammerstein's contributions, and perhaps their most lasting one, which became a valued convention, was the importance of a serious story to drive the show: Nellie's realization of and effort to move beyond her racism in *South Pacific*; Billy Bigelow's regret over his abusive behavior in *Carousel*; Maria and Captain Von Trapp's decision to flee Austria rather than enlist with the Nazis in *The Sound of Music*. They also aimed to create believable characters with psychological depth; even though actors would burst into song, they employed a realist acting style in the book scenes. In this way, the musical acknowledged and was influenced by Method acting techniques that were promulgated in the United States in the mid-twentieth century.[21] By the 1950s, book musicals employed a story to propel the show; the musical numbers grew out of the situation, portrayed the musical's world, and reinforced the show's tone; the songs were necessary to the plot and the characters, not simply added in for amusement or a star turn. Characters sang and danced to express themselves, and each song's music and lyrics reflected and represented each character and her relationship to other characters and to the world of the play. Finally, the production's set, lighting, and costume design conveyed an identifiable time and place.

In the decades that this book surveys, 1950s–2000s, virtually all Broadway musicals had to contend with the formidable legacy of Rodgers and Hammerstein. Because their musicals are among the best known and most frequently produced in high schools, colleges, and community theatres, their conventions have been internalized by musical theatre audiences. (*Oklahoma!* is performed somewhere in the world at least once a day.) The compositional, theatrical, and performance conventions that Rodgers and Hammerstein and their colleagues developed in the 1940s, '50s, and early '60s remain the touchstones against which book musicals are measured. Since then, many musical theatre critics and historians continue to analyze and judge the sophistication of musicals based on their integrative qualities. By 1978, though, theatre historian Margaret M. Knapp complained about musical theatre history's "evolutionary" narrative and the "current critical obsession with the need for integration of elements in a musical production," which led critics to disregard powerful "ephemeral elements" in a performance.[22] Like heterosexual romance, the formal conventions of the integrated musical developed and practiced and refined in the mid-twentieth century have become so identified with the form that their existence seems a natural part of the musical's architecture and not an invention that became naturalized over time. Many conventions of the 1950s musical are so much a part of our culture that they have become fodder for jokes, and more than a few ironic and self-reflexive musicals of the twenty-first century poke fun at those very conventions, especially the neo-Brechtian *Urinetown* (2001), which constantly refers to musical theatre convention, like when Officer Lockstock warns Little Sally, "You're too young to understand it now, but nothing can kill a show like too much exposition" (10).[23] Similarly, Monty Python's *Spamalot* (2005) finds the female principal, Lady of the Lake, commenting on her lack of a song.[24]

However mid-twentieth-century artists aimed for formal integration, musical theatre is, at its essence, built on the contrast between speaking and singing, between everyday speech and the poetry of lyrics, between walking and dancing.[25] As a genre, musical theatre is insistently, exuberantly performative, always already aware of itself as performance, even in those musicals that observe fourth-wall realism in the spoken scenes. Raymond Knapp calls the musical "brazenly artificial,"[26] and D. A. Miller describes its "frankly interruptive mode-shifting" and the "fundamental structural opposition between narrative and number."[27] Gleefully divided and contradictory, musical theatre is, as Scott McMillin points out, indebted to Brecht's theories of "alienation" and not to Wagner's "total artwork," despite mid-twentieth-century artists' citing Gesamtkunstwerk as their ideal. Audiences understand and embrace this curious, essential bumpiness between modes.

In *The Musical as Drama*—the first study to systematically consider the musical as formally and functionally divided—McMillin identifies the two defining practices of musical theatre—the genre's glue, as it were—as "repetition" and "difference." McMillin explains that repetition between musical numbers allows the show as a whole to take on a particular sound. Difference refers to the distinction between the book and the musical numbers and the contrasting performance modes that each entails, which provides the narrative and emotional scaffolding for the play. Musical theatre's building blocks of difference and repetition work in tandem to create the delightful tension between the predictable and the new, between spontaneity and anticipation, between expectation and confirmation. Live performance enhances and intensifies these pleasurable dualities in the tacit, paradoxical agreement (between performance and audience) that characters express themselves naturally and spontaneously *and* that each performance is the result of specific artistic choices, rehearsals, and hard work that is technical and repeated.

McMillin coins the term "coherence" to describe how a musical is held together by patterns of difference and repetition of its parts. Dismantling the historiographical hegemony of "integration" as musical theatre's key quality, McMillin argues that songs can come out of a situation and make narrative and characterological sense without the musical as a whole being the least bit integrated.[28] "Story" still matters—and matters immensely—but what makes the book musical unique is not its "integration" but the specific "coherent" relationships among the parts. Book musicals typically contain a logical story (or two), a unified score, and characters with psychological through lines. Nellie Forbush sings of her exhilaration in "I'm in Love with a Wonderful Guy"—the song extends the moment when she speaks of her love but in a different performative mode. In contrast, Joanne wryly observes the couple fighting on stage from outside the scene in "The Little Things You Do Together" in *Company*—the song comments on the action. And Melchior and the other schoolboys in *Spring Awakening* blare their unspoken rage that their teacher never hears in "Totally Fucked"—the song allows the characters to express their private feelings in an alternative world. Each chapter in *Changed for Good* identifies formal shifts in the genre historically, from integrated book musical to concept musical to megamusical, yet this history is one of building more than replacement, with new arrangements among the parts. Chapter 6, for example, argues that the formally integrated book musical—Rodgers and Hammerstein's model—provides the base for *Wicked* in 2003.

Context and Commercialism

The Broadway musical is a commercial, profit-seeking, artistic commodity, entertainment form, and cultural product that participates in a larger conversation about gender and sexuality. Because the musical is a mainstream form that needs to cater to middle-class audiences' desires and expectations, one might expect only escapist, pleasant, seemingly apolitical subjects and stereotypical representations of women, and sometimes this is the case. And yet, the musical also explores social issues of the day, including women's rights and changing roles in U.S. culture, sometimes directly and sometime obliquely. Whatever the subject, the Broadway musical venerates female performers and provides substantial roles for women.[29]

Musicals are not "only entertainment," but they are entertaining. Because musicals are pleasurable and fun and also very expensive and time-consuming to produce, they are in a deceptively sensitive and intimate conversation with their cultural, historical moment. *Changed for Good* argues that U.S. women's history, women's roles, and representations of women in other media have conversed and resonated with the Broadway musical in its form and content since the 1950s.

Broadway musical theatre occupies a unique and even peculiar position in U.S. culture. Although musicals originate as live and singular events, they have been recorded, revised, excerpted, and adapted into other formats that allow greater, even mass exposure. Thus the history of the Broadway musical is also the history of television and the cast album, of Hollywood film and U.S. tourism, of Disney and YouTube. Considered one of two U.S.-born art forms—the other being jazz—Broadway musicals and their film versions have been exported globally, with film musicals like *The Sound of Music* (1965) and *West Side Story* (1961) standing in for "America" in an international imagination. Broadway musicals were very much a part of everyday popular culture in the 1950s. Television, whose presence increased exponentially over the decade, regularly featured Broadway actors on talk shows like Edward R. Murrow's *Person to Person*, scenes from Broadway musicals on the *Ed Sullivan Show*, or product-sponsored variety shows to celebrate the oeuvre of a musical theatre team, such as the *Ford 50th Anniversary Show's Tribute to Rodgers and Hammerstein* (1954), which featured then-queens of Broadway Mary Martin and Ethel Merman in a fourteen-minute medley duet. Into the 1960s, LPs of original cast albums regularly landed on the *Billboard* charts' top ten. For example, for the week ending January 19, 1963, *The Sound of Music* was at number five and *My Fair Lady*, number fourteen, even seven years after the musical opened. The film soundtrack of *West Side Story* (1961) was at number one that week. The relationship among these different entertainment forms became synergistic by the 1990s, with Hollywood musicals serving as material for Broadway musicals and vice versa in *Hairspray* and *The Producers*, and pop singers' repertoire becoming the score for jukebox musicals, like *Mamma Mia* and *Jersey Boys*.[30]

The only constant since the 1950s has been economics, as both production costs and ticket prices have risen, For example, in 1956, it cost $401,000 to produce *My Fair Lady*, but in 1969, *Coco* cost more than $900,000.[31] Ticket prices doubled between 1945 and 1960.[32] While the most expensive seat was $6 in 1950, by 1965 it was almost $10 and another $2 more the following year. In 1969, it was still possible to get a nosebleed seat for $2, which was less than a first-run movie ticket at the time. In the mid-1970s, ticket prices rapidly increased, from a top price of $17.50 in 1975, to $20 in 1976, to $25 in 1978, and to $30 in 1980.[33] In 2001, *The Producers* sold "premium seats" for over $150 and by 2010, $300 orchestra seats were not uncommon. Still, throughout its twelve-year run, *Rent* sold $20 seats in the first two rows to the first takers on the day of the performance, for which some spectators, mostly students, camped out overnight along the street.[34] Proportionately, ticket prices have risen less than costs; for example, the revival of *Guys and Dolls* in 1992 cost around twenty times more than the 1950 production, but tickets prices only cost nine times more.[35]

In spite of the ever-increasing costs of producing and attending a Broadway musical and the checkered history of the Times Square neighborhood, audiences continue to flock to shows. In the mid-1970s when Forty-second Street was lined with porn shops and x-rated movie theatres, *A Chorus Line* sold out and became the longest running musical until it was surpassed by *Cats* in 1997. In 1994, then-mayor Rudy Giuliani brokered an urban revitalization deal with Disney's Michael Eisner, who brought theatre and shopping—*The Lion King* (1997, in the extensively renovated New Amsterdam Theatre) and the adjacent Disney Store—to Times Square, remaking the once seedy area. Times Square became tourist and family friendly.[36] By 2011, tourists from around the world mingle with New Jersey suburbanites and even New Yorkers who take in a Broadway musical. Whether they see *Phantom* in its twenty-second year or *In the Heights* in its twenty-second month or *Women on the Verge of a Nervous Breakdown* in its twenty-second day, people go to Broadway to experience musical theatre.

Musical Theatre's Archive

Musical theatre is local and ephemeral. Neither global marketing nor the 1990s Disneyfication of Times Square nor the omnipresence of the Internet alters the ineluctable fact of musical theatre's liveness and its material specificity. On a given night, the exact same *Phantom of the Opera* plays in ten different productions all over the world, seemingly differentiated only by the time zone and the language sung by the actors. After *Phantom* opened in London in 1986, producer Cameron Mackintosh and composer Andrew Lloyd Webber decided to open many productions all at once, and they insisted that every production of the show replicate the original, as chapter 4 explains. Using computerized lighting effects and set changes, laying down the entire musical score as a soundtrack, and directing actors to follow their predecessors' performances to every detail, Mackintosh and Webber remade musical theatre into quasi-cinema, which they defended as "quality control." And yet each spectator has a unique experience and perceives that evening's performance as singular. By the early 2000s, almost all middle-class households had DVRs or some method of recording television, and DVDs for movies were ubiquitous, but theatre is a stubbornly time- and place-bound event. Perhaps audiences value the activity of being "in the moment" even more intensely in a thoroughly media-saturated culture, which allows endless repetitions of almost any experience. Theatre can't be rewound, reread, or revisited. One must pay attention; the moment is fleeting.

Musical theatre is deeply, intimately collaborative, and the Broadway musical as a performance "text" coalesces through countless decisions of many collaborators—librettist, composer, lyricist, orchestrator, director, choreographer, designers, actors, and producers. The group of artists who make a musical are much more numerous than any other theatrical genre, so that it's virtually impossible to locate the source of an artistic choice. When focusing on character, for example, one can't know which specific choices came from the actor or the director. The musical evades pinning credit (or blame) on a specific artist. Also, a production team makes artistic choices that are, by necessity, expedient and practical. Songs are written, revised, and rehearsed if they "work" and rejected if they don't.[37] Scenes and musical numbers are deleted if the show is too long, or added if a moment isn't clear. Several days before *The Phantom of the Opera* opened in London, for example, several major dances were cut because the show was too long. The dancers, who were all professional ballerinas, were upset, angry, and powerless.[38] Finally, a first night's performance becomes the canonical version of the show.[39] Official changes—adding or taking out a song, for example—are seldom made after opening night, but the show grows and changes and gathers nuance as it is performed again and again and the actors become more comfortable. As Bruce Kirle argues, and few would disagree, Broadway musicals are "unfinished show business," "works-in-progress." In 1970 Brooks Atkinson observed with bemusement: "[I]t was not money that made something memorable out of *My Fair Lady, Wonderful Town, West Side Story, The Music Man, The Most Happy Fella, The Sound of Music, Fiddler on the Roof, Man of La Mancha,* and *Hair.* It was enthusiasm. No one would undertake the intricate, painful, gargantuan, hysterical task of putting on a musical play unless he had more enthusiasm than most people have about anything."[40]

Although I acknowledge these processual dynamics of musical theatre, the examples in *Changed for Good* are from the "original" Broadway production of each show. The characters who appear in these pages—Anita and Glinda, Charity and Dorothy, Nancy and Diana, and many others—become inseparable from the women who originated those roles, creating them for the first time on the Broadway stage: Chita Rivera and Kristen Chenoweth, Gwen Verdon and Stephanie Mills, Georgia Brown and Priscilla Lopez. The women's vocality—timbre, tone, range—as well as their embodiment—physicality, style, attitude—constitute key archival material for a feminist history of the musical.[41]

I experienced many but certainly not all of these musicals live. Memories of performance—mine and critics' and other spectator-fans'—contribute significantly to the arsenal of materials for interpretation and analysis in *Changed for Good.* Other resources, with caveats, include published scripts and scores when they are available; archival photographs, even as many photos were staged for publicity purposes; cast albums, even as they are not an accurate recording of the show because they are recorded separately from the performance and often have different orchestrations; artists' accounts of the production process; feature stories and interviews; podcasts; taped performances at the New York Theatre on Film Library (TOFL); and YouTube clips. Reviews of Broadway productions, especially from the influential *New York Times*, offer a subjective assessment that often became the historically accepted interpretation and judgment of the show. Reviewers fill in production details and situate the musical in context, often unconsciously revealing unspoken cultural and theatrical expectations, since they write from their historical moment. In fact, the most illuminating and provocative comments are often those expressed nonchalantly.[42]

Musicals as Performance, or Analyzing Musicals

Musicals are made of spoken text and musical numbers and bodies on stage, and the ever-shifting relationship among these key elements—what musicologist Stephen Banfield calls melopoetics, or the relationship between music and speech, and melokinetics, the relationship between music and movement—forms the toolbox of conventions from which musicals are created.[43]

The most memorable element of a Broadway musical is a song. As a particular event, a song uses the tools of music (notes, meter, rhythm, key) with the tools of language (words, images, metaphors, rhymes) in the context of a play with a story. A song takes place at a certain moment and has a notable effect; it is performed by particular actors with unique bodies, voices, gestures, styles, and deliveries. Within a single musical number and in the relationships among musical numbers in one show, the pleasure of song and of dance accrues through repetition, the anticipation of repetition, the anticipation of closure, and closure.[44] Because Tin Pan Alley standards were the basis for mid-twentieth-century Broadway show tunes, and because most composers for musical theatre were trained as classical musicians and learned to write tonic-driven music, these songs follow a predictable structure of melodic and harmonic organization.[45] Melodies in musicals tend to be relatively simple and straightforward, as compared to say, concert music, as Mark Grant observes: "Melody must have something stable and immutable to imprint itself on the ear and the memory."[46] Songs return to and end on their key's "home," which Western ears can anticipate as a musical line moves toward it. These musical expectations, with few exceptions, provide auditory pleasures even when the songs depart from a standard thirty-two-bar form—which they often do after Rodgers and Hammerstein—and are built into the songs of the American musical theatre.

Songs in musicals are functional in that they *do* something: introduce or explain a character, develop or expand an emotional moment, propel the story or complicate it.[47] In their notes and orchestration, lyrics and vocabulary, songs evoke the musical's setting and convey the moment's tone or mood. Just as musical numbers have an informational or emotional purpose, they provide the scaffold for the total theatrical event. An opening number helps the audience to get situated in the musical's world; characters' first songs introduce their hopes and desires; characters who sing together belong together; act 1 ends on a high note; act 2 begins with a lighter or diversionary number to allow the audience to settle back in; near the end of a show, a song hits the musical's climax. In addition, songs in musicals vary across voices from solos to duets to trios, sounding with sufficient regularity to give audiences relief from speech (and, except for sung-through musicals, vice versa). Much information and music can be communicated in a song very quickly: the common equation is that a three-minute song is equal to fifteen minutes of dialogue. Whatever their literal function, songs also shift how time feels. The occasion of a song opens space in the play and gives the audience a chance to engage in a different experiential mode. Critics of the sung-through musical such as *The Phantom of the Opera* or *Miss Saigon*, in fact, fault the form for its single mode of communication—music— and for not differentiating between what should be expressed in spoken language and what in song. Defenders of the subgenre claim that the consistent mode is more natural and less disruptive to the audience's experience.

The lyrics of a song are equally important in establishing meaning and communicating feeling because lyrics are written from the character's point of view and so offer an intimate window into the character. Even a narrator figure like Che in *Evita* or the Narrator in *Into the Woods* offers his own perspective; the ensemble narration of *Sweeney Todd* introduces a clear (if gruesomely hair-raising) angle on the protagonist's life (and death). Stephen Sondheim confesses his one lyric-writing mistake: Maria in *West Side Story*, because a naïve and unsophisticated young woman would never invent and sing the cleverly rhyming lyrics of "I Feel Pretty": "I feel charming/Oh, so charming/It's alarming how charming I feel" (195).[48] In addition, while lyrics are tightly, intricately constructed in their meter and rhyme, they are not poetry. Poetry is condensed and lyrics need air, Sondheim emphasizes, and the audience needs to hear the lyric, take it in, and think it through.[49] Finally, how a character sings delivers important information to an audience: a character who sings badly, such as Ado Annie in "I Can't Say No" in *Oklahoma!*, or not at all, such as Baroness Schraeder in the film version of *The Sound of Music*, signals one who is out of step—literally, out of tune—with society and perhaps not to be believed or trusted.[50]

A Feminist and Queer History

This book tells a new story of the Broadway musical by turning attention away from heterosexual couples and presumptive heterosexual romance and toward women. By valuing performances between and among women, this approach is undeniably queer: "As the very word implies," writes David Halperin, "'queer' does not name some natural kind or refer to some determinate object; it acquires its meaning from its oppositional relation to the norm, the legitimate, the dominant."[51] In addition to its very method, *Changed for Good* uses "queer" with entirely positive connotations, primarily to reference intense female homosocialities, friendships, intimacies, and kinships that are performed in a given musical. A few Broadway musicals present actual lesbian couples, like Cordelia and Charlotte in *Falsettos* (1992), Maureen and Joanne in *Rent* (1996), or Celie and Shug in *The Color Purple* (2005), discussed in chapter 5, through romantic songs or book scenes in which the women profess their love. But as chapter 1 argues, two women singing together in a duet, their voices intertwined and overlapping, their attention toward one another, can also signify as queer.

Changed for Good also uses "queer" to describe women and girls who tell life-affirming stories about singing with friends, doing summer camp talent shows, or performing in musicals at school. This affect-laden performance practice does more than enhance female friendships. It enables them through the doing of performance. Perhaps this is primarily a middle-class activity but it crosses race, as women who are white, African American, Latina, and Asian American have all written about or expressed their love for musicals and musicals' influence on their lives and development. Girls and women who benefit from such attachments are queer in a feminist way—they find strength between them. *Changed for Good* argues for the need to understand girls and women's homosocial affiliations and affective practices facilitated by musical theatre in a generative, expansive, creative, and nuanced way.

Chapter Summaries

Changed for Good explores musical theatre history decade by decade, from the 1950s to the 2000s, looking at and listening to what women did on the Broadway musical stage in that era. In each chapter, I put a group of musicals in conversation with U.S. women's history, paying special attention to the decade's mainstream events and representations of women on film, television, and best-selling books; that is, the cultural arena with which Broadway musical theatre converses. In each chapter, a historical section sets the cultural scene and demarcates the cultural politics of each decade, describing the hegemonic assumptions that circulated about gender and sexuality; that is, the ideas through which musicals would have been produced and received.[52]

While every Broadway musical interacts with representations, political events, advertising, music, television, novels, and magazines of its own moment synchronically, it also operates as a genre diachronically; that is, each musical builds on and responds to previous musicals and their earlier uses of formal conventions. The performative history of musical theatre's conventions—not unlike Judith Butler's now classic formulation of gender as the "stylized repetition of acts"—becomes naturalized ("sedimented," for Butler) over time, but is always reenacted, repeated, and reproduced, with a difference.[53] What Susan McClary calls "conventions" can also be understood in other scholars' frameworks, which she notes: Raymond Williams's "structures of feeling," Fredric Jameson's "political unconscious," Roland Barthes's "mythologies," Thomas Kuhn's "paradigms," Kaja Silverman's "dominant fictions," or Ross Chambers's "social contracts" to understand artworks' production and reception.[54] McClary affirms, "Whatever we label these structures, they are intensely ideological formations: whether noticed or not, they are the assumptions that allow cultural activities to 'make sense.' Indeed, they succeed best when least apparent, least deliberate, most automatic."[55]

Each chapter in Changed for Good, then, concentrates on a particular convention of the musical that bubbled to the surface at that time: the 1950s female duet, the 1960s solo female dancer, the 1970s ensemble number, the 1980s scenography, the female principal's first song and the eleven o'clock number in musicals in the late 1990s–2000s. And, of course, the decade divisions are the inevitable result of convenient organizing that is at once useful and also deceptively and inaccurately clear-cut. Every musical is constructed of conventions that have been arranged and rearranged, deconstructed, reconstructed, reorganized, thrown out, put in, revised, transformed, and repeated over time. Changes in the genre of the musical are intertwined with changes in women's roles and activities in U.S. culture.[56] So, for example, while ensemble numbers are performed in virtually every musical of every period, in the 1970s, many musicals went further to conceive of the entire musical as an ensemble project. Not coincidentally, these musicals were created during an era when feminism and progressive communal ideals entered mainstream thought. Organized by decade from the 1950s to 2008, this study goes from *Guys and Dolls* to *In the Heights*, lingering on the blockbuster *Wicked* to analyze this remarkable musical—both its conventional structure put to feminist and queer uses and the girl fans who use it in their lives for empowerment.[57]*Changed for Good* argues that gender and genre are inseparable, that as representations of and performances by women changed in the musical from the 1950s on, they altered the musicals' elements and so transformed the very form.

This book begins in the 1950s, during musical theatre's "golden age" and U.S. culture's "protofeminism." In the 1950s, most musicals used the format of a "book musical," where a story, which typically followed a heterosexual romance (or two) to marriage, organized the musical. The songs mapped the emotional journey of the musical, introduced characters, developed relationships, and conveyed the place, time, and tone of the show. While often projecting a faraway place or a distant past, these musicals touched on serious topics of the day, even if metaphorically or humorously. The book musical and its attendant conventions continued to provide a framework for some musicals into the twenty-first century.

Although 1950s musicals were invariably focused on the developing heterosexual romance, they included a range of song types for variation and interest. Among these song types is the female duet, which appeared in many musicals of this decade, including *Cinderella, Gypsy,* and *The Sound of Music.* The female duet complicated and resisted the seemingly pat heterosexual love story by presenting two women in an intimate musical performance, many of which come very close to the end of the show. Just as the lovers are supposed to be getting together once and for all, two women sing together and they harmonize, or get along very well musically. The sentimental form of the 1950s musical is more complicated from the perspective of gender than it might seem at first. Also, in a decade that was extremely conservative about gender roles, where marriage then motherhood was the unquestioned route for most white and middle-class women, the female duet offers a different form of intimacy and connection and alternative, protofeminist roles for the singers.

Chapter 1 examines the 1950s classic, formally integrated Broadway musicals, *Guys and Dolls* (1950), *Wonderful Town* (1953), and *West Side Story* (1957), which many believe are the greatest musicals of all time and the apotheosis of the form, to demonstrate how the convention of female duets undermines the presumptive heterosexual narrative in musicals first produced during a conservative period in U.S. history.

In the 1960s, the book musical was still dominant, with the story's structure taking precedence and songs deployed to enhance the emotional aspect of the story, such as when characters' emotions become too powerful for them to speak and they burst into song. But during this decade, different kinds of stories also appeared, and more musicals featured a woman as a central character rather than only as part of a heterosexual couple. Of course, musical theatre was never a hotbed of feminist performance, but the struggle over gender roles was part of the culture in the 1960s, and musical theatre inevitably absorbed and reflected those issues, too. In the generally conservative form of the musical, women's new roles tended to be portrayed with both elation and anxiety. 1960s musicals featured women on stage alone in song and dance, but weren't sure whether to celebrate them or to punish them.

Chapter 2 explores the social phenomenon of the Single Girl in the 1960s and considers how a number of musicals in the middle of that decade, including *Sweet Charity* (1966), *Cabaret* (1966), *Hello, Dolly!* (1964), *Mame* (1966), *Oliver!* (1963), and *Man of La Mancha* (1965) represent that figure (or a middle-aged version of her) on the Broadway musical stage. (Most historians locate the "sixties" as 1964–1972. These musicals premiered at the beginning of this period.) This chapter focuses on the convention of dance and movement and asks how those elements at once express ambivalence about the single woman and greatly empower her.[58]

In the 1970s, issues that were radical in the 1960s became a part of mainstream culture. Also in the 1970s, musical theatre became increasingly expensive to produce (as it did in every decade), and was no longer a dominant part of popular culture because young people's taste in music had changed by then. While songs from musicals in the 1950s and even into the 1960s regularly landed on the hit parade, and original cast albums routinely topped the charts, in the 1970s, only a few show songs became hits, such as "Day by Day" from *Godspell*. Musicals of the 1970s experimented with new formats, most notably forgoing a dominant heterosexual romance for a story of a group or community. In a decade during which Americans became more self-centered as well as more community-oriented, musicals of the 1970s reflected these two impulses.

Chapter 3, then, considers 1970s musicals structured around an ensemble: *Company* (1970), *Godspell* (1976), *The Wiz* (1975), and *A Chorus Line* (1975). Each of these musicals stretches the musical stylings of Broadway to include pop, folk, and rock music, and the typical heterosexual love story to focus on a nonbiological family or community grouping, questioning whether or not "me generation" individualism trumps gender. This chapter focuses on the convention of the song-and-dance ensemble number. Female characters in musicals of the 1970s were part of an ensemble, but they also occupied key roles, defining the overall feeling and meaning of the show, which this chapter explores.

If musicals of the 1970s were influenced by downtown experimental theatres that began in the 1960s during a hippie, anticapitalist social moment, the musicals of the 1980s responded to a new global capitalism, supported by the economic and government policies of the Thatcher and Reagan regimes. In this decade of excess and expansiveness, the most influential Broadway musicals of the 1980s originated in London—hence, the phrase "British invasion" to describe this phenomenon. "Megamusicals," as they've been categorized, radically shifted all aspects of production and reception, allowing many identical productions of one musical to play all over the world simultaneously. In this type of musical, the actor's job changes, too, as she becomes a cog in the machinery or a prop in the mise-en-scène. While both male and female actors are diminished in the megamusical's production practices, women in these shows are even less important than in earlier years. Women's shrinking position in musical theatre corresponds to the backlash against feminism that took place during the 1980s in the United States.[59]

Chapter 4 analyzes the female characters in the two biggest megamusicals of the decade, *Les Misérables* (1987) and *The Phantom of the Opera* (1988). This chapter argues that the elaborate scenography of the megamusical diminishes women on the Broadway musical stage. Focusing on the solo "numbers" within an undifferentiated score (that is, unlike earlier musicals, those in the 1980s have several melodies on which the whole score is built; thus characters are not uniquely defined musically), I consider the wimpy, pathetic, seemingly irrecuperable women of these musicals.

By the 1990s and then the millennium, with "multiculturalism," "diversity," and Third Wave feminism in the air, the slightly-behind-the-times Broadway musical stage made a concerted effort to represent people of color. A number of musicals opened in a variety of forms and formats and told stories that centrally featured women of color. These musicals used the tools that had been around since the 1950s—the opening declarative solo number and powerful eleven o'clock number—and affirmed African American, Latina, and Jewish women as self-determining, self-assertive individuals and Broadway's stars.

Chapter 5 discusses a group of musicals produced around 2000 that foreground race and ethnicity as well as gender: *Parade* (1998), *Caroline, or Change* (2003), *The Color Purple* (2005), and *In the Heights* (2008). By studying key conventional moments in each musical—the female protagonist's first and last numbers—this chapter maps out the interdependence of race, gender, and sexuality in these contemporary shows.

Chapters 6 and 7 focus on *Wicked*. Chapter 6 demonstrates how this musical is the exemplar of musical theatre's generic conventions put to feminist and queer use. This chapter explores how *Wicked* combines girl power, Rodgers and Hammerstein's organizing principles, and megamusicals' marketing strategy. *Wicked* ties together other themes explored in the book, such as race and Jewishness, the individual and the ensemble, female duets, and the dispensable male lead, and ends with the formation of a queer female couple. Chapter 7 then introduces the voices of girl fans to the mix as a reminder that audiences of musicals matter above all. In an analysis of girls' participation on Internet fansites and their interpretations and uses of *Wicked*'s divas during the musical's first years of production on Broadway, I demonstrate the energy and acuity of girl fans of musicals, and how they carry the torch of the form's continuation and its ongoing reinvention as a vehicle for female empowerment.

A Feminist Musical Theatre History: Changed for the Better?

Near the end of *Wicked*, Elphaba and Glinda sing a duet, the sweet and mournful "For Good," in which they express their love for and dedication to one another: "Who can say if I've been changed for the better?/I do believe I have been changed for the better" (176). They sing together, harmonizing easily, and the song's performance cements their relationship forever. Although they'll soon separate, they have made an imprint on each other's lives. They conclude the song with, "Because I knew you/I have been changed for good" (176).

More than fifty years earlier, two other female characters in a Broadway musical sang a duet near the end of the show that bonded them: the characters were Adelaide and Sarah, the musical was *Guys and Dolls*, the song was "Marry the Man Today," and the year was 1950.

Both *Guys and Dolls* and *Wicked* were huge hits on Broadway. Both shows featured sparkling female characters of opposite temperament and musical style. The duets in both shows were located near the end of the musical, settled relationships, made decisions, and tied up the plot. Could these musicals be more different? One set in Damon Runyon's New York City, theatricalized by Abe Burrows and Jo Swerling, the other in L. Frank Baum's mythical land of Oz, revisioned by novelist Gregory Maguire and then scripted by Winnie Holzman. One musicalized with the brassy, jazzy tunes of Frank Loesser, the other composed in pop-rock style by Stephen Schwartz.

This book's story is how musicals moved from a female duet that *interrupts* the romance narrative to female duets that *construct* the romantic narrative;

from the female duet that resists the heteronormativity of the 1950s integrated musical to the female duet that *culminates* the show's love story.

What happened from 1950 to 2003 so that the Broadway musical would still depend on the late-game female duet to do its emotional, narrative, and characterological work? How could the Broadway musical be so much the same and yet so different fifty-three years later?

This book attempts to answer these questions.

CHAPTER 1

The 1950s: "Marry the Man Today"

By the time *My Fair Lady* opened at the Mark Hellinger Theatre on March 15, 1956, audiences knew what to expect from a Broadway musical destined to become among the most famous and beloved musicals of all time. They knew that an overture would play snippets of all of the songs, beautifully flowing from one to the next. They were ready for a straightforward book scene to follow the overture, which would introduce the musical's time and place and the main characters in the first few minutes. They wouldn't be surprised by a male and female lead, both strong-willed, but from two different, incompatible worlds. They knew that some problem would throw the two together and the pair would spend the next two and a half hours tussling it out. They expected another more comic plot to run alongside the main plot, occasionally intersecting it. They were ready for some big ensemble numbers, lively dance, and lavish costumes and set design. They knew that act 1 would end on a moment of suspense and act 2 would begin gently, as members of the audience recovered from their intermission drink or smoke or toilet break. They could predict that act 2 would be shorter, have fewer songs, and more reprises. They knew that the plot would clip along, everything would get wrapped up, and the feuding couple would unite and marry.

My Fair Lady conformed—with delight and loveliness—to almost all of these expectations of the 1950s musical. Eliza's first number, "Loverly," introduces her smart and willful character in a fantasy about warmth and chocolate that she gains when she learns to speak properly. The Eliza who sings the first song is musically consistent with the one who sings "I Could Have Danced All Night" in celebration of her achievement. "The Rain in Spain" begins as Eliza still struggles to form words properly, then she succeeds, and finally the three—Higgins, Eliza, and Pickering—sing and dance a celebratory tango, perfectly fulfilling the expectations for a formally integrated musical, moving directly from speech into song and including dance in the most natural and organic way. Critics raved, lines for tickets formed around the block, and the show ran for 2,717 performances until 1962, which broke all records. Julie Andrews was launched to stardom, and *My Fair Lady* became a textbook case for the perfectly constructed musical.[1]

Well, almost perfectly constructed. While the songs in *My Fair Lady* capture the feeling of Edwardian London and express the characters' uniqueness in music and lyrics—who else but Henry Higgins could speak-sing, "The Scots and the Irish leave you close to tears/There even are places where English completely disappears./In America, they haven't used it for years!" (110)—the ending of the show is famously ambiguous.[2] Eliza does return to Higgins's house and implicitly plans to stay, even as he barks at her, "Where the devil are my slippers?" in a final tableau that troubles feminist directors as much as the end of *The Taming of the Shrew*, since the stage directions indicate, "She understands" (191). George Bernard Shaw, whose *Pygmalion* is the source for the musical, felt so strongly about the ending that he wrote a "sequel" explaining that Higgins is an entirely inappropriate mate for Eliza, and that she could never marry a "confirmed old bachelor with a mother fixation" (94). Later, in his own defense, Alan Jay Lerner, the lyricist and librettist, audaciously responded, "Shaw and Heaven forgive me—I am not certain he is right" (97).[3] The very fact that Lerner can imagine a happy, romantic ending for Eliza and Higgins affirms the influence of musical theatre's conventions, even to the degree that they were well established by the mid-1950s. Eliza and Higgins don't marry by the end of *My Fair Lady* and it's not clear that they will. Moreover, Eliza's return is entirely unmotivated and seems unlikely, given how much Mother Higgins supports her leaving Henry. That audiences believe that they see Higgins and Eliza in love underlines the power of conventions and more specifically the conventional heterosexual romance narrative that orders and ends the story of many 1950s musicals.

Many musicals in the 1950s have more believable romances, including the ones in this chapter: *Guys and Dolls, Wonderful Town,* and *West Side Story.* But these musicals also have another convention, which *My Fair Lady* lacks, that undercuts the force of the heterosexual narrative: the female duet.

In the formally integrated musical of the 1950s, heterosexual romance and the structure of the musical are intertwined. Form organizes content, and emotion and musicality pull the spectator along. And yet many of these musicals also contain female duets, which offer women an appealing alternative affiliation. The female duet disrupts the apparent seamlessness of that structure, to show not only how the midcentury musical allows queer interventions but how those disruptions are part of, in fact integral to, the very organization of 1950s Broadway musical theatre. As Wayne Koestenbaum urges, "May music escape, for good, the fate of presumed straightness. May music at last be subject to the critic's seduction."[4]

The homosociality or homoeroticism of a female duet forces a wedge into the 1950s musicals' resilient heterosexual project. In a decade known as pre-feminist or protofeminist (or, simply, not yet feminist), female duets make women all the more central in the musical and gesture toward different relational possibilities. By valuing a female couple and female relationships, whether or not the women are actually friends in the narrative, these songs perform women in collusion and coupledom.

Women in the 1950s

Gender roles in the 1950s were sharply delineated and among the most conservative of any period in U.S. history. Following a period of relative flexibility during World War II, when women were needed to fill the many jobs left empty when men went to war, employers during this era replaced working women with the men who returned from abroad, especially in factory and manual labor jobs. The U.S. economy expanded and the country's mood was confident, but women's choices shrank. Middle-class women in the 1950s were expected to be wives and mothers. Just as Rosie the Riveter's flexed bicep advertised women as workers in the early 1940s, June Cleaver's apron told women that their realm was the kitchen.

Gender roles were rigid and clear. White middle-class heterosexual women were supposed to be homemakers and mothers and to find complete satisfaction in those roles. Although many women worked outside the home during World War II, once men returned from the war to reclaim their jobs, women were summarily fired or pressured to leave. The woman who wanted to continue working, according to one 1947 journalist, appeared "thoughtless and greedy . . . , extravagant, a poor mate for her husband and a bad housekeeper."[5] At the same time, federal support for child-care facilities ended. By the mid-1950s, middle-class white women were discouraged from working outside the home, and middle-class white men were supposed to support the family financially. In his study of women in U.S. history, William H. Chafe summarizes, "Although some change had occurred, it was within a structure of assumptions and values that perpetuated massive inequality between the sexes."[6]

"Mother," both valued and condemned for every social ill, was the key identifying role for women in the 1950s. For example, women were expected to be loving and supportive caretakers and sufficiently involved in their children's lives, but not too overprotective or they would turn their boys into homosexuals. Sexuality, the family, and national security were all subconsciously linked during this period. Historian Stephanie Coontz explains, "A 'normal' family and vigilant mother became the 'front line' of defense against treason; anticommunists linked deviant family or sexual behavior to sedition."[7] The stability of the family, then, not only guarded against foreigners from other countries with other values but also protected society from perceived threats from within. Chafe explains, "Machismo, patriotism, belief in God, opposition to social agitation, hatred of the Reds—these were the definitions of true Americanism."[8] Senator and anticommunist crusader Joseph McCarthy's "witch hunt"—the House Un-American Activities Committee—intended to root out any hint of political liberalism, whether expressed through politics, art, or sexuality.

Television became ubiquitous and its influence expanded through symbiotic advertising and network shows. In the entire decade of the 1940s, three million television sets were sold; in the 1950s, though, more than five million were sold each year.[9] Messages about gender were both direct and indirect in their persuasiveness. Advertisements for the newly invented and aggressively promoted Betty Crocker cake mixes interrupted programs like *The Goldbergs*, where Mama Berg controlled the Bronx neighborhood as well as the family with Jewish wit and determination. If not a wife or mother, then a woman might be a pinup girl, exemplified by Marilyn Monroe, or a young, lively teenager, like Gidget or Patty Duke. On the edge of adulthood, these women appealed to the newly configured youth demographic recognized by advertisers as potentially profitable.

Most female characters on television were firmly embedded in a nuclear family, the social unit that came to represent the United States par excellence in the 1950s. More than dote on her husband, a woman in the 1950s was expected to focus on her children and on maintaining the happiness and stability of the family. The family's centrality was evident across racial, ethnic, and class lines, as shown in the successful 1950s television series *Life with Luigi*, about Italian working-class families in Brooklyn; *Mama*, about a Norwegian immigrant family in San Francisco; *Amos 'n' Andy*, about blacks in Harlem; *Hey, Jeannie*, about Irish working-class families in Brooklyn; *Life of Riley*, about working-class migrants in Los Angeles; and *The Goldbergs*, all of which featured working-class, ethnic families.[10] Family life also organized the plotlines on the successful shows that featured white and middle-class families: *Father Knows Best, Leave It to Beaver, The Adventures of Ozzie and Harriet,* and *The Donna Reed Show*. Women dominated the families in some shows, such as the *The Goldbergs* (which Gertrude Berg also produced), *Mama* (based on the play *I Remember Mama*), and *Beulah* (a black maid for the white Henderson family, which featured Ethel Waters, then briefly Hattie McDaniel, and then Louise Beavers).[11]

On television, in movies, and in print advertising, the heterosexual couple was the norm, and virtually all female characters were coupled with men. Still, *All about Eve* (1950) was about two women (even if one was obsessed), *Some Like It Hot* (1959) featured men in drag, and Alfred Hitchcock movies of the decade like *Vertigo* (1954) and *Rear Window* (1958) featured men together in intense working relationships. As in the Broadway musical, heterosexual romance was the norm. The few representations of gays and lesbians in mainstream culture showed them as sick or as predators, such as Lillian Hellman's *The Children's Hour* (1934, film 1961). Although offscreen, actual gays and lesbians formed subcultures, frequented bars, and created performance, especially in major cities, the official and unofficial policy of the United States was aggressively homophobic.[12] Fear of communists blurred with fear of homosexuals, and both were viewed as a threat to national security.

Although women seldom appeared with other women in a sustained way in popular culture of the 1950s—they were most likely seen in a catfight over a man—the most famous and successful television show of the decade, *I Love Lucy*, featured female friends Lucy Ricardo and her neighbor Ethel Mertz—as well as the Cuban Ricky Ricardo—one of the few Latin Americans on mid-twentieth-century television. Many story lines during the series' six-year run (1951–1957) focused on the female duo. Opposite in temperament and style, Lucy and Ethel frequently got into big trouble to avoid getting into bigger trouble with their husbands over money, food, household management, or Lucy's desire to be a performer. Because of the slapstick style of certain aspects of the show's humor, many of Lucy and Ethel's adventures threw them together in physicalized choreographies. *I Love Lucy* showed week after week the value of a female friendship. Like female duets of 1950s musicals, Lucy and Ethel, even as housewives, bonded and learned from one another. The private realm of the home and the dominance of the family and the heterosexual couple couldn't stop a connection between women.

Representations of women in 1950s Broadway musicals both paralleled and diverged from those in other media. While many musicals do feature the ingénue or the girl-next-door in the soprano romantic lead, such as Maria in *West Side Story* (1957) and Sarah Brown in *Guys and Dolls* (1950), and a few musicals offer temptresses, such as Lola in *Damn Yankees* (1955), just as many contain strong, dominating women like Anna in *The King and I* (1951), Anita in *West Side Story*, and Ruth in *Wonderful Town* (1953). In contrast to the many representations of perfect and perfectly coiffed mothers on television and film, few mothers appear in musicals, except for Broadway's most famous mother: *Gypsy's* Mama Rose, described by reviewer Walter Kerr as "the mastodon of all stage mothers."[13] Female caretaking is prevalent, though, especially in Rodgers and Hammerstein musicals like *South Pacific* (1949, both Nellie and Bloody Mary), *The King and I* (both Anna and Lady Thiang), and *The Sound of Music* (1959, both Maria and the Mother Abbess), but these women also have jobs as a nurse, a governess, or a teacher.

Musicals in the 1950s

Of all decades in U.S. cultural history, the 1950s is the decade most associated with the Broadway musical. Musical theatre, as an entertainment genre whose conventions were refined during this period of economic expansion and national pride, sustains its reputation of being buoyant and optimistic. While in fact fewer musicals opened in the 1950s, more made a profit and more have continued to be performed in revivals and school and community productions. For every decade since the 1950s, in fact, commentators have declared the Broadway musical dead.

While Broadway was lively with new musicals opening weekly, musical theatre participated in U.S. culture in other forms, too. Original cast album LPs, released soon after a musical opened, brought the music of Broadway into homes of millions of Americans. The cast album of *My Fair Lady*, for example, sold five million copies and spent 480 weeks on the Billboard charts.[14]

Television also interacted with Broadway musicals, with numerous tribute shows whose sponsors were typically part of the title, such as the *Ford 50th Anniversary Show* in 1954, in which Mary Martin and Ethel Merman performed a fourteen-minute medley, capped off by a duet of "There's No Business Like Show Business" from Irving Berlin's *Annie Get Your Gun*, first sung by a character whom Merman originated in 1946 and Martin played on national tour. The *Ed Sullivan Show*, which began broadcasting in 1948, and was a mainstay in many households for twenty-three years, introduced U.S. audiences to the Beatles but also presented songs and scenes from many Broadway musicals.[15] In 1960, for example, Sullivan aired a scene from Alan Jay Lerner and Frederick Loewe's *Camelot*, which followed the team's hit *My Fair Lady* four years later, but which suffered some bad luck, negative word of mouth, and lukewarm ticket sales. Julie Andrews and Richard Burton sang on the show, and the next day, the line for tickets went around the theatre's block.

Rodgers and Hammerstein, the musical theatre's accepted geniuses—as marketers and self-promoters as much as creators[16]—expanded their reach through extended Broadway runs, touring companies, television appearances, and cast albums. Rodgers and Hammerstein wrote and produced five hit musicals in the 1950s: *The King and I, Pipe Dream* (1955), *Cinderella* (television, 1957), *Flower Drum Song* (1958), and *The Sound of Music*, as well as the less successful *Me and Juliet* (1953). Although three of their greatest hits— *Oklahoma!* (1943), *Carousel* (1945), and *South Pacific*—opened on Broadway in the 1940s, in addition to the film musical *State Fair* (1945) and the less well known *Allegro* (1947), by the 1950s, these musicals were a part of mainstream culture for thousands of Americans who'd never been to Broadway. Because Rodgers and Hammerstein created so many musicals in such a short time, because they had countless imitators who sought the same success, because their musicals became mainstays of amateur and college productions, and because their musicals were made into film versions—the most famous and successful, *The Sound of Music* (1965)—the legacy of Rodgers and Hammerstein is incomparable and lives on. While Rodgers and Hammerstein weren't the originators of the formally integrated Broadway musical, they were among the leaders in developing the genre and they participated in the solidifying of conventions of text, music, and performance that still function as benchmarks today—if not of a musical's success, then its use of musical theatre's elements in a less or more conventional way. So intimately linked with the form and with the conventions that mark the Broadway musical as a genre, their names have become a shorthand for musicals of the 1950s.

Heterosexuality structures and ideologically underpins the plots of musicals of the 1950s. Two principals, one male and one female, are introduced early in the show by solos that convey through music how they are opposites who will eventually unite. Their divergent personalities, overdetermined by their differences in gender, symbolize larger cultural and social divisions— between high and low class in *My Fair Lady*, between law and freedom in *Guys and Dolls*, between discipline and impulse in *The Music Man* (1957), between nature and the city in *The Sound of Music*—which are resolved by the end of the show. Gender difference, then, signifies all difference, and heterosexual union, which culminates in the requisite romantic duet and then the choral finale, signifies and more importantly, performs the unification of the entire community in "Climb Ev'ry Mountain," "Seventy-Six Trombones," or "Guys and Dolls."[17]

In actuality, although the audience anticipates from the beginning that the heterosexual couple will unite based on heteronormative viewing practices, or "tradition," as Joseph P. Swain puts it, a musical itself seldom represents their romance but rather enacts and plays out all of the obstacles to their union.[18]

A musical's story of heterosexual romance takes place in a world consisting of two clearly delineated homosocial communities. Some of the practical reasons for this binary are to provide different kinds of sound and songs and stagings for the audience to enjoy and to fill out the musical's world. The actual scenes, songs, and dances focus on the heterosexual couple's lack of compatibility and on their better fit within their respective homosocial spheres, which are represented through singly gendered chorus numbers, trios, and duets. Women's chorus numbers from this era (and the 1940s and early 1960s, also considered within musical theatre's "golden age") in which a female cohort accompanies the female principal include "I'm Gonna Wash That Man Right Outta My Hair" from *South Pacific*; "Paris Original" from *How to Succeed in Business without Really Trying* (1961); "Take Back Your Mink" and "A Bushel and a Peck" from *Guys and Dolls*; "I Feel Pretty" and "America" (Broadway version) from *West Side Story*; and "Many a New Day" from *Oklahoma!* Trios include "Gotta Have a Gimmick" from *Gypsy*; "A Problem Like Maria" from *The Sound of Music*; "Matchmaker, Matchmaker" from *Fiddler on the Roof* (1964); and "There's Gotta Be Something Better Than This" from *Sweet Charity* (1966), to name only a few. The leading lady, backed by the easy harmonizing of her cohort, struggles musically to differentiate herself from them and to establish the requisite but obstructed heterosexual connection.

But a feminist perspective on the musical values the ensemble numbers and the woman's connection to her crew. While the heterosexual couple's meeting, greeting, and mating provide the raison d'être and architecture of midcentury Broadway musicals, many of them also feature a duet between women. The heartfelt duet between women occurs regularly enough in musical theatre to be considered an established element of an extraordinarily conventionalized form. Female duets in musicals from the 1950s might seem merely to provide a diversion from the musical's narrative trajectory. Like rousing chorus numbers, self-defining and self-expressive solos, and incidental charm songs, the female duet no doubt functions in part as an expected musical variation on the male-female romantic duos that organize the musical's purpose. But the intimacy created by two women singing together also troubles the formally integrated musical's heterosexual closure, at the very least offering a different kind of affective connection or possibly undoing the musical's heterosexual presumption altogether.

The Function of Female Duets in the Formally Integrated Book Musical

Female duets in the resolutely heterosexual formally integrated book musicals of the 1950s can have different functions. One type, an expression of female competition, conforms to the conventions of what I call a "collaborative duet." In such a duet, the two women collude on a plan or support each other emotionally, whether the mood of the women's interaction in the song is loving or edgy. In another type, the "pedagogical duet," one woman persuades the other to change her mind, and a lesson occurs. These songs are classified by purpose—collaboration, pedagogy— because musical numbers in the integrated form are intentionally tied to story, character, and setting, and so they are emphatically functional.

Female duets could be categorized in any number of ways: by composer and lyricist, by tone or style or setting of the show, by the relationship between the women (are they sisters? friends? Do they even know each other?), by musical key or tempo, by rhyme scheme or lyrical structure, for example. Organizing them by purpose and effect emphasizes that they are situated within a whole evening's performance of a musical play and should be heard and seen (or imagined) within the show. That they are part of the score of an integrated musical makes this issue important, too. Plenty of hit songs came out of 1950s Broadway musicals, including "I Whistle a Happy Tune" from *The King and I*, "A Bushel and a Peck" from *Guys and Dolls*, and "Stranger in Paradise" from *Kismet* (1953). But each of these musical numbers has a dramaturgical purpose; it tells a story within the musical. Female duets move the action along; were it not for the musical number, more dialogue would be needed.[19]

In short, these songs gain power because they're not in isolation. While two women singing together can definitely create a homosocial or homoerotic charge, these songs are intimate or queer because they are within a story, sung by characters in a specific moment. In both kinds of duets, the musical's attention radically shifts to accommodate the two women, and their song displaces the heterosexual couple. When the women's duet comes very late in the show, their connection provides a representation of intense homosociality that dislodges the heterosexual couple's already fragile union. When a female duet takes place early, it makes female intimacy viable for the rest of the show.

When two voices are heard together, they signify a couple, and two women's voices, in close proximity as they hit notes within the same octave, create a particularly intimate aural relationship on which the female duet capitalizes. In a given duet, the relationship between the two voices constantly shifts as they sing in unison, in typical thirds, in the same melody line one after another, or in different melodies altogether in counterpoint. The listener hears how they are the same and different simultaneously, their voices marking a refusal to be only one or only two. The erotic charge of such intertwined voices is unmistakable, palpable; they give voice to what Suzanne G. Cusick describes as a "power/pleasure/intimacy triad."[20] Joke Dame describes the effect of "equal voices, or rather equal timbres," as "homoerotic *jouissance de l'écoute*."[21] In arguing for casting women in formerly castrati roles in opera, Dame notes how, when two women sing together, "melodies [are] twirling around each other," and the "dissonances are very close and cause frictional moments of [an] almost physical nature. In the cadential notes, a unison, the lovers literally merge into each other and fuse into the prime." When the two voices in the same octave sing together, Dame continues, "As one in their melodic lines, as one in timbre, color, and pitch . . . they symbolize perfect love."[22]

The female duet occupies a space in between the norm and the deviation. It is more intimate and direct than the all-women's chorus number and more active and transformative than the male-female love song. One song in the score alters the pace in a show and stalls heteronormativity's forward-moving chronology in what Stephen M. Barber and David L. Clark describe as "queer temporality," or "a crossing of temporality with force."[23] These female duets temporarily halt the heterosexual romance and offer a different relationship, a special attachment. They require the audience to pause and disallow the conventionalized drive toward heterosexual closure. These songs are deconstructive in that they disrupt the heterosexual romance, but they are also reconstructive, even utopian, in their reimagining of a different musical relationship and connection.[24] In musical theatre, a song—the supreme condensation of music and lyrics, of orchestra and human sound, of performers' voices and bodies—both intensifies the present moment and expands the emotional effects. It provides "a 'moment,' a 'persistent present,' or 'a queer temporality that is at once indefinite and virtual but also forceful, resilient, and undeniable.'"[25]

The female duets in *Guys and Dolls*, *Wonderful Town*, and *West Side Story* are from some of the best-known, best-loved, and most-often-produced musicals of the 1950s. Praised then and now for their integration of song and dance and dialogue, these shows are aggressively heterosexual and homosocial, built on two pairs of lovers.

The Female Collaborative Duet in *Guys and Dolls*

In musicals of the 1950s, the collaborative duet features women in tandem, either contriving a plot (sometimes to trick their men), egging each other on to take action in some way, or sympathizing with each other's perspective. No persuasion is necessary; the situation is clear to both women, who bond through their collaboration. The duet moves across time as a musical and lyrical elaboration and repetition.

This song type finds precedent in opera's convention of "dueling sopranos," heard, for example, as the "Jealousy Duet" in Bertolt Brecht and Kurt Weill's opera–musical theatre hybrid, *The Threepenny Opera* (1928).[26] In the shift from opera to musical theatre, though, the typically triangulated relationships in which two women vie for the attention of one man are replaced by a quadrangle—the double plots of heterosexual romance that appear in many mid-century musicals from Rodgers and Hammerstein on. The four-way character configuration, especially in the intensely homosocial worlds of musicals, renders the two women a female couple, which they perform in a duet. Their coalition is musically emphasized, as women's vocal ranges in musical theatre, or their "vocal compass," are markedly reduced from opera, and the key and the tessitura, or area in which most notes occur, are lowered to allow lyrics to be easily understood.[27] Although women characters are invariably constructed in opposites—virgin/whore, princess/evil stepsister, smart/gullible, worldly/innocent—they sing within an aurally unified range. The women are not only companionable but coconspirators or cocreators, their mutual reality confirmed.

The alternating lines and unified chorus of which many female collaborative duets are composed stress how the women's voices are at once the same and distinct, how their characters are different but in agreement. Many of these songs, including "Marry the Man Today" from *Guys and Dolls*, are quick and upbeat, even though the song is in a minor key, in a lilting fox-trot with lyrics that reference contemporary issues and items specific to the cultural lexicon of the musical's world. Others, such as the musical parody "Ohio" from *Wonderful Town*, are plaintive ballads composed in thirds, an aurally easy and pleasant arrangement that suggests unity and camaraderie. Both songs are witty in their humor, and set in contemporaneous musicals, timely.

Guys and Dolls, with music and lyrics by Frank Loesser and a libretto by Abe Burrows and Jo Swerling, consists of a character- and place-defining score rife with syncopation and the frequent use of triplets.[28] The plot follows Nathan Detroit (played by Sam Levene on Broadway), who organizes "the oldest established permanent floating crap game in New York," as the male chorus sings in a hymnlike refrain. To raise money to rent a hall for the game, Nathan bets his fellow gambler Sky Masterson (Robert Alda [actor Alan Alda's father]) that he cannot date missionary Sarah Brown (Isabel Bigley). Sky succeeds and the two fall in love, but Nathan holds the crap game in the mission hall, and Sarah, furious, leaves Sky. Sky then convinces Sarah to take him back by promising her a church-ful of sinners at her next meeting, which he delivers by wagering $1,000 against the souls of the men in a crap game and winning. In the meantime, Nathan avoids marriage to his longtime girlfriend, Miss Adelaide (Vivian Blaine), who suffers from a psychosomatic cold because he will not tie the knot. By the end of the show, the sinners pray, the crap game is played, and the two heterosexual couples marry.

Guys and Dolls met with unanimously rave reviews when it opened in 1950. Critics loved how every element of the show—score, lyrics, libretto, choreography, and design—captured the world of Damon Runyon (author of two short stories that were source texts for Guys and Dolls) and candy-coated it for Broadway. The musical won the Tony Award for Best Musical as well as the New York Drama Critics' Circle Award. In his 1970 history of Broadway, the-atre critic Brooks Atkinson observed that "the genius of Guys and Dolls was to portray [the characters] without glamour, and the genius of Loesser was to characterize them musically with candor and relish." Because musical theatre's "standards had gone up sharply by 1950. . . every song had to be just right, because every song defined a character. There was not a commonplace nor a superfluous song in the score."[29] Musical theatre scholars agree that the four principals are "perfectly in balance."[30] As Geoffrey Block writes, "Even those who love to hate Broadway musicals make an exception for Guys and Dolls and consider this show one of the most entertaining and perfect ever."[31]

The female principals, Sarah and Adelaide, form perfect opposites: Sarah is the rigid, uncompromising Christian missionary whose tongue and libido are loosened by a trip to Havana and several rounds of drinks, allowing her to re-alize that she loves Sky. Her gorgeous soprano solos are richly melodic songs of romance that express her keen desire barely hidden under her chilly surface. In contrast, Adelaide (who has no last name in the musical) sings a belting alto, which some performers intentionally make tinny or shrill in her numbers. All of her solos are novelty or character development songs, including the hilar-ious "Adelaide's Lament," in which she sings, "In other words, just from stalling and stalling and stalling the wedding trip/A person can develop la grippe . . . la post-nasal drip," and then Loesser's incredible line, "You can spray her wher-ever you figure the streptococci lurk" that then rhymes with "You can give her a shot for whatever she's got, but it just won't work" and "tired of getting the fisheye from the hotel clerk."[32] Adelaide also sings in her role as a nightclub performer, including the breakout hit from the show, "A Bushel and a Peck." Adelaide's songs and her one-two punch lines provide much of the show's humor, such as:

Adelaide (*To Sky, after Nathan has let her down again*): Will you see
   Nathan before you go?
Sky: Maybe.
Adelaide: Tell him I never want to talk to him again and have him call
   me here.[33]

The women represent, as Knapp observes, "religion" and "display"—"a slightly
more genteel parallel to the familiar 'Madonna/Whore' trope."[34] If Adelaide is
not played by a strong actor, she can easily become silly and dismissible. Typically in production, however, the stronger actor plays Adelaide, and her character upstages the more conventional ingénue Sarah.

Although the men's gambling links the two romantic plots of *Guys and
Dolls*, the two women occupy completely separate spheres throughout most
of the show. Moreover, Sarah's crusade against depravity implicitly includes
Adelaide's profession as dancer/pseudostripper in its purview. Their duet
follows a quiblobet ("two separate melodies performed successively and
then, to the ear's delight, simultaneously"[35]), or what Knapp calls a "combination number," in which each woman sings her key number—"Adelaide's
Lament" and Sarah's "I've Never Been in Love Before"—which reveals how
they are musically compatible even as they seem to be opposite: their
self-expressions can, surprisingly, harmonize. When the women come together to sing "Marry the Man Today," they make known how their similarities are more important than their differences, how their opposite
characteristics are "both subsets of dollness," as Knapp admits, "which
(somehow) connect at a deeper level."[36] Their song explains how they are
both eminently practical—in contrast to their gambling, wandering (and
desirable) men. (The men also sang a duet in the show about their aversion
to coupling, which was cut on tour because Sam Levene, who played Nathan
Detroit, could not sing it well.)[37] Because this duet, like "A Boy Like That/I
Have a Love" and many other female duets, takes place near the show's end
and is the last new song of the score (that is, not the very last number in the
show but the last nonreprise), it thus confirms a significant opposition to
heteroromance (fig. 1-1).

The lyrics of "Marry the Man Today" are timely and funny and anything
but romantic. The men are equated with not-yet-altered clothing and not-yet-
ripe fruit; they are seen as a project, malleable and able to be manipulated.
Marriage is a business proposition. The women want to domesticate their
men, to make them into well-behaved middlebrow citizens, subscribers to
Reader's Digest and fans of Guy Lombardo. The song's straightforward struc-

Figure 1.1 In *Guys and Dolls* (1950), Adelaide (Vivian Blaine) and Sarah (Isabel Bigley) join forces in "Marry the Man Today," the musical's near-end female duet. Courtesy Photofest.

ture, the frequent repetition of the title phrase ("marry the man," always in triplets that readily trip off the tongue), and the presence of hard and simple end rhymes allow the audience to easily anticipate where the song will go musically and encourage an emphasis on the song's lyrics and the performed connection between the two women. From the beginning of the half-spoken intro section, the women's mutual understanding of their perspective is established as each adds lines in alternation. Adelaide sings, "You've simply got to gamble," then Sarah, "You get no guarantee"; Adelaide continues, "Doesn't that kind of apply to you and I?" and Sarah corrects her grammar, singing on the same notes, "You and me."[38] Here and throughout the number, the women repeat with a difference; one follows the other and sings the same notes but with lyrics revised, and each new line develops the women's characters and their relationship.

Sarah's correction of Adelaide's grammar introduces the ever-growing humor of the song. In the verse, each sung line is preceded by a measure of vamp, a cartoonlike slide of notes that here connotes sneakiness. The vamp also gives the audience a moment to digest the lyrics and the actors several beats during which they can cross the stage, touch each other on the arm or waist for emphasis, exchange glances, make eye contact, or, more typically in this show, mug for the audience by opening their eyes wide and exaggerating their expressions. Adelaide begins, "Marry the man today/Trouble though he may be/Much as he likes to play/Crazy and wild and free."

Each line moves up the scale, almost exploding to the slightly higher refrain. The two initiate the refrain in unison, each time with slight and funny variations on the lyrics: "Marry the man today, rather than sigh in sorrow," then Adelaide comes in with the punch line and the rhyme: "Marry the man today and change his ways tomorrow." The sharing of lines in the song is powerfully mutual, an alternating structure in which each one in turn begins the verse and introduces the idea, both in language and in melody, then the other adds to and completes the thought. In the next refrain, they sing in unison, "But marry the man today/Handle it meek and gently," then Adelaide adds, "Marry the man today and train him subsequently." The women alternate lines, too, each seeming to compose the song as it goes along; their voices become increasingly intertwined and in dialogue as the song proceeds. They finally both sing, "Marry the man today, give him the girlish laughter," and Sarah finishes the rhyme, "Give him your hand today and save the fist for after." When they sing in unison, even though the tempo stays the same, the feeling of the song's pace picks up intensity and vigor, with a sense of propelled movement. As the women become excited, their ideas feed on one another, generating energy and force and pushing against the song's meter.

When the verse repeats, Sarah initiates the line; then, rather than adding the next line as before, Adelaide echoes Sarah's first line to create a two-person minifugue or round. As in the combination song that precedes the duet, their voices overlap and create lovely harmonies, but here they sing the same lines, one after the other, in what Block calls a "simple and static counterpoint."[39]

Through repeating and elaborating the idea, both in music and in lyrics, Adelaide and Sarah grow closer during the duet.

This number, as it is usually performed, stresses the women's intense pleasure as they find themselves together in similar situations, completely different yet absolutely alike. Also because it takes place so near the end, the audience feels the show begin to wind down and so focuses intently on the women as a pair. In performance, the actors tend to demonstrate their admiration of each other, both in character and as singer-actors. Literary scholar Terry Castle foregrounds women's pleasure of such onstage attention in a performer's "ability to give voice to her pleasure, to reveal herself on stage, without shame or self-censoring, as a *fan* of other women."[40] The other (B) section of the song proceeds in a 4/4 march as the beat, music, and lyrics (sung on eighth notes) combine to portray determination and a businesslike approach. In combination with the verse and chorus, these sections sound self-consciously funny as the women set themselves up for battle in mock seriousness:

> Adelaide: Slowly introduce him to the better things
> Respectable, conservative, and clean
> Sarah: Reader's Digest
> Adelaide: Guy Lombardo
> Sarah: Rogers Peete
> Adelaide: Golf!
> Sarah: Galoshes!
> Adelaide: Ovaltine!

The lyrics are packed with verbs—gamble, marry, handle (him), track (him) down, train (him), expose (him)—and a sense of action and activity. When Adelaide and Sarah catalog the things a woman might "have" to hold on to her man ("Carefully expose him to domestic life/And if he ever tries to stray from you"), in ascending order of consequence—"have a pot roast," "have a headache," "have a baby"—the number of children expands from one to two to six to nine, until Sarah exclaims, "Stop!" Here and throughout the number, their creativity builds; the song itself becomes the expression of possibility. At the same time, the humor of the things a woman might "have" renders the whole heterosexual enterprise both utterly practical and very silly.

The women's specific parts in the song are differentiated only by the texture of their voices—on the cast album, Blaine's flat nasal belt and Bigley's head voice with some vibrato. When they sing in unison, on some notes their voices blend perfectly; on other notes, the distinction is audible. One striking moment of vocal unity occurs when they actually laugh on the syllable "laugh" in the phrase "girlish laughter." Mordden describes a "baaing mordent on the first syllable of 'laughter' so that the two in effect 'sing' a laugh."[41] (A mordent is "a type of ornament which, in its standard form, consists in the rapid alternation of the main note with a subsidiary note a step below.")[42] When, at the end of the song, Blaine and Bigley each repeat "and change his ways" in an echo several times in turn, building and rising in what Mordden calls a "two-octave violin glissando," and then break apart into harmony on "tomorrow" in thirds, their linkage—a musical consummation, for sure—is actualized.[43]

Through the various forms of unanimity that are voiced in this song—taking turns, echo, unison—and the collaboration of ideas that build and repeat, the song performs that the women are more suited and more in collusion with each other than with their men. They finish each other's thoughts; they replicate each other's melodies. The simple song takes them to a place where they understand that, like their men, they need to become gamblers—but in marriage and domesticity. In performance, though, the larger point is made in this last song in the show—on their own, they find support, absolute understanding, and mutuality.

The Female Collaborative Duet in *Wonderful Town*

With music by Leonard Bernstein, lyrics by Betty Comden and Adolph Green, and a book by Jerome Chodorow and Joseph Fields, on whose novel *My Sister Eileen* the musical was based, and directed by George Abbott, *Wonderful Town* follows the adventures of two sisters who arrive in New York City in the 1930s to find their fame and fortune (fig. 1-2).[44] The role of Ruth in *Wonderful Town* was written for Rosalind Russell, a not atypical method of creating a Broadway musical in the 1950s. At the time, Russell wasn't known as a singer but all of the reviewers found her voice more than adequate and her comic timing superb for the role of the intellectual journalist sister of the slightly dotty ingénue actress, Eileen, played by Edith Adams. In part because the musical is set in the 1930s, its tone is lighthearted, its dialogue tongue-in-cheek, its music effervescent, and its relationships externalized. The Greenwich Village of *Wonderful Town* is populated by colorful characters: several dancing male choruses; an Irish, harmonizing police force; a supporting chorine; her pseudomacho fiancé (who appears dressed in his shorts); and a brash, overprotective, easily tricked mother. Eileen's interest in (all) men and their animal-like desire for her never seem dangerous, even when she is arrested and put in jail for inciting a small riot. Ruth, in the other hand, may worry that she is too smart and too tough for

Figure 1.2 In *Wonderful Town* (1953), sisters Eileen (Edith Adams) and Ruth (Rosalind Russell) make a new life together in New York City, far from their home town in "Ohio." Courtesy the Lionel Pincus and Princess Firyal Map Division, the New York Public Library, Astor, Lenox and Tilden Foundations.

any man to fall in love with her, as she sings in the hilarious charm song, "One Hundred Ways to Lose a Man," but like all the best heroines in Broadway musicals, her pathos pales in comparison to her charming feistiness. From the start, the audience falls in love with her, and according to musical theatre's convention, knows that the man whom she dislikes from the start of the show (in this case, the editor Robert Baker) will unwittingly fall in love with her by the end, too, which he does.

Still, the key relationship in *Wonderful Town* is between Ruth and Eileen, who perform as a couple, opposites linked together, like Sarah and Adelaide, Maria and Anita in *West Side Story*, Louise and June (and Rose and Louise) in *Gypsy*, Maria and Liesl (and Maria and the Mother Abbess) in *The Sound of Music*, and Vera and Mame in *Mame* less than a decade later. In all of these musicals, the dominating, presumptive heterosexual romance is interrupted by a memorable duet between women.

Wonderful Town is structured around scenes where the two women separate and experience the world from their different perspectives, then come together to share stories and to support each other. With a very few exceptions, virtually all of the duets in the musical are theirs. The first song after the opening "Christopher Street," which introduces New York City's bohemians and alludes to its gay life as well, is "Ohio," a mournful and funny duet in which Ruth and Eileen sing primarily in thirds. Later, each of the women sings songs with a group of men—the Irish policemen with Eileen; the navy men with Ruth doing the Conga. At the end of the musical, when Ruth and Robert Baker get together, the song, "It's Love," is sung triangularly: Eileen sings a line on the stage of the Vortex nightclub, then Robert Baker enters and taps Ruth, who is sitting in the audience, on the shoulder, then she sings a line and they kiss. But the song and so their coupling is enabled by Eileen, since she informs Baker that he loves her sister, whether or not he realizes it. In effect, then, Robert and Ruth actually don't sing a love duet of their own.

Unlike the female collaborative duet that falls near the end of *Guys and Dolls* and so undermines the heterosexual narrative, "Ohio" is sung near the beginning of *Wonderful Town*. As Ruth and Eileen's first number, even before either one sings a self-introducing solo, "Ohio" asserts the primacy of the relationship between the two women. It creates the expectation early on that other relationships will be secondary and that the story to be tracked is of the two women together and their coming of age: how they change in their adventures in the city, in their jobs, in the new neighborhood, and with their potential male love interests. In this way, an early female collaborative duet works differently than one near the end of the musical; this one sets the stage for the story and the characters' connections rather than alters them.

In the number, Eileen and Ruth sing their regret at having left their small town. The song's lyrics are poignant but also funny because of the rhyme scheme: "Why? Oh why? Oh why oh?/Why did we ever leave Ohio?" (107).[45] This is a love song to Ohio, their home, their boring and idyllic and comfortable past. Like the words, the melody circles around just a few notes, bringing the two women back to "home," to each other. When they sing "Ohio," the audience doesn't yet know how these two sisters are opposites: one pretty, the other smart and ambitious; one soprano, the other alto; one flirtatious, the other (like Sarah Brown in *Guys and Dolls*) transformed into a sexual being only via alcohol and an exotic locale. Their music expresses a connection that is both sustaining and mournful.

Other examples of 1950s female collaborative duets include "If Momma Was Married" from *Gypsy*, a funny waltz in which Louise and June voice their desire for their mother, Mama Rose, to get married. They sing, "Momma, get out your white dress!/You've done it before/Without much success/Momma, God speed and God bless,/We're not keeping score/What's one more or less?" (48).[46] In the "Stepsisters' Lament" in *Cinderella* (a Rodgers and Hammerstein musical produced for television in 1956 starring Julie Andrews), the stepsisters complain in syncopation, "Why would a fellow want a girl like her, a girl who's merely lovely?/Why can't a fellow ever once prefer a girl who's merely me?/What's the matter with the man?"[47] In "What Did I Ever See in Him?" at the opening of the second act of *Bye Bye Birdie* (1960), both Rosie and Kim express their mutual frustration with their men in a speeding melody of eighth notes. Similarly, in "Take Him" from *Pal Joey* (1940), a musical that is often cited as an early and influential formally integrated, serious book musical, a deceptively sweet and perky melody wittily complements Vera and Linda's anger toward the playboy Joey, as each urges the other to "take him, but don't ever let him take you." Vera sings, "Lots of good luck, you'll need it/and you'll need aspirin, too."[48]

The Female Pedagogical Duet in *West Side Story*

Near the end of the second act of *West Side Story*, the 1957 collaboration of the composer Leonard Bernstein, the lyricist Stephen Sondheim, the librettist Arthur Laurents, and the director-choreographer Jerome Robbins, Anita (Chita Rivera) and Maria (Carol Lawrence) sing a wrenching, climactic, show-stealing duet (fig. 1-3). The musical, based on *Romeo and Juliet*, follows two gangs, the Jets and the Sharks, as they battle for urban turf. Maria, who is Puerto Rican and sister to Bernardo (the leader of the Sharks and Anita's lover, played by Ken Le Roy), falls in love with Tony (Larry Kert), who is Polish and the former leader of the Jets. Despite their hope that their romance can transcend racial and cultural differences,

Figure 1.3 In *West Side Story* (1957), Anita (Chita Rivera) rebukes Maria (Carol Lawrence) for loving "A Boy Like That," but Maria responds with "I Have a Love" and changes Anita in the duet. Courtesy Photofest.

Maria and Tony's love affair instigates a string of violent events, including a rumble during which Tony kills Bernardo. By the end of the show, Chino, Bernardo's best friend, kills Tony, and Maria, wielding Chino's gun, threatens to kill everyone gathered as she asserts that she has "now learned to hate." The last moment finds Maria bent over Tony's dead body; then the chorus sings a slow reprise of "Somewhere," and the boys from both sides join to carry off Tony's body. (In the 1961 film version, the police arrest

Chino, assuring the audience that when white boys die tragic deaths, boys of color are arrested.)

When it opened in 1957, *West Side Story* was met with positive but predictably anxious reviews, and it lost almost every Tony Award to *The Music Man*, Meredith Willson's romanticized portrayal of a small-town con man—Harold Hill, played by the indomitable Robert Preston—who turns into a community builder and then, of course, the romantic lead. Still, Robbins won a Tony for best choreographer, and Oliver Smith won for best scenic design for *West Side Story*.[49]

Critics commented on Robbins's brilliant use of dance to tell the story; on Bernstein's complex and unified, "high art" score built on the short theme of a tritone plus a half step up (the first three notes of "Maria"); on Sondheim's capturing of an urban youth vernacular; and on the musical's contemporary, acerbic content and despairing ending. Shortly after it opened, Latino critics lambasted the creators, and especially Sondheim, for their negative representation of Puerto Ricans as the musical's other. Sondheim revised the lyrics for "America" for the film version and eliminated what had been read as offensive lines about Puerto Rico, such as "island of tropic diseases"; "Always the hurricanes blowing": "And the money owing/And the babies crying/And the bullets flying" (167).[50] The all-female chorus number in the stage version became an argument that divided along gender lines in the movie, which made the women seem naïve about the racist realities of living in "America." The film was directed by Robert Wise (who also directed *The Sound of Music*) and won the Academy Award that year. Debates about *West Side Story*'s politics continue to rage, and productions have been canceled, as the musical is both brilliant and also deeply problematic.[51]

The duet that takes place near the end of *West Side Story*, which is the last new song introduced in the musical, functions pedagogically. Maria, the soprano and the naive "virgin"-in-love who can see beyond skin color, persuades Anita, the alto and sexually experienced woman bound to her ethnicity, that love conquers all. At the point of the duet in the musical, Anita returns home to Maria but finds her bedroom door locked and, suspecting correctly that Maria is with Tony, knocks. Tony sneaks out of Maria's bedroom window after they promise to meet at Doc's drugstore to run away together. Maria unlocks the door, and Anita enters, knowing immediately that Tony just left, and "turns accusingly to Maria," who says, "All right; now you know." Anita answers "savagely," "And you still don't know: *Tony is one of them!*" (212).

The song begins with fierce orchestrations that echo the violent, irregular rhythm and tritones of the show's musical themes.[52] Then Anita sings, as the stage directions specify, "bitterly," "A *boy* like that who'd *kill* your *bro*ther,/For*get* that boy and *find* an*oth*er!/One *of* your *own* kind—/Stick *to* your *own* kind!"

(212). Anita verbally and musically attacks Maria, and the lyrics' offbeats (noted in italics) stress her fury as well as emphasize how English serves as her second language. Anita is overwhelmed with grief, anger, and hatred, and she repeats the verse's melody: "A boy like that will give you *sorrow*—/You'll meet another *boy* tomorrow!/One *of your own* kind,/Stick *to your own* kind" (212). After Anita sings a still forceful but more flowing second section, which repeats the words "boy" and "kill," and adds "love," "heart," and "smart"—all simple words that capture strong emotion—Maria takes up the same melody but in her own words: "It isn't true, not for me,/It's true for you, not for me,/I hear your words—/And in my head/I know they're smart,/But my heart, Anita,/But my heart . . ." (213). The women engage in a struggle over meaning and interpretation, but in the same rhythm and by the same musical means. According to the music, their feelings incorporate the same degree of commitment and belief. They sing to each other directly, each trying to convince the other of her perspective—it is a life-or-death debate. The "boy" is the object of the argument (and many duets between women are ostensibly "about" men), but the address is "you." From the first verses, the song anticipates that Maria will prevail, as her lyrics are all one-syllable words, which fit more precisely with the notes and therefore sound more rational and measured, not out of sync like Anita's.

If the song's first verse establishes the tense alliance between the women and allows each to enunciate her feelings to the other, the second verse puts them in intertwined opposition. Maria's last phrase of one verse carries over to the next verse continuously: "But my heart knows they're wrong/And my heart is too strong" (213). At the same time, Anita sings her first verse in counterpoint, her melody related harmonically to Maria's but not identical. When Maria takes up the same impassioned melody in the same furious rhythm, she simultaneously unites with and opposes Anita. Her lyrics convey her different perspective, her divergent perspective in fact, yet she and Anita express their commitment in the same musical vocabulary. They both struggle to be heard by the other, to be understood, as they sing over and around each other. The last few phrases of this section move into an almost-conversation or operatic recitative mode, as Anita speak-sings, "Very smart, Maria, very smart!" and Maria responds in a high soprano release, "Oh no, A-ni-ta, no—you should know better!" and then, slowing and definite, into almost speech, "You were in love—or so you said," and then, slowing down even more, "You should know better . . ." (213). Their intimate conversation locates them as a musical couple, each striving to be understood by the other.

The song's second part, which is virtually a different song altogether—"I Have a Love"—develops and deepens Maria's pedagogy of emotion that she sets out in the first section. Counterpoint moves into a melody in unison; oppositional lyrics become the same words; notes in discordantly intense relation resolve into an aurally pleasing and logical harmonious chord. Maria's melody recalls the motif from "Somewhere," the love duet of tragedy, but in an altered rhythm.[53] Maria's lyrics—"I have a love, and it's all that I have./Right or wrong, what else can I do?"—express her dedication, and Anita eventually joins her in harmony of parallel thirds in the last section: "When loves comes so strong,/There is no right or wrong"; then they crescendo to, "Your love is your life!" completing the song on the same note, an octave apart (214).

The last section transforms a song of conflict and conversation into an expression of love as they join together musically—Rivera's thick, rough-edged belt and Lawrence's clear, plaintive soprano—and sing their agreement to each other with the same notes that the (heterosexual) lovers sang to each other earlier. Anita eventually submits to Maria's reasoning, but not without great difficulty and persuasion on Maria's part, and when they sing together in a major key, it is in the calmest, most-ordered rhythm of the song. They hit the same note on "right" (of the phrase, "There is no right or wrong"), one moving down and the other moving up in her voice part. As musicologist Wilfrid Mellers asserts, "Musically, the positive elements, now and at last, prove stronger than negation."[54]

The dramatic action that follows the song underlines their emotional union. Anita, now changed by Maria, reveals to her that Chino has a gun and is hunting for Tony, but before Maria can leave to meet him, Lieutenant Shrank enters her bedroom and begins to question her about the dance at the gym. Maria signals to Anita, who supports Maria by leaving to deliver a message to Tony; Anita becomes Maria's partner. Subsequently, the Jets harass and almost rape Anita, and in her fear, frustration, and fury, she lies and tells them that she came to find Tony to tell him that Maria is dead. Anita's outburst propels the series of events that leads to Tony's death and Chino's arrest. Bernstein's funeral dirge musically reinforces the audience's knowledge that the two communities are hopelessly divided, even after a tragedy that affects them both.

In most productions of *West Side Story*, the duet between the two women tends to be staged like a dramatic scene, which emphasizes the intimate connection between them. (The film version, which most directors of the show have seen [numerous times, no doubt], gives a sense of the physicalized logic of the scene-song. Although of course a director could stage the song differently, the music and lyrics suggest the physical connection between Anita and Maria.) They are in close quarters—Maria's tiny bedroom—and in the first part of the song, Anita paces around the room, throwing looks and gestures to

Maria that emphasize the force of her words and melody. Anita sings to Maria, the song is a direct address, an attack, a warning, a lesson. Unlike songs that are sung for the audience or for a casually observant character in the diegesis, this song makes sense only as one that creates a relationship, a mode of communication. The actor playing Maria would usually stand up for her musical entrance, "It isn't true, not for me," confronting Anita to her face (213). From this point on, a logical staging of the song would involve the women facing each other directly (within the stage's necessity of "cheating out"; that is, turning slightly to face the audience), perhaps moving toward and away from each other, but always circling around, linked together and joined in the space of this room, this song. By the end, they are likely sitting or standing, facing each other, looking intensely into each other's eyes, holding hands, and singing the same note. The song is invariably concluded with an embrace.

In the context of *West Side Story*, this song refers to a man; it is about Maria's love for Tony, and the song's lyrics allow one woman to teach another why loyalty to her man is fundamental. Yet the song's performance elides the man and concerns only these two women, the female characters, the women actors onstage. They sing to each other, and they listen to one another. Most important, one woman is convinced, persuaded, and changed by the other. The song develops an emotional shift, a change brought about by one woman's influence on another. This number is intensely homosocial, as is the whole musical of *West Side Story*; except for the dance in the gym and a few short scenes, Tony and Maria are barely onstage together, and neither are the other heterosexual couples. Again, convention buttresses the sense of the musical as a great love story more than the actual representations and actions onstage. The heterosexual relationships in some ways authorize the salient and frequently represented and performed homosociality (for both women and men, both Sharks and Jets) in *West Side Story*. Maria and Anita's strong relationship, their queer connection, whose existence precedes this song in the musical, is intensified and coalesces here, rendered even more pronounced because of their bond as Latinas. Finally and not incidentally, the double entendre of the lyrics opens alternative listenings: the last song of the show finds two women singing a love song to each other in one's bedroom.

While "A Boy Like That/I Have a Love" is an unusual and remarkable song, especially in the jagged, complex rhythm in the song's accompaniment at the beginning, its overall project, performance, and effect articulate this subgenre of women's duets: the female pedagogical duet. As one woman teaches the other a lesson, the latter's character shifts. By the end, they sing together, their unified voices assuring that they agree, the lesson has been learned, the couple has been solidly formed.

In most integrated musicals, the second act consists primarily of reprises that wrap up the heterosexual narrative. This structure renders the musical's heterosexual romance plot weak, frequently unconvincing, and utterly dependent on heteronormative cultural conventions and expectations for its believability (even in the not-so-believable world of musical theatre). The female pedagogical duet, then, upends the heterosexual romance entirely, altering and feminizing the affective organization of the musical by linking the two women in intensely grounded affiliation and mutual understanding.

Other 1950s female pedagogical duets include, for example, *The Sound of Music*'s reprise of "Sixteen Going on Seventeen," sung near the end of the show, when Maria promises Liesl that the "adventure" of falling in love will happen if she can "wait—a year—or two" (132).[55] (This song also refers to an earlier, extremely intimate scene between the two women in Maria's bedroom, which, not coincidentally, follows the first rendition of the song between Liesl and the Nazi youth, boyfriend-on-a-bike, Rolf.) Another pedagogical duet occurs early in the show in "My Favorite Things," when the Mother Abbess teaches Maria how to be brave as she faces her new life with the Von Trapp family. In Rodgers and Hammerstein's television version of *Cinderella*, Cinderella and her godmother sing "Impossible," transforming the refrain into "It's possible" through a female duet of imagination, determination, and hopefulness. Later in the show, Cinderella convinces the stepsisters to see the evening from her perspective (that is, of the Prince falling in love with her, which of course they never experienced) in "A Lovely Night."[56] In the mid-1960s, "Matchmaker, Matchmaker" operates as a female pedagogical trio in *Fiddler on the Roof*, as Tzeitl, Tevye's eldest daughter, teaches her sisters to be careful what they wish for in an arranged marriage. In *Sweet Charity*, Charity teaches her friends and coworkers, Nickie and Helene, to have higher ambitions than being taxi dancers in an effervescent trio.

In the later twentieth and into the twenty-first century, many musicals offered two women the principal roles (or two of the principal roles in addition to men) and positioned them explicitly as a singing and dancing couple. The duos were enemies turned collaborators like Velma and Roxie in *Chicago* (1975) and Elphaba and Glinda in *Wicked* (2003); they were sisters like the conjoined twins Daisy and Violet Hilton in *Side Show* (1997) and Celie and Nettie in *The Color Purple* (2005); they were a lesbian couple like Charlotte and Cordelia in *Falsettoland* (1990), Maureen and Joanne in *Rent* (1996), or Celie and Shug in *The Color Purple*, and more. Whether or not two women are the principals, female duets are a key convention of the Broadway musical.

Female duets flourished in a decade identified with heterosexual presumption in culture and on the Broadway musical stage. By looking at and listening to how these songs work, by examining how they fit into the whole show, and by attending to their importance as a convention of the form during an era of intense creativity and unequaled popularity, a feminist perspective can tell a different story of the 1950s.

Meanwhile, social and cultural struggles that would lead to 1960s hippie culture, the civil rights movement, and the women's liberation and gay rights movements were forming. While the nuclear family was fundamental for certain sectors of the population, and while conservative policymakers emphasized the need for America to maintain its stability, its autonomy, and its borders, many women and African Americans were articulating a different vision of American society. Just as the complacent '50s were a simmering pot of gender and race frustrations that exploded in the 1960s, the seemingly seamless 1950s form of the musical had cracks. By the mid-1960s, heterosexuality still prevailed (presumptively) but other musical and theatrical structures were employed as well. Feminism was beginning to take root. The next chapter looks at the single female in musicals of the mid-1960s, specifically her physicality through staging and dance.

CHAPTER 2

The 1960s: "If My Friends Could See Me Now"

In the years following *Oliver!*'s 1963 debut on Broadway, the torch song "As Long as He Needs Me" was covered by countless singers of both genders, including composer Lionel Bart and Shirley Bassey before the show opened in New York, then Anita Bryant, Sammy Davis, Jr., Doris Day, Michael Feinstein, Judy Garland, Liberace, Ann-Margret, Peter Nero, Dionne Warwick, and many more. Quickly moving out of the context of Bart's imported-from-London smash hit adaptation of Charles Dickens's novel, the song took on a life of its own as an expression of the singer's loyalty to a lover. Its popularity as a single was a remarkable achievement in a decade when Broadway musical theatre no longer provided the popular music of U.S. culture. Hearing the song sung by the Drifters or Steve Lawrence, it's easy to forget the dramaturgical context of the number. Nancy, the female principal in *Oliver!*, sings more songs in the musical than any other character. She performs this wrenching solo not once but twice in the show, both times addressing her boyfriend–common-law-husband–cum-abuser, Bill Sikes. For the reprise, he threatens her, she sings the song, and then he murders her. The fact that Nancy is killed in *Oliver!* doesn't mitigate actor Georgia Brown's powerful presence when she delivered the song as the first Nancy in London and on Broadway, but it does point to unnerving contradictions between the narrative and the musical numbers in Broadway musicals of the mid-1960s.

This chapter travels through a cluster of musicals from the mid-1960s— *Oliver!* (1963), *Hello, Dolly!* (1964), *Man of La Mancha* (1965), *Sweet Charity* (1966), *Cabaret* (1966), and *Mame* (1966)—in which the female protagonist's body is something to contend with, as women's bodies in musicals have always been, something to be looked at, but more, something that is active, moving, influential. In some cases, it's a body that dances, slides down a banister, or gathers a charmed crowd around her. And in some cases, it's a body that is raped, pushed in a lake, or killed.

The female body was of interest and fascination in the mid-1960s on the musical theatre stage and in U.S. culture, too. While feminism as a mainstream idea or everyday practice had yet to emerge—that would happen in the late 1960s and into the 1970s—women's liberation as a political movement was in the air as women fought for and began to gain rights legally, socially, and culturally. As early as 1961, John F. Kennedy established the President's Commission on the Status of Women to study women's roles, gender differences, and equality, especially disparities in pay. (This issue has yet to find resolution. In 1963, when the Equal Pay Act was passed, women were paid an average of fifty-nine cents to a man's dollar. As of 2007, women made seventy-eight cents to a man's dollar, which means that the pay gap only closed by nineteen cents in forty-four years.)[1] In 1966, the National Organization for Women was formed to address national issues of concern.

Many white, middle-class women aspired to be upwardly mobile, suburban housewives and mothers,[2] but others found common ground in Betty Friedan's shattering exposé of college-educated women's frustrations, *The Feminine Mystique*, published in 1963. Friedan began the project by interviewing her classmates who graduated from Smith in the 1950s and found that many of them were bitterly unhappy and numbingly bored. The book struck a nerve and fueled women's resistance to traditional gender roles and everyday practices of sexism.

If Friedan voiced the anger of married women, Helen Gurley Brown became the spokesperson for the unmarried woman in the mid-1960s. Although married herself when she wrote the best-seller *Sex and the Single Girl* in 1961, Brown spoke to unmarried women who wanted to have careers and adventures before settling down to be married and have children. The book encouraged women to embrace their autonomy and to be sexy and to have sex before marriage. The Food and Drug Administration (FDA) approved the birth control pill in 1961, which meant that young, unmarried women could follow Brown's exhortations to wear their skirts short, to attract men, and to have sex. For many women, "chastity was no longer the gauge of a woman's value."[3] Yet even with the invention of the Pill, an uncompromising double standard persisted for sexual behavior and autonomy.[4] As historian Beth Bailey notes about the early 1960s, "It was not only the advisers [to women on their sexuality and sexual practices] and experts who equated virtue and value. Fifty percent of the male respondents in Kinsey's study wanted to marry a virgin."[5] Everyday practices reinforced the virgin/whore dichotomy.

During the same period, postwar sociologists and psychologists claimed to have discovered a loss of confidence and assertiveness among men, a so-called crisis of masculinity, or "flight from manhood," as conservative commentators called it, which they blamed at once on the trauma of war, on career women who threatened men's roles in the workplace, and on dominating mothers. For example, some men responded anxiously to Brown's advice to single women: "Though one might think that men would have been delighted by Brown's message—she was, after all, telling women to say yes to pre-marital sex—men raised to expect modest, demure, diffident female companions were in fact taken aback by Brown's vision of sexual equality," writes historian David Allyn.[6] Perhaps not surprisingly, this "crisis" bubbled to the surface just when women and African Americans began agitating for equal rights.

Representations of women in Broadway musicals reflected these contradictions, both showing women as conscious agents in their lives and careers and punishing them for being too assertive or too sexually active. The group of musicals that opened in the mid-1960s all feature scenes or songs with a single woman on stage that focus on her moving body, either through dance or through movement or blocking in the book scenes. Taken together, they form a continuum of representations from the least to the most performatively powerful. These musicals also reveal a discrepancy, which happens frequently in musical theatre, between the ideological work of the image or representation (in these examples, of a single woman) and the ideological effect that emerges from the power of performance. These examples make that tension exceedingly clear, as all of these musicals follow a story that in some way condemns a single woman for her sexuality or her independence—the narrative punishes her for her actions or her desires—and at the same time, the choreography—whether in song or spoken scene—allows the female actor powerful performance opportunities. Thus the audience might *think* that the woman is being punished but *feels* how the performance celebrates her. This chapter explores the range of these theatrical practices, focusing on examples of the single woman's body on stage.

1960s Broadway Musicals

The mid-1960s marked a turning point for the American Broadway musical, as U.S. society experienced a seismic shift, and U.S. culture both shaped and reflected that shift. Neither avant garde nor classical, neither progressive nor conservative, the musical struggled during this period aesthetically, financially, and politically. Commentators at the time debated whether the musical was dying or already dead, the same or different. In 1970, longtime theatre critic Brooks Atkinson bemoaned musical theatre of the 1960s, writing, "In the sixties, the quality of music deteriorated into a kind of standard monotone, as if it were a job but no longer a pleasure to write for the theater. The range of the music was narrow, the themes mechanical, and Broadway sounded all alike." In what seems a somewhat hyperbolically dim view today, Atkinson found it "difficult to distinguish" the scores of Jerry Bock (*Fiddler on the Roof*) from Jule Styne (*Funny Girl*) from Jerry Herman (*Hello, Dolly!* and *Mame*) from Burt Bacharach (*Promises, Promises* [1968]). "A kind of musical cant prevailed," he declared, "as if the times were too stereotyped for individuality. Music was standardized on a level of mediocrity."[7] Around the same time, critic and playwright William Goldman, in his funny, wry, and personal exposé of the 1967–68 season on Broadway, wrote, "Musical comedy is in trouble today because the songwriters aren't there. The old men are dead or doddering, the young ones mostly dull."[8] Indeed, Oscar Hammerstein II's death in 1959 marked the end of the most prolific and influential creative partnership in the history of the Broadway musical. Others noted that the Rodgers and Hammerstein formula, whose innovative techniques produced a generation of musical plays with musical numbers integrated into the narrative, had become a rigid set of rules and conventions. Film critic Pauline Kael called the musical the "white elephant of Broadway," which "clumped to go into numbers 'naturally.'"[9] Contemporary theatre historians agree. Carol Ilson finds the musical by the mid-1960s entering a period of "decreased creativity," and Gerald Bordman writes, "Beset by the collapse of so much order and decorum," the Broadway musical "fell apart."[10]

Social changes of the decade—the civil rights and women's liberation movements, the Vietnam War and attendant protests—rendered many of the topics of earlier musicals, like *The Music Man* and *The Sound of Music*, quaint and their optimistic tone sentimental.[11] The typical 1950s Broadway musical's celebratory effervescence was seen as nostalgic, old-fashioned, and escapist during the "bloody international strife and turbulent national unrest" of the 1960s. "The Vietnam conflict kept escalating, and in the U.S. riots flared across cities and even on campuses," writes theatre historian Keith Garebian.[12] When the musicals in this chapter opened on Broadway, Lyndon Johnson was president, the United States was gaining globally in wealth and power, Martin Luther King Jr. called for passive resistance, and the Cold War mentality prevailed. In 1966, the same year that *Sweet Charity* and *Cabaret* opened, the Black Panther Party was formed, and Stokely Carmichael, chairman of the SNCC, began popularizing the phrase "Black Power." That same year, former movie star Ronald Reagan was elected governor of California, instigating a political shift to the right in that state, and Peter Brook's disturbing and inventive Tony-winning production of *Marat/Sade*, a critique of political power gone awry, was playing on Broadway. The country, rife with contradictions, was on the cusp of cataclysmic changes. "It was an era of radical dissent," writes Garebian, "and popular culture reflected this metamorphosis."[13]

While many musicals continued to be created along the Rodgers and Hammerstein model, including *Hello, Dolly!* and *Mame*, commercial, aesthetic, and social forces began to put pressure on the musical to adapt and change. First, the Broadway musical's increasing production costs combined with rampant inflation in the 1960s. The detailed and multiple realist sets required by historically and geographically specific 1950s musicals such as *Wonderful Town* and *My Fair Lady* were exorbitantly expensive to design and build, so producers put up smaller shows with fewer, more basic sets or even better, a single unit set.[14] Boris Aronson's set for *Cabaret*, for example, was spare, most notable for a large mirror suspended above the stage and set at an angle so that spectators saw their own distorted reflections staring back at them. Second, the growth of the suburbs meant that middle-class people increasingly consumed culture where they lived and not in Times Square (if they lived in the tristate, New York metropolitan area, the location for many Broadway spectators). Broadway musicals competed against local activities, including Little League and community theatres, suburban shopping centers and movie houses, and suburban dinner theatres, for spectators' time, attention, and money. Moreover, rising ticket costs transformed Broadway theatregoing from a middle-class leisure activity to a luxury outing.[15] Third, the music of musical theatre, which for decades had been the popular music heard on the radio and danced to in clubs, no longer appealed to the younger generation, which advertisers were quickly consolidating into an identifiable consumer market and whose tastes tended toward the newer electronic sounds of rock 'n' roll.[16]

The musicals in this chapter adhere to many of the structural conventions of Broadway's mid-twentieth-century integrated book musicals and lean toward experimentation, too. Except for *Cabaret*, as in formally integrated musicals of the 1950s, songs emerge out of the action, propel the plot, develop characters, and delineate the play's setting; dances similarly seem to occur naturally and develop story, character, setting, and mood. The musicals alternate dialogue with song and dance, moving smoothly from spoken word to music, even as they perform both a tension and a unity between the realist world of the dialogue and the metaphorical world of the musical numbers. And yet these other five musicals (besides *Cabaret*, that is) do begin to fracture the form, to violate the fourth wall of realism, and to comment on themselves as musicals. *Sweet Charity* is blatantly and abruptly episodic, with design elements that foreground the performance's awareness of itself. *Man of La Mancha* uses metatheatre, improvisatory experimental theatre techniques, and a real-time intermissionless play to act out the adventures of Don Quixote. The most formally conventional shows—*Mame, Hello, Dolly!,* and *Oliver!*—feature big, densely choreographed ensemble production numbers. *Mame* and *Hello, Dolly!,* the quintessential feel-good musicals, might be considered throwbacks but each has a weirdly huge diegetic musical number. In fact, Jerome Robbins turned down the job of directing *Hello, Dolly!* because he said he could not understand what the title song was about and why these waiters were singing to this woman and why she belonged there. As what became labeled the first "concept musical," *Cabaret* exaggerates these distinctions so that each diegetic song performed in the Kit Kat Klub comments on the action in the realist book scene that precedes it. Across this range of styles, tones, and formal uses of musical theatre's conventions, these shows are unified by their concern with and contradictory treatment of the female body on stage.

While mid-1960s musicals sustain earlier shows' heterosexual presumption, they move away from heterosexual romance as the main organizing narrative and a community's celebration as the finale. Rick Altman notes that 1960s musicals represent love cynically: "No longer are music and spectacle generated by the energy of a successful courtship guaranteed by the communitarian joy of an energetic musical spectacle."[17] While heterosexuality plays a role in each musical, the protagonist has her own identity, and her goals and desires mobilize the plot. The romantic duet, a mainstay of 1950s musicals, is eliminated in these musicals, replaced with odd, not-quite love songs, like "I'm the Bravest Individual" in *Sweet Charity* or "Perfectly Marvelous" in *Cabaret,* where the women tell the men what to think and feel, or woman and boy songs, like "My Best Girl/Beau" in *Mame* or "I'd Do Anything" in *Oliver!,* or Mame and Vera's queer female duet, "Bosom Buddies." The focus on the single woman requires a reorganization of song types. These musicals' unabashed focus on the female principal—on her life, her work, her friends, and her desires— rather than the heterosexual couple replaces earlier musicals' heteronormative nostalgia with an impulse that anticipates later 1960s feminist social change.

The Single Girl

Picture the quintessential popular culture images of a young woman in the mid-1960s: Twiggy, Marlo Thomas on television in *That Girl* (1966–71), the women in Mary McCarthy's novel *The Group* (1963), and Jennifer North (played by Sharon Tate) in the 1967 film adaptation of Jacqueline Susann's steamy novel

Valley of the Dolls (1966).[18] This figure, the Single Girl, was a staple on television and in popular culture of the decade. The Single Girl was sexually active and unmarried, independent and financially secure. She rejected Donna Reed's aprons and Lucy Ricardo's whining antics for her own apartment, her own paycheck, and her own birth control: "the Single Girl presents a utopian fantasy of a woman free from the social and sexual constraints that appeared to limit her mother."[19] With her monthly issue of *Cosmopolitan* and Brown's *Sex and the Single Girl* tucked under her arm, the Single Girl wore her skirts short and her boots high. Marrying a rich, handsome, successful man would be the next stage in the life of the Single Girl—as Brown did at age thirty-seven—but in the meantime, she should have a job, have sex, and have fun.

A variation on this 1960s female character type was "the Perky Girl." Jane and Michael Stern describe her as "a public image, a way of presenting a happy face to the world. It was a façade of optimism possible only in an era that had yet to invent such concepts as finding oneself and self-realization. In the pre-Me Generation days, it was a worthy enough goal to simply radiate cheer with the consistency of the sun."[20] Women from 1960s pop culture who fall into this category include Samantha (Elizabeth Montgomery) on the very queer *Bewitched* (1964–72), who was married but independent because of her magical powers and with a bumbling, effeminate husband (the second Darrin was Dick Sargent, who was gay) and a witch mother, played by the gay icon Agnes Moorehead; the childlike but powerful Barbara Eden in *I Dream of Jeannie* (1965–70); and even the dim-witted Elly May Clampett (Donna Douglas) on *The Beverly Hillbillies* (1962–71), which featured another gay icon, Nancy Kulp as Jane Hathaway.

Musical theatre's Single or Perky Girls populate this chapter, including middle-aged Mame, freewheeling and briefly married, and Dolly, widowed through most of the musical and married at the end. Neither ingénues nor comic sidekicks, these women sing alto, follow character arcs, and are highly active.

The Single Girl type exhibits traits that each female protagonist in these musicals possesses. First, she is employed, and her workplace is the location of her monetary and emotional security. She is practical, as well, with "concrete things on her mind, like paying the rent."[21] As Hilary Radner writes, "Crucial to the Single Girl's autonomy is her efficacy in the workplace. She is salaried.... A working girl, she exacts a paycheck from a boss rather than grocery money from a husband."[22] Second, the Single Girl is sexually active, and "sexuality is part of her capital, her expertise (performance) rather than her chastity enhance[s] her value."[23] Third, the Single Girl sees marriage in her future. She "does not consider the possibility of a world without men,"[24] argues Radner, and "she cannot ultimately challenge an order grounded in the primacy of masculinity."[25] Fourth, the Single Girl depends on her friends. Commentators or critics who found the mid-1960s Broadway musical hopelessly out of step with the times didn't notice the Single Girl there.

Women of color were barely visible as the 1960s Single Girl type.[26] In 1968, several years after these musicals opened, Naomi Sims was the first African American woman to appear on the cover of *Ladies Home Journal*.[27] Also in 1968, *Julia*, the television series starring Diahann Carroll, premiered; she was a widowed single mother, who worked as a nurse. (Images of the sexualized black woman or the Mammy figure were all too available in culture; what was lacking was the image of a self-determining woman of color.) In 1967–68, Pearl Bailey played the title role in a highly acclaimed all-black production of *Hello, Dolly!* According to theatre historian John Bush Jones, the number of black musicals declined in the 1960s when artists instead put their energy toward alternative, politically charged cultural sites.[28]

Choreographies

"One of the much-observed characteristics of the new sixties female icon— whether fictional or real-life heroine—was her ever-mobile, active, and graceful body," writes Moya Luckett.[29] The single women in this chapter dance or move, and their physicality, blocking, and gestures—their choreography, that is, whether set to music or to story—define their characters as much as song or speech. Musical theatre history imagines women as physically strong on stage, in a group, perfectly aligned in a kick line or alone, a still, grounded solo belter.[30]

The sharp kick line and the stolid, arms-spread belter haunt the various configurations of the character and actor's bodies in these 1960s musicals, which locate movement more "realistically" in relation to the characters' psychologies and within the diegeses of the musicals. For Charity and Sally Bowles, dance expresses her character, both on and off the stage of her employment, either the Fandango Ballroom or the Kit Kat Klub. Charity and Sally are performers whose overt displays of their bodies are celebrated on stage, even as they are punished and excluded from a successful romance. The next two musicals, titled after their female protagonists—*Hello, Dolly!* and *Mame*—feature a diva figure who sidesteps or remakes the heterosexual romance typical of musicals. The story is built around her, and the musical at once admires her, fetishizes her, and is confused by her. For Dolly or for Mame, her body—both the actor's and the character's—is set in the middle of an extravagant ensemble number that celebrates her. In addition, her body is a source of activity: Dolly and Mame both make things happen and propel the people around them to action. Finally, Nancy in *Oliver!* and Aldonza in *Man of La Mancha* are supporting characters who each sing several showstopping tunes, and yet the musicals utterly victimize them. Their class position sexualizes them, and they are tied to men but not married. Both Nancy and Aldonza dance in a tavern but are as forcefully embodied as victims of violence by men, aestheticized on the musical theatre stage. By focusing on the female characters and the convention of choreography, these musicals offer a new perspective on the 1960s Single Girl.

Sweet Charity

Based on Federico Fellini's film *Nights of Cabiria* [*Le Notti di Cabiria* (1957)], *Sweet Charity* opened at the Palace Theatre in January 1966. What critics called the musical's "slender plot" revolves around Charity's attempt to find a man—any man—who will love and marry her, as a large neon sign over the set reads, "The Story of a Girl Who Wanted to Be Loved."[31] She works as a taxi dancer at the sleazy Fandango Ballroom, and meets men night after night who want her but not in the way she wants. Charity meets the "famous movie star" Vittorio Vidal one night when she accidentally (literally) bumps into him, and he invites her to a club and then to his apartment, but only to make his temperamental girlfriend jealous. Charity also looks for a man at the 92nd Street Y and meets Oscar, the musical's male principal. Their relationship begins neither with love at first sight, nor the animosity typical for a 1950s Broadway musical but rather in a scene in which they are trapped in an elevator. He is claustrophobic and nearly hysterical, and she buoys him up, encouraging him to sing, "I'm the bravest individual I have ever met!" (61).[32] They click, and Charity tells Oscar that she works in a bank, hiding her real occupation from him, and soon they decide to marry. When she finally confesses that she is an almost-sex-worker, Oscar admits that he had already discovered her job and realized that he can't marry her. As Oscar says, "I have this childish, incomprehensible, idiotic, fixation about purity. . . . But every time I think of you—with all those other men—" (111). The musical ends with Charity alone but optimistic.

The musical was Bob Fosse's idea, transforming Fellini's prostitute protagonist into a less overtly sexualized dime-a-dancer, dividing the male lead into two separate characters, and moving the setting from Rome to New York. Fosse conceived the project as a comeback vehicle for his then-wife, Gwen Verdon, then forty-one years old, who had won Best Actress Tony Awards for *Can Can* (1953) and as Lola in *Damn Yankees* (1955).

Famous for her quirky hoarse voice, shocking red hair, and charismatic presence as well as her extraordinary dancing, Verdon was the first and most important interpreter of Fosse's choreography and the inspiration for much of his style.[33] Verdon's look in the show—short hair and sassy skirts—echoed the boyish angularity of famous fashion model Twiggy that was then all the rage. Theatre historian David Ewen summarizes: "From the moment Miss Verdon slipped onto the stage dancing . . . she remained in front of the footlights practically throughout the entire production (without a change of costume): singing, dancing, and projecting a galvanic personality that left the audience breathless not only for her performance but also for her sustained energy and dynamism."[34] According to Glenn Litton, "Fosse pushed everything at such a clip that the book's contradictions and empty spaces washed away behind his vivid, sinuous production numbers."[35]

The show solidified Fosse's reputation as a director-choreographer. His numbers in *Sweet Charity* ranged from jazz to soft-shoe to an extended dance piece that presented many then-current, popular social dance styles like the Frug. Featuring Fosse's jazzy hallmark sharp contrasts of motion and surprisingly appealing, awkward movements, Verdon's style conjoined with his in *Sweet Charity* to influence choreography in the 1960s, shifting pointed feet to flexed, with turned-in toes, jutted-out hips, slouched shoulders, head cocked to the side, and a slack-jawed expression that David Van Leer calls the "desexualization of eroticism."[36] Van Leer writes, "Some of the dance's gestures might seem to imitate traditional sexual movement—hip swings, wrist and ankle flips, slow sensual turns. But what we remember is the stylization, not the movements they imitate."[37] This new look altered the physicality of femininity on the Broadway musical stage.

Sweet Charity's comedic, heartwarming, and contemporary script was written by Neil Simon, playwright of the immensely popular *Come Blow Your Horn* (1961), *The Odd Couple* (1966), and *Barefoot in the Park* (1966), quintessential contemporary comedies of quick-witted, sharp-tongued, zany characters and almost slapstick situations. The script feels 1960s New York all over, with jokes about the city, references to 1960s television, psychotherapy, the Ninety-second Street Y, and a spiritual hippie counterculture (in "Rhythm of Life"). Cy Coleman, who wrote the music for *Wildcat* (1960) and *Little Me* (1962), produced a memorable score by using many musical forms prevalent in Broadway musicals of the mid-1960s—a march for "I'm a Brass Band," a mock gospel for "Rhythm of Life," and a bassa nova for Charity's soliloquy.[38] Lyricist Dorothy Fields, perhaps the most witty, prolific, and influential female musical theatre lyricist, who cowrote the libretto for *Annie Get Your Gun* (1946) with her brother Herbert, and wrote the lyrics for Fosse and Verdon's *Redhead* (1959), conveys a modern-day sense of character, setting, and plot.[39] Litton notes, "Like Charity, the numbers brimmed with old-fashioned, untempered eagerness to please."[40] *Sweet Charity*, primarily fueled by Verdon's fame and charisma, ran for 608 performances and won Fosse a Tony for Best Choreography.[41]

Sweet Charity ultimately makes a feminist case for sexual freedom and financial independence, but its ideological route is circuitous and riddled with obstacles, reflecting the contradictory messages about women and female sexuality that circulated in 1960s culture. At first, *Sweet Charity* appears to be blatantly, almost terrifyingly misogynist. The musical is framed by two almost identical scenes in which Charity's then-current boyfriend throws her into the lake in Central Park.[42] These two violent actions render literal the dominant theme of the musical: that Charity wants a man but will be rejected by all, from the sleazy, conniving thief who pushes her in the water at the beginning, to the sweet and neurotic man who shoves her in at the end. Although no doubt the bookend scenes were intended to be comic, they place a woman's body in the predictable, dreary position of hapless object-victim, and that she desires these men renders her all the more pathetic. Interestingly, though, these "victim" scenes foreground the typical status of Charity's body as active and self-assured, a theatrical embodiment of athletic self-possession. Charity's ostensible weakness, then, is contradicted by the actor's strength in performance, especially in singing and dancing; her inability to attract and keep a man is contradicted by the appeal of her character to the audience; her awkwardnesses are contradicted by her excellent, strong, and graceful dancing. In this way, *Sweet Charity* repeatedly and insistently enacts a paradox between saying and doing, yet the result is not cynicism: the exuberant action—the "doing"—performatively brings feminist possibilities into being.

Sweet Charity's anxious incongruities, perfectly predictable in a mid-1960s Single Girl musical, center on the theme of purity, from the protagonist's silly name, Charity Hope Valentine (which is met with a snicker from a policeman in the first scene), to Oscar's absurd refusal to see beyond her work (Fosse: "No matter how much he loves Charity, this guy cannot deal with the fact that she does what she does"[43]) to the sentimentality expressed by her friends at work. After Oscar proposes to Charity, her friends and coworkers at the dance hall throw her a going-away party. The taxi dancers, prostitutes, pimps, and small-time criminals sing and dance a bouncy chorus number, "I Love to Cry at Weddings," certifying in rousing good cheer that even society's "impure" are hopeless romantics. The scene, like many others in the musical, is a joke at mainstream society's expense and also expresses sincere emotion. When Charity's friends' affection for her is shown most clearly, Oscar decides that he can't be with her in what looks to him like a sordid sexual world. Oscar's attachment to "purity" seems absurd in the face of their sincere caring, and the audience is positioned with and sympathetic to Charity and her friends, caught up in the catchy song.

Charity desires domesticity, and she wants to be commodified, not as a sex object but as a wife. She would rather trade her financial independence in an exchange from laborer to wife, but because of her work, the middle-class man won't have her. In the end, Charity is ideologically "punished" not for her sexual prowess, which is never actually represented, but for her guileless anachronistic desire for a 1950s model of life. *Sweet Charity* does not condemn women for being sexual; it urges them to want something other than 1950s conventional marriage and to embrace being a Single Girl.

The first song of *Sweet Charity*, as is typical for a Broadway musical, introduces key elements of her character and shows her as a Single Girl. Charity enters the stage dancing to an almost cartoon-like melody; she is first seen as a moving body, and then later, she sings. Her opening song, "You Should See Yourself," a bossa nova with a driving, 6/8 beat, creates a sense of movement and motion. Unlike a typical "I am/I want" song, a declaration of the self and her desires, Charity's first song is directed to her soon-to-be-violent and soon-to-be-ex-boyfriend, and it expresses her character obliquely, as she urges "you" to see the good in himself. In a moment, this unnamed man will break up with her, steal her wallet, and dump her into the lake.

What does Charity's first song convey about her character? First, she is active, not passive, and she asserts her view of the man as she sings, "You should see yourself in my eyes!/You're a blue ribbon Pul-it-itzer prize!" (4). Second, she is propelled by dreams, ideas, and fantasies; in spite of rejection and even violence, she reemerges unscathed and hopeful again, her imagination alert, singing, "Dreams . . . I had not!/Dreams . . . now I got!" (5). Third, her opening soliloquy explains how she expects both sex and marriage. She expresses a new, liberated version of female sexuality in which the woman is active and desirous, speaking during the song's bridge, "You know what I did today? I looked at furniture. Bedroom sets, kitchen sets, bedroom sets, living room sets, bedroom sets" (4). The line is funny in its repetition and also frankly conveys her interest in sex. Fourth, she shows herself as financially stable: "I've got the money for the down payment right here. My dowry" (4). With sufficient finances, Charity remains outside the exchange of women between men; she can give (or sell) herself away. Finally, in the performance of this song, the actor and character merge into a figure whose physicality dominates the stage, then the show: as the character dances her way through her life, the performer dances her way through this musical. Charity's first number introduces her character by way of the actor's confident physicality and initiates the tension between form and content that the musical plays out. Even as the audience witnesses visually and experiences kinesthetically the pleasure of Charity's physical strength and gracefulness, it also encounters lyrics that generate a character with stereotypical female neediness. That the musical's introduction of its female principal is not directly followed by a parallel song with the male principal signals its structural distinction from most 1950s musicals and its focus solely on the woman.

After "Big Spender," the famous female ensemble number, Charity's second song, which shows her working, develops the contradiction between what is said and what is done. In her "Soliloquy," sung to herself as she dances with a client, she tells the story of the ex-boyfriend whom she met when he invited her to tea and she ended up buying him jockey shorts and paying for his cab. She recounts that he moved in with her and then, as the music shifts, "He needs toothpaste/And a tooth brush and pajama tops" (4), and finally, as the music changes to a tango, she tells how he demanded "pocket money! Poker money! Smoking money!/Skating money! Bowling money! Movie money!/Haircut money! Shoeshine money!" (22). As critic Mark Steyn describes the number, "Charity's banal recollections of a pedestrian relationship [are set] to a gently shimmering bossa nova. . . . The contrast between the tackiness of the relationship and its sophisticated musical setting makes it funny and sympathetic."[44]

In Charity's other numbers, her articulated fantasy of conventional domesticity is constantly and repeatedly undercut by the performer's power and the embodiment of the Single Girl. This musical spends most of its time letting the leading lady sing and dance alone; to be herself, Charity doesn't need a man, she needs to perform. For example, when Charity finds herself alone in Vittorio Vidal's bedroom, she sings a rousing "if they could see me now,/That little gang of mine—/I'm eating fancy chow/And drinking fancy wine—" (38) (fig. 2-1). In this song, Charity dances her way around the swanky bedroom, creating a stagey vaudeville number, using a cane and collapsible top hat as a prop. Unlike in the waltz, the polka, the tango, or other couple dances typical in Broadway musical choreography in the 1950s, the movement in this number

Figure 2.1 In *Sweet Charity* (1966), Charity (Gwen Verdon) enjoys a solo dance in Vittorio's apartment and wishes "If My Friends Could See Me Now." Courtesy Photofest.

is individual, highly theatrical, and direct. The choreography references new solo dances of the mid-1960s like go-go, which provided an escape from the heterosexual strictures of couple dancing.[45] Charity struts, kicks, marches, and twirls, all to her own pleasure, all movement propelled and sustained by herself, not by a male partner.[46] Later, after Oscar proposes to Charity and for one brief moment she thinks she will marry, she sings not a sweet love duet but a solo march: "I'm a brass band/I'm a harpsichord/I'm a clarinet . . . I'm the bells of St. Peter's in Rome/I'm tissue paper on a comb/And all kinds of music keeps pouring out of me" (101). The prospect of marriage turns her into music, even as an (unspecified) "somebody loves me at last" (101).[47] Romance for Charity is less about the specific man and more about the feeling. In the end, romance matters only because it allows her to perform.

Although throughout the show Charity's individual musical dominance and the actor's choreographic prowess undercut the failed marriage plot and the violent actions against her, the very end of the musical defies the musical theatre convention of the eleven o'clock number. Rather than a final solo announcing Charity's resilience, like "Rose's Turn" in *Gypsy*, or the reprise of "Don't Rain on My Parade" in *Funny Girl* ("My Man" in the film version), the last moment introduces the Fairy Godmother, who says to the "wringing wet" Charity (who has lifted herself out of the orchestra pit-cum-lake), "[d]reams will come true tonight!" (113). "She waves the wand at Charity" and "throws a handful of stardust on her," but then turns her back to the audience, revealing a large signs that reads, "Watch 'The Good Fairy' tonight—8 o'clock—CBS" and "flutters off the stage" (113). While the last image reveals how "dreams" are thoroughly structured by commercialism and media, Charity, undaunted, begins to dance as she did at the beginning, striking the same pose as she did at the musical's opening, as the stage's neon sign reads, "And so she lived . . . hopefully . . . ever after" (113). The musical's putatively sad ending and the assumption that she'll never get a man strain to reproduce the adage that some women are for marrying and some for sex. But the final moment belies the expressed vulnerability of its heroine and refuses to condemn her. The Broadway audience celebrates her presence and her dominance, as the final moment encapsulates what the audience already knows: *Sweet Charity* is not about the heterosexual couple, but about women alone. In the words of Helen Gurley Brown, "A single woman is known by what she does rather than by whom she belongs to."[48] Charity's final, simple gesture of picking up her suitcase, the almost iconic Single Girl pose, the relaxed and confident movement that propels the actor is greeted with thunderous applause, turning it into a vehicle for self-assertion, worn lightly at the end of this show.

Cabaret

Cabaret, with a libretto by Joe Masteroff, is based on John van Druten's play *I Am a Camera* (1951, starring Julie Harris), developed from Christopher Isherwood's

Berlin Stories. It follows American aspiring writer Cliff Bradshaw to Berlin in 1929, where he meets Sally Bowles, a vivacious and aggressively charming British cabaret performer who embodies the 1960s Single Girl.

Conceived and directed by Harold Prince, *Cabaret* is among the first "concept musicals"; that is, a musical structured to illuminate a theme or an idea more than to tell a conflict-driven story, and which tends to deal with serious subject matter and frequently refuses pat or happy endings. In addition, concept musicals experimented with new relationships among a musical's constituent parts of song and dance and book scenes.[49] For example, while all of the musical numbers in *Sweet Charity* extend an emotional moment or move the plot along, as was conventional in 1940s–60s formally integrated book musicals, in *Cabaret*, John Kander and Fred Ebb's songs fall into two categories. The first connects to the musical's two parallel realist romance plots, both of which fail. The relationship between Sally and Cliff ends when she aborts her baby and refuses to leave Berlin to go to America with him and create a nuclear family (although to many spectators, Cliff's expressed desire to marry Sally is a weak attempt to mask his homo- or bisexuality).[50] In the musical's secondary relationship, Fräulein Schneider, who owns the boarding house where Sally and Cliff live, breaks off her engagement to Herr Schultz, a Jewish man who is so fully assimilated to German culture that he fails to see how the Nazi regime will affect him, even after bricks are thrown through the windows of his fruit store.[51] These songs include Sally's early number "Perfectly Marvelous," Fräulein Schneider's "Who Cares Why Not," and the older couple's "The Pineapple Song."[52]

The second category of song and the marker of this musical's structural innovation takes place in the Kit Kat Klub. These are the Emcee-led diegetic numbers performed in a sleazy setting, each directly commenting on the action of the domestic scene that precedes it, such as "The Money Song" and "If You Could See Her through My Eyes." Brechtian in style and Weillian in tone, these comment songs position the theatre audience as the cabaret audience, implicating the viewers as citizens in pre-Nazi Germany being entertained by "decadent" performers. In this space that Prince referred to as "limbo," set designer Boris Aronson angled a large mirror above the stage, as noted earlier, which forced the 1966 audience members to see themselves literally reflected as they watched the musical. *Cabaret* is as much about mid-1960s America as it is about pre-Nazi Germany.

A few mid-1960s critics chafed at this dark, ironic, political, and self-reflexive piece, but *Cabaret* won eight Tony Awards, including Best Musical, and it quickly became the "hottest ticket" on Broadway in 1966 and ran for

1,166 performances.[53] "A stunning musical," Walter Kerr called it in the *New York Times*. "Brilliantly conceived.... It opens the door ... to a fresh notion of the bizarre, crackling, harsh, and yet beguiling uses that can be made of song and dance."[54] Bert Convy played Cliff, and Joel Grey created the role of the Emcee that made him a star on stage and later on screen in the film version.

Many of the contradictions that appear in *Sweet Charity* among narrative, character, and performance are also evident in *Cabaret*, and the female principal, Sally Bowles, like Charity, exemplifies the 1960s Single Girl. Like Charity, Sally has childlike qualities, but here, she is a self-indulgent woman who only thinks of liquor, fur coats, and parties. As she says to Cliff when he refuses to smuggle money for the Nazi Party, "You mean—politics? But what has *that* to do with us?" (95).[55] *Cabaret* conflates the personal—Sally's resistance to becoming an American housewife—and the political—her blithe attitude toward the Nazis, so that Single Girl femininity stands in for amorality. (In comparison, as noted earlier, *Sweet Charity* critiques its protagonist for her desire for 1950s domesticity.) And yet in spite of the fact that the musical is told from Cliff's perspective and the Emcee emerges as the unforgettably terrifying voice of reason's demise, it is Sally Bowles, played by British film actress Jill Haworth, who crosses between the two worlds and who sings the musical's memorable title song. The musical is laced through with ambivalence about the representation of 1960s femininity.

From the beginning, Sally is a fiercely embodied character, and because many of her songs are diegetic, her job as a performer and dancer, as a physically laboring body, is constantly foregrounded. In contrast to Charity, whose thankless and demeaning job opens the floodgates for her fantasies, to which she dances with exuberance, Sally adores her job and the role she plays as "herself" on stage. But as in *Sweet Charity*, the place of staged performance in *Cabaret* is seedy, and Sally is supposed to be a mediocre performer, a paradox that challenges a Broadway audience that expects a superlative voice. Many reviewers complained about Haworth's less-than-stellar performance, and Kerr called her the "one wrong note" in the production.[56] But, as Prince commented, the actor playing Sally must perform badly to be believable: "Sally Bowles was not supposed to be a professional singer. She wasn't supposed to be so slick that you forgot she was an English girl somewhat off the rails in the Weimar era."[57] Prince opted for dramatic realism over conforming to audience expectations.

In addition to framing Sally as a performer, her opening number, "Don't Tell Mama," simultaneously functions as a conventional "I am/I want" song, and so blurs from the start the difference between the performer Sally Bowles, "the Queen of Mayfair," as the Emcee introduces her, and the "real" Sally

Bowles (fig. 2-2).[58] The number is structured in two sections, with the first part spoken: "Mama thinks I'm living in a convent," as Sally reveals from the start that she is not Jewish and not directly affected by the events to come. As the song continues, "Don't Tell Mama" moves into a clever, lilting, jazzy tune in syncopated 4/4 time. The bouncy, short-syllabled lyrics of the refrain, each of which ends with the line "Don't tell mama," allows the song to pulse and push on. Sally sings in a direct address to "Please sir," "Hush up," "Shush up," and the end of each verse is punctuated by references to corrupt family members whose lifestyles are worse than hers. The song resembles in tone the throwaway number "A Bushel and a Peck" from *Guys and Dolls*—a self-consciously child-like, sexual come-on number that became the biggest hit from that show. This one differs, though, from the jaded power of the women in *Sweet Charity*'s "Big Spender," even as all three numbers address the male audience/clients directly. The lyrics stress Sally's difference from her mother, and even as she sings in character, this song foreshadows that Sally will reject the pressure to be a mother by the end of the musical. "Don't Tell Mama" maps the persona of the Single Girl, who is distinguished from her mother as sexual and autonomous.

Figure 2.2 In *Cabaret* (1966), Sally Bowles (Jill Haworth) takes center stage at the Kit Kat Club in "Don't Tell Mama." Bert Convy, sitting right, as Cliff. Courtesy Billy Rose Theatre Division, the New York Public Library for the Performing Arts, Astor, Lenox and Tilden Foundations.

Ron Field's choreography for the number communicates Sally Bowles's cli-chéd sense of sexiness.[59] Field explained how his choreographic process for *Cabaret* entailed putting himself in role: "I thought, I am a choreographer at the Kit Kat Club, which is a second-rate club in Berlin in 1930, how would I approach this? I thought, Well, I'd go to see a lot of American movies. I would see what was going on in America, since America has always been the place where *dancing* stars." He continued, "I would kind of overdo it. Everything took on heaviness, a harshness."[60] Although no taped version of Jill Haworth's performance is available, a 1968 clip of the London production that followed the one on Broadway and starred Judi Dench shows Field's choreography.[61] As the song begins, Dench enters through a glittery curtain of ribbons, wearing a long, slinky, fringe-bottomed red dress with a fluffy white boa thrown over her shoulder, and stands on an upstage platform alone. She holds a long cigarette holder from which she puffs occasionally. She slinkily moves downstage where the other Kit Kat girls are gathered, half serious and half laughing, lips curled.

As a fairly conventional musical theatre choreographer, Field incorporates steps that were part of a 1960s Broadway movement vocabulary to suggest sex-iness more than show it overtly (as Fosse did in *Sweet Charity* and the film version of *Cabaret*, although Field's style was not as stylized and was very pretty when compared to Fosse's brash and aesthetically unappealing move-ment). The movements in the song are seductive, teasing, and directed to the men in the audience. Dench and the other women, who are dressed in sailor tops and satiny shorts, frequently sink into one hip, with the legs bent and to-gether, and alternate this closed downward movement with a stance with arms raised and extended, which is regularly accented with a flirty turn of the wrist. The movement is pleasurable to watch and predictably feminine. Except for one moment of hip gyration, Dench's hips move right and left and not forward and back (that is, not contracting and releasing, which much more approxi-mates sex). As for the chorus, except for a section during which each woman of the chorus wraps her arms around herself in a kind of hug, then bends her knees and pops up, their movement is similarly "pretty." For most of the song, Dench moves in front of, is encircled by, or moves behind the line of the other women. In every way, the focus is on her, in the costume, vocally, and choreo-graphically. Until the final number, all of Sally's numbers in the cabaret are solo turns embedded within a group number. In this way, the uniqueness of her character is constantly asserted.

By the end of *Cabaret*, the book scenes have shown Cliff as growing, changing, and learning, and Sally as unchangingly flighty, fun-loving, needy, and charmingly manipulative—just as she was in her first song with Cliff, when she puts words in his mouth, "I've met this perfectly marvelous girl" (38). Sally's last song number, the famous title song, shifts again the balance among the contradictions of Sally's character. While the narrative world of the musical attempts to condemn or at least pity Sally's apolitical and fallen-woman condition, the theatre audience takes pleasure in her virtuosity in song and her strength in dance.

Through much of the musical, Sally is dancing, moving, sitting on Cliff's lap, or drinking oysters and raw eggs to cure a hangover, but the last song finds her standing still in a spotlight, at once devastated and exhausted, celebratory and exuberant, and sincere. She sings, "What good is sitting alone in your room?/Come hear the music play" (106), and during the song, she decides to end the pregnancy. Cliff will leave, but she remains and can sing and perform on stage. By the end of the musical, like Charity (and like Fanny Brice in *Funny Girl* [1964]), Sally is alone. The heterosexual relationship has failed but the vibrant body of the female performer succeeds theatrically. She is, in the end, determined to live, since "life is a cabaret" (106). Finally, like the mirror that reflected the 1966 Broadway audience back to itself, Sally's abortion likely would have resonated with the then-recent FDA approval of the birth-control pill, to which, of course, a 1920s Sally would not have had access. The fact that she doesn't move or dance at the end of the musical suggests that her Single Girl body betrayed her. *Cabaret* warns of the dangers of a woman's freedom.

Hello, Dolly! and Mame

In the mid-1960s, composer Jerry Herman wrote scores for two musicals that remain among the most frequently performed and best-loved shows of the twentieth century.[62] *Mame* resembles *Hello, Dolly!* in other ways: both were adapted from well-known and successful nonmusical plays; both were choreographed by visionary artists (Gower Champion for *Dolly* and Onna White for *Mame*); both feature a strong, singular, middle-aged woman; both female leads are controlling, verbal, irresistible, and clever; both musicals are sweet and funny; both are set in time periods distinct from the 1960s when they were produced (*Hello, Dolly!* in the 1890s; *Mame* in the 1920s–40s); both were enormously successful and continue to be produced regularly; both contain a title song that places the female protagonist in the center. In addition, while both are formally integrated book musicals, both replace the Rodgers and Hammerstein conventional romance narrative with a woman's story surrounded by several subplots. Dolly and Mame do get married, but neither marriage changes the female lead and marriage is ultimately insignificant in the musical as a whole. These are shows about a single woman on stage.

Hello, Dolly! and *Mame*, produced two years apart, star women who are variations on the Single Girl of the 1960s, a middle-aged woman whose quirky eccentricity and financial independence not only win her freedom in the musical but utter star power on stage. Like the other musicals in this chapter, *Hello, Dolly!* and *Mame* perform anxiety about gender and ambivalence about strong women. Well known but shortchanged by labeling them "diva vehicles," *Mame* and *Hello, Dolly!* offer bold solo numbers and rich characters for middle-aged women, as evidenced by the sheer number of great female performers who played these roles over the years, including Carol Channing, Mary Martin, Ethel Merman, Ginger Rogers, Pearl Bailey, and Barbra Streisand in the movie version as Dolly, and Angela Lansbury, Ginger Rogers (again, this time in the 1969 London production of *Mame*), and Lucille Ball in the film as Mame. In addition, both of these musicals are, perhaps ironically, best known not for the songs that the women themselves sing but for the infectious title songs that a chorus sings to and about them. Both musicals frame scenes of the woman coming down a staircase self-consciously and with absolute control, making a spectacle of herself, even as the number both celebrates and objectifies her; and in other scenes, the woman is physically active. Because Mame and Dolly are middle-aged women, the musicals don't sexualize them; rather each woman's forceful personality reverses the age-old masculine-active/feminine-passive binary.

Hello, Dolly! is based on Thornton Wilder's play *The Matchmaker*, and follows the travails of the widow Dolly Levi, who sets up couples and then makes a match for herself in the personage of the rich Horace Vandergelder. Impresario producer David Merrick launched the project. Before Merrick decided to hire Jerry Herman to write the music for *Hello, Dolly!*, he wasn't sure that Herman, whose best-known score was the Israel-set *Milk and Honey* (1961), could "do Americana." Herman later said, "He thought I was too *ethnic* for the piece," but Merrick gave him a copy of the script, and Herman composed four songs in three days, including the title number and "Put on Your Sunday Clothes." In a fifteen-minute audition, Merrick heard the music and hired him on the spot.[63] *Hello, Dolly!* became one of the best-loved musicals of all time. It won ten Tony Awards, including Best Musical and Best Actress for Channing, and ran for 2,844 performances, becoming the longest running musical at the time. Gower Champion, who was among the first director-choreographers (like Bob Fosse, Michael Bennett, and more recently, Kathleen Marshall), won acclaim for his work.[64]

The character of Dolly Levi is active and in charge throughout the musical, and her very identity is one that influences other people and affects their lives. Her story in the musical charts her realization that she needs to "arrange" her own life and remarry as well as facilitate other people's marriages. As Wilder said, "My play is about the aspirations of the young (and not only the young) for a fuller, freer participation in life."[65] The opening number of the show, "Call On Dolly," is sung by the chorus of 1890s New York City townspeople "in stylized poses" as the curtain rises: "Call on Dolly/She's the one the spinsters recommend/Just name the kind of man your sister wants/And she'll snatch him up" (3).[66] Other characters sing about and identify Dolly before she sings about herself, and when she enters in the middle of the song, the crowd applauds. She is immediately framed as active, as a doer, and as a performer. She introduces herself: "Marriages arranged!" and "Financial Consultation, Instruction on the Guitar and Mandolin, Short Distance Hauling, and National Monuments Restored!" (4). The wacky list again underlines her activity, which crosses money, music, manual labor, and patriotism. The moment is both clever and silly, an exaggeration that produces ambivalence about her character, raising the question of whether the musical is laughing with her or at her. Later in the scene, she explains that this is how she makes a living: "Some people paint, some sew . . . I meddle!" and continues by singing her "I am/I want" number, "I Put My Hand In." Dolly describes herself as a woman interested in both "pleasure and the profit it derives" and explains that she arranges such diverse things as "furniture and daffodils and lives" (7).

For the first part of the musical, Dolly acts on and influences other people. She advises and colludes with Irene Molloy about her marriage prospects (the women are two sides of the same widowed coin, and each wants to marry to be financially supported and be able to stop working), and she teaches Barnaby to dance so that he can get a girl (58). She sets up romance rather than participating, narrating her plans to her "late husband Ephraim Levi"—that is, to herself and the audience—and quoting his favorite aphorisms to anyone who pays attention. At the end of act 1, though, she "asks" Ephraim to allow her to marry Vandergelder. Again, this action is amusing and contradictory. On the one hand, she behaves as if she needs a man to give her power to make a new life; on the other hand, she is clearly the master of her own future. She can perform the widow even as she acts with complete autonomy. Act 1 ends with Dolly's showstopping "Before the Parade Passes By," an anthem that gradually grows to a rousing march, and she declares that she wants to participate in life and not sit and watch it pass by her (63). In act 2, once Dolly knows her mind, she only needs to lay the trap, and there is no doubt that she will get what she wants. She tricks Vandergelder into marrying her, but he seems delighted by it in the end, and eventually reprises the title song in honor and admiration of her (114).[67] *Hello, Dolly!* moves between a sweet, even sentimental presentation of love, romance, and marriage, and an utterly practical one. For Dolly, marriage is never anything other than a business arrangement.

In act 2, the musical's famous title song and choreography recenter Dolly's body as both acting subject and fetishized object. The waiters excitedly announce her arrival (repeating the pattern that opened the musical: a description of her and anticipation for her precedes her). Rudolph exclaims, "It's true, yah! She just stepped out of a white and gold carriage, pulled by six black horses with scarlet plumes," to which the Cook responds, "After ten years! Ach, Rudolph! It's like old times again" (85). Dolly, the party girl Cinderella who brings the Harmonia Gardens back to celebratory life, arrives, and the stage directions read, "Music up as every eye goes to the head of the stairs, the portieres move and Mrs. Levi steps through, handsomely gowned, red hair done up magnificently on top of her head. She descends stairs as Waiters, etc. await her first words" (85), and she begins to sing the title song.

Dolly's entrance, while emphasizing the single woman's presence, differs from, for example, Sally Bowles's in *Cabaret* because Dolly is middle-aged and widowed, and so outside of a blatantly sexualized role. The choreography in this number emphasizes how Dolly is both subject and object. According to Champion biographer David Payne-Carter, the famous number was created partly by serendipity when rehearsal pianist Peter Howard began to play burlesque music to accompany Dolly's descent down the staircase: "Its very incongruity—racy music accompanying a middle-aged widow descending stairs into an elegant restaurant—seemed to add a dimension of which Herman and Champion had never dreamed."[68] Champion choreographed the rest of the number with Dolly moving in counterpoint to the mass of waiters. They dance around the pasarelle (the ramp built around the orchestra pit out from the stage's apron, which gave the set a turn-of-the-century feeling) and cross in opposite directions, Dolly leading the movement, her singularity constantly set off from the men as a group.[69] When they join together for the kick line, the unity of movement contrasts the earlier crossing and countercrossing, representing Dolly's return to her life.[70] Meanwhile, the lyrics express the continuity of the present with the past and Dolly's (aging) body: "You're still glowin', you're still crowin', you're still goin' strong" (86). Both she and they sing, "Dolly'll never go away again" (86). Neither a heterosexual couple nor a community perform this rousing central song, but rather a group of men express their affectionate appreciation of a middle-aged, single, charming, sexually unavailable woman. Referencing the Ziegfeld Follies and Marilyn Monroe singing "Diamonds Are a Girl's Best Friend," with the attending men respectfully admiring from a distance, Dolly's age excludes her as a viable sex object for them, and the men are positioned as mascots and seemingly gay. Dolly's singular self and body become an object for a group of men to appreciate.

In addition to her body's centrality in this showstopping number, the character occupies an extraordinarily physicalized presence in the musical. The climactic scene in Harmonia Gardens, where Dolly entraps Horace during the meal, for example, is a hilarious choreography of food, silverware, and condiments (fig. 2-3).[71] A series of photographs of this scene in the Billy Rose Theatre Collection of various actors who played Dolly, laid out to create a kind of storyboard and read alongside the script, captures the movement of a single woman "dancing" and the comedy of the scene. Dolly never stops talking and she never stops eating, two activities that foreground her bodily presence. She claims she can't eat a thing and proceeds to eat everything. He says he doesn't like beets and she serves him beets. Dolly sprinkles salt and eats enthusiastically, and her mouth is open and she is talking the whole time. She gestures as she talks; she points all over the place; she takes off her gloves (which is a big project since they go above her elbow); she reaches out over the table; she dishes food onto his plate; she pours salt on his plate. Food flies on and off her plate and his plate and across the room, and she talks so fast that he can't keep up. In an exchange repeated several times in the scene, she says, "However we won't discuss it anymore," and then, "However since you brought the matter up, there's one more thing I ought to say," to which he answers, "I didn't bring the matter up at all!" She comes back with, "One more thing I ought to say before we forget all about it. . . ." (92–93). Vandergelder is situated as a spectator and the object on which/whom she acts in the scene. Dolly is both character and choreographer; she directs movement, maneuvers people around (as does Mame), manipulates Vandergelder's intentions, and exerts control over their lives. The refrain or punch line of the scene, "You go your way . . . (She points Right with one hand) . . . And I'll go mine! (A windup with the other hand, then she points in the same direction as the first hand)" (91–92) gesturally crystallizes how she crafts the scene to her pleasure.

The character of Dolly Levi unsettles conventions of female types that were typical in Broadway musicals until this point. The role that would usually be played by a character actor is the star, and while she sings frequently in the show, the role doesn't require a legit voice. Herman believed that he was writing the score for Ethel Merman, and he composed numerous solos for Merman's expansive range and powerful belt. When Merman declined the

Figure 2.3 In *Hello, Dolly!* (1964), Dolly (Carol Channing) eats and talks in an elaborate choreography of food and utensils as she convinces Horace (David Burns) to marry her. Courtesy Photofest.

role, saying that back pain after *Gypsy* kept her from performing again, Herman was devastated.[72] Still, director and choreographer Gower Champion "cast not only according to type and ability, but according to the energy a performer was able to pour into the audience."[73] Carol Channing won the role through her quirky presence and strong physicality, what Herman appreciated as her "larger than life, almost cartoon-like quality."[74]

Numerous actors of different types—in addition to Channing (opened January 16, 1964), Ginger Rogers (who replaced Channing beginning on August 9, 1966), Martha Raye (1967), Betty Grable (1967), Bibi Osterwald (1967), Phyllis Diller (1969), Ethel Merman (who finally came around in 1970), and Mary Martin—played Dolly successfully because the role is exceptionally malleable. Dolly is an actor and is acted upon, a subject and an object. Her type resonates with the 1960s Single Girl, and refers to and critiques housewives of the 1950s and '60s. Just as the character of Dolly charms and manipulates those around her, each actor can charm and manipulate Dolly to accommodate her voice, her style, her physical humor.

In 1967, Merrick opened an enormously successful all-black production starring Pearl Bailey who, many critics noted, played herself with charismatic verve and in great voice (fig. 2-4). Merrick, who was always committed to hiring black actors, produced Dolly because "a white man's story about the upper class could be done with an all-Negro company. Well, as you know, it did work."[75] Through the 1960s, employment for black actors on and off Broadway fluctuated as much as it had in the 1940s and 1950s, and despite agitation by Actors' Equity for integrated shows (the union succeeded in banning segregated audiences in 1961), no positive trends could be identified. All-black shows had more success providing opportunities for black actors, which frustrated Equity's Committee on Racial Equality (CORE) chairman Frederick O'Neal, who commented in the New York Times in 1967, "How long does one wait for voluntary compliance with these things?" and added that "those outside the theatre are going to force the issue," alluding to CORE's picketing outside the theatre of How to Succeed in Business without Really Trying in 1962 to protest the musical's all-white cast. In March 1968, statistics were terrible; of the 523 actors working on Broadway, 57 were black, seven Latino, and one Asian. [76]

For many, the all-black Dolly was a very positive event. The New York Amsterdam News reviewer Jesse H. Walker enthused, "It's a triumphant musical and a personal triumph for Pearl Bailey, who, while really being Dolly is still Pearlie Mae—from the moment she comes on and ad libs 'I got a few words to say in this show,' throughout the show as she rolls her eyes, her hips, her lyrics and everything else, until the finale and her standing ovation from the SRO audience."[77] Clive Barnes in the New York Times agreed. But in the late 1960s, many detractors viewed the production as offensively segregationist, which Barnes even notes in his review, saying that he was reluctant to support the project but was charmed by the production. Actors' Equity and O'Neal also disapproved, especially after the progress made toward integrated casts. Bailey, for her part, demurred, and pointed to the terrific performance opportunity for her and

Figure 2.4 In the all-black production of *Hello, Dolly!* (1967), Pearl Bailey in the title role marches around the stage's extended apron, getting attention from all assembled in the musical's title song. Courtesy Billy Rose Theatre Division, the New York Public Library for the Performing Arts, Astor, Lenox and Tilden Foundations.

other black performers. Baseball star Jackie Robinson also praised the production in a column for the *New York Amsterdam News*: "Magic is the word for Miss Bailey. She casts a spell. Charming, mischievous, genuine, and lovable, she does an incredible job." He explained, "'Dolly,' as you know, is all Negro cast. It wasn't too long ago that some people would have regarded this fact as a step backward. But 'Dolly' is a long leap forward. It is such a beautiful company with its combination of colors from fair, through yellow, tan, brown and black."[78] Merrick and Bailey proved that the middle-aged Single Girl type, asexual by definition, could include an African American woman.

Mame

Mame, Herman's second huge hit of the mid-1960s, was directed by Gene Saks, with a book by Jerome Lawrence and Robert E. Lee, based on their play, *Auntie Mame*, which was based on Patrick Dennis's novel of the same name. In the introduction to the script, Lawrence and Lee defend their musical's celebration of life and the necessity for a character like Mame during the tumultuous mid-1960s. They write, "This seems to be the Year of the Mole—a time of blindness and confusion, of fuzzy aims and fading faith. Our theater lately has been in a dark age, reflecting only shadows. Mame somehow lifts a flame in that blackness. She has optimism! zest! bounce!"[79] For the librettists, an escapist musical during this time was a political gesture. Angela Lansbury embodied Mame with appropriate gusto, and Bea Arthur played her best friend and best enemy, Vera Charles.[80] *Mame* opened on May 24, 1966, and ran for 1,508 performances.

Like Dolly, Mame is a middle-aged Single Girl of the 1960s who controls her world and whose singular body dominates the show. Moreover, like *Hello, Dolly!, Mame* both adores and values its protagonist and reveals some anxiety about her power by undermining her autonomy and objectifying her in the title song. Lawrence and Lee suggest their ambivalence: "Even when she isn't quite sure where she's going, Mame knows, by God, she'll get there!"[81] But *Mame* differs from *Hello, Dolly!* as well. First, although she is Irish (Levi is her married name), Dolly is a Jewish-seeming character, whose penultimate scene finds her eating voraciously, talking nonstop, and manipulating a man through wit, cleverness, and speed to get what she wants. Mame, in contrast, is an urbane and sophisticated Manhattan WASP who drinks too much, parties too much, breaks rules, and yet manages to be accepted by the southern gentry and the family of her beau, Beau. While Dolly can do anything to make money and support herself, Mame can only spend money. When the stock market crashes and Mame tries to work by playing the "Lady in the Moon" in a musical comedy in which Vera is starring, she gets tangled in the scenery. As the stage directions read, "But as Mame stares down [from the suspended moon to the stage floor below], her fear carries her away and her obligato goes wild. Mame hangs onto the swaying moon for dear life, but her hat falls off and she ends up clinging to the underside of the crescent" (42). For the audience, this scene is hilarious and relies on the actor's physical humor, like Dolly's in the restaurant, and yet, Mame's failure signifies her inability to function as a laboring body. These two musicals expand the range of middle-aged single girls by way of class and ethnicity.

Figured as active throughout the musical, Mame enters by sliding down the banister in a flourish, dressed in gold pajamas and carrying a bugle, into the center of the party in her house to celebrate "a holiday I invented" (6) (fig. 2-5). She is creative and imaginative, lives for the moment, is a passionate, open-hearted adventuress. In her first song, "It's Today," a variation on an "I am/I want" number, Mame expresses her life philosophy and engages the whole group: "Well it may not be anyone's birthday/And it's far from the first of the year" (6). She warmly adopts her orphaned nephew Patrick and takes care of Agnes Gooch when the shy girl finds herself pregnant. Like Dolly, she is smart and, if necessary, conniving: when confronted with the conservative, racist family of Patrick's fiancée, she buys the property that abuts theirs to open a home for unmarried pregnant women both to make a political point and to

Figure 2.5 In *Mame* (1966), Angela Lansbury in the title role slides down the banister in her flamboyant entrance in "It's Today." Courtesy Billy Rose Theatre Division, the New York Public Library for the Performing Arts, Astor, Lenox and Tilden Foundations.

anger them. Both Dolly and Mame do marry but marriage plays a small role in these musicals; the male principal sings little, and the single woman emerges as the musical's center.

Both Dolly and Mame win their men though physical activity—Dolly's elaborate restaurant stage choreography and Mame's fox hunt. Although the audience doesn't see Mame, who's never ridden a horse and to whom Beau's suspicious mother intentionally assigns a "crazy" horse, they hear an account of what happens. Jeff, a character in the ensemble, sings, "Look at her go,/Look at her fly,/Out of the woods,/Into the sky," as Mame somehow stays on the horse. Another ensemble character sings, "She's ruined your bougainvillea/ And she's smashed your plums," and Mother Burnside exclaims, "astounded," "Mother of Jefferson Davis, she's passing the FOX!" (69–70). Beau concludes, "This lovely lady has restored elegance and humanity to the gentlemanly sport of the hunt" (71). Mame is more man than men. She finds quick acceptance among her future husband's family after she performs a great feat of athleticism—that is, after she becomes her body.

The musical's title song celebrates Mame after she passes the fox and then rescues the creature. If the title song in *Hello, Dolly!* celebrates the heroine's return, "Mame" welcomes the protagonist to a new social scene, but both women are admired for their independence and charm. If Dolly brings the Harmonia Gardens back to life after her ten-year-absence, Mame's very presence reshapes emblems of southernness. Beau's friends and family sing, "You make the cotton easy to pick,/Mame,/You give my old mint julep a kick,/Mame" (73). (Both *Hello, Dolly!* and *Mame* cheerily sidestep the complexities of class [waiters in New York] and race [celebratory references to picking cotton] in their ode to a single woman.)

About this song, Herman said, "I didn't want to write another title song after *Hello, Dolly* because I kept on saying to the producers, It's never going to happen a second time. Lightning does not strike twice."[82] So powerful was Herman's music and lyrics, though, that Onna White's choreography in *Mame*'s title song bears striking resemblance to Champion's in *Hello, Dolly!*; that is, the music fairly tells the dancers how to move. Appropriately for this number, White "was known for her large-scale, intricate dance routines and her meticulous planning."[83] With relatively simple steps in fantastic, complex configurations, many bodies move in opposing directions at once, conveying a grand sense of movement and propulsion. The crowd travels across the stage in a big line, and the song revolves around Mame, who is sung to and about. In the musical's title song that ends act 1, the female star doesn't sing it at all.

Visually, Mame's body stands out, as her costume in this scene stresses her difference, too. The men wear white riding pants and red tails, and the women are dressed in flouncy pinks. Mame, in contrast, sports an androgynous black and white riding outfit with long black skirt and jacket. She looks different and unique, as the scene and the song tell the story of a leading lady who is admired but who is set apart in a big group number.

Oliver!

Oliver!, the British-born musical by Lionel Bart, had already made back its investment for David Merrick by the time it opened in New York. A three-year hit in London, *Oliver!* began its Broadway production with out-of-town tryouts in Los Angeles, San Francisco, Detroit, and Toronto.[84] The cast album was released months before the Broadway premiere and was already on the charts by the time the show opened on January 6, 1963. In spite of lukewarm reviews in New York, most of which questioned the very project of musicalizing Dickens's novel, *Oliver!* was well received by Broadway audiences and ran for 774 performances. It was nominated for ten Tony Awards and won for scenic design, musical direction, and score. *New York Times* reviewer Howard Taubman found the adaptation sentimental and "obvious," accusing it of settling "for stridency, smoke, easy laughs and facile show-business razzmatazz."[85] The production imported Sean Kenney's "vivid scenery," which received some critical compliments.[86] Taubman praised the revolving turntables with set changes in full view of the audience and no curtain dropping—both scenographic novelties at the time—claiming that they were "an enormous aid to evoking the atmosphere of London; they change and move so swiftly and freshly that they seem to lead an imaginative life of their own."[87]

In addition to commenting on the scenery, reviewers weighed in on the transformation of Fagin, who, like Dickens's character, was Jewish in the West End production, but whom Merrick changed into an ethnically unspecific swindler so as not to offend Broadway's considerable Jewish audience base.[88] As a photo spread featured in the *New York Times* in December 1962, a month before the musical's opening, noted, creator Bart, himself Jewish, eliminated "Fagin's identity as a Jew; . . . he is now a Cockney and more humorous than sinister."[89] Taubman, though, criticized the choice to shape Fagin as "a complacent low comedian" with his big pickpocketing number "a jolly rumpus room."[90] He noted that Fagin's second act number, "Reviewing the Situation," musically belied the producers' effort to deracinate the character, since it "bears close resemblance to a Jewish folksong." The number contains "a lush violin obligato [that] seems to stress racial strains that the author obviously never meant to suggest."[91]

Whatever sensitivity the creators and commentators expressed about the representation of a Jewish character in *Oliver!*, they shared none about the character of Nancy, one of two featured women in the musical who is verbally abused, slapped, beaten, and eventually murdered. Critics' lack of attention to Nancy's victimization is remarkable because she is the female lead in the musical, but such an observation would have been anathema to mid-1960s male critics. Taubman summed up his review of Georgia Brown by describing her as "earthy" (fig. 2-6).[92]

Although she enters the musical relatively late, near the end of act 1, Nancy is a key figure in the musical's plot. First, she entraps Oliver when he leaves the house of wealthy Mr. Brownlow (who turns out to be his grandfather), failing to realize that once he landed under the rule of Fagin, the miser, Bill Sikes would never allow the boy to escape alive. Back at Fagin's place with Oliver, Nancy defends the boy against Sikes's rage. Soon, though, she is overwhelmed by guilt and regret for returning Oliver to a life of fear and abuse, and Nancy then returns to Brownlow's house, confesses her actions, and arranges to bring Oliver back to the rich man by meeting at London Bridge that night. The story hinges on Nancy's actions, decisions, and reversal of those decisions.

Oliver! reiterates that Nancy is her body, both as an active character and a victim of Sikes's violence. She is introduced vocally, cursing nonsense words from offstage, "Plumming and Slam!"[93] and enters with her younger friend and sidekick, Bet, who might be her better mate than Bill Sikes. By presenting Nancy coupled with Bet—a viable partner—the musical stresses her heteromasochism. Fagin shouts, "The ladies! Wake up boys the ladies are here," to which Nancy responds, "We'll have less of that if you don't mind. Where's the gin?" The stage directions indicate that "Nancy drinks half the bottle of gin in one gulp," as Fagin warns, "All in moderation my dear. Too much gin can be a dangerous thing for a pure young girl." Nancy's excessive behavior, which even the horrible Fagin recognizes as unhealthy, frames her as irresponsible and only able to quench her bodily desires. Later, when Nancy recants her kidnapping of Oliver, she cements her symbolic role as the whore with a heart of gold (like Charity, a bit like Sally Bowles, and like Aldonza in *Man of La Mancha*).

Musically, Nancy is central to the show. She performs some of *Oliver!*'s best-known and most moving songs and more of them than any other character in *Oliver!* Nancy's significant musical presence not only allows her to express herself, it also elevates her status in the society of thieves and beggars who populate

Figure 2.6 In *Oliver!* (1963), Fagin (Clive Revill) and Nancy (Georgia Brown) scheme about how to "Live a Fine Life" of petty crimes, pickpocketing, and trickery. Courtesy Photofest.

the musical. Near the end of act 1, she initiates the first of two saloon songs— "It's a Fine Life"—a semisarcastic account of their lives as member of London's urban poor (and the song is reprised in act 2). She also sings "I'd Do Anything" with the Artful Dodger, a tongue-in-cheek critique of the fancy society that she detests and for which she longs. She models a parodic performance, which

Oliver and Bet imitate. Nancy's voice also opens act 2 with the lively polka "Oom Pah Pah," in which all assembled in the tavern join. In three of her four numbers, Nancy serves as leader and teacher. These three of Nancy's musical numbers are full-out production numbers with choreography and movement. The first two numbers blur the diegetic and nondiegetic, as they are spontaneous performances for the assembled group. "Oom Pah Pah" is diegetic, performed for the pleasure of patrons at the tavern. These three numbers emphasize how deeply the character lives in her body.

Nancy's musical numbers, framed as performances, set up expectations about the character's sincerity, as the character is well aware when she is performing. When she sings the heartbreaking ballad "As Long as He Needs Me," convention tells the audience that this number will be her most sincere expression of emotion because it's clearly nondiegetic. "As Long as He Needs Me" became a hit single when the cast album was released in the United States before the show opened in Los Angeles, and audiences were introduced to Georgia Brown, the "husky-voiced powerful English actress."[94] One reviewer called her "Britain's answer to Judy Garland."[95]

In a simple and haunting melody, the song conveys the female need to be needed, which becomes disturbingly masochistic in the context of the musical: Nancy first sings the song directly after a confrontation with Bill Sikes. In spite of her objections, he and Fagin force her to retrieve Oliver. He hits her, and she sings.

Nancy is an active agent and singer in *Oliver!*, yet the plot requires that she be beaten several times over the course of the musical and killed near the end. The musical roundly condemns her victimization; she is a tragic, mother-madonna-whore figure, and Bill Sikes is at best an evil, violent man and more likely an insane misogynist. Given that Nancy, Fagin, and Sikes all live in the same social realm, Nancy's sympathy for Oliver is overdetermined as feminine, as is Bet's sobbing when Nancy dies: Bet is the only one who cries over Nancy's death. Still, the audience must witness Bill hit Nancy and later, strike her down and kill her. Like the rape of Aldonza in *Man of La Mancha*, the physical and emotional violence against Charity in *Sweet Charity*, and the ethical and political condemnation of Sally Bowles in *Cabaret, Oliver!*'s representation of violence against Nancy reveals the musical anxiety about strong, assertive women in the 1960s.

Man of La Mancha

Man of La Mancha, based on Cervantes's *Don Quixote*, was created by Dale Wasserman, with music by Mitch Leigh and lyrics by Joe Darion. With more than a nod to experimental theatre techniques of the 1960s, *Man of La Mancha* is about theatre and about the very power of performance. Wasserman originally wrote a ninety-minute nonmusical version of the piece for television, but as he explains in the preface to the published script, "It was produced with considerable éclat and garnered a number of awards but left me profoundly dissatisfied, for the strictures of television and its assertive naturalism defeated both my design and my intentions."[96] Wasserman wrote a script for a Broadway production but again felt that the story needed a different form, one "disciplined yet free, simple-seeming yet intricate, and above all, bold enough to accomplish that ephemeral objective which is called 'total theater'"; that is, it needed to be a musical.[97] Wasserman and his collaborators struggled to finance the musical, since producers found it "too radical, too 'special' and, most crushing of all, too intellectual."[98]

Still, *New York Times* reviewer Taubman wrote, "And now Cervantes and his ineffable Don Quixote have been transported to the popular musical theater. With the exception of a few vulgarities and some triteness, they have made the transition in *Man of La Mancha* with remarkable spirit and affection." Linking the musical to the aesthetic values of the day, namely formal integration, Taubman pronounced that "Mitch Leigh and Joe Darion have made every conscientious effort to integrate their songs into the texture of action and character." Taubman concluded, "At its best, it is audacious in conception and tasteful in execution."[99] In 1970, Atkinson considered *Man of La Mancha* one of two worthwhile musicals to come out of the 1960s (*Hair* was the other one). *Man of La Mancha*, he wrote, "expressed a kind of wistful admiration for the foolish gallantries of Don Quixote; and, among the many songs played and sung with skill and freshness, it presented one song, 'The Impossible Dream,' that made a universal statement. It celebrated hope for a better life."[100]

More than any other musical in this chapter, *Man of La Mancha* is about a crisis in masculinity. While Oscar is neurotic, Cliff naïve (for some of *Cabaret*), Vandergelder malleable, Beau overly sweet (and quickly killed off so that Mame can maintain center stage alone), Bill Sikes violent, and Fagin feminized by way of his Jewishness and "mothering" of his boys, Cervantes is literally doubled as Don Quixote. Feminist theory observes that masculinity is the unmarked norm and femininity the performed other, but this musical presents masculinity as a performance that must be shaped, practiced, and rendered believable and sympathetic for its audience, both the theatre audience and the audience of prisoner-judges. The musical is so preoccupied with the challenge of masculinity and the search for ideals that it can only cast its one woman,

Aldonza, in a terrifyingly limited role, violent herself and a victim of violence and abuse throughout the musical. And yet as in all of the musicals in this chapter in this decade, she sings some of the most memorable songs in the show and in the end, becomes a mouthpiece for the dead Cervantes and reprises "The Impossible Dream," the biggest hit from the show.

Like Nancy, Aldonza is poor, but this character is a prostitute in the "real" world of the musical. Often a victim, she has learned the hard way how to protect herself. The stage directions describe her as "a savage, dark alley-cat, survivor if not always victor of many back-fence tussles" (18). She enters carrying a pot of stew, sets down the tureen, and spits into it. Then she angrily sings her first declaratory song, a jagged, jolting melody, "It's All the Same": "One pair of arms is like another,/I don't know why or who's to blame,/I'll go with you or with your brother,/It's all the same, it's all the same!" (19). She continues with appropriate bitterness, "So do not talk to me of love,/I'm not a fool with starry eyes,/Just put your money in my hand,/And you will get what money buys!" (19) (fig. 2-7).

After this number, Aldonza sings only one other solo in her own voice, "Aldonza." This number functions as a second declaratory number on the same theme of her own destitution. After Don Quixote insists on calling her Dulcinea, she rebuts, "(*Passionately*) I am not your lady!" and sings, "I was spawned in a ditch by a mother who left me there/Naked and cold and too hungry to cry;/I never blamed her, I'm sure she left hoping/That I'd have the good sense to die!" (65–66). She begs Don Quixote, "So please torture me with your 'Sweet Dulcineas' no more!/I am no one! I'm nothing! I'm only Aldonza the whore!" (67). This song relates melodically to her first number, underlining how the character has not changed by this point in the show. The musical refuses to allow Aldonza variety in her expression because she exists to prove that Don Quixote knows her better than she knows herself. She believes him and willingly fulfills his vision of her only after he loses sanity and his will (70). It is her sympathy for him, not her own agency, that propels her change (not unlike Christine's final [and sole] action in *The Phantom of the Opera*—see 1980s chapter).

More troubling than Aldonza's flat, stereotypical characterization is her brutalization in the musical's well-known rape scene.[101] With the sole purpose of allowing Don Quixote to rescue Aldonza from the violence of the other men, she "asks" for it by briefly and temporarily succumbing to Don Quixote's fantasy world. When the prisoners show themselves to be as they are—violent and misogynist—it's the woman's body that suffers. Even Taubman, no feminist for sure, observes, "The binding of the wounds, by the way, is turned into a blistering, orgiastic dance for the muleteers and the shapely, mobile Miss Diener, who is dragged and hauled as violently as any performer in town."[102]

Figure 2.7 In *Man of La Mancha* (1965), Aldonza (Joan Diener) sings of her brutal and violent life. Courtesy Billy Rose Theatre Division, the New York Public Library for the Performing Arts, Astor, Lenox and Tilden Foundations.

The music of the scene remains primarily in major keys, harmonically underlining Don Quixote's bravery over Aldonza's victimization.

And yet Aldonza is constructed in contradictions. On the one hand, her musical story shows her to be a pawn and an object more than an acting subject. Her role in this musical, more than that of any other woman in this chapter, is to set off the men's activities and struggles. Like Nancy in *Oliver!*, she is introduced and described in relation to her body—her physicality is key to her character. But while Nancy from the beginning occupies the space of the "mother" in *Oliver!*, Aldonza slowly changes and softens (that is, becomes more appropriately feminine) over the course of the musical. Only by the end can she truly attach to Quixote and grieve his death. Also, while Nancy relies on her own will, intelligence, and agency to defend Oliver and to communicate with his grandfather, Aldonza is portrayed as stubborn and stupid, resisting Don Quixote's persistent invitations to join his world. Because the audience knows his is the "correct" world, her refusals mark her not as worldwise but as limited, rigid, and unimaginative.

On the other hand, Aldonza is a featured character in the man's world of *La Mancha*. She participates in "The Combat" and "The Dubbing." She also sings reprises of "Dulcinea" and "Man of La Mancha," and she initiates the company finale, the reprise of "The Quest" ("The Impossible Dream"), and in some ways emerges as the final voice of the musical.

Musicals of the 1960s navigated society's struggle over gender during the decade, rendered more precarious in a commercial, traditionally middle-class (and white, Jewish, gay) entertainment form. Some musicals pulled toward a more progressive vision by building on the already well-founded tradition of strong and vibrant women performers and women's roles, and other musicals pushed back by punishing women in the narrative, even as they featured women as singers in the center of the action. In the 1970s, as the next chapter shows, gender equity emerged in musicals that concerned the community as well as the couple and the single girl.

CHAPTER 3

The 1970s: "Everything Was Beautiful at the Ballet"

A Chorus Line, the 1975 Tony- and Pulitzer Prize–winning collaboration of Michael Bennett, Marvin Hamlisch, and Ed Kleban, calls up two iconic images. The first, which became the logo for the show, takes place early in the musical: seventeen dancers are strung across the stage, standing along a white line painted parallel to its downstage edge. Their poses vary, hands on hips or arms crossed, ankles neatly tucked together or one leg flung out and open-angled, weight equally distributed on both feet or sunk into one hip. However their postures and costumes differ, they all display the strong, lithe bodies of dancers and the eager, anxious expressions of those auditioning for a Broadway show. The second image is from the end of *A Chorus Line*, or even beyond the end, during the curtain call of the company singing and dancing to "One," the homage to the star who's not there. The entire cast, including those who were not chosen for the fictitious musical, enters one by one for the curtain call. They wear identical costumes of gold lamé and sparkles, close-fitting vests, and top hats, their fast-moving bodies creating a luminescent glow in a series of grapevines, chassés, leaps, and the obligatory yet impressive kick line. It's impossible to identify who is who. A photo of this number, the group in a diamond formation, each dancer standing on the right leg with the left leg bent at the knee, the right arm raised with top hat in hand, left hand on hip, was also used in advertising the musical during its record-breaking run of 6,137 performances. *A Chorus Line* ends as the lights fade on the image of dancers moving in perfect, shining unison, "leaving the audience with an image of a kick line that goes on forever," as the stage directions say (145).[1] The transition from one image to the other, from motley crew to well-oiled machine, telegraphs the story of *A Chorus Line*, a story of individuals struggling to be noticed for their ability not to be noticed; that is, their ability to fit perfectly with the group in a coordinated choreography.

This chapter looks at women in a collection of musicals that opened between 1970 and 1975 and that explore the relationship between the individual and the group—*Company* (1970), *Godspell* (1971 [Off Broadway], 1976 [Broadway]), *The Wiz* (1975), and *A Chorus Line*. These musicals, exceedingly different from one another in content, tone, and musical style, all exhibit the contradictory impulses that characterize the 1970s: an increased concern with one's self and a growing engagement with social issues. These four musicals replace the heterosexual romance narrative that dominated musicals of the 1950s and into the 1960s with an ensemble-based story, and the ensemble number, the convention on which this chapter focuses, occupies pride of place, musically, choreographically, and thematically. In contrast to the paired romantic leading ladies in 1950s musicals and the singular Single Girls in 1960s musicals, women in this cluster of shows operate within a group or a community, and power among the characters is dispersed across genders. In the 1970s, as feminism entered the mainstream, musical theatre presented women and men in more collaborative social units. In each musical, though, women also step out of the ensemble and put a feminine spin on the musical's emotional and political effects.

1970s

The 1970s were "an eminently forgettable decade," writes historian Bruce J. Schulman in the introduction to his book that of course proves otherwise, "an era of bad clothes, bad hair, and bad music impossible to take seriously."[2] "Wince-worthy fads" of the 1970s, writes Julia Sheeres, included "pet rocks, string art, streaking and platform shoes."[3] In terms of governmental politics, the 1970s saw the troubled presidency and humiliating resignation of Richard Nixon and the lackluster presidencies of Gerald Ford (1974–1977) and Jimmy Carter (1977–1981). The Watergate break-in in June 1972 and the Nixon administration's attempt to cover it up led to a public and political scandal that lost the public's trust in politicians thereafter.

However cynical most Americans were toward national politics, though, many were active and engaged on a local level and valued community and collaboration. Sheeres writes, "Although most of these crazes seem tragically quaint (key party, anyone?), the '70s were also characterized by a touching receptiveness to new ideas."[4] Progressive social movements of the 1960s including the civil rights movement, women's liberation, and the early gay rights movement, propelled by the Stonewall Rebellion in 1969, filtered into broader consciousness.[5] The green movement gathered steam: after the furor aroused by the 1962 publication of Rachel Carson's *Silent Spring,* the Environmental Protection Agency was formed in 1970.

Race consciousness and race pride also became more mainstream in the 1970s. New York was suffering economically and politically in the early 1970s, and the African American community was particularly hard hit. Yet the vibrant activism of the 1960s civil rights movement led to programs that ensured desegregation and more opportunities for urban blacks. In 1972, Shirley Chisholm became the first African American woman candidate for president, and Barbara Jordan the first African American woman from a southern state to be elected to the U.S. House. Elaine Brown took over the Black Panther Party in 1975 and retracted her earlier antifeminist stance, writing, "The value of my life had been obliterated as much by being female as by being black and poor."[6] Soon after *The Wiz* opened in 1976, Jordan became the first African American woman to give the keynote speech at the Democratic National Convention. The Combahee River Collective was formed in Boston in 1974 and issued its statement in 1977, which outlined a black, lesbian feminist movement, motivated by its members' specific oppression and articulating a politics inclusive of black men and Third World women. They described the phenomenon of "interlocking oppressions" of racism, sexism, classism, and heterosexism—that such subjugations are mutually constitutive and not merely additive for black women's lives—which was among their crucial contributions to feminist and critical race theory.

Increased awareness of race found its way into popular culture. On television, for example, *All in the Family* pushed the envelope in portraying the underbelly of white America's everyday, casual racism. When Alex Haley's monumental novel *Roots* was published in 1976, Americans of all races clamored to read the epic story of his family, who began in Africa, were brought to the United States as slaves, and survived, eventually leading to Haley's birth. Inspired by Haley's work, more Americans across races and ethnicities began tracing their roots, investigating local histories of towns, and creating family genealogies. Diana's assertion of her Puerto Rican identity in *A Chorus Line*— when she fails to improvise bobsled riding in an acting class, she quips, "Maybe it's genetic. They don't have bobsleds in San Juan" (65)—speaks to this national impulse. The musicals explored in this chapter all bear the markings of race awareness: the hard-won commercial success and visibility of *The Wiz* attracted both black and white spectators, *Company* self-consciously concerns only white and upper-middle-class Manhattanites, and *Godspell* and *A Chorus Line* feature multiracial casts.

Some commentators in the 1970s were concerned with value placed on the individual, such as sociologist Christopher Lasch, who famously called it "The Culture of Narcissism," in disgust and despair. Tom Wolfe, who coined the term "The 'Me' Generation," was exhilarated by the individual who looked for self-knowledge and self-fulfillment, sometimes through political action, sometimes through spirituality, and sometimes through individual achievement. Wolfe wrote, "The old alchemical dream was changing base metals into gold. The new alchemical dream is: changing one's personality—remaking, remodeling, elevating, and polishing one's very self . . . and observing, studying, and doting on it. (Me!)"[7] In addition, the tension between social movements and individualism meant that many people found individual purpose and meaning in social movements. *Godspell* speaks to this trend, as it concerns the quest for spiritual fulfillment in a humanist presentation of the Gospels. While the question of selfhood and self-identification was integral to the zeitgeist of the time, the culture was not as obsessed with "me" as it would become in the extravagant 1980s; the 1970s were compelled by the relationship between "me" and the community.

Feminism became more visible and accepted in mainstream culture, too. At the beginning of the decade, the first women's studies program was established at San Diego State College. Gloria Steinem began publishing *Ms.* magazine in 1971; Title IX was passed in 1972, making sex-based discrimination in federally funded education programs illegal, which dramatically improved funding for women's sports in schools and colleges. The first rape crisis center opened in Berkeley, California, in 1972, with more in major cities close behind; abortion was legalized in *Roe v. Wade* in 1973.[8] Alternative and independent institutions of all kinds—publishing houses, record labels, theatres, magazines—sprang up, and a range of feminist ideologies were articulated and practiced.[9]

The increased visibility of feminism with a focus on individual life choices shifted social mores and practices around heterosexuality, marriage, and relationships. Long-standing dating rituals morphed into group socializing and "relationships," a new word first used in everyday parlance in the 1970s, which included cohabitation before marriage, open marriages, and group sex. Women were allowed to and even encouraged to have and express sexual desires, to be sexual agents rather than only passive recipients of male attention. The gay rights movement picked up speed after the Stonewall Riots in 1969, and gay men and lesbians "came out of the closet." Among television's biggest hits of the decade was *The Mary Tyler Moore Show*, with Mary unmarried and with a boyfriend with whom she was obviously having sex. Novels in which the female protagonists underwent consciousness raising and life transformations were extremely popular, including *Rubyfruit Jungle* (1973) by Rita Mae Brown, *The Women's Room* (1977) by Marilyn French, and *Small Changes* by Marge Piercy (1973).[10] In popular music, Helen Reddy's "I Am Woman, Hear Me Roar" (1972) and Aretha Franklin's "Respect" (1968) became feminist anthems.[11]

Advertising's response to feminism underlines how once radical feminist ideas became mainstream. Until 1969, print ads geared toward women typically featured a woman selecting a product to please her boyfriend, but in 1970, Madison Avenue's strategy shifted and virtually every ad showed a woman making a choice for herself. The ad industry suddenly realized that it could exploit feminism, so every product, including those that weren't especially feminist (vaginal douches, for example) were marketed as being "liberationist" and empowering.[12] As an advertisement for Pond's hand lotion addressed its imagined consumer in 1969, "They're a whole new genre of unfettered, free-spirited, savvy women who know how to cut through the phony baloney of the beauty business and get right down to basics."[13] Once feminism made it to Madison Avenue, it could surely make it to Broadway.

The Ensemble Number

A staple in the repertoire of musical theatre's elements, the ensemble number presents a community on stage.[14] A creative team's choice to have the entire cast sing together, whether standing, moving, or dancing, enforces the idea of "the people" through the volume of voices and the volume of bodies, the aural and visual space taken up by the whole group.

The ensemble at once transcends gender and relies on it: when voices blend together, the attitude, story, perspective, and emotion are unified, and different identities don't matter. Still, the force of an ensemble number depends on male and female voices spanning the octaves, singing some sections in harmony and others in unison, coming together and dividing. The ensemble number, of course, has infinite variety, from straightforward melodies sung in unison like "Tomorrow Belongs to Me," Kander and Ebb's chilling imitation of a Nazi-era folk song from *Cabaret*, to the gorgeously layered polyphonic quintet "Tonight," which ends act 1 of *West Side Story*. Other intricate, multivoiced ensemble numbers include "One Day More" from *Les Misérables*, "A Weekend in the Country" from *A Little Night Music*, and "No Day Like Today," from *Rent*.[15] In a balance between chaos and unison, voices that break out and then come together create the dynamism and power of the ensemble number.

The ensemble number not only affects the aural texture of a musical, it also shapes the scene visually. In the opening number and title song of *In the Heights*, for example, Usnavi's friends and neighbors enter the street scene one by one, dancing, buying coffee, listening to the radio, greeting friends. The stylized, intricately choreographed "good morning" routine introduces the cast in their varied ages, genders, ethnicities, and styles. When the number morphs into a densely harmonized, beat-filled ensemble refrain, "In the heights/I flip my lights and start my day/There are fights/And endless debts and bills to pay/In the heights/I can't survive without café," Thomas Kail's direction and Andy Blankenbuehler's jazz and hip-hop choreography alternate phrases of unified movement with individualized steps. Musically and choreographically, the first song presents a varied community that is nonetheless a community. In contrast, in the final song of act 1 in *Evita*, the entire cast, save Eva, stands still with fists raised in protest. Director Harold Prince's stage picture of men, women, and children, banners flying, and the despairing revolutionary Che downstage and victorious Eva on the catwalk above, encapsulates Eva's power and the citizens' loyalty to her.

Interestingly, the presence of numerous actors on stage heightens the audience's awareness that in the theatre they have the freedom to look where they like. Even as directors, choreographers, and designers try to focus spectators' gazes by using movement, proximity, size, and light, as well as aural volume and tone—that is, spectators tend to look to see where the sound is coming from, who is singing, and so on, using both sight and sound in tandem—spectators can choose for themselves where and how to place their attention. This simple theatrical fact, along with liveness, distinguishes theatre from film and television and no doubt accounts for much of the pleasure of theatre spectatorship.

Like any other component of a musical, the ensemble number's aural power arises from its difference from other musical numbers in the show, as well as its difference from speech. When the full cast sings the entire number—as it does at the finale of *Oklahoma!*—it creates the sense of a world on stage. When the chorus joins a singer, transforming a solo number to an ensemble piece—as in "Sit Down You're Rockin' the Boat," from *Guys and Dolls*, or "Coffee Break" from *How to Succeed in Business without Really Trying*—then the growth of the sound creates a story, depending on whether other singers join in gradually or all at once. In addition to what's conveyed by the ensemble number itself—the community's celebratory resistance to mainstream culture of "La Vie Boheme" in *Rent*, the young people's determination to live well in spite of the loss of their friends and a repressive society in "Purple Summer" in *Spring Awakening*, the waiters' affection for Dolly Levi in the title song in *Hello, Dolly!*—the ensemble number establishes its effect based on what precedes and what follows it, whether music, speech, silence, a blackout, or applause.

While almost every musical has an ensemble, the narrative, character-ological, and affective functions of ensembles have differed considerably across eras and conventional practices of musical theatre since the 1940s. In most formally integrated musicals, for example, the ensembles play a number of different roles, including filling in the crowds and setting the scene in which the principals act. In the opening scene of *My Fair Lady*, for example, members of the ensemble play Covent Garden workers, street cleaners, merchants, and beggars. Later, ensemble members play the servants in Higgins's house, Doolittle's working-class, tavern-going friends and neighbors to whom he sings, "I'm getting married in the morning," so "get me to the church on time" (174), and the snobby, high society Londoners who are horrified by Eliza's emotional outburst at the horse race and who later dance at the Embassy Ball.[16] In other musicals, actors are cast more specifically within the ensemble, and each actor plays one role. In *West Side Story*, for example, the whites and the Puerto Ricans make up two distinct ensembles, with different looks, sounds, and movement vocabularies. The two groups appear together only in "The Dance at the Gym," Jerome Robbins's choreographic tour de force that demonstrates the irony of the young people's mutual antipathy. The two camps are alienated from one another, despite the same teenage desires and impulses.[17] A proponent of Method acting, Robbins famously forced the two groups of actors to stay apart during rehearsals, and he encouraged their mutual suspicion offstage to enhance their performance of hatred on stage.

The musicals of the 1970s capitalize on and complicate the conventions of the ensemble number that were well established by this point in musical theatre history. The musicals that are the focus of this chapter not only contain ensemble numbers as a part of the show. These musicals expand the typical chorus number to render the ensemble itself the musical's principal.

Company

Company uses the ensemble as its basic organizing unit: the "Bobby Baby" theme provides the unifying musical thread in an otherwise nonplotted and fragmented show. Other ensemble numbers punctuate Bobby's emotional journey or emphasize how he's not changing, as he encounters the couples and his girlfriends one by one. Because the characters are not developed and only appear in one or two scenes, except for Joanne, they form a conglomerate of gendered attitudes toward marriage—that is, it's less significant what each represents and more important what they add up to. Each character provides a snapshot, deeply gendered. Even though *Company* is ostensibly about Bobby, it's really more about marriage writ large.

Company is a concept musical that meditates on the theme of marriage and commitment. Based on a series of short stories, vignettes of married life and single womanhood are unified by Robert (or Bobby), a bachelor friend to all of the couples and the potential love interest for the single women. With no apparent order to the scenes or songs, *Company* finds a slender narrative thread by tracking Robert's occasionally expressed changes of heart and concludes when he decides he is ready for "someone to hold you too close" (114).[18] A collaboration among director Hal Prince, composer and lyricist Stephen Sondheim (one of his earliest productions), librettist George Furth, choreographer Michael Bennett, and set designer Boris Aronson, *Company* was met with a mixture of admiration and confusion when it opened. Because it was organized around a theme more than a story, because the characters didn't change and weren't psychologized, and because the songs commented on the action rather than emerge from it, some critics misunderstood it and some audiences were confused by it. Still, it managed to make back its investment, and was one of only two musicals to profit in the spring season of 1970 (the other was *Applause*). During this grim season, seven of the fourteen new musicals that opened ran a week or less, three closing after just one night.[19] *Company*'s success was remarkable, given how many conventions it broke that were part and parcel of the Broadway musical at the time.

The script explains the casting: "Robert is the only member of the company who doesn't double. The remaining thirteen members of the company each have a particular character to play, as well as doubling as Company. There is no singing or dancing ensemble" (np: "Musical Numbers"). The stage directions acknowledge the convention of the existence of a singing and dancing ensemble in this musical; the creators knew they were doing something different. Although *Company* lacked a conventional ensemble, the whole cast sang several musical numbers as well as a frequently reprised musical theme that threaded through the whole show. The feeling of the ensemble is strong in *Company*.

The very title of the sharp-edged musical implies the importance of the ensemble. The word carries multiple meanings, according to the *Oxford English Dictionary*, each of which applies to this layered piece. It refers to a guest or guests, aptly describing the many scenes that depict Robert as a visitor in his friends' apartments. The framing scene of the musical, Robert's thirty-fifth birthday party, which is supposed to be a surprise and to which he doesn't show up at the end, takes place in his own apartment. The party scene repeats at the beginning and end of each act, with Robert's friends—that is, his company—all around. The word also means "companionship," again appropriate since the musical focuses on Robert's ambivalence about having a companion, specifically about being in a heterosexual couple.

The word "company," as a term into which is built inclusiveness, also denotes what's outside of it or excluded by it. Having company to one's home means that they don't live there, just as being the invited company means the home isn't yours. And the term "company" is more formal than "friends." Keeping company is the opposite of being alone, and this distinction structures the musical. The company Robert keeps, the characters in *Company*, includes five heterosexual couples who are his married friends, and three women whom he dates. Even though these other characters don't interact, or even seem to know one another outside of being Robert's mutual friends, their performances in the musical, particularly in the ensemble numbers, render them a community.

Company's memorable "Bobby Baby" ensemble refrain repeats a number of times and aurally links the different scenes of marital bliss or dysfunction and Robert's quest for self, romance, or coupledom.[20] At the beginning of *Company*, Robert enters and listens to a number of phone messages, which introduces Sondheim's practice of making music from ambient noise and the sounds of everyday conversation. Bobby then hears "a series of ghostly offstage individual voices intoning 'Bobby' a capella" (4). These scattered voices produce a haunting, disembodied sound and immediately put the focus on the protagonist and his perspective. While the voices have an echoing, enveloping quality, they're neither soothing nor attacking—yet. Set within a narrow vocal register and with simple, unadorned accompaniment, the voices almost speak as the notes move in a circular, minor melody, and so evoke the feeling of everyday, even banal life—the life that this musical captures in its series of scenes of quotidian domestic normalcy. The friends eventually enter carrying presents, group themselves around Robert, and offer birthday wishes "tonelessly," as meaningless and unfelt as Robert would hear them (4). Still, Robert doesn't feel oppressed by his friends so much as ambivalent about them. The stage directions indicate that "gradually, they all start becoming more human, looking and reacting to Robert and to each other" (5). When the Company sharpens into a living, active and reactive force, the "Bobby Baby" theme begins, which moves directly into the title song.

The song "Company" alternates sections between Robert and the rest of the cast, which express the complicated mutual dependency between them. Accompanied by a grating, repeating telephone busy signal—another everyday sound that recurs in the musical, threaded through like the "Bobby" theme—the characters each call "Bobby" "Bobby baby," "Bobby bubi," "Rob-o," "Bobby love" in a louder, faster, more insistent version of the earlier "Bobby" theme. The characters sing overlapping phrases that fill in details of their relationship with him: "Bobby, there's a concert on Tuesday," "How about some Scrabble on Sunday?" "Why don't we all go to the beach—" (11). The lyrics are positive and happy, and list pleasant activities and events, but the music sounds discordant and oppressive, with a foreboding, almost threatening quality. This section is extremely rhythmic; the rock influence and relatively simple melody lend the song a driving feeling. No clear distinctions emerge among the characters; each simply demands Robert's attention. They conclude by finally singing in unison, accompaniment still pulsing: "Bobby come on over for dinner," "Just be the three of us . . ." They then conclude, slightly discordantly, with "We loooooooooove you!" (13). Here, Robert introduces the refrain of the song, a jaunty, pulsing melody alternating two-beat phrases with longer ones, many of which end on unresolved notes. He sings, "Phone rings, door chimes, in comes company!" (13) Musical phrases repeat and move up the scale, and notes are held for longer and longer periods, creating anxious musical tension that contradicts the lyrics of affection and attachment. Robert concludes this section alone: "Those good and crazy people, my married friends!" and "With love filling the days," "'To Bobby, with love,'" and "That's what it's really about, isn't it?" (13–14).

The ensemble moves back into the "Bobby baby" theme, but this time around, Robert responds, trying to answer his friends' questions and requests. As he replies, "Name it, Sarah," "Try me, Peter" (15), the other characters are singing, too, so his answers can barely be heard over the din. After several repetitions of the Bobby theme, which is layered with increasingly complicated plans, bits of information, invitations, and queries, the group repeats the "Bobby, come on over for dinner" verse (19). This time, they all move to what Robert sang alone before: "Phone rings, door chimes, in comes Company!/No strings, good times, just chums, company!" (19). While the group repeats what Robert sang earlier, he simultaneously sings, "You I love and you I love and you I love," almost as a mantra or chant. The whole cast concludes, "Company!/Life is company!/Love is company!" (20). The number "Company" is thus at once buoyant and oppressive.

Prince and Bennett's staging of this opening number stressed the interdependent themes of isolation and connectedness. The different couples were first visible in small areas that represented their separate apartments on Boris Aronson's cube-like, scaffold structure, "a Constructivist chrome and glass jungle gym" of "various levels, platforms, and elevators, a postmodern pattern of separation and isolation."[21] As they sang the next-to-last verse, the couples crossed from their "apartments" to a center, second-level area that, once all of the actors gathered there, was lowered to the floor like an elevator. When they sang the final chorus together, then, the actors moved all at once, creating a strong visual image of the group.

The group emerges as a constant musical and emotional force in the musical. The ensemble is at once symbolic and demographically specific, representing the very urban, sophisticated New Yorkers who would be in the theatre audience. They enter in the next scene after Sarah wrestles her husband, Harry, to the ground, and Joanne (originally played by Elaine Stritch and a role that will forever be haunted by her performance) drily sings the comment song, "The Little Things You Do Together": "The concerts you enjoy together,/Neighbors you annoy together,/Children you destroy together,/That keep marriage intact" (28). The ensemble joins the harsh critique halfway through, and the song ends with Larry: "Shouting till you're hoarse together"; Joanne: "Getting a divorce together"; Group: "That make perfect relationships./Uh-huh . . . Kiss-kiss"; Joanne: "Mm-hmm" (30–31) (fig. 3-1). The ensemble later performs a vaudeville pastiche number, "Side by Side by Side," which segues into another song of their devotion to Robert, "What Would We Do without You?"

The repeated "Bobby Baby" theme, which occurs six more times during the musical, reminds the audience that Bobby is haunted by his friends' demands as well as by their projections of their own feelings, expectations, desires, and disappointments onto him. Robert serves as a tabula rasa for relationships: the men envy his freedom and the women desire him. The men want him to want the kind of young and sexy woman they want, and the women want him to want a woman like them. Until the final song, the audience learns very little about Robert himself. Even then, what he articulates in "Being Alive" is undeniably vague.[22] Earlier, when he rashly proposes to Amy—who has just expressed her terror at the thought of marrying Paul by singing the wildly funny patter song, "Not Getting Married Today"—Amy responds by explaining, "Thank you, Robert. I'm really . . . it's just that you have to want to marry *some*body, not just some*body*" (68). Although supposedly Robert has learned something about himself by the end of *Company* and can admit that he needs to be vulnerable and open to "being alive," it's still hard to imagine who would marry him. The fact is that Robert is not a character drawn with detail. He does sing three solos, which give a sense of how he

Figure 3.1 In *Company* (1970), the Ensemble observes "The Little Things You Do Together," led by Elaine Stritch (Joanne), above. Then, from left to right: Steve Elmore, Beth Howland (Amy), John Cunningham, Merle Louise, Teri Ralston, and George Coe. On the floor: Larry Kert (Robert), Barbara Barrie (Sarah), and Charles Kimbrough (Harry). Courtesy Billy Rose Theatre Division, the New York Public Library for the Performing Arts, Astor, Lenox and Tilden Foundations.

is changing, but compared to earlier musicals that might chart the character's development through song, the dominance of the ensemble in *Company* means that Robert is more often the audience for a song than he is the singer.

The fact that Robert seems to have only two options, either being alone or getting married, locates *Company* on the early cusp of the 1970s. While marriage was very much the norm until the early 1970s, by the middle of the decade, fewer people believed that marriage was an essential stage in life. "Relationships" replaced dating, with the implication that one could engage in a series of intimate involvements and not be on a quest for a permanent, legal mate.[23] The musical at once aggressively reinforces heterosexuality as the norm, and denaturalizes heterosexuality by depicting many different kinds of straight relationships, none especially successful or fulfilling. Many critics argue that Robert is gay because of his refusal or inability to commit to a woman. In the 1970 production, the girlfriends in "You Could Drive a Person Crazy," sang, "You could understand a person, if that person was a fag," at once suggesting that he might be gay and foreclosing that idea. For the 1995 revival, that line was changed to "if he happened to be gay" to avoid offense, and a scene was added between Peter and Bobby to allow Bobby to state emphatically that he was not homosexual. But even with a putatively straight Bobby, the musical's unwavering cynicism about heterosexuality fosters a queer reading.

In the end, the central person in this musical is a man, and his struggle is a masculine one, a painful circumstance that only being a man gives him the privilege to experience. The central question of marriage, coupledom, and commitment is specifically masculine in *Company*. If the musical is Bobby's journey, or all in Bobby's head, then what do the women contribute? What is *Company* saying about women? How is their perspective gendered? As an exploration of marriage in its various stages, from early love and weddings to conflicts and divorce (although the vignettes are not in chronological order), *Company* allows both male and female characters to sing and express various perspectives, but the most eloquent and nuanced views are the women's.[24]

Each of Robert's three lovers has a solo that articulates a "single girl's" perspective (and that might have been the perspective of Charity Hope Valentine, in *Sweet Charity* in the previous chapter), each less or more independent, less or more desirous of marriage, but they all want (or had wanted) to marry him. Even the swinging single stewardess, April, would like to stay longer at his apartment. April's number, "Barcelona," is a duet with Robert in which they negotiate their weirdly predictable dynamic: despite protestations, she wants to be with him and he wants her to leave. Even though he says he wants her to stay, he doesn't expect that she will, which the audience knows, so she looks foolish for taking him at his word. Marta's "Another Hundred People" reflects on New York City more generally, and not from an especially gendered perspective, suggesting that both women and men suffer the emotional ravages of isolation in the big city. In "You Could Drive a Person Crazy," the single women unite in their frustration with Robert. Of the coupled women, Amy's "Not Getting Married Today" is a terrific charm song with little emotional (although plenty of musical) heft that foreshadows that she will, of course, capitulate and marry Paul. By contrast, Joanne's alarmingly bitter "Ladies Who Lunch" gets to the heart of *Company's* critique of a bourgeois, disconnected society. Her bookended numbers attack the expectations that organize their lives, even as she implicates herself in her scathing critique of their (and her) shallow materialism. Joanne is ultimately as important as Robert as the "voice" of the musical.

Like marriage, the women in *Company* are represented with ambivalence. They are a part of the ensemble and stand out from it. That masculinity is taken for granted means that the men get less to say or sing in the show, but the musical displaces its anxiety about heterosexuality onto the women and places them in uncomfortably self-destructive roles. Although none of them are "women's libbers," and they express a range of perspectives on marriage and are far from naïve or romantic, their songs generate pity and laughter more than a serious consideration of their plight, and certainly not marrying isn't an option for them. Perhaps the women in *Company* would have benefitted from a consciousness-raising group.

The strongest performative unit in *Company* is the ensemble, the Company, but Sondheim uses the conventions of musical theatre to theatricalize the difference between what is said and what is done. The characters have the same desires and expectations of Robert, but no relationship to one another, and nothing ultimately ties them together. They sing and dance together in a form that typically unites characters into a community, but never become one. In many musicals, the ensemble number comes at the end of the show, but here, the ghostly version of the "Bobby" theme is heard at the beginning of the last scene, but the company never sings together again.

But *Company*, like many of Sondheim's musicals, performs against itself. Because the characters' differences are sketched more than developed, because they sing together frequently, because the music they sing is repeated enough to register for the audience, and because the audience hears it again and again, each time, the force of the ensemble is felt. Even as *Company* wants to say that people can't be together, the convention of the ensemble number performs that they can. In the end, *Company* is utterly ambivalent about the value of company.

Godspell

The spirit and tone of *Godspell* could not be more different than *Company*'s, and yet the two musicals have much in common in their structure and their musical and emotional investment in the ensemble. But while *Company* presents uptown New York sophisticates and speaks to issues around relationships and marriage in the 1970s, *Godspell*'s society is decidedly downtown, and oriented toward spirituality, rebirth, and a soft-touch counterculture. If *Company*'s women exhibit a range of gendered anxieties associated with being single in the city or frustrations with being married, *Godspell*'s women project feminist satisfaction. *Godspell* merges feminist principles with spiritual rebirth. Like *Company*, *Godspell* asserts the importance of the group, and like *Company*, the women hold a unique and crucial place in expressing the voice of the musical. And like *Company*, *Godspell* revolves around a central male character who does little besides unify the others gathered around him (fig. 3-2).

Figure 3.2 In *Godspell* (1976), the newly formed community assembles to perform Jesus's teachings. Shown from left: Robin Lamont, Bobby Lee, Valerie Williams, Lois Foraker, Don Scardino, Elizabeth Lathram, Laurie Faso, Marley Sims. Courtesy Photofest.

The balanced gender and race casting in *Godspell* reflects the mainstream in-filtration of feminist and antiracist movements. By the early-to-mid 1970s, most women considered themselves feminists, and feminist activism permeated almost every aspect of U.S. society: religion, scholarship, culture, and daily life. As historian Ruth Rosen describes it, "Like a swollen river, the women's move-ment had spilled over its banks, creating hundreds, then thousands of new trib-utaries, as it flooded the nation. All over the country, women were discovering feminist perspectives on race, ethnicity, labor, spirituality, education, ecology, and peace." She adds, "'Feminism' and 'sexism,' language not widely used even in the late sixties, had now becomes commonplace household words."[25]

Godspell's humanist version of Christian theology, which makes the mu-sical easily revivable, also points to its 1970s roots. Desire for authentic spiritu-ality, the remaking of organized religion, and translating the Bible into everyday practices were very much in the air at the time. During a time when Western religion was being criticized, *Godspell* offered a positive and affec-tionate depiction of Christianity and made it readily accessible.

Godspell was created by John-Michael Tebelak when he was a graduate stu-dent at Carnegie-Mellon University.[26] After a short run at the downtown ex-perimental theatre La MaMa, producers Edgar Lansbury (brother of Angela) and Joseph Beruh thought the idea had potential but that it needed a stronger score. Stephen Schwartz, who had been an undergrad at CMU, was hired to write the music, and *Godspell* opened at the Cherry Lane Theatre off-Broad-way on May 17, 1971. In spite of mixed reviews, *Godspell* became a huge hit through word of mouth (not unlike what happened for Schwartz's *Wicked* in 2003, as chapter 6 discusses). It moved to the larger, off-Broadway Promenade Theatre on August 10, 1971, for an extended run, and then transferred to Broadway in June 1976, where it played for another 527 performances.

This barebones show has had remarkable staying power, performed contin-ually, especially in schools, universities, and churches. Based on the Gospel according to St. Matthew and Luke, *Godspell* is framed by John the Baptist's "discovery of Jesus" and Jesus's crucifixion. Its tone is earnest, its style playful, evoking Viola Spolin's improvisatory theatre games. Spolin, a Chicago-based director and educator, published what became the bible for theatre educators, *Improvisation for the Theater* (1963), with more than two hundred theatre games and exercises "focusing on the concept of play to unlock the individual's capacity for creative self-expression."[27] *Godspell*'s "poor theatre" aesthetic, with a playground-like set of two sawhorses, some planks, and a chain-link fence upstage, and motley, clownish, mismatched costumes makes it relatively inexpensive to produce. In addition, *Godspell*'s long-term appeal and relevance is in the musical itself: its playful re-presentation of Bible stories, its catchy folk-rock score, its positive representation of community, its unusually flexible gender roles, and its nonrealist, presentational acting style; that is, the very qualities that made it a groundbreaking musical in the early 1970s.

Godspell eschews many conventions of musicals before the late 1960s. Its time and place are unspecified; the songs and stories are arbitrarily arranged; the songs don't further a plot; there is no narrative or story; there is no character development. John Bush Jones considers the musical a "revue," and Elizabeth Wollman categorizes it as a rock musical with spiritual overtones.[28] Musical theatre scholars have paid little attention to *Godspell* because of its catchy and accessible music, its admittedly sentimental, love-conquers-all message, its lukewarm and occasionally dismissive reviews in the 1970s, and its strong association with amateur theatre. But while *Godspell* moves away from many of the conventions of earlier musicals, it engages with performance practices introduced on Broadway by *Hair*, which suggests that these elements were in the air for young artists at the time. Both musicals feature youthful characters who seek their identities through the group with which they associate: the lost, modern-day disciples in *Godspell*, and the Tribe of Greenwich Village hippies in *Hair*. Both musicals give each character a solo or duet and balance the musical numbers across the entire cast. They use a then-contemporary musical vocabulary with a range of styles and tones, although *Hair*'s score is more based in rock music and *Godspell*'s in folk. Both musicals use little scenery, minimal props, and simple lighting. Both also break the fourth wall to engage the audience directly. Still, the two musicals differ in tone, mood, and attitude. Rebellious, angry, brash, and overtly political, *Hair* deals with race, sex, drugs, the generation gap, and most of all, the war in Vietnam. *Hair*'s viability for revival depends in part on attitudes toward war; the Public Theatre's 2008 production in Central Park, for example, gained more traction because of the audience's frustration with the war in Iraq. In contrast, *Godspell*'s Gospel source secures a certain timelessness, and the playful innocence, Christian message, and vaudeville-like structure that make it readily producible almost anywhere may mean that it's not trenchant enough for a Broadway revival.[29]

Godspell isn't especially heterosexual or gay but it is a queer musical. Like *Hair*, it places a male couple in the center. John the Baptist/Judas is the only character besides Jesus who instigates action. Theirs is the only identifiably consistent relationship in the musical, and the two perform their clever intimacy in the catchy, soft-shoe, combination song, "All For the Best." In *Hair*, Claude and Berger are not only connected as best friends, but because *Hair* foregrounds sexuality and sexual relationships, they are overtly triangulated with Sheila. In addition, the women who emerge as distinct characters in *Hair* (including Sheila) pine after men who are oblivious or more involved with their male friends. As for *Godspell*, aside from John and Jesus, the musical side-steps sexuality, coupling, and romance; the ensemble as organizing rubric is all-encompassing.

Like *Hair, Godspell* takes as its subject the creation, perpetuation, and cele-bration of community, and the entire piece is built around the ensemble. As Schwartz writes in a 1999 addendum to the script, "Above all the first act of *Godspell* must be about the formation of a community. Eight separate individ-uals, led and guided by Jesus (who is helped by his assistant, John the Baptist/ Judas), gradually come to form a communal unit."[30] Although Jesus is the cen-ter of the musical and offers the lesson of each of the parables, all of the players participate throughout. Beyond delivering the moral, Jesus is no more psycho-logically developed than the rest of the characters and the musical doesn't deal with his life beyond his early baptism and later crucifixion. His individualism emerges more in his performative function—what he does and how he insti-gates action—than in older musical theatre's conventional character growth through self-declaratory songs. Schwartz explains, "It is important that Jesus be the leader at all times, that the energy and attitude of each 'game' come from him, particularly in the first half of the first act." Each parable should convey "a clear sense that it is done for and with the master's approval." Schwartz cau-tions that the cast must not appear too silly nor should Jesus be played with "misplaced reverence," as "too 'serious' or passive." Schwartz adds, "He is, if you will, the Chief Clown, and must drive the action at all times."[31]

From the opening moment, Godspell presents itself as an ensemble mu-sical. After a brief, miked and reverbed introduction from the actor playing Jesus—"My name is known: God and King"—who is seated upstage, back to audience, mic hidden (1), the ensemble aspect of the musical opens with each actor wearing a sweatshirt that labels him or her a famous philosopher— Thomas Aquinas, Socrates, Nietzsche, and so on.[32] Each expresses a well-known phrase or idea from that philosopher, which gradually becomes louder and more muddled; the audience soon realizes that the company is playing out a philosophical debate in which each tries to overshout the others, resulting in cacophony and confusion. Schwartz writes of this prologue, which was left off the cast album to ensure its "'cross-over' as a pop album"[33] that "it is necessary to see what the individuals are like when there is no community—how lost they are and how easily they descend into violence and chaos" (1). The actor playing John the Baptist enters, playing a shofar, and he sings the prayer-like "Prepare Ye (the Way of the Lord)." Here *Godspell* signals its commitment to a

Jewish-in-origin Jesus and to a secular spirituality based on the humanity of Jesus's teaching more than any kind of religious orthodoxy. John "baptizes" all of the eager actors with a wet sponge from a pail of water and then recognizes the actor playing Jesus and asks to be blessed by him. In this moment, the difference between Jesus and the rest of the cast, which may not have been previously observable, is made manifest, thus reinforcing both the Christian lesson that Jesus is always potentially among us and the performance lesson that any actor can play any role.

Once the actors don colorful clothes and use clown makeup to mark themselves, they have "become" the disciples, and spend the rest of the musical acting out parables in speech, pantomime, dance, and song, like a spiritually based commedia dell'arte troupe.[34] (Schwartz notes that the "hippie" costumes of the original production were in keeping with the time, and he urges contemporary productions to find their own look.)[35] Each actor has a chance to take the stage either in speech, movement, or song. The script indicates that almost every parable requires the participation of the whole cast, but the precise staging is flexible. For example, in the Rich Man's parable, Joanne narrates and, in the original production, the female cast members straddled the supine and bent-kneed male cast members to create "puppets" composed of the women's upper bodies and the men's legs (39). The stage directions note, "Obviously, other choices are available to the individual director, but it is important that the OTHERS participate in acting out the story" (39). Each actor-character-disciple, then, has the chance to control the proceedings and all support that player by participating in the parable, by joining the song, or by behaving as an engaged and supportive audience.

Importantly, almost none of *Godspell's* parables or songs are exclusively solos or duets. Schwartz chooses to veer away from these conventional musical theatre song structures. Instead, almost every song begins as a solo, then grows as singers join, from "Save the People" to "Day by Day," from "O Bless the Lord My Soul" to "Turn Back, O Man."[36] The songs and stories are organized emotionally (rather than to delineate a plot), and each player expresses strong feeling, from curiosity to wistfulness to exuberance. When the ensemble joins the soloist as a kind of call-and-response, the volume and the emotions deepen and expand. Thus almost every song in *Godspell* concludes with a rousing sense of all-inclusive commitment to the moment. The emotional and kinesthetic engagement is intensified by the fact that none of these songs begins as an ensemble number. Each musical number requires one person to set the melody and the tempo, and *Godspell* suggests that anyone can step in and offer a prayer. The ensemble supports and participates in each song in a slightly different way each time, highlighting the multiple roles a community can play in relation to each of its members. In this way, *Godspell* performs what musical theatre does at its essence: invites those assembled to join in. The group is flexible, playful, and engaged. *Godspell* offers a very positive portrayal of community until they turn against Jesus.

Godspell's assignment of songs reflects a gender-neutral community, which the mainstreaming of feminism enabled. Even songs that suggest a gendered performance, such as the sweetly feminized "Day by Day" or the Mae West take-off "Turn Back O Man" could be sung by men without changing the purpose or address of the song, and women could lead "Light of the World" or "On the Willows." Still, one assumes that in most productions, men play both Jesus and Judas, which inevitably adds a patriarchal bent to the production. Yet the warm and loving authority of the Jesus character, and his facility in leading the group, are more important than the gender of the actor playing him.[37]

Godspell reconfigures a conventional actor-character relationship, which also enhances its sense of inclusiveness. The characters do have names, which were the names of the original cast members, and each takes on some simple, basic character traits based on his or her solo number. Schwartz explains, "In any given production, each actor will bring his or her own personality trait to the character, but it is helpful for the director to look for certain salient personality characteristics when casting each role." He continues, "This allows the individual cast members to be different enough from one another for the audience to distinguish them."[38] Still, each actor plays a range of roles during the musical through solo numbers, group songs, and varied parts in the parables, including some that require cross-gender performance or a satirical imitation of, for example, Richard Nixon or famous actors of the time. Because this practice of pretending so dominates the musical, no actor develops an identifiable psychological through line. The audience watches the actor, not a character, at all times, and this direct relationship encourages a connection based not on psychological identification but rather on an affective admiration and contagious desire to play. *Godspell* makes it all look easy and invites the audience to imagine themselves as part of a similar community.

The musical goes even further in creating an affective space for audiences to relate to the actors by using environmental staging to place the actors in the house at various points in the musical.[39] Actors go into the auditorium after being baptized and return dressed as in their disciple/clown costumes. Sonia sings one verse of "Turn Back O Man" while walking up the aisle and directs the patter—"Is your seat comfortable, sir?" "Mmm, I like that!"—to specific audience members (67). In the patter before the Rich Man's parable, the actors mutter complaints about money to people in the audience. At the end of the show, Jesus is carried out down the theatre aisle (94–95). In these and other instances, the script specifies that actors should ad lib lines that are current and relevant, as *Godspell* strives to remake itself via the actors for a new audience in each production. Again, this quality, built into the concept of the musical, keeps it fresh for each audience community. Finally, during "Light of the World," the last song of act 1, the cast invites the audience onto the stage during intermission to drink wine, guaranteeing that all productions address their audiences in a direct and celebratory manner.

The connection that *Godspell* makes with the audience during intermission, encouraged by audience members' actually walking onto the stage, ensures a sympathetic investment that carries them through the darker, emotionally grueling act 2. If act 1 traces the happy, relatively conflict-free formation of a utopian community, act 2 presents fissures and divisions. Although almost every musical number still opens into an ensemble piece, more songs are somber in tone, including "By My Side," "We Beseech Thee," and "On the Willows." Once the actor playing Judas—played by the same actor who played John the Baptist in act 1—is identified as the traitor, the musical shifts to a clearer narrative. Jesus asks the disciples to stay awake with him, which they fail to do. Their sleep is typically staged in theatre-game fashion (pace Spolin), with the actors lying on the floor in a circle, their heads in the center, left side down and right hand draped across the waist of the person on the floor in front of them. They breathe in unison, each inhalation and exhalation marked by the collective raising and lowering of their right arms together. This simply staged moment, like much of *Godspell*, reinforces its close-knit sense of the community.

The Wiz

Like *Godspell*, *The Wiz* capitalizes on the audience's foreknowledge of the story and its appreciation for the contemporary angle, here, an all-black adaptation of *The Wizard of Oz*.[40] Also like *Godspell*, *The Wiz* is a zesty, accessible musical, which is frequently produced by colleges and church groups and has received little scholarly attention.[41] But while *Godspell*'s community consists of a flexible, gender neutral group and a male leader, *The Wiz*, like its source material, finds Dorothy as the head of an assembled family (fig. 3-3). Her leadership resonates with 1970s feminism and even more with black women who were heads of their households. Dorothy's journey is gendered, initiated when Auntie Em

Figure 3.3 In *The Wiz* (1984 revival), the created family of Dorothy (Stephanie Mills), the Tinman (Howard Porter), the Cowardly Lion (Gregg Baker), and the Scarecrow (Charles Valentino) will "Ease on Down the Road" to see the Wiz. Courtesy Photofest.

gives her a dress, and is a classic, circular structure that eventually returns to order, transformed and renewed. Dorothy reprises her first song at the end—the last word in the musical is "home." *The Wiz* is the only musical in this chapter where the leader or initiator of this community is a woman, which alludes to the significance of women as mothers, breadwinners, and leaders in the African American community in the 1970s.

The Wiz was the pet project of producer Ken Harper, who worked at the New York radio station WPIX as the director of music and public affairs, and he envisioned it as a television show. Unable to raise the money, Harper rerouted *The Wiz* to Broadway and acquired financing from Twentieth Century-Fox in exchange for movie, record, and publishing rights.[42] Harper invited Charlie Smalls to compose the music and write the lyrics. Geoffrey Holder designed the costumes, and later replaced the director to fix the show. Stephanie Mills, who starred as Dorothy, was fifteen years old at the time. Except for Holder, none of those involved were Broadway veterans. Even more than *Godspell*, *The Wiz* was a risk.

The Wiz uses the plot and characters of the iconic 1939 MGM movie, and musical numbers happen in the same places but with some telling differences. It opens in Kansas, with Dorothy, a dreamer with her head in the clouds, who has a fraught relationship with her Aunt Em. Early in the musical, Aunt Em sings "The Feeling We Once Had," expressing her disappointment in Dorothy's distance from her as the girl has grown up. Thus Dorothy doesn't get an equivalent of "Somewhere Over the Rainbow"; her first "I am/I want" song in *The Wiz* doesn't come until after she's landed in Oz and sings "Soon as I Get Home." She is introduced as a character who always wants to return, as opposed to the original Dorothy, who first wants to escape. The Good Witch of the North is Addaperle ("add a pearl"), "the Feelgood Girl," a hilarious prostitute ("I do tricks!" she exclaims brightly), who resembles Billie Burke's famous characterization in her good-hearted spaciness, and the Wicked Witch of the West is here named Evelline ("Evil leaning"). Glinda, Addaperle's sister, who appears near the end of the musical to sing "If You Believe," informs Dorothy that the silver slippers she's been wearing can (and always could) magically return her home.

Although *The Wiz* follows its movie source in plot, character, and structure, it jettisons Harold Arlen's Tin Pan Alley and Broadway-style score for soul, gospel, rhythm and blues, and funk. The transformation from white Hollywood musical to black Broadway incorporates a new vocabulary of speech, song, and movement, as well as new meanings for the tropes of "home" and a spiritual journey in a hostile environment. As one critic in the *New York Amsterdam News* wrote, "The basic difference in the two productions is the black influence. The black influence upon an average production is just as important as the dressing is to the salad, the barbeque sauce is to the ribs, and the icing is to the cake. The key ingredients to the black influence are sensuality, quality, professionalism, relaxation, and enthusiasm."[43]

Still, *The Wiz* is a fantasy, with catchy, appealing songs and a sweet, innocent tone, an antidote to the racial struggles of the time. Few black musicals were produced in the 1970s, as many artists felt that integration had failed, and

they embraced the Black Power ideology of separate spheres and aligned themselves with the Black Arts Movement. Like *Bubbling Brown Sugar* (1976), *Ain't
Misbehavin'* (1978), and *Eubie* (1979), *The Wiz* opted for racial pride and a
"feel-good" vibe rather than an overtly political message.[44] Ironically, perhaps,
although the producers of *The Wiz* may not have seen themselves as socially
significant, and that wasn't their explicit goal in the content of the show, they
were indeed creating socially significant art in that it got produced and succeeded on Broadway.

The Wiz generated much excitement. In fall 1974, the *New York Amsterdam
News* crowed that "black producers are taking over Broadway," with *The Wiz* as
a prime example.[45] As the show was rehearsing in Baltimore for its premiere,
though, word got out that there were big problems, and closing date notices
were already posted on the New York callboard on opening night, January 5,
1975. To make matters worse, the *New York Times'* reviews were terrible. Clive
Barnes found "the treatment of the story" "tiresome" and "the total result a
little cold." He was "unmoved for too much of the evening," which he quali-
fied: "I was respectfully unmoved, not insultingly unmoved." He described
Smalls's music as "all too insistent and oddly familiar," and William F. Brown's
book as "somewhat charmless." His review concluded, "There are many things
to enjoy in 'The Wiz,' but, with apologies, this critic noticed them without actually enjoying them."[46] Walter Kerr was even harsher, writing, "The contemporary overlay, alas, is feeble at every turn; the show wanders about in search
of a dateline, not to mention a decent laugh."[47] By January 6, *The Wiz* seemed
too besotted with production problems and a hostile (read: racist) press to survive.

The resuscitation and subsequent commercial success of *The Wiz* created a
community that in some ways mirrored the action within the musical itself,
gathering steam, support, and members of the "family" as it went along on its
journey into a hostile territory. The *New York Amsterdam News* ran an editorial
shortly after *The Wiz* opened, urging black theatergoers to see the musical and
excoriating white reviewers for rejecting the vernacular-based show. The editor wrote that "the establishment critics raised substantive questions about
their ability to objectively and accurately assess the innovative work. We take
a positive stand and recommend this unusual satire highly." The editorial concluded with urgency: "This play is one which should be supported by the Black
community since its demise may come as a result of the inability of the 'mainstream play killers' to respond to a white story satirized by Blacks, produced by
Blacks, sung by Blacks and seen predominantly by Blacks on opening night.
That audience welcomed 'The Wiz' with open arms (seven curtain calls)."[48] A

stream of critics then chimed in with positive reviews encouraging readers to see *The Wiz* and noting that white reviewers did not understand references to black culture and life. Mel Tapley, for example, wrote, "It looks like critic Rex Reed is leading the pack of fastest guns in the West trying to shoot down 'The Wiz,' the effervescent and delightful musical at the Majestic."[49] Jessica Harris called *The Wiz* "soul food." She exclaimed, "From the moment that Aunt 'Em (Tasha Thomas) opens her mouth, it is clear that the people who wrote and the people who perform in this musical know all about grandmothers and aunts and Aretha and LOVE."[50] The production also ran a blitz of TV commercials, the second television advertising campaign in Broadway history. (The first was *Pippin*, which featured the now-iconic white-gloved jazz hands.) Supporters of *The Wiz*, like Dorothy, reached out and invited new spectators to come along on the journey.[51]

In response, black spectators bought tickets in droves, and church and community groups organized theatre outings and reserved large sections of the theatre. Both grassroots support and positive word of mouth turned the show into a huge hit, and it ran on Broadway for five years. In this way, *The Wiz* motivated the formation and enactment of a community of black theatergoers and critics who defied the hegemony of white critics and whose resistance underlined the white perspective of mainstream papers and negated the presumption that a white perspective is objective or universal. Several spectators wrote letters to the editor, praising the paper for refusing to succumb to the opinions of white critics and noting the importance of the black press to offer a different perspective. They admitted that they might not otherwise have seen *The Wiz* because they believed the white critics, but the paper persuaded them and they thought the show was great. In its weekly theatre listing, the paper blurbed *The Wiz*, "'The Emerald City Is Rockin, And Little Dorothy Is Dancing Down The Yellow Brick Road Like It Led To Soul Train' quotes John Laycock of the Winsor Star."[52] When *The Wiz* won seven Tony Awards six months later, including Best Musical, the black press was still enjoying its renegade yet influential stance. That this musical did ultimately succeed commercially proved that white audiences would see and enjoy the show, too. Years later, theatre scholar Thomas S. Hischak describes *The Wiz* as "a vivacious musical," "filled with sassy, self-mocking dialogue," and a "Motown-sounding pop score overflowing with energy and joy."[53]

The Wiz presents the creation, solidification, and then eventual separation of a community. Dorothy strikes out alone, but she gathers companions along the way, and the group grows to four. Each time that a new character joins the crew, they repeat the song "Ease on Down the Road." (There are other ensemble numbers in *The Wiz* but this one provides a musical thread through the show and is about community formation.) Jazzy and rhythm and blues–inflected, the song has a simple, AABA, repetitive structure in a lively tempo and catchy melody, with all four lines end-rhymed. In the first rendition, Dorothy sings it to the Scarecrow as an invitation to join her. After a brief, electric guitar introduction, Dorothy sings, "Come on, ease on down, ease on down the road" (26).[54] The line itself has movement and pull, as the first "ease" is sung on an offbeat and the second on a downbeat, giving it a more emphatic feeling. "Road" is drawn out onto two notes, creating suspense in the first note. The line repeats. Then the B line, "Don't you carry nothin' that might be a load," also alternates words on the downbeat and syncopation, further conveying a sense of movement and propulsion. Just as the melody and rhythm compel the listener to move, dance, walk, or skip, the lyrics articulate the same purpose.

The song's four-line verse expands on the refrain and, in each new rendition of the song, the lyrics explain how each character might "ease on down the road," given the specific challenges of his condition: for the Scarecrow, "Cause there may be times/When you think you've lost your mind" (26); for the Tinman, "Pick your right foot up/When your left one's down" (30); for the Lion, "And you wake one morning/Just to find your courage gone" (36). The last line of each verse offers hope and encouragement, more general than specific: for the Scarecrow, "Just you keep on keepin'/On the road you choose" (26); for the Tinman, "But just keep on steppin'/And you'll be just fine" (32); for the Lion, "And just stick with us/and we'll show you how to smile" (36).

The black version of "Follow the Yellow Brick Road" and "We're Off to See The Wizard" is as appealing and catchy as the original songs, but "Ease on Down," as opposed to "follow" or "we're off," makes use of the "cool," relaxed hipness of black vernacular at the time. The song is more physically specific too; the jauntily repeated lines call up a "hokey-pokey" movement. The original choreography by George Faison included a "road" made of dancers dressed in yellow that flanked the characters and supported them through their journey, and the principals' movement involved skipping and a forward-moving, African-derived step-ball-change. In each reprise, a new character adds himself onto the line without changing the overall movement. This version, in both song and dance, stresses a relationship among the characters, as they support and encourage each other. In each reprise, the song expands from solo to duet to trio, taking on depth and volume, and the audience witnesses a community growing.

Like *The Wizard of Oz* (and like the other musicals in this chapter), *The Wiz* presents the individual in relation to her "community." Each character joins the other travelers not intending to be part of a community but because he has an individual desire that he hopes the Wiz can answer. Each character has strengths, so the whole is stronger than any one of them. The solo numbers in *The Wiz* (again, like its predecessor) capitalize on each character's unique self, and Dorothy sings several songs about her feelings of alienation and exclusion. Her song of encouragement to the lion, "Be a Lion," is all about being yourself, and when the good witch sings to Dorothy about going home, she sings, "Believe in Yourself" (and the number is a reprise of the Wizard's version, which he sings to the assembled desirous crew).

Like Bobby in *Company*, Dorothy in *The Wiz* ends the musical alone but in a new emotional state, ready to connect to the community she'd left. By creating and leading her own "community," Dorothy truly grows up. Bobby, a middle-class man (white in all New York versions), is forever left searching, grappling with social expectations of men in the early 1970s; yet Dorothy, a black woman, leaves her home, finds a new community, and returns energized to commit to her home.[55]

A Chorus Line

In a review of the 2006 revival of *A Chorus Line*, John Lahr aptly sets the musical in its mid-1970s context:

> "Why shouldn't you be the best you can be?" Zach asks Cassie, his former lover whom he first plucked from a chorus at the age of twenty-two. Cassie replies, "That's not a decision, that's a disease. God, good, better, best—I hate it!"
>
> Back in 1975, "A Chorus Line" aspired to be part of Broadway's legend of good times, and also something completely different. Seeping into its cutthroat dance-off was not just a new look but a new sound—the post-Vietnam sound of retreat. Cassie's spiritual fatigue reflected the culture's nostalgia for a simpler, happier life, one undamaged by the nation's imperialism, one that would replace the destiny of me with the destiny of we.[56]

A musical about performers who become a temporary community through the audition experience and the self-disclosures that Zach the director requires of them, *A Chorus Line* emplots the pull between the individual and the group so fully that the story and the theme merge. The musical is powerful in its scenic simplicity and the fact that it's about what it represents—dancers and dancing. Bodies create shapes on the stage, and the actor-dancers' bodies, the bodies of the ensemble, create the set.

A Chorus Line is important in Broadway musical history for several reasons. First, while it was not the first musical to move from a not-for-profit theatre to Broadway—*Hair* did it six years earlier and ran for an impressive 3,000 performances, and won the 1969 Tony for Best Musical and Best Direction of a Musical—*A Chorus Line* was nominated for twelve Tony Awards and won nine, including Best Musical, Best Direction, Best Book, Best Score, and Best Choreography. The musical also won countless other awards, including the 1975 Pulitzer Prize for Drama, and it became the longest running musical until it was beaten by *Cats*.[57] In the late 1980s, when *The Phantom of the Opera* and *Les Misérables* opened on Broadway with falling chandeliers, fog, flashing lights, and rotating barricades, *A Chorus Line* drew crowds who simply saw bodies moving, a single white line drawn across the proscenium, and a wall of revolving mirrors. It closed on April 28, 1990, after 6,137 performances.[58]

Just as *The Wiz* was the brainchild of Ken Harper, who then managed almost single-handedly to keep the production alive, *A Chorus Line* grew from up-and-coming choreographer Michael Bennett's idea to create a show based on the stories of chorus dancers, or gypsies. If Harper managed to find a new audience for Broadway, Bennett found an entirely new subject. In 1974, countless Broadway performers were unemployed, and Bennett, a young, immensely talented choreographer who worked on *Promises, Promises* (1968), *Company*, and *Seesaw* (1973), decided to invite dancers to meet in a loft to talk about their lives in dance. At the time, he confessed to friends that he was considering making a musical about dancers, but the people who gathered mostly showed up to tell their stories. Once the project moved toward becoming a musical, the performers were paid $100 to participate in the workshops, which was more than they were paid not working. Because the economic situation was so dire on Broadway at the time, many dancers were willing and eager to spend time together, to eat and drink, and talk.[59]

The activity of gathering to share stories for personal affirmation as well as impetus for larger political action—the consciousness-raising group—began as a feminist practice in the late 1960s. In 1968, Carol Hanisch, who had been a civil rights worker in Mississippi in 1964–65, coined the phrase "the personal is political," and Kathie Sarachild, also a civil rights worker, peace activist, and member of the feminist group the Redstockings, originated the term "consciousness-raising."[60] Sarachild wrote a series of articles that urged women to see their personal circumstances not simply as individual choice (or failure) but as a social and political condition. Historian Ruth Rosen writes, "This is what consciousness-raising meant—looking at your life through your own eyes, reflecting on the choices you had made, realizing who had encouraged and discouraged your decisions, and recognizing the many obstacles and constraints that had little to do with individual temperament or talent."[61] By the early 1970s, consciousness-raising groups were ubiquitous in cities and suburbs, and countless articles, essays, and novels, such as "The Politics of Housework" and "The Myth of the Vaginal Orgasm," authorized the women's experiences that were coming to light.[62] Although the dancers who told their life stories and shared their experiences for the sessions that became *A Chorus Line* were not meeting as a precursor to political activism, this activity was part of American culture at the time and provided a preexisting format to explore their situations. Dancers, like women, had much in common and could commiserate about their lives, and heighten their awareness of the occupational hazards—both economic and physical—of being gypsies.

The setup of dancers at an audition for a Broadway musical's chorus is at once completely "real" and utterly contrived in *A Chorus Line*. On the one hand, the musical takes place in real time and charts a believable (in musical theatre terms) story of dancers getting to know one another and growing into a community through a shared, difficult, competitive experience. On the other hand, the musical employs a fragmented structure in a metatheatrical reality with introspective voiceover sections that allow the audience to hear the dancers' private thoughts and feelings. Zach's demand that the dancers talk about themselves means that *A Chorus Line*, as a whole, expands and reiterates musical theatre's conventional first number of the show, the "I am/I want" song. Connected only by Zach's prodding for each dancer to talk, the characters' disclosures are presented chronologically according to the character's age when the story took place. The ensemble effect is played out when each and every character shares a story and the rest of the characters listen and watch.

The opening number of *A Chorus Line* captures the precise tension between the individual and the group that the musical explores for the next ninety minutes. (*A Chorus Line* was one of the first musicals to eschew an intermission.) The lights come up with the whole cast facing away from the audience, learning a dance combination. The piano plays a familiar vamp, and the first word of the show is "again"; like a fly on the wall, the audience lands right in the middle of the action. After turning to "face away from the mirror"—that is, toward the theatre audience—the cast performs the combination they have just been taught, and the explosive, intense choreography bumps up the emotional intensity and bursts with the group's kinesthetic power. The upstage mirror doubles the number of visible bodies, creating an ever-greater sense of organized chaos and moving limbs. Then, when the dancers sing their first line in unison, "God I hope I get it" (9), they express in voice what the audience already has observed in their bodies: that they are all having the same experience, trying to do the steps perfectly and together, and perfectly enough to stand out.

During the opening, characters are slowly distinguished from one another: Connie dances "with her mouth"; Sheila sulks if she's not assigned to the front row; Richie leaps too high; Cassie doesn't sing with the others. Still, this mininarrative in the opening moments of A Chorus Line works entirely differently than the openings of many musicals that introduce characters clearly and one by one so that the audience knows quickly who each character is and what he or she is doing. In contrast, with A Chorus Line, the audience can only begin to identify characters slowly, not even knowing yet who will make the first cut. Bennett intentionally plants a character—"headband boy"—who is very distinctive but who gets eliminated in the first round. Here Bennett plays with the audience's expectations that identifiable characters will remain in the musical. This choice approximates reality and also gives the audience contradictory signals about whom to identify with.

Not only does the opening sequence introduce characters, set the scene of the audition, and paint a mood of excitement, anxiety, and the desire to be chosen, it also incorporates the audience into the ensemble by teaching them how to look at choreography closely. The numerous repetitions of the same phrase of music and choreography with pauses for Zach to correct the dancers teach the audience to see the combination through the eyes of the dancers, who scrutinize themselves and one another. Bennett purposefully created an almost-impossible combination and the dancers make mistakes, and yet gradually improve with each round. The last group of male dancers, according to Bennett, performs the combination perfectly. By the end of the opening, the audience is primed to look at dance "as if" they are themselves dancers.

As the characters come into focus, their identities are always circumscribed by their relationship to the ensemble. At the end of the opening section, once Zach makes the first cut, he calls the dancers by their assigned numbers, except for Cassie, whom he calls by name, which signals that he already knows her and that she will be a key character (16). Staccato chords repeat, and the chosen line of seventeen, facing the audience, moves a few steps upstage, then walks strongly backward (upstage) as if preparing for the grand move forward, and then strides downstage in unison on the beat to stand along the white line, holding their headshots in front of their faces. Next, one by one, they slowly lower the photos, revealing their real faces, which are sweaty and anxious in contrast to the perfectly coiffed and polished images on the headshots. The ubiquitous white line becomes the musical's central metaphor and its unifying staging element, as characters splinter off for their solo numbers but always return to the line (fig. 3-4).

The overall structure and narrative of *A Chorus Line* move away from earlier musicals' tracing of a heterosexual love story. While Cassie and Zach are indeed a couple—or rather, were a couple—the musical only depicts their struggle since the relationship has ended. Each recounts what was disappointing in the other in unfortunately stereotypical roles: Zach is ambitious and work-centered; Cassie can't become the star he thinks she should be. He is striving to be a director and become more autonomous in his work; she remains a performer and dependent on who might cast her—in this case, Zach. They can't communicate. In fact, the most intimate moment of the musical comes when Paul breaks down as he tells the story of his parents' discovery that he performed in drag. Humiliated and bereft, Paul crumples and Zach comes onto the stage, where he's not been since he briefly demonstrated the opening sequence of

Figure 3.4 In *A Chorus Line* (1975), the company stands on the line, singing "I Hope I Get It." Courtesy Photofest.

choreography. He puts his arm around Paul, and they walk a bit upstage. When Larry, Zach's assistant, enters to ask if the others can return from their break, Zach keeps his head next to Paul's and motions back to Larry to stay away. The moment reveals Zach's sympathy at last and also confirms that this musical is fundamentally about paying homage to the dancer. *A Chorus* Line doesn't pretend to be a heterosexual love story but was instead, in 1975, a contemporary story about individual people's lives.

Even as *A Chorus Line* is ensemble-driven, individual characters emerge over the course of the performance. It builds narrative tension, since each story finds its characters older than the last, thus following a life chronology in the real time of the audition. As the dancers get increasingly tired, they learn more about one another, become more invested in the audition, and their stories become more charged, intimate, and vulnerable. When each character sings a solo or a duet, or dances, or tells a story, virtually every story explicitly concerns his or her gender, race, ethnicity, and sexuality. Women and men both sing in *A Chorus Line*, but women dominate the music and, except for Paul, shoulder the musical's emotional heft. The men sing charm songs and tell funny or moving stories, such as the first perky and optimistic solo, "I Can Do That."

A Chorus Line enunciates the ensemble's significance and the centrality of its women in "At the Ballet," a trio sung by three women about their childhoods in which all of the dancers participate, suggesting they all have had similar experiences. Composer Marvin Hamlisch said that the song set the tone for all the music in the show; once the song was written, the creators understood the shape and color of the piece as a whole. Sheila, Bebe, and Maggie sing the same wistful melody; then their harmonies grow and build, one layering on the other. The lyrics of the refrain are simple: "I'd be pretty"; "I'd be happy"; "I would love to"; and all sing, "At the ballet" (49). During the song, which is staged with the three women simply facing front, set along an upstage right to downstage left diagonal, the rest of the cast mimes a ballet class in the shadowy upstage area. They enact bodily what the women sing and remember experiencing as children. The women's difficult, abusive childhoods stand in for all of the dancers' youths.

"Hello Twelve, Hello Thirteen," an elaborate montage that falls right in the middle of the musical, builds on the ensemble effect seeded by "At the Ballet." That this sequence occupies considerable time in *A Chorus Line* reinforces how the musical values the theme of the individual finding his or her identity. The characters suffered the same rite of passage—adolescence—and the everyday traumas of finding themselves, yet each character experiences something unique, whether it's a crush on a movie star, walking in on parents having sex, or the childhood desire to grow up and become a kindergarten teacher. In her memoir, *Time Steps*, Donna McKechnie, the original Cassie, said that the song was composed from the dancers' own words.[63]

"Hello Twelve, Hello Thirteen" moves constantly among the movement of individuals, groups, or the whole cast, with an ever-present cacophonous sound (or the feeling of chaos over the beautifully orchestrated harmonies) and frenetic energy. A choreographed phrase toward the end of the number captures how the song balances the individual with the ensemble, as the whole cast forms a single line from upstage to downstage, with only the first person in line visible. One by one, the dancers break away from this line in their unique step and then move back into the neutral zone of the horizontal line across the stage.

The musical asks if Cassie's individuality threatens the ensemble. Her tour de force, "The Music and the Mirror," is set up as a private showing for Zach (fig. 3-5). She has the stage all to herself, and the flats revolve to mirrors so that she is reflected many times. Her choreography includes leaps and turns, back-bends, and head rolls; that is, movements that are unique and individualized

Figure 3.5 In *A Chorus Line* (1975), Cassie (Donna McKechnie) gets her star turn and the "chance to dance" in "Music and the Mirror." Courtesy Photofest.

and that were, in fact, conceived to accentuate Donna McKechnie's strengths as a dancer.[64] Cassie's lyrics, "All I ever needed was the music, and the mirror,/ and the chance to dance for you" (96), are linked to her character's history, but these are the words of every dancer there—the desire to dance, the desire to perform. McKechnie said she felt isolated from the group when they were developing and rehearsing the show because she did have more experience and a longer, previously more successful career than the other cast members. In addition, she had a star turn in the show. In the end, she said, her isolation contributed effectively to her character's development.[65]

An early version of the number, which Bennett choreographed to be an absolute showstopper, had McKechnie surrounded by a group of male dancers who were dressed in black jumpsuits and also served as stagehands, moving multiple mirrors on and off the stage at various points in the number. McKechnie later wrote that "I came across like Ann-Margret and her boys, and it didn't suit the character or the drama, though it might have been a big hit in Las Vegas."[66] Soon, Bennett realized that the power of the number depended on Cassie dancing solo, finding her truth through the number, and finishing the song exhausted and sweating, having given her all to the dance. McKechnie worked with composer Hamlisch to change the song's tempo at various points, "going into a slow 4/4, which feels sexy, showing another kind of determination after a driving rhythm, then building again toward a climax." The orchestration didn't have strings, but Hamlisch wrote a trumpet solo. McKechnie wrote, "In my mind there was an emotional dynamic between those two levels in the music, a really exquisite ambivalence with Cassie's sexuality emerging from the rhythm of the drums and her yearning reflected in the plaintive trumpet line."[67]

The issue of Cassie's stardom in the musical came to a head in reality during Tony season that year when Bennett pushed hard to get McKechnie nominated for Best Actress, which she won over Chita Rivera and Gwen Verdon in *Chicago* and Vivian Reed in *Bubbling Brown Sugar*. There were six actors who had large roles in the show, but the others only had parts big enough for the Tony committee to allow them to be nominated for "featured" performers.[68]

The final solo number, which turns into a group number and became one of the breakout hits from the show, "What I Did for Love," is initiated and led by a woman, a Latina. Diana answers Zach's question, "What do you do when you can't dance anymore?" (129) after Paul twists his knee and is taken from the stage. (Paul obviously cannot be cast in the fictional show: the Puerto Rican who only reluctantly reveals himself as gay after Zach badgers, pushes, prods, and harasses him to talk is then "killed" off.)[69] As with the other group numbers in *A Chorus Line*—"I Hope I Get It" and "Hello Twelve"—this song captures the entire group's common feeling. The song's force comes from its placement near the end of the musical (and after Paul's traumatic story) and the fact that, for once, the dancers don't dance. Their emotions are so intense and primal that they must stand still to sing the song. Diana opens the song and sings the first verse; she is the voice of all of the characters, and she can articulate why they do what they do. In *A Chorus Line*, the women's songs invariably introduce the voice of the musical ("At the Ballet"), assert absolute individuality ("Music and the Mirror"), and, in this song, express what everyone feels.

In this scene, just before the characters meld into one in *A Chorus Line*'s spectacular and devastating conclusion, they stand still. In this picture, they create neither the geometric formations of the finale nor the line to which they continually return through the musical, but rather are spread all over the stage, each alone, each separate. The musical's last nondiegetic song, "What I Did for Love," places them across the stage so the audience can take in each one.

The final number of *A Chorus Line*, "One," theatricalizes with gold lamé and glitter the simultaneous satisfaction and heartbreak of the ensemble. Each actor enters the stage one by one, including those who were cut in the first round of the audition. The spectator immediately realizes that it's nearly impossible to distinguish one character from another. After an evening of becoming attached to these individuals, and trying desperately to see who is chosen and who is cut, as the final moments of the audition rush by, the audience understands that all of the labor of self-individuation was for naught. The chorus sings, "She's the one," and yet that actor-character, the putative leading lady, is not in this number and was never a part of this audition (145). And yet even though the dancers all look alike, the movement of so many identical bodies is thrilling. *A Chorus Line* requires an ensemble to be a chorus line, its essential self.

The ensemble musicals of the 1970s found new configurations of relationships on stage and moved away from the heterosexual narratives that dominated early musical theatre. In addition, women "starred" in these shows in ways that both underlined their femininity and allowed a more androgynous person to emerge. Still, none of these shows were "feminist" musicals. In fact, self-labeled explicitly and intentionally feminist musicals of the 1970s suffered the same close-mindedness from white male critics as did *The Wiz* from white critics. Myrna Lamb and Sheila Bingham's *Mod Donna*, which opened in 1970, received a positive review from Clive Barnes in the *New York Times* but other reviewers used the occasion to reject the show completely and to taunt the women's lib movement. In 1978, Nancy Ford and Gretchen Cryer's *I'm Getting*

My Act Together and Taking It on the Road was greeted with hostile responses from critics but enthusiasm from audiences, and the musical was a smash hit, ran for three years, and launched many other productions of the musical.[70] Through the 1970s, women's liberation and feminism inched their way into every corner of culture, but as the next chapter explores, in the 1980s, the United States experienced a conservative turn in politics and in culture. *A Chorus Line* ran through the entire decade but competed with spectacular megamusicals whose women occupied stereotypical roles and had no ensemble on which to depend.

CHAPTER 4

The 1980s: "The Phantom of the Opera Is There Inside My Mind"

One of the last hit musicals of the 1970s was Andrew Lloyd Webber and Tim Rice's *Evita*. Starring a young, astonishingly charismatic Patti LuPone, the sung-through musical follows the rags-to-riches life of Eva Perón, wife of Argentina's authoritarian president Juan Perón, inspirational leader, and star. A backstage (since Eva's life is figured as a performance) biomusical in the clothes of a megamusical, *Evita* gathered excitement well before its September 1979 opening because, as Webber and Rice had done with *Jesus Christ Superstar* in 1973, they released the cast album first, before the musical became a theatrical product in its own right.[1] What evolved into common practice in the 1980s created preshow buzz and predisposed audiences to enjoy the theatrical version because they were already familiar with the score. Moreover, the "concept album" from which director Harold Prince fashioned the stage production also became another entertainment commodity altogether.[2]

Eva as embodied by LuPone was reminiscent of grand and powerful women in musicals of the late 1950s and early 1960s like Mama Rose, Mame, and Dolly. Prince said, "She was born dirt-poor, illegitimate, in a macho-oriented South American country—a far from beautiful woman who transformed herself through diet, dye-pot, persistence and savvy into a glamorous figure. . . . What I did was make it hard for the audience to make up their minds about Evita. . . . I wanted you against your will to think she was glamorous."[3] In the story, she sleeps her way to the top of the military and political food chain and marries then-Colonel Perón to gain power and fame, but the heterosexual romance of the musical matters not at all. Eva's true match is her nemesis, the political radical Che, a fictitious character modeled on revolutionary Che Guevara, and played by the formidable Mandy Patinkin, who recognizes Eva's gestures as "a circus" and "a show."[4] They dance a symbolic, out-of-real-time waltz in act 2 to express their mutual antipathy and unsurprising interdependence. Although the location is Latin America, white actors played the principal roles in the musical, and one critic at the time wrote that "it's about as Latin as a steak-and-kidney pie."[5]

The most famous, iconic image from *Evita*—so recognizable that *Wicked* humorously references it in the beginning of act 2—finds Eva dressed in a sparkly, strapless, white ball gown, her blond hair pulled back in a severe bun, standing atop a catwalk with the crowd of Argentine citizens and supporters below her. The actor's arms are raised and bent at the elbows, palms pointing upstage in a pose of benediction, as she powerfully belts the haunting melody, "Don't cry for me, Argentina/The truth is I never left you."[6] Eva's emotionally fake but performatively honest ballad segues into the ensemble's act 1 finale march, "A New Argentina." The number packs an emotional punch by aligning the theatre audience with the ensemble-citizens, subjecting them to the power that arises from Evita's performance of vulnerability when she sings, "Have I said too much?/There's nothing more I can think of to say to you."[7] Although the character of Eva is practically irredeemable, the actor shines, and *Evita* might have presaged a hopeful future for women in Broadway musicals in the 1980s. Looking back, though, *Evita* was a proto-megamusical that anticipated the next aesthetic and commercial transformation for the Broadway musical. The megamusical would alter many of the genre's conventions of production, form, and reception and simultaneously would kiss the feminist musical goodbye.

Fast forward to the late 1980s and the arrival on Broadway of the two biggest hits of the twentieth century: *Les Misérables* (1987) and *The Phantom of the Opera* (1988). In the 1980s, the "British invasion," as it was called, brought megamusicals—also labeled "technomusicals" or "poperettas"—to New York from London, where they were already smash hits. This new style of musical theatre, launched by producer Cameron Mackintosh and dominated by the works of composer Andrew Lloyd Webber, revivified Broadway, breaking all records for audience attendance. If *Evita*, an early megamusical, gave a strong and charismatic woman pride of place in the show and built the narrative and the music around her, in *Les Miz* and *Phantom*—so well known that they're typically referred to in shorthand—old, stereotypical gendered binaries emerge: men are active and women are passive; men function in the world and women are relegated to a domestic space; men are artists and politicians and women are their muses. Within these conservative gender binaries, women are represented as the well-worn and limiting types of the virgin and the whore, and the women with whom the heroic men fall in love are virgins.[8] Big themes, big sets, and big music mask the misogyny embedded in these musicals, which shrink their women musically and physically; that is, women take up minimal musical space and even less performative space. Not surprisingly, the 1980s is also known as the decade of antifeminist backlash, most famously exemplified by Glenn Close's chillingly unforgettable performance as the insane, homicidal, single, working woman Alex in the movie *Fatal Attraction* (1987). But while *Fatal Attraction* demonized feminism and gave Close the meaty role of a character that audiences detested, *Phantom* and *Les Miz* ignored feminism and gave women milquetoast roles that audiences loved. *Phantom* and *Les Miz* converse with 1980s culture that sought to diminish the significance of women as social and political actors.

Les Misérables and *The Phantom of the Opera* radically displace the strong and visible, acting and active, prominent women in musicals of the earlier twentieth century, but in two different ways. *Les Misérables* casts women only as supporting characters with few songs, little stage time, and limited activity in the narrative; in truth, *Les Misérables* is an excessively masculinist musical. In *The Phantom of the Opera*, one woman stars as Christine, and a few others take on small character roles. While Christine is a key character—indeed, the linchpin of the plot—and while the actor who plays her sings frequently, the role is a stereotypical muse. Christine is the object of Raoul's and the Phantom's affections, triangulated between them as they duke it out for control over her.

Within the diegesis, then, women are diminished in these musicals. It's not only that these shows are not about women—at all—but that their representations of women are retrograde. The women barely do anything, rather their "action" is only emotional. The women in *Les Miz* grieve for a man, and Christine in *Phantom* feels unspecifically in love with Raoul—that is, the attraction and romance is developed neither dramaturgically nor musically—and she is afraid of the Phantom. Each female character expresses one emotion (except Christine, who has two emotions, love and fear) and on one emotional level (intense). The historical settings create a seemingly logical excuse for women not to do much (women weren't on the front line in the French Revolution of 1832), but a glance at musicals from *My Fair Lady* to *Cabaret* reveals that any character can be active and complex in any historical time and place. The reduction of women on stage is especially troubling in a performance form that historically valued female characters, put them center stage, and offered great performance and character opportunities for women actors. If musical theatre traditionally gave women more to do, and even ingénues had to project their voices and so convey a certain physical strength, in the 1980s that was no longer the case.

This chapter explores the women—both characters and actors—in these two record-breaking, groundbreaking, paradigm-shifting musicals in relation to the convention of scenography. While earlier chapters in this book have investigated conventions embedded in the musicals' texts themselves—song forms, movement, narrative organization, relationships between characters—this one also considers a crucial aspect of a show that one can't know without experiencing the performance: the production elements of set, lighting, and sound design. These elements create the musical's world in which the audience lives for a few hours, and they make meaning and manipulate emotion as forcefully as acting choices or musical phrases. The 1980s became known for remarkable technological achievements in design.

In addition to the negative stereotypes that *Les Miz* and *Phantom* perpetuate, then, the expansive scenography of the megamusical that drives the show shrinks the female body on stage. Much of the power of 1980s musicals relied on innovative design elements, and although to a certain degree, these megamusicals reduce the presence of the human being altogether, this practice—the diminution of the human form in relation to scenery—is gendered. How does the female performer, who once visually and aurally dominated the musical theatre stage, fit into these musicals? This chapter argues that each musical takes a different tack to shrink women's importance on stage: *Les Miz* pushes women outside of the scenographic frame, and *Phantom* overwhelms the woman with spectacle.

The 1980s

The 1980s were the decade of Ronald Reagan and Margaret Thatcher, of government shrinkages and economic expansion, of increasing disparities between the rich and the poor. After the well-intentioned but ineffectual presidencies of Ford and Carter, who both served only one term, former movie star Reagan exuded sunny Southern-Californian optimism. At the same time, in fog-drenched Britain, Thatcher's government also supported fiscal growth and unfettered capitalism. A feeling of financial gain on both sides of the Atlantic—whatever the weather—accompanied the megamusical British imports "across the pond" and drove their commercial success, starting with *Cats* in 1982.[9] Thatcher's culture helped to produce big glossy megamusicals, and Reagan's culture eagerly consumed them and made their creators rich.[10]

The 1980s also witnessed the erosion of progressive social policies and a move away from political centrism, replaced with an individualistic, pick-yourself-up-by-your-bootstraps mentality. While the economy expanded, the political and social agenda of the 1980s New Right was unabashedly conservative. According to historians Michael Omi and Howard Winant, the "new right dream seemed within reach: to consolidate a 'new majority' which could dismantle the welfare state, legislate a return to 'traditional morality,' and stem the tide of political and cultural dislocation which the 1960s and 1970s represented."[11] This era saw "the assault on liberalism and 'secular humanism,'" and "the obsession with individual guilt and responsibility where social questions were concerned (crime, sex, education, poverty)."[12] Omi and Winant continue, "Liberalism was seen as beholden to minorities, for whom it provided 'handouts,' while conservatism was thought to embrace traditional individualist (and thus 'colorblind') values of hard work and sacrifice."[13] In 1985, in fact, Reagan said that some civil rights organizations were no longer needed because they had accomplished their goals.[14] More Americans identified as "conservative" rather than "liberal," and the majority disavowed social movements of women and racial minorities that seemed to conflict with "traditional values."[15]

Through the 1970s, mainstream culture absorbed many feminist ideals and practices, and by 1980, feminism was in many ways taken for granted. The 1980 presidential election witnessed the first gender gap in voting, when fewer women than men voted for Reagan. A 1986 *Newsweek* poll found that 56 percent of women considered themselves feminists, 71 percent said the women's movement had improved their lives, and only 4 percent described themselves as antifeminist. That same year the *New York Times* agreed to use Ms. instead of Mrs. or Miss to identify women in its articles.[16] In the home, many middle-class kitchens were equipped with Cuisinarts and microwave ovens for heating frozen foods quickly, so women spent less time in the kitchen and on housework in general.[17]

Achievements for individual women in politics and literature mounted as well. In 1981, Sandra Day O'Connor became the first female Supreme Court justice. In 1986, Barbara Mikulski from Maryland was elected to the U.S. Senate, doubling the number of women from one to two; she was the first Democratic woman to serve in the Senate who didn't succeed her husband. In 1983, Alice Walker won the Pulitzer Prize and the American Book Award for her novel *The Color Purple* (1982), and Toni Morrison's groundbreaking novel *Beloved* was published in 1987 and also won the Pulitzer that year.

On the other hand, in many ways, U.S. culture in the 1980s retreated into conservative values and narrower roles for women. For example, some women who had benefitted enormously from feminism began to disavow it. The term "postfeminist generation" first appeared in 1982 in an article in the *New York Times Magazine* in which the author interviewed a group of women in their twenties. While these women believed in absolute gender equality and expected it for themselves, they felt that they could succeed just by being strong individuals and that feminism was over and done with.[18] Meanwhile, actual legal battles were lost. In 1982, the Equal Rights Amendment failed to gather the necessary number of states for ratification, and in 1986, the Supreme Court ruled in *EEOC v. Sears* that Sears did not discriminate against women.[19] After 1980, fewer women received judicial appointments, and from 1980 to 1981, the number of women selected for White House staff fell from 123 to 61.[20]

Ten years later, journalist Susan Faludi looked back and depicted the 1980s as a decade of a backlash against feminism; her book was subtitled *The Undeclared War against American Women*,[21] and the moniker resonated for many. Faludi and other feminist commentators at the time observed culture, including clothing styles and other trends, as expressing ideology; that is, the "backlash" that she described in the book's title was not a conscious campaign against women, but rather an ideological shift to the right. Faludi discusses, for example, the fashion of childlike clothes for women, which gave them the appearance of youth and conveyed that they were not responsible or serious.[22] Similarly, the creation of musicals that reduced the action of women on stage in the 1980s was not (likely) the conscious practice of the artists involved but rather a cultural project that both shaped and was shaped by the historical moment.

For Faludi, the media, advertising, and popular culture pushed back against women and against feminism, sending the message that women could not have successful careers and happy personal lives and that feminism was to blame. In 1986, for example, *Newsweek* warned that single, college-educated women over forty were more likely to be killed by terrorists than to marry. The magazine retracted the article, which was titled "Too Late for Prince Charming?," in 2006, but the very fact that such an article could be printed and would raise such alarm (which it did) gives credence to an ominous antifeminist mood.[23]

Television shows in which women clearly could not "have it all" dominated the airwaves in the 1980s. Although television featured more women who tried to live as feminists, including Kate and Allie, Murphy Brown, and Molly Dodd—all single mothers—and Roseanne Barr, the hilarious and famously bitchy working-class mother, each character failed personally or professionally or both.[24] Several highly praised television series from the 1980s implied that career women should be punished for their accomplishments, and competent professional women suffered despite great reserves of strength. *New York Times* critic Ginia Bellafante notes that "[o]n 'L.A. Law' Grace Van Owen (Susan Dey) was given a nervous breakdown; Dr. Wendy Armstrong (Kim Miyori) of 'St. Elsewhere' killed herself after she couldn't save a child's life; others were saddled with breast cancer, infertility, divorce, loneliness."[25] Popular cultural studies scholar Andi Zielser observes, "Working women on both the big and small screens spent the 1980s being scorned, humiliated, and punished for the dual sins of being ambitious and female."[26] The show *thirty-something*, which premiered in 1987, never achieved high ratings, but it captured the zeitgeist of the late 1980s, and presented educated, middle-class women who were unhappy no matter what their life choices. All of the women were neurotic, indulgent parents; Princeton-educated, stay-at-home mom Hope Steadman (played by Mel Harris) was alternately guilty about not being driven or ambitious enough and about not being a good enough mother.

Other shows that premiered after 1985, such as *The Golden Girls, Sisters*, and *Living Single*, presented a group of women, but the characters were under-developed, as if, Zeisler argues, "Each woman acted as but one facet of what a real woman's personality might be."[27] Films of the decade often pitted women against one another, like the noble mother who kills Alex at the end of *Fatal Attraction*. As Christine Stansell puts it, "In films of the 1980s, heroines of unusual ideas and unconventional behavior were bound to end up alone, insane, murdered, or left in the dust by younger, perkier, more pliant rivals who snag the man while heroines falter and flop," giving the example of Melanie Griffith winning the man and the job over executive Sigourney Weaver in *Working Girl* (1988).[28]

Madonna invented and reinvented herself in the 1980s, taking full advantage of the new form provided by MTV that linked moviemaking, music production, fashion, and performance. Every aspect of Madonna's performances was tinged with both irony and self-empowerment, from her innocent and directly sexualized *Like a Virgin* (1984, her second album), which included the Marilyn Monroe takeoff single "Material Girl," to her role as the cool, fancy free troublemaker in the film *Desperately Seeking Susan* (1985). Madonna at once represented a strong and independent woman, a woman with her own desires both sexual and otherwise, and a woman who relied on the retrograde images and accoutrements of conventional, sexualized femininity.[29]

Even self-claimed feminists contributed to an antifeminist backlash. Wendy Wasserstein's award-winning Broadway play, *The Heidi Chronicles* (1989), for example, follows the protagonist's journey through feminism, a career as a feminist art historian, and various disastrous romances, to a final scene in which she has adopted a baby and may find some semblance of happiness after feminism and an intellectual life have failed her. Over and over, representations of women said that feminism was over, a futile, even wrongheaded project, and that women couldn't have it all. These representations of women in the 1980s as unhappy and troubled both reflected and influenced the times.

A Short History of Set Design

Through the "golden age" of the mid-twentieth century, as Broadway musicals became more story-driven, their scenography attempted to accurately represent their place and time. Larger and more detailed sets provided a realistic locale for characters and their stories, whether a Salvation Army church—the Save-a-Soul Mission—in Damon Runyon's Manhattan in *Guys and Dolls* (1950, designed by Jo Mielziner), or the family living room of a midwestern home in *Bye Bye Birdie* (1960, designed by Robert Randolph). Through the era when realistic, psychologized acting was valued in musical as well as nonmusical theatre, set designers imagined and built onstage spaces that characters would believably inhabit.[30]

The busiest and most accomplished set designers of the mid-twentieth century crossed over from nonmusical theatre to musicals and back again, underlining the serious artistic purpose to which composers and lyricists from Jerome Kern and Oscar Hammerstein II on aspired. Mielziner, for example, who designed the remarkable Expressionist-influenced sets for Tennessee Williams's *The Glass Menagerie* (1945) and Arthur Miller's *Death of a Salesman* (1949), also created the Tony Award–winning set for *South Pacific*. For the show, Mielziner collaborated with director and colibrettist Joshua Logan and Rodgers and Hammerstein to move smoothly from the Seabees' beach to Bali Hai, from Emile's plantation home to Commander Harbison's military office, underscored by music to emulate filmic crossfades. Although few musicals of the 1940s or 1950s achieved this level of visual flow, many musicals relied on "crossover" music with small scenes played downstage of the curtain to allow the set to change behind it, sparing the audience from waiting in the dark with only music to accompany a big set change. *The Sound of Music*, for example, designed by Oliver Smith, features a sweet scene of the children, still frightened by a thunderstorm, gingerly walking from Maria's room to their own—that is, downstage of the closed curtain—warbling "The Lonely Goatherd" in shaky voices. By the time they crossed from stage left to right, the next scene was set and the curtain raised. Like Mielziner's, Smith's designs were wide-ranging, from many more musicals, including *West Side Story* and *Camelot*, to dramas, such as Tennessee Williams's *The Night of the Iguana* (1961), to comedies like Neil Simon's *Barefoot in the Park* (1963) and *Plaza Suite* (1968).

The practice of mimetic, realist set design has persisted as the baseline for musicals into the twenty-first century, but in the late 1960s and 1970s, sky-rocketing production costs coupled with the pervasive influence of avant garde, collaborative, and "poor theatre" performance-making techniques of the Living Theatre, the Open Theatre, and the Performance Group led to more conceptual and spare designs. *Cabaret*, for example, discussed in chapter 2, shows both of these influences. Boris Aronson's set featured a realist backdrop, working doors and windows, and some furniture pieces in the scenes in Fräulein Schneider's boarding house—a realistic design to represent a 1920 Berlin location. But in the "limbo" cabaret scenes, as we saw in chapter 2, Aronson's large mirror above the stage reflected the audience as a constant reminder that the political dynamics of 1929 Berlin were not all that different than those of the United States in 1966, which clarified the political metaphor of the Hal Prince–directed production. Aronson's stunning conceptual design for *Company*, explored in chapter 3, used steel beams and plexiglass to suggest apartments in New York City, its inhabitants at once crowded and discon-nected from one another.

Other musicals through the 1970s and into the 1980s increasingly found ways to thematize spatially the musical's content. In *A Chorus Line*, for ex-ample, discussed in chapter 3, the entire set consisted of a single white line painted across the stage and a wall of mirrors upstage. This absolutely simple set presented the mirror-backed stage on which the dancers danced and revealed their innermost selves and the white line on which they were instructed to stand, literally and emotionally putting themselves on the line, a metaphor that the musical expanded and exploited. During the show, the mirrors, each mounted to revolve, turned around to reveal a plain wall, and then later turned again to the mirrored side and moved into a curved arrangement for Cassie's "The Music and the Mirror" to reflect multiple, fragmented images of Donna McKechnie's moving body. *A Cho-rus Line* was also the first musical to use a computerized light board, and Tharon Musser's design cued the musical's action and shaped its emotional power.[31] Not insignificantly, unit sets, spare sets, or sparsely decorated sets saved money, but their simplicity also kept the audience's attention focused on the performers.

Cats and the Megamusical

In 1982, *Cats* changed everything. Mackintosh, who imported the show from London's West End, as well as *Starlight Express* (1987, ran for 761 performances), *Miss Saigon* (1991, ran for 4,092 performances), and the two musicals discussed in this chapter, said, "History proves that every 20 or 30 years you have to remake the rules,"[32] and he was true to his word. Mackintosh's product was genre-shifting, upending long-practiced methods of musical theatre creation, production, marketing, and reception. Aesthetically, megamusicals featured huge sets, spectacular lighting effects, a sung-through score composed of accessible pop-rock music, a few musical themes that repeated to create an aural tapestry, lush orchestrations, and irresistible emotional power. Set and lighting cues were "locked down" and recorded on computer, so that nothing changed from one performance to the next and the same show could be played by different actors in different cities at the same time. Because the whole show was musically scored, the action moved at a prescribed pace, ensuring no variation among actors' performances and promising spectators the same show anywhere and at any time. In these ways, the megamusical approximated film production, distribution, and reception.

The first of these vast and vastly successful productions, *Cats*, whose tagline was "Now and Forever," actually ran almost forever, or for eighteen years, and typified the megamusical. The Winter Garden Theatre was rebuilt to accommodate an enormous rotating platform on which designer John Napier constructed a trash dump, suggested to him by the title of T. S. Eliot's poem "The Waste Land." (Eliot's poems in *Old Possum's Book of Practical Cats* [1939] provided the text for the songs.) *Cats* had a bare-bones story, but charmed audiences of all ages in its portrayal of felines of different personalities, each of whom sang a song or did a dance. Dance, in fact, dominated the production, featuring Gillian Lynne's acrobatic choreography of "whirling cat dervishes."[33] Frank Rich wrote in the *New York Times* that *Cats* succeeded because it "transports the audience into a complete fantasy world that could only exist in theater and yet, these days, rarely does."[34]

Although the characters in *Cats* are, well, cats, they are decidedly gendered and in absolutely conventional ways, identified less by appearance or gesture and more by costume details and their songs in the irresistibly infectious score. Yet the dynamic of *Cats* is of an ensemble with featured characters, not entirely unlike *Company* or *A Chorus Line*. There is the patriarch Old Deuteronomy, the white kitten Victoria whose solo begins the Jellicle Ball, a boyish mischievous Mr. Mistoffelees, and many others, but no hetero-feline romance in *Cats*.

Rather the vague story of redemption is about a contest to see which cat will get to the "Heaviside Layer," or cat heaven. Grizabella, the Glamour Cat, first played by Betty Buckley, an old, scraggly, Bette Davis–type, wins after she sings the show-stopping "Memory." When the actor sings on a raised platform trash can up center stage, she is surrounded by the other cats who are still and attentive. Theatre historian Gerald Bordman writes that "she is lifted skyward in a blaze of illumination on a smoke-spewing tire."[35] The focus of the whole theatre is on the actor, and, except for the continuously swirling stage smoke, the scenery is at rest. In some ways, then, the star of *Cats* is a woman. "Memory" was an international breakout hit, covered by countless singers, and recorded in dozens of languages. Almost two decades after musical theatre's songs regularly garnered mainstream popularity, Webber wrote a song permanently etched in cultural history.

Cats "mewed all the way to the bank," earning $6.2 million in advance sales. In 1997, it surpassed *A Chorus Line* as the (then) longest running musical in Broadway history, and as of its final performance on September 10, 2000, it had grossed $380 million on Broadway (and nearly $3 billion worldwide).[36] *Cats'* blockbuster success was due to its spectacular effects, its family friendly content, and its revolutionary marketing and advertising strategy. Rather than a boldface, splashy blurb from a review or a list of actors and artists or even a catchy, exclamatory phrase, the show's poster was an all-black background and cat's yellow eyes with dark silhouettes of dancers in its irises. No words needed translation into other languages, as this internationally legible image was reproduced on products of all kinds— souvenir T-shirts, coffee mugs, and other paraphernalia—and its striking logo, its branding, guaranteed instant recognition everywhere. These products became markers of spectators' cultural capital, who then inadvertently publicized the brand themselves, whether or not they had actually seen the show. Megamusicals offered so many merchandising tie-ins that, over time, the production itself did not need to turn a profit, as long as it was sufficiently visible through souvenirs for audiences to recognize the musical and continue to buy other items.[37] As historian Graham Thompson notes, "The show was branded like any other consumer product. . . . [T]he sheer degree of corporate backing that a musical like *Cats* could deploy did mark a different order of economic and cultural interaction."[38] Moreover, Mackintosh always spent money on advertising, even when a show was sold out. "There's no better time to beat the drum than when people can't buy tickets," he explained. "You have to let them know they can't buy a ticket. That's what the difference between a hit and a megahit is all about."[39]

British imported megamusicals reinvigorated Broadway in the late 1980s and early 1990s. After the sharp decline in the number of musicals produced in the 1970s, as well as profitable ones, the ones that became hits recouped costs relatively quickly and began to turn a profit. During the 1980s, production costs increased around 500 percent, from an average of $1 million at the start of the decade, to *Cats'* record- setting $4 million in 1982, which *Phantom* broke in 1988 at $8 million.[40] Rising production costs were most attributable to labor, from retrofitting theatre spaces, to constructing huge, technologically complex sets with hundreds of moving parts, to building lavish costumes, to hanging thousands of lighting instruments, to training technicians to operate the many computers that ran the show each night. Although a somewhat more robust economy and technological developments supported the growth of set- and design-driven megamusicals, these shows ultimately became less expensive to play over a long, multiyear run than musicals of earlier decades. As set designer Richard Isackes notes, "Because stage hand labor has gotten increasingly expensive, automated scenery has become increasingly attractive to producers. Although the upfront cost is far greater than for conventional scenery, in a long-running show this initial capital investment is easily offset by the long term reduction of very heavy labor cost."[41] Producers, faced with higher and higher costs, were reluctant to take artistic risks and instead bet on big, accessible shows that were already hits in London.

Theatre tickets went up, too: one could see *A Chorus Line* for $10 in 1975 but ticket prices were between $25 and $45 ten years later.[42] During the economic boom of the mid-1980s, though, more Americans could afford to go to the theatre. Musically accessible and visually spectacular megamusicals, along with rising ticket prices, both attracted new audiences and altered the expectations of regular theatergoers, who, for their money, wanted a grander theatrical experience of grandiose sets, special effects, and loud, lush sound.[43]

Production and Performance Conventions of the Megamusical

The theatrical conventions of scenographic spectacle, computer-recorded and computer-generated cues, and mass brand marketing that Mackintosh introduced with *Cats*, as mentioned earlier, approximated film. Part of the appeal of megamusicals, asserts Jonathan Burston, was their similarity to other entertainment experiences of the 1980s and after. Burston explains that new technological advances could "promote a distinctly non-theatrical, quasi-cinematic realism to the stage—a particular kind of visual 'seamlessness' . . . that aimed to erase all evidence of wires, pulleys and other cues to the existence of a long-standing theatrical tension between the actual and the contrived."[44] Megamusicals also eliminated most blackouts, as scenery seemed to fly in magically, and one scene literally faded or moved into the next. Interestingly, both Napier (*Les Miz*)and Björnson (*Phantom*) are credited as "production designers," underlining how these huge musicals are reluctant to use traditional theatre artists' terminology and rather rely on the job description of film production. It's not simply that they designed the sets (and Björnson the costumes as well), but that they conceived the entire look of the show.

Yet the audience's experience of a Broadway megamusical was (and is) theatre and not film, which intensified its power and effects all the more. However the scenography imitated a movie's nonstop, seamless movement, spectators' experience was live, and they directly witnessed set changes and lighting shifts caused by relatively simple (if expensive) stagecraft. These effects offered spectators a close and upfront view, even more thrilling than film because the play and the audience coexisted.

Megamusicals' visual spectacle and special effects transformed, or rather, dwarfed, the human body on stage. Drawing the audience's eye away from actors' bodies and the labor of performance and toward fog, flashing lights, and smoothly moving set pieces that assembled, disassembled, and reassembled in full view, the set itself became a performer. Computers, writes scenic historian Christopher Baugh, "enable sceneography to explore its own vocabulary and, through the duration of movement, to become a performer within the performance."[45] The production values of the megamusical caught on. In 1989, critic Mel Gussow revisited eight long-running Broadway musicals and noted that *A Chorus Line* was the only one that did not use a fog machine.[46] These filmic visual components worked in tandem with the music, as few numbers stopped for applause.

The music of 1980s megamusicals also shifted in terms of style, technology, and performance mode. Building on the rock sounds of 1970s musicals like *Jesus Christ Superstar* and *Godspell*, composers moved away from melody-driven Broadway standards to a rhythm-driven, soft-rock, "conspicuously 'global' pop" style.[47] The scores are densely orchestrated with strings and woodwinds that provide a thick and active sound.

Megamusicals have less and more music than book musicals: fewer distinct songs but a lot of music because, even when the performers aren't singing, most of the action is underscored. While these musicals don't use the reprise as Rodgers and Hammerstein did, their reuse of melodic phrases or whole songs fills the spectator with a sense—likely unconscious on a first listen—of familiarity. Due to the transposition of the same musical phrases and figures across characters or dramatic moments, these scores go against the conventions established by Rodgers and Hammerstein and their peers that music and lyrics should reflect a character and that a musical number should be unique to that character's voice and to that moment in the play. Critic Mark Steyn, for example, observes that in a sung-through megamusical, the "relationship between music and lyrics loosens." He writes, "In a conventional musical, the lyricist . . . can't merely set dialogue to music or be descriptive or soliloquize; he has to find a lyric idea that vindicates the move into song."[48] In a book musical, "you have to justify the music," but in sung-through musicals, Steyn's critique continues, "no *musical* distinction is made between conversational trivialities and big character soliloquies: banal chit-chat and key moments of emotional stress are carried by the same melodic phrase, effectively according them the same weight. The precise tension of a musical—the raising of the stakes, as dialogue turns to underscored speech, then to verse, then to chorus—has simply been abolished."[49] The sung-through musical is, for some, integration gone awry, especially when the same melody is reused with different lyrics—or "contrafacta"—as is frequently done in *Les Misérables* and *Phantom*.[50] But *Les Miz* lyricist Alain Boublil has different aesthetic goals: "The sung-through musical is a different convention from the dialogue/song musical. It's not necessarily better . . . but it's another art form. What I don't like at all is when you don't know why they've started singing or why they've started talking. The change from one to the other can make you too aware of the form, and so makes it less believable." He explains, "The magic of the sung-through form is that it allows you to treat a very serious story. There has to be a good reason why people are singing on stage. But it has to seem so natural that you almost forget that they are singing."[51]

If composers of megamusicals reconfigured the conventional relationship between music and lyrics, audiences of megamusicals developed new expectations of the theatrical experience, in part because of those new conventions and in part because of changing audio technologies. Because the cast album tended to be many theatregoers' initial experience of a megamusical, audiences wanted to hear in person an approximation of this familiar, balanced, through-a-stereo-speaker sound. In the theatre, then, live musicians were moved away from the audience, who would hear the music not directly through the instruments but through the speakers, as if hearing a CD. Of course, instruments and human voices mediated through computers and projected entirely through speakers profoundly altered how musicals sounded. The overall texture of the music replicated FM radio, an intimately close and clean, "scrubbed" sound.

The presence of audio technology necessarily affected the role and labor of the actor. Traditional ideas about projecting one's voice out into the theatre no longer mattered, as actors with body mics had the freedom to turn upstage, whisper, or stand anywhere on stage and still be heard in a huge theatre almost as if they were speaking in each spectator's ear. A successful musical theatre actor no longer had to develop the technique and skill of projection, and even actors with quiet voices could be stars on the megamusical stage. Actors could modulate the tone or timbre of their voices, but computers could (and did) manipulate the voice as well to emulate the smooth sound of FM radio and reduce the quirks of an actual human being's voice. In addition, unlike earlier days of miked sound where actors shared a channel, 1980s musicals set each actor's voice on his or her own channel. In the past, then, the volume of the whole channel could be adjusted but not each separate voice, so actors themselves had to create a balance among their voices. In the 1980s, though, the sound technician altered each voice alone, making it louder or softer and adding reverbs, echos, and other sound effects as desired.[52] Ultimately, technology rather than the actor's labor produced the sound. The technology eliminated the actor's freedom to control her volume and to modulate the aural space she could occupy at any one time. As for theatre audiences, they could hear each voice perfectly, but in a group scene, even with effort, found it difficult or impossible to see the actor-source of the sound.

Les Misérables

Les Misérables, which was created by the team of French composers Claude-Michel Schönberg and Alain Boublil (whose original, shorter French version was performed in a Paris sports arena and was seen by half a million people there), codirectors Trevor Nunn and John Caird, set designer John Napier, and lighting designer David Hersey, and with the imprimateur of the Royal Shakespeare Company as the original producing venue, earned mostly admiring reviews and won a gaggle of awards.[53] Frank Rich in the *New York Times*, for example, led with, "If anyone doubts that the contemporary musical theater can flex its atrophied muscles and yank an audience right out of its seat, he need look no further than the act 1 finale of *Les Misérables*." Rich went on to laud the "gripping pop opera," especially the "fusion of drama, music, character, design and movement" that "links this English adaptation of a French show to the highest tradition of modern Broadway musical production."[54] Howard Kissel of the *Daily News*, though, hated the show and called it "drivel— singsong, repetitious, and emotionally dead,"[55] and theatre historian Gerald Bordman describes it as "behemoth, pretentious, and outrageously amplified."[56] Kissel and Bordman's complaints were typical for those who were disdainful of megamusicals: that the music is repetitious and that size stands in for quality. Still, *Les Miz* won eight Tony Awards, including Best Musical, Set, and Lighting Design, as well as the New York Drama Critics Award for Best Musical, and five Drama Desk Awards. Given how the dynamics of the megamusical prioritized design over actors, it's not surprising that, even though *Les Miz* fairly swept that year's Tony Awards, no actors were recognized.

Based on Victor Hugo's epic novel, the musical follows the travails of noble, escaped convict Jean Valjean and his enemy, the obsessive police officer, Javert, who eventually kills himself out of frustration and despair. Their lifelong chase is interwoven with the struggle of student revolutionaries and workers in Paris and punctuated with family drama—Valjean adopts Cosette when her mother, Fantine, dies; romance—grown-up Cosette and rebel student Marius fall in love; unrequited love—poor, feisty Eponine has a crush on Marius; and bawdy, scene-setting humor of the tavern owners in "Master of the House."

Les Misérables is equally famous for its mesmerizing music, its barricade, and its logo. The iconic waif, the child version of Cosette, was plastered on all publicity material in New York, including full-page newspaper ads, posters, T-shirts, coffee mugs, buttons, and other "Les Misérabilia," which revved up ten months before the musical opened. Between Mackintosh's mammoth publicity machine and transatlantic word of mouth—the musical was already a huge hit in London—the Broadway production of *Les Miz* sold $6.7 million worth of tickets a full five weeks in advance of its New York premiere. The first day that tickets were available, future spectators spent $447,275 on tickets for a production that they might not see for months. With an average ticket price of $46.50, the advance sales amounted to more than 144,500 tickets sold.[57] This amount was more than double the single-day record previously set by *Cats* in 1982. *Les Miz* was an "event" more than simply entertainment.[58]

Cosette's image was later adapted for each country where the show was performed. She held a torch like the Statue of Liberty for the Broadway production, sat astride a horse dressed as a Mountie for Canada's, wore Viking horns for Denmark, and donned Maria Von Trapp's skirts in *The Sound of Music* for Austria. For the U.S. national tour, she was adorned with identifying regional symbols, wearing big sunglasses for Los Angeles or peeking out upside down from the Liberty Bell for Philadelphia.[59] Yet as this chapter demonstrates, the centrality of the girl on the musical's publicity material belies the character's relatively minor role in the show itself.

Women play small and insignificant roles in *Les Miz*. First, they appear late: Fantine's first song halfway through act 1 is a woman's first solo, long after the male characters have been introduced and have sung and the story is well on its way. Second, the three featured female characters—Fantine, Cosette, and Eponine—are delineated from the other minor female characters and ensemble players by their virginal innocence, not literal virginity but a kind of spiritual goodness, a narrow female stereotype. Third, the women only exist to set off the complex decisions, spiritual struggles, and brave actions of the men.

The women in *Les Miz* are at once sharply differentiated from one another and made to seem the same. The hopelessly romantic Fantine had a brief love affair that results in a daughter, Cosette, as she discloses in her first number, "I Dreamed a Dream." The child's father long gone, Fantine sacrifices all for Cosette's survival, even turning to prostitution, which goes against her every impulse. Tough and feisty but not enough for this world, Fantine ultimately succumbs to disease and quick death. Jean Valjean, a stranger to her, adopts Cosette and raises her as his own, and she grows up to be the pure woman Fantine was meant to be. The third female principal, the street urchin Eponine, occupies a different category of woman but her desires overlap with Cosette's because they both love the revolutionary student, Marius. Because Eponine is poor, though, she is not a viable romantic partner for Marius. Even tougher and more resilient than Fantine, Eponine tries to involve herself in his life by doing favors for him, even finding out where Cosette lives, and she later shows up at the barricade and volunteers to spy for the revolutionaries. Eponine, then, acts in *Les Miz* more than the other two women. But she is motivated solely by her love for Marius and her desire to be around him and help him and not at all by the larger, important politics that govern the men's actions. In the world of *Les Miz*, men are active and struggle physically, spiritually, and politically. Men sing to each other and are in relation to one another and the stakes are high: death and life; imprisonment and freedom; oppression and revolution. The big challenges, big themes, and big issues are aligned with men and masculinity.

Although the love story of Marius and Cosette provides one of *Les Miz*'s narrative threads, the musical strives to assert its serious, political purpose. The two portray young romance, each in love for the first time. Significantly, though, Marius has a fully engaged life and friends and interests outside of his relationship with Cosette. His friends tease him about his love, arguing in "Black and Red" that there are bigger, more important things to worry about. Indeed, even as *Les Miz* represents the young lovers, the musical itself values more fully the political battle—the plot of Marius and Enjolras (and even Eponine). As Mackintosh said, "Every nation can see their own personal struggle in it. There isn't a country in the world that doesn't have its own parallel in the story that Victor Hugo wrote."[60] To be sure, the heterosexual plot doesn't emerge until relatively late in Les Miz—near the end of act 1—and its triangulation is also resolved late, after Eponine's death in act 2. Unlike the musicals of the 1950s where the individual lovers each signified political differences that the musical eventually resolved through their union, in Les Miz, the lovers are a mere diversion from the real plot, which is "political" and decidedly homoerotic.

The central story of Les Miz has nothing whatsoever to do with women, but is rather the spiritual and moral battle between Valjean and Javert, which the set was designed to represent. Codirector John Caird said, "The main meat of the story . . . is Valjean's progress."[61] Codirector Trevor Nunn told Napier that "he needed to design a chase, a way of encapsulating the idea that one man, a fugitive, is on the run from another man through the entire work." Napier came up with the idea, according to Nunn, of "two towers [that] would fold back on themselves as they came to the center of the stage [and that] could be hugely high."[62] The towers provided ample opportunities to stage the men running, crossing, leaping, and climbing. Theatre historian Bordman observes, "David Hersey's equally imaginative lighting gave a special menace to the sewers through which Valjean must escape."[63]

The musical's act 2 climax, when two giant towers, weighing three tons and driven by computer, glide, merge, and interlock to form an enormous barricade on which the bodies of dead rebel students lie, signals how Les Misérables scenographically values men and their world. In his review, Rich described how "in a dazzling transition, the towers tilt to form an enormous barricade," and concluded that "the proletarian simplicity of the design's style masks an incredible amount of theatrical sophistication."[64] Because the musical prioritizes place and setting over characterization, the design elements are more than integral: they are essential to the production. In effect, the musical's scenery stars as another performer with whom the men get to play.[65] The male characters interact with and through the set on the barricade, tower, and the tavern. Valjean carries the wounded Marius through the sewers of Paris, evoked by fog and dim gray lighting, and sings the prayer-like "Let Him Live," asking to trade Marius's life for his own. Even the villain Javert kills himself by jumping off a high bridge upstage, a moment that invariably elicits gasps from the audience when the actor disappears below the stage floor.

Male actors in many of the group scenes create a kind of human scenography, where bodies form striking visual tableaux. Caird explained how the artists used slow motion to create impressive effects with many bodies: "It's a combination of the revolve moving and David Hersey's lights whizzing round on top of them and you heighten the impact with slow motion. On the barricade, how do you achieve a whole lot of people dying violent deaths, and all in the moment, without there being a lot of blood and so on? By using a device like slow motion the impact is so strong."[66] As Rich described it, actors on the revolving stage are choreographed "so that spatial relationships mirror human relationships in the pressing march of history."[67]

Within *Les Miz's* performative architecture, women occupy a sonic and visual space outside of the key action and themes and off and away from the complex and entrancing machinations of the set that the musical values. The musical's principal women are excluded from these impressive, visually engaging, and thematically significant scenes. Each female character has a song that is staged with the woman alone. In this way, *Les Miz* deserts the actor by isolating her from visual elements altogether. *Les Misérables* diminishes women by exiling them from the set and forcing them outside of the world of the play.

In *Les Miz*, Schönberg and Boublil introduced the practice of reusing musical phrases and motifs throughout the show, linking music to emotional moods or themes rather than to individual characters. All musical theatre composers make use of a coherent array of keys, instruments, harmonic arrangements, and stylistic flourishes to create a sound that unifies the show, such as Jerry Herman's ragtime, cakewalk-based, and nostalgia-inducing score for *Hello, Dolly!*, Jerry Bock's minor thirds that sound "Jewish" in *Fiddler on the Roof*, or Jim Jacobs and Warren Casey's 1970s imitation of 1950s rock 'n' roll in *Grease*. In addition, most composers craft a score with musical linkages between characters to present the audience sublimally with a deeper sense of the relationships between characters. For example, in *My Fair Lady*, Alan Jay Lerner subtly transforms Eliza and Higgins's music into the other's, expressing musically how they have influenced one another.[68] *Les Miz* makes this practice aurally identifiable for most spectators, as Valjean and Javert, men who are at once opposites and also intimately, fatalistically connected, literally repeat each other's entire melodies. Numerous other musical themes repeat across the score. The lyricist for the English-language production, Herbert Kretzmer, called the repeated themes "spinal music, music that runs through the show like a backbone." The use of such reprises, Kretzmer ventured, "is, I believe, one of the many reasons for the show's hold over audiences."[69]

Although *Les Miz* is formally a pop opera, with recitatives instead of spoken dialogue, several clearly delineated songs do exist in the musical, albeit few of them that repeat in different scenes, sung by different characters. The female characters do sing sections of recitative, but more often, their stage moments are framed musical numbers. The women in *Les Miz* perform almost as if in concert, apart from the story. Dramaturgically, they function to strengthen the characterization of the men. Fantine's sole purpose, for example, is to show Valjean's extraordinary generosity when he agrees to raise her soon-to-be-orphaned daughter, Cosette, as his own. Forced into prostitution, from which she gets neither satisfaction nor power, she drinks liquor to steel herself for sex and scratches the face of one of her customers when he mistreats her. Because Fantine is essentially an innocent, she is an unsuccessful prostitute, and the other women judge her and try to cheat her when she sells her jewelry and her hair just to survive and feed her daughter. The musical underlines repeatedly that she is a pure woman, not fit to be among the "lovely ladies," as the rollicking and bitter song goes, who easily sell themselves. *Les Miz* separates Fantine and prevents her from bonding with other women.

Fantine sings two solos in her short-lived act 1 appearance, each of which finds her emotionally lost and physically isolated onstage. In "I Dreamed a Dream," which revival reviewer David Ronney called "the show's first major assault on the tear ducts,"[70] she expresses desire for the man who deserted her, Cosette's father. When the song begins, with a folk guitar accompaniment, it sounds different than the score so far, suggesting musically that this character doesn't belong in this play. The actor sings the first part of the number kneeling on the floor and then she stands, all the time in a narrow spotlight, apart from theatrical elements that would locate her within the world of the play.[71] In her second solo, "Come to Me," a dying Fantine sits on a small cot and implores Valjean, whom she's just met, to care for Cosette. She sings to him, so a relationship is implied, but again, the narrow spot isolates her and separates her from him. Then, immediately after Fantine dies, Javert enters, and he and Valjean fight over and around her dead body; she is literally an object in the middle of their struggle and their duet. Although her death sets into motion key aspects of the plot, the performance of the song is isolated. According to the creators, in earlier versions of the musical Fantine had a bigger part and more developed backstory, "to better understand what's happened to her," as Kretzmer explained. They cut that material because "somehow in the song 'I Dreamed a Dream' you get the sense of what has happened to her."[72] Trevor Nunn concurred: "I also felt Fantine had too many utterances early on, especially as Fantine was going to depart the show."[73] In short, they agreed, "the

whole show was too loaded emotionally towards Fantine."[74] Fantine's scenographic detachment underlines that her brief presence in the musical is more
symbolic than characterological, emphasizing themes of spirituality, redemption, and sacrifice, but mainly supportive of Valjean's character development.

Cosette, played by one child actor and one adult, embodies the innocent
woman Fantine would have been had poverty not forced her into prostitution
and death. Young Cosette, suffering orphan, sings "Castle on a Cloud," a sweet
lullaby in which she longs for a mother to care for her. The scene takes place in
the tavern after hours, where she's been forced to clean up after drunken
patrons. But once she begins to sing, the background fades into the dark. Like
Fantine's numbers, little Cosette's solo is staged with the girl alone in a pool of
light, virtually out of the action of the musical. To construct the lyrics,
Kretzmer explained that "it was deemed wiser to avoid more obvious rhyming
patterns. My first draft contained the expected rhyme of 'toys' with 'boys,' but
again on Trevor's suggestion, it was decided to frustrate expectation; so instead
of the predictable rhyme we had, 'There is a room that's full of toys/There are a
hundred boys and girls.' The very employment of rhyme implies and suggests
that the singer possesses a mind that is organized and ordered in some formal
way. But the child Cosette is a badly treated little girl, with no pattern to her
life, no schooling or education, so you try to avoid the expected rhyme, which
would indicate too advanced and orderly a mental development in one so
young. Instead, you substitute something deliberately askew, off-center and
adrift."[75] This effective lyric construction simultaneously heightens Valjean's
fatherly effect on her, since she can sing in rhymes as the show proceeds. In
addition, as Kretzmer remarked, in the original French song, Cosette dreams
about a prince rescuing her, but it made more sense to him that a little girl
would long for a mother and not a man.[76] Dramaturgically, this choice allows
the older Cosette to be completely innocent, seemingly having never expressed
desire for a man. When Marius awakens her desire, it plays like a rebirth and so
gives more power to his influence on her.

Once Cosette grows up, she is the perfect ingénue with one purpose only:
to fall in love with Marius, a function the musical neatly fulfills by not giving
her a true solo: "In My Life" and "Heart Full of Love" are both sung with
Marius and the triangulated Eponine. The first of these, "In My Life," begins
with Cosette in the garden in front of her father's house, indicated by a tall
iron fence and a stone bench, and the actor moves around the stage more in
this song than the women typically do in the show. Nervous and fluttery, she
paces to the bench, sits, stands, moves upstage to the gate of the house, then
back to the bench. Rather than forging a clearly motivated connection to the

scenography, however, the actor inhabits the stage space lightly and tentatively. Here, as in a later scene when she sits with Marius at a small table in
act 2, she is far removed from the vibrant, attention-getting scenography of
Les Miz.

Eponine, the most active female character in the musical, is constructed in
relation to the other two. First, she and Cosette are stereotyped opposites, as
Kretzmer explained that Cosette (once she is Valjean's daughter) "is a protected child, unaware of the brutishness and crudity of street life that Eponine
has always known."[77] Eponine functions as the impure other, a striving girl
who desires a man beyond her station and whose presence never registers as
a threat to Cosette but rather underlines that the male hero must love the
ingénue.

Second, Eponine serves as Fantine's living ghost, the sacrificial woman;
Fantine's theme song while dying, "Come to Me," is the same melody as
Eponine's song of unrequited love, "On My Own." Kretzmer explained that "in
the mind of the audience . . . they are combining the melodic cadences of that
tune into a mental, almost semiremembered dream landscape, which they
couldn't put a memory to, but something inside their recent memory is telling
them that they've heard that song before."[78] Nunn affirmed that using the same
song for both women would "keep a connection of sacrifice" between the two.[79]

Aside from her inextricable theatrical (but nonexistent emotional) connection with the other women, Eponine's role in Les Miz was consciously diminished and depoliticized by the creators. First, they telescoped her character
through a leitmotif rather than giving her more complete songs to sing. Schönberg explained, "Eponine is always introduced by the same instruments. . . . It's
a shortcut to tell you a situation that would take two or three minutes to explain
on stage and you can express it in fifteen seconds of music."[80] Second, they
transformed the original French version of "L'Air De La Misère," which
Kretzmer described as "a song about the hunger and misery of the poor. We
gave the song to a different character entirely and made it a lament about unrequited love sung by a tough little dreamer."[81] The creators revised a political
song about poverty into an individual plaint about love. A woman in Les Miz
might have expressed political sentiment but instead she is contained in the
emotional realm.

Eponine's performance of "On My Own," which invariably stops the
show, removes her from the musical's marvelous scenography. Like the
women in the other numbers in Les Miz, the actor presents more like a concert singer and less like a character expressing herself in a theatrical world.
The stage empties behind her and, dressed in an ankle-length coat and

woolen hat, face dirty, arms crossed, she walks a loop on the revolving floor from stage left to downstage center. Her walking on the revolve conveys the sense that she is walking farther, while in actuality she actually covers little ground on stage. She stops center stage, standing in a narrow spotlight, and looks up and out to sing the number. Several times, the actor pulls the coat around her for protection. The song is repetitive, catchy and sad, and builds to an impressive volume and intensity as the character expresses her unrequited love for Marius in the same melody Fantine sings on her deathbed as she begs Valjean to care for her daughter. Over and over in *Les Miz*, the women sing only about and for men. Eponine sings, "I love him but every day I'm learning/all my life I'll only be pretending/without me this world will go on turning/A world that's full of happiness that I have never known," with the climactic note held loud and long. The top note, in performance, allows and encourages the actor to break character as she demonstrates her breath capacity.[82] In several different productions of *Les Miz*, when the actor's sustained note earned applause, she broke concentration, the corners of her mouth turning up with pleasure. She sang the last verse moving in and out of character, Eponine singing of her love for Marius "on my own" and the actor unable to contain her delight in the audience's adoration of her. Oddly, the musical can allow the actor such metatheatrics because she matters so little to its larger purpose. In the end, women are denied characterization and integrated into the musical's theatricality.

Eponine does get one opportunity to interact with the musical's remarkable scenery—in her death scene (fig. 4-1). Although her involvement with the students' rebellion is not because she is political, but because she wants to be on the barricade to be near Marius, she gets caught in the crossfire. Marius takes her into his arms, soothing her and kissing her gently, and they sing, "A Little Fall of Rain," leaning against and framed by the barricade, and she dies. The message is clear in this lovely and moving scene: the women only get to be in scenes with *Les Miz*'s big set when they die.

The Phantom of the Opera

If *Les Misérables* exiles women from the scenography by isolating their musical numbers as concert-like pieces outside of the theatrical frame, *The Phantom of the Opera* overwhelms the one featured woman by surrounding her with spectacular scenery, dramatic lighting effects, and sumptuous costumes that dwarf her.

Figure 4.1 In front of the barricade in *Les Misérables* (opened on Broadway in 1987), Eponine (Frances Ruffelle) dies in the arms of Marius (Michael Bell), her love for him still unrequited. Enjolras (David Burt) stands by. Photograph by Michael Le Poer Trench © Cameron Mackintosh Ltd.

For *The Phantom of the Opera*, composer Andrew Lloyd Webber joined forces with lyricists Charles Hart and Richard Stilgoe, director Harold Prince, choreographer Gillian Lynne, set and costume designer Maria Björnson, and lighting designer Andrew Bridge. When tickets went on sale in New York in November 1987, it was already the "must-see" show of the year—Princess Diana had seen it twice in London—and more than $920,000 worth of tickets were sold on the very first day, more than twice as much as *Les Miz* a year earlier. The preshow buzz was accompanied by negative publicity for Sarah Brightman, Webber's then-wife cast as Christine. Actors' Equity objected to a non-American actor in the role but Webber won. Since *Phantom* was Brightman's first legitimate acting job, critics were primed to skewer her, and gossip fueled ticket sales all the more. When *Phantom* opened on January 26, 1988, it had already earned $16 million.[83]

Phantom garnered mixed if frequently mocking reviews but prevailed as the first absolutely critic-proof show. Frank Rich's review in the *New York*

Times led with, "It may be possible to have a terrible time at 'The Phantom of the Opera,' but you'll have to work at it. Only a terminal prig would let the avalanche of pre-opening publicity poison his enjoyment of this show, which usually wants nothing more than to shower the audience with fantasy and fun, and which often succeeds, at any price."[84] Mel Gussow called it "a phantasmagorical experience."[85] Undeterred, audiences went crazy and loved it and tickets sold and sold. *Phantom* won seven Tony Awards including Best Musical and Best Set, Costume, and Lighting Designs. Like *Les Miz*, no actors were singled out for awards, which acknowledged design's predominance and perhaps anticipated the ease by which actors could and would be replaced in this new musical theatre commodity. As of January 2011, the musical had been playing for more than twenty-three years. The musical's website estimates that *Phantom* has been seen by more than 100 million people in 149 cities in 25 countries, with a gross profit of more than $5 billion.[86]

Although *Phantom* is lampooned for being a musical about a chandelier, the total scenography was much more than a big flying lamp. The production cost $2 million just to renovate the Majestic Theatre, already the largest theatre on Broadway, to be able to accommodate the machinery required to run the show. The basement wasn't deep enough to house the requisite machinery, so it was gutted, the stage floor was ripped up, and a steel grid was built to support the building's roof and back wall. The new stage floor had ninety-seven specific holes and four trapdoors, all of which were used in the show.[87] By the time *Phantom* opened, two hundred people worked there each night, between actors, musicians, dressers, run crew, prop and carpentry staff, ushers and doormen and janitors.[88]

Prince and Björnson both emphasized how the design aimed not for spectacle but rather to convey eroticism and mystery through the use of shadow and light, drapes, and old-fashioned effects like footlights to evoke the feeling of a Victorian theatre and candlelight and fog in the Phantom's lair. Björnson was the only woman in a group of strong-willed men, and Webber felt that her design was "feminine" and that she "responded to the submerged sexual repression in the story in a remarkable way."[89] Andrew Bridge's lighting design, which used only around four hundred lighting instruments rather than the typical seven hundred or so in most Broadway shows, sculpted a shadowy stage to create "a sense of menace, secrecy and sexuality" and to elicit audiences' curiosity, wonder, and even disorientation. Prince said that the designers intentionally left spaces blank—that is, in darkness—for the audience to fill in with their imagination.[90]

For Prince and the designers, the atmosphere became a principal character in the musical. Rich found the design "a tour de force throughout," and described how "Ms. Björnson drapes the stage with layers of Victorian theatrical curtains" and then "constantly shuffles their configurations so we may view the opera house" from many different perspectives.[91] Foster Hirsch describes Prince's contribution to the design, which sounds a lot like actor coaching: "Like the Phantom himself, Prince's production ('a black box with tricks,' as the director calls it) makes use of sleight of hand: now you see it, now you don't."[92] Hirsch explains how "Prince sculpts theatrical space and time, from scene to scene transforming the height and depth of the playing area as he divides and rearranges space, creates frames within frames as drapes descend from the flies, reverses perspective, and fuses episodes with fades, dissolves, montage effects, or abrupt cuts."[93] Indeed, the first notable action in *Phantom*, the stunning effect of the chandelier, suddenly brightly lit and rising from the dusty stage floor, has been variously admired, scoffed at, and ridiculed, and has become a synecdoche for musical theatre's spectacle. Dramaturgically, the chandelier's reanimation takes the action to the past, as Raoul is suddenly young again and the opera house alive. But theatrically, when the real theatre audience watches the chandelier rise, it sees the size and scale of the Majestic Theatre, and then, the relatively small actors on stage. This moment has the opposite effect of what musical theatre usually tries to do: make the actors seem larger than life. Here, a scenic effect renders them small.[94]

What was heard on this enormous stage? Rich, for one, appreciated the set more than the music and found "a victory of dynamic stagecraft over musical kitsch."[95] Gesturing toward the classic musicals like *West Side Story* and *Fiddler on the Roof*, to which he had favorably compared *Les Misérables*, Rich quipped, "It would be equally ludicrous, however—and an invitation to severe disappointment—to let the hype kindle the hope that 'Phantom' is a credible heir to the Rodgers and Hammerstein musicals that haunt both Andrew Lloyd Webber's creative aspirations and the Majestic Theater as persistently as the evening's title character does." He summarized *Phantom* as "a characteristic Lloyd Webber project—long on pop professionalism and melody, impoverished of artistic personality and passion."[96] Webber biographer Michael Coveney, though, describes *Phantom*'s score: "The balancing of operatic pastiche with [Webber's] own idiosyncratic rock romanticism . . . with unusual intervals and adventurous harmonics that help the melodies unfold."[97] Musicologist John Snelson observes that the piece is made of "musical building blocks" that build on one another through repetition, "gaining subtlety through the interaction of the material rather than modifications of the material itself."[98] Coveney notes, "The music is on a constant switchback between the surface sunniness of romantic opera and the heart of darkness in the Phantom's labyrinth."[99]

The Phantom of the Opera is a beauty-and-the-beast tale, undergirded with a story about how the beauty, Christine Daaé, comes of voice, both figuratively and literally. From the moment that Christine is plucked from the chorus—a distracted ballet dancer who doesn't know why or how she sings so beautifully—to the last scene, when she bravely tells the Phantom that she might have loved him in spite of his disfigured face but can't love him because of his disfigured soul and then kisses him full on the mouth, her journey is tracked by her increasing ability to say/sing what she thinks and feels.[100] When Christine finds her own true voice in "Wishing You Were Somehow Here Again," she also finds the strength to resist the Phantom's power and see the Phantom for what he is—a man whose physical disfigurement has warped his soul. Her (musical) independence means that she can leave his underground lair and return to the above-ground world with Raoul, to live happily ever after as his countess. That she trades a brilliant career as an opera singer, which only the Phantom could enable, for a life of domesticity with Raoul is never presented as Christine's dilemma. Rather, in spite of her evident musical talent, she remains curiously unambitious and passive. From the beginning, she has "her head in the clouds."[101] When the Phantom makes her sing, it's not clear if she derives any pleasure or satisfaction from it, or if she even wanted to move from the chorus to a starring role. The musical keeps Christine's performative agency vague; she is mostly in a daze. The audience learns that her beloved father was a famous violinist—and that she clearly has a father fixation—but she never expresses the desire to perform, so quickly does the narrative focus on her being the object of desire of the two men who vie for her. Christine's struggle becomes, then, not one of career versus love, but of what kind of love she'll have: a sexualized, father-inflected, subconscious tug, or a rational, appropriate romance. And in some ways, this too is a false choice, because the other narrative—that of the Phantom's haunting and violent control over the opera house—shows that he is, well, crazy, obsessive, and disfigured, and clearly not an appropriate choice for her.[102]

The musical also brackets the prospect of Christine's career by representing the opera as a ridiculous place. The sets are over-the-top; the music is cheesy; the managers are bumbling and inept; the diva is egocentric and untalented. When the company struggles with the Phantom's musically difficult, modernist opera, Don Juan Triumphant—and Webber clearly intends the Phantom to be ahead of his times musically—they lack the knowledge to appreciate it and the skill to pull it off.[103] No matter, Christine, the innocent with the heavenly voice, can't stay in this place of mediocre performance, the musical says. She must be in the Phantom's underground (lakefront!) lair or Raoul's chateau (by way of a rooftop). Either way, she is headed for a future as a housewife.

Although the actor playing Christine is on stage for much of the musical and sings more than any other character—in fact, the Phantom has only around forty minutes of singing and she has at least twice that—she is ultimately too passive for the character to emerge as anything other than a fetishized object of desire. Moreover, for each of her numbers, she is surrounded by such fantastical settings that the actor's physical power is diminished in relation to the huge, spectacular set.[104]

Christine's first number, "Think of Me," introduces her defining trait: passivity. During a rehearsal, Carlotta, the diva, sings in the operatic style the Phantom detests, and he makes a huge backdrop crash to the floor. Terrified and furious, Carlotta quits, but Meg, another dancer and Christine's friend, chimes in, "Christine Daaé can sing it." Meg's mother, Mme Giry, the ballet master and messenger of the Phantom's letters, adds, "She has been well-taught." Only then does Christine step timidly forward to sing, but admits in a barely audible whisper that she does not know who has taught her. She begins tentatively, then gains strength in voice and confidence. A quick blackout shifts the scene into the opera's performance, and when the lights come up, she is alone in a spotlight, now the star, richly costumed and objectified for the Phantom, Raoul, the other players, and the applauding audience to gaze upon. Everything—the set, the other actors, and the scene itself—moves around her and she remains, simply, singing. In addition, what she sings in the conventional spot for an "I am/I want" song is a performance and not even one that was truly hers. Not having her own song implies that Christine has no self to express.

In Christine's second song, "Angel of Music," when she and the audience meet the Phantom, spectacle overwhelms characterization. In her dressing room—a small platform on wheels that glides onstage, pre-set with a hat rack and a small dressing table covered with tiny perfume bottles, framed pictures, and a tea set, and a full-length mirror facing the audience—Christine feels the Phantom's presence as he sings to her. He suddenly appears in the mirror; the audience sees her reflection and also his ghostly visage behind her. She is drawn to him, the mirror slides open, and she walks through it. The moment is theatrically amazing, breathtaking even, but it draws the spectator's attention away from Christine's emotional journey. Like her, we are seduced to go through the mirror, without conscious will or choice.

Christine and the Phantom sing the musical's title song as they journey by river to his lair in yet another visually sumptuous number in which the actor is a mere prop. The stage begins in blackout. Ever so slowly, the lights come up, barely illuminating a fog-filled stage and a small figure all the way upstage, a full sixty feet away from the downstage apron. The figure's movement is at first so slow it's almost imperceptible, but gradually it comes into view: a small boat, the Phantom standing and holding a pole that he uses to maneuver the boat, and Christine seated in front of him. As the boat moves slowly on a zigzag route through the fog toward the front of the stage, dozens of candelabras rise up on either side, their multicolored flickering lights illuminating the boat's route through the sinister, imaginary lake. Rich called the scene "a masterpiece of campy Hollywood iconography—it's Liberace's vision of hell,"[105] and Coveney attests, "It was a filmic, ritualistic, soft-handed approach to a difficult but thrilling scene, and the staging of it matched the music all the way."[106] The Phantom towers over Christine; she is a small body curled in the boat's bow. He lifts his arms up and over, appearing to push the pole along the "lake," propelling the boat with strength and direction: he knows where they're going. As they sing, she looks dazed, totally under his spell and his control (fig. 4-2). While both actors are props in a gorgeous stage picture, the gendered difference is stark: the man controls the boat and so appears active, while the woman sits still, being driven by the man's will and desires and singing the music he's instilled in her.

Figure 4.2 Accompanied by the musical's title song, the Phantom (Michael Crawford) steers the boat, with Christine (Sarah Brightman) a passenger, across the underground lake to his lair in *The Phantom of the Opera* (opened on Broadway in 1988). Courtesy Joan Marcus/Photofest.

Other aspects of the scene lessen the woman's stature. First, between the dressing room and boat scenes, the actors must make a long backstage cross. To achieve the appearance that one minute Christine is walking through the dressing room mirror and the next minute she and the Phantom are in the boat (like a jump cut in film), body doubles and prerecorded voices are used. Since the stage is so dark and the actors voices come through speakers anyway, this sleight of hand (and sound) might go unnoticed, but it compromises the very liveness of theatre. Second, the title song doesn't jibe with Christine's character arc. As Snelson tries to make sense of it: "Why does someone enamored of an Angel of Music sing that 'the Phantom of the Opera is there—inside my mind'? Surely it was the Angel of Music that she referred to a few lines earlier when relating, 'In sleep/he sang to me,/In dreams he came.'"[107] As Snelson's observations suggest, technological marvels take precedence over the principal woman's characterization. Finally, the song's disco beat and odd, pulsing electronics that mingle with romantic violins employ a different musical vocabulary—pop music—than the rest of the operatically oriented score.[108]

As the song ends, and the pair arrives at the Phantom's underground abode, Christine again is figured as an object in the scenography, even as she sings higher and higher. Bjornson explained that she and Prince created the setting with "a suggestive simplicity: a cracked mirror, a dummy in a wedding dress prepared for Christine and, at the back, iron bars with a great, black vista behind them, closing [Christine] in, a caged bird, a portcullis."[109] Crystallizing the image of Christine as a singing servant, the Phantom helps her off the boat and commands her to sing. As she trills "ah" on an upward rising melody, she faces him upstage of her. He turns her around, as if she is a doll to face the audience in the song's final piercing phrase. Coveney describes how "Sarah Brightman's highest register expressed the weird orgasmic side effects of his bestial act of possession."[110] Until this point in the story, Christine is supposed to be under the Phantom's spell, which the stage picture accurately conveys. The problem here is that the actor is under the design's spell, a small item in enormous, visually arresting scenography.

The musical's systematic objectification and diminution of Christine—both the character and the actor—become more marked as the narrative progresses and she supposedly gains autonomy and her own voice. Her next solo, late in act 2, takes place in the the cemetery where her father is buried and where she goes to ask his advice about her life by singing "Wishing You Were Somehow Here Again." This song is meant to be her turning point when she resolves to move on and live, but again, *Phantom* undermines her strength musically and scenographically. First, while the song grows louder with each verse and climaxes in a key change that signifies her determination, it sends another musical message, too: this section is similar to "Angel of Music," the melody of the Phantom's seduction of her, and thus detracts from her self-reliance since she continues to sing a version of his music. Second, she is surrounded by enormous gravestones and crucifixes, and the stage floor is textured with shadows and the outlines of more gravestones. Again, intensely atmospheric scenography distracts from her power. Finally, the musical refuses to allow Christine to revel in her newfound strength because the Phantom and Raoul immediately begin to fight over her. The Phantom throws fireballs—actual explosions from his staff—and then disappears in a flash of light. In the scene that is supposed to present Christine's turning point, the audience is unlikely to remember that she went to the cemetery to make a decision about her life. Her expression of agency is undone by the fantastic theatricality of their battle.

In the last scene, her last solo, Christine finally acts but in a stereotypical self-sacrificing way.[111] The Phantom kidnaps her again, and Raoul follows. Returning to the Phantom's place, the audience sees the big grated fence upstage, dripping candles and weird shadows, bizarrely shaped statues, the dummy of Christine as a bride, and fog and more fog. Stage left is the Phantom's piano on a small octagonal platform surrounded by an iron rail topped with melted candles, almost like a shrine. The Phantom taunts Raoul to approach him, and then entraps Raoul in a punjab lasso. Only Christine can free Raoul by agreeing to love the Phantom, which she does, singing "Angel of Music." The Phantom, moved by her willingness to sacrifice herself, frees Raoul, then commands them to go. Raoul and Christine exit, but then she returns with the wedding ring he had placed on her finger earlier. The Phantom sings, "Christine, I love you," sobbing, his disfigured face revealed, and she responds in the same music from the beginning of the show. Nothing in the score suggests that she has changed. And in this last scene, where she actually *does* something, the setting is more amazing than ever. What spectators see is more interesting than her explanation of her feelings. And in the end, she leaves and the Phantom gets the big emotional payoff.

The Megamusical's Technological Replication and Actors

The actors who play Fantine, Cosette, and Eponine in *Les Miz* and Christine in *Phantom* not only contend with the challenges of scenography (whether they are evicted from the set or overpowered by it) and stories that ultimately privilege men, but they also confront the challenges of the megamusical as a multinational performance product. Their creativity is stifled first, by a locked down, soundtracked production that allows no flexibility in timing, and second, by a rehearsal process that is solely imitative and not inventive.

Musicals in the past always sought to enhance their profit through road productions—national or international tours—and either concurrent or subsequent productions across the Atlantic. As discussed earlier, Webber and Mackintosh, after the astonishing success of *Cats* in London and New York, changed the game by opening many "sit-down" (long-running) productions at once all over the world, in Toyko and Stockholm, Chicago and Los Angeles, and also on Broadway and in the West End. Their franchising entailed absolute control over the product, with the same design, lighting cues, and choreography; in fact, they "cloned the show," as Webber described it.[112] "Technologies combine to facilitate an account of the production, a *model-buch* to archive the performance," Baugh observes, "and one which has enabled the production to become a highly marketable and exportable commodity."[113] Computerized cues coordinated both scenography and music, and the sung-through format produced a score that was prerecorded, "saved," and replayed nightly in the exact same way. Actors could not pause for a moment or change tempo at all because every element of the production was tied together.

Long-running megamusicals hired many actors over time, but the "procedures for remounting megamusicals owed more to Fordist logics of the production line than to the craft-based models of reproduction that had preceded them," as Burston writes.[114] According to Burston and Susan B. Russell's firsthand account of performing in *Phantom*, actors are instructed not to study the script or develop a new approach to a character, but instead to reproduce the exact performance of their predecessor, from gesture and movement to facial expression and intonation.[115] Generations later, actors have no knowledge of the original purpose of or motivation for blocking choices, pieces of stage business, or singing style. This assembly-line-like model of production seems especially anathema to theatre when the actors, too, become cogs in the theatrical machinery. Although long-running, identical megamusicals offer(ed) actors more work stability, according to those whom Burston interviewed, the very essence of their acting was compromised, and they felt like these were "McTheatre jobs."[116] Russell writes, "Certainly, an actor on celluloid can transform an audience member, and actors in *Phantom* transform audience members at every show, but the audience member cannot transform a celluloid actor in return. A living actor locked in a temporality other than the 'now' is lost in both translation of art and transformation of spirit. And is not the present-tense possibility for transformation what circumscribes live theatre? Is not live theatre made living by the endless possibilities within time, place, and space?"[117] All actors, regardless of gender, feel the effects of the megamusical's scale and reproducibility. But women actors suffer the consequences more when their characters lack agency.

The megamusicals of the 1980s altered the Broadway musical in every way and launched a subgenre that continues to thrive with new musicals and old ones, too. Reviewing *Les Miz*'s revival, David Ronney admiringly accused the show of "shameless emotional exorbitance. The pop opera milked tears with the same indefatigability as the smoke machines that kept its stage drenched in soupy atmosphere. The show that helped re-popularize musical theater as blockbuster spectacle has since been so parodied it's almost a parody of itself. And yet, undeniably, it still works, stirring audiences for 20 years and counting."[118] In the meantime, other musical theatre artists continued to work with the tools and conventions of the form, influenced by the megamusical and its technological advancements. While most musicals in the 1990s and after employed computerized effects, many also pushed back to recenter the actor, and especially the female actor.

CHAPTER 5

The 1990s–2000s: "I'm Beautiful and I'm Here"

On the website for the *The Color Purple*'s national tour, after clips of images from the musical scroll through and TV announcers rave about the show, talking heads of different genders, races, and ages pop up on the blue-backed screen, one by one, speaking Celie's transformative lines of self-assertion with her final song playing in the background. First, a blond, well-coiffed, middle-aged white woman appears, wearing pearl earrings, a pearl necklace, a stylish jacket, and a broad smile. Looking directly at the camera, she says, "I am black, I may be ugly, um, I'm poor, but I'm here." Then a white family of four pops up, playfully arguing about the correct order of the lines. In unison, with the bearded father enumerating the traits, they chant, "I may be a woman," but the eighteenish daughter in glasses immediately corrects them, "No, I may be ugly," and they all concur, "Yes, I may be ugly," and, as they're all talking at once, the daughter adds, making her hands into fists, "And she's . . . but I'm he-e-e-re!" Next a number of faces quickly roll by intoning, "But I'm here," from a light-skinned African American woman with long wavy hair and glasses to a heavyset Asian American man to a white woman to an African American man. The camera pauses longer for Gloria Steinem, who declares, "It's saying, I—and the 'I' is very important—am here."[1] The last face is that of a twenty-something curly-headed African American woman in a hoodie and long beads, who gets more time to explain: "I'm here and I matter. And it's, it's such a little phrase but it's, it's like if you say it, you feel it."[2] The publicity, which attempts to universalize a musical about the life experiences of a "poor black woman" living in the South from 1909 to 1949, seems at once embarrassingly ingenuous and also astonishingly PR-savvy. As a commercial entertainment product, *The Color Purple* at once wants to address African American women and everyone. It's no surprise that *The Color Purple* was produced by the media conglomerate that is Oprah Winfrey.

While *The Color Purple* is the only musical discussed in this chapter that had the backing of that particular corporate giant, all of them—Jason Robert Brown and Alfred Uhry's *Parade* (1998), Tony Kushner and Jeanine Tesori's *Caroline, or Change* (2003), and Lin-Manuel Miranda and Quiara Alegría Hudes's *In the Heights* (2008)—experienced what became standard procedure for musicals by the twenty-first century: a multiyear development process, enormous production costs, a large team of producers and backers, and an eye cast to the road.[3] What hadn't changed since 1950 was each show's need to attract a wide audience to fill the house to sustain a run. The shock of the video advertisement for *The Color Purple* is that it's not a shock at all. How could a "poor black woman" stand in for all spectators, that is, for all people? *The Color Purple*'s liberal rhetoric is consistent with musical theatre's "political" leanings. Around the millennium, the individualist message that *A Color Purple* espouses and the Internet as mode of communication also signal a Third Wave feminist moment.

Third Wave Feminism

As a political ideology that sees itself as an extension and development as well as a sometimes corrective to and revision of Second Wave feminism, Third Wave feminism originated as a movement by women of color to incorporate race and ethnic consciousness into a gendered critique. Coined and first articulated by Rebecca Walker (daughter of Alice Walker, author of the Pulitzer Prize–winning novel *The Color Purple*, on which the musical is based) in her edited anthology *To Be Real: Telling the Truth and Changing the Face of Feminism* (1995), Third Wave feminism understands equality broadly. Explicitly non- or anti-dogmatic about gender and sexuality, Third Wave feminism is equally concerned with trans, queer, and shifting affiliations. From tastes in clothes to tastes in television, from choices about work to choices about domestic life, Third Wave feminists are irrefutably individualist. For some, Third Wave feminism encourages embracing irony, the playful reappropriation of typically misogynist representations, and aggressively against-the-grain spectatorship. For others, Third Wave feminism takes on a more earnest cast, a determined navigation of gender and race together. Contradiction and hybridity undergird Third Wave feminist praxis.[4] At the same time, Third Wave feminists place themselves in a longer history of feminist movements.

Self-identified Third Wave feminists differentiate themselves from postfeminists. "Postfeminist culture's centralization of an affluent elite [exemplified by

Sex and the City] certainly entails an emphatic individualism," write Yvonne Tasker and Diane Negra, "but this formulation tends to confuse self-interest with individuality and elevates consumption as a strategy for healing those dissatisfactions that might alternatively be understood in terms of social ills and discontents."[5] In their edited anthology *Interrogating Postfeminism: Gender and the Politics of Popular Culture*, Tasker and Negra argue that postfeminism serves only white, heterosexual, middle-class women, since the basis of the project is an individualist, commodity- and consumption-based identity. Its most well-known proponents are Naomi Wolf, Katie Roiphe, and Camille Paglia, self-nominated "power feminists" who habitually blame women for their own oppression and deny that social structures limit one's choices and mobility. By definition, women of color and working-class women—the characters represented in the musicals in this chapter—are excluded from a postfeminist rubric.

With Third Wave feminism as a cultural backdrop, this chapter examines a cluster of four musicals that feature a woman of color protagonist: African American Celie in *The Color Purple*, Jewish Lucille in *Parade*, African American Caroline in *Caroline, or Change*, and Latina Nina in *In the Heights*.[6] These musicals offer four different racialized inflections of gender, and in these musicals, race or ethnicity is textual; that is, being Jewish, African American, or Latina is part of the subject of the musical, marked and determining and inextricable from the character herself. The female characters in these musicals negotiate hard life decisions, and their choices are exceedingly limited. Since being able to make a choice at all is a remarkable feminist gesture in these musicals, all four shows valorize the individual self, the woman who finds her identity through a journey of personal struggle and eventual self-knowledge. Each musical shows the costs of a woman of color's action, agency, and self-determination.

Millennial Multiculturalism, Ethnicity, and Broadway Musical Theatre's Liberal Humanist Individualism

By focusing on two African American, one Latina, and one Jewish female principal, this chapter takes a multicultural approach. By 2000, "multiculturalism" and "diversity" were buzzwords that elicited criticism on the right and the left. From the left, for example, Walter Benn Michaels argues in *The Trouble with Diversity* that Americans' love affair with race and with diversity deflects their refusal to deal with the real problem of the country: economic disparity and class. He writes, "The trouble with diversity, then, is not just that it won't solve the problem of economic inequality; it's that it makes it hard for us even to see the problem."[7] Michaels finds feminism problematic because it aligns women on Wall Street with women in Walmart, both of whom are paid proportionally less than their male counterparts. But the real problem, Michaels argues, is the disparity between Wall Street and Walmart employees, regardless of race, gender, or any other vector of identity. He writes, "The idea here is not, of course, that feminism is intrinsically bad . . . . The idea is rather that our efforts to solve the problem of discrimination—indeed, our formulation of the problem *as* a problem of discrimination—is not so much a contribution to justice as it is a way of accepting injustice."[8] As an example, Michaels teases out the nuances of the Leo Frank case (discussed in detail below), on which *Parade* is based. "Every American Jew knows this name," notes Michaels, and he argues that the real issue was not anti-Semitism but rather class inequity. Frank made about thirty-five times what Mary Phagan, the victim, made—$180 a week to her 10¢ an hour. Reframing the watershed event for American Jews in a larger perspective, Michaels points out that Frank was one of four Jews lynched during a period in U.S. history, 1880–1930, when around thirty-five hundred black people were lynched.[9] *Parade* references money and class and offers an ambivalent portrayal of the wealthy Jewish woman who emerges as its protagonist.

All four musicals in this chapter query how class operates, and financial independence is a critical goal for all four women. But class and race are frequently intertwined. As political scientist David S. Mason observes in *The End of the American Century*, the concept of "representation" in the United States is anything but representative. Because running for office requires so much money, it has "a number of deleterious effects on democratic principles and ideals," and half of the so-called representatives are lawyers, all are white-collar workers, and none are "ordinary working people." As of 2006, African Americans and Latinos were sorely underrepresented—although together they made up about 25 percent of the U.S. population, there were fewer than 14 percent African American and Latino House members. Women, who make up half the U.S. population, held less than one-sixth of the seats in the House.[10]

By the twenty-first century, "race" as a biological fact was unsustainable. Cultural critic and literary scholar Paul Gilroy, for example, argues *Against Race*, as his book is titled, and asserts that molecular biology has proven race as "absurd." Moreover, Gilroy finds a "change of climate in the meaning of racialized signs," and that "blackness is an asset" for celebrities such as Spike Lee and Tyra Banks. Still, Gilroy asserts, a positive valence attached to stars' blackness does "nothing to change the everyday forms of racial hierarchy."[11] Instead, he utopically envisions a "pragmatic, planetary humanism" that also abolishes "sexual division,"[12]—goals not too distant from Third Wave feminism.

And yet while critiques of race, diversity, and multiculturalism are well taken, musical theatre lives in representation, in semiotic referentiality. However progressive cultural critics insist that race is illusory, theatre is stubbornly materialist. Bodies appear on stage, and audiences interpret them through culturally and historically specific assumptions about race. Musical theatre presumes mimesis; musical theatre presses on authenticity. For example, Karen Olivo, who originated the role of the ambitious and sexy Vanessa in *In the Heights*, was raised in Los Angeles and knew no Spanish before being cast in the show. In a documentary that followed the musical's production process, she said, "Because I didn't speak Spanish and I've never gone to the countries that I'm from, I've always felt like a bit of a fake, like a fake Latina."[13] No matter: she looks "Latina," she learned Spanish (or at least learned her lines in Spanish), and garnered accolades for her "authentic" performance.

The fact that Broadway, never a groundbreaking artistic forum and even more of a middle ground by the millennium, produced a number of musicals with women of color protagonists is remarkable. The Broadway musical, exorbitantly expensive to attend at seventy-five dollars a seat, was undeniably an elitist cultural product, geared toward tourists with disposable income. The neighborhood changed in the mid-1990s, when Disney purchased vast amounts of real estate in the Times Square district and teamed with then-mayor Rudolph Giuliani to "revitalize" and "clean-up" the area, ridding it of porn shops, X-rated movie theatres, and homeless people, and making it safe for children, tourists, and suburbanites. Times Square's "Disneyfication" continued into the twenty-first century, and national retailers like the Gap, Toys "R" Us, and a Hershey's candy store replaced local merchants. With the Times Square area family-friendly, tourism increased dramatically, and more spectators from around the United States and around the world experienced Broadway musicals.[14] The megamusicals discussed in the previous chapter benefited from these changes and continued to run, while the musicals discussed in this chapter went in other directions, artistically and politically.

As a result, these four musicals juggled competing pressures all at once: the artists' desire to represent seldom-seen female-of-color protagonists; the audience's expectation, if unarticulated, that a Broadway musical will feature a quintessentially American tale of individual victory; the producers' need to break even if not make money; and U.S. society's sharply divided politics around race and diversity (that is, an increasingly diverse population,

conservatives' unembarrassed xenophobia especially after 9/11, and pro-
gressives' endless plea for tolerance). *Parade*, the earliest of these musicals,
opened at the end of Bill Clinton's presidency, and *In the Heights* was called
the "first Obama musical." In between, the United States experienced
George W. Bush as President and Condoleezza Rice as the Republican poster
girl for feminism and diversity.

This chapter knowingly incorporates race and ethnicity across identity categories with utterly different political and theatrical histories. Still, as literary
scholar Dean Franco asserts, U.S. history is one of comparative ethnicities,
and Americans understand themselves and each other through what he calls
an everyday comparative approach.[15] Because women of color—African
American, Latina, and Jewish—are so rare on the musical theatre stage as
leading ladies, placing these musicals as a mutually conversant group is useful
to see and hear how they speak in similar and different ways.

The Conventional First and Last Songs

This chapter explores two of musical theatre's ubiquitous, crucial, and well-
exploited conventions: the female protagonist's first number and the eleven
o'clock number. Because musicals move across time, those edges of the performance become especially memorable and resonant in terms of characterization, story, and emotional effect. Since musical theatre values and celebrates
the individual, the distance from the first to the last number telescopes the
character's growth. The four women featured here undergo profound changes
(although Caroline says she won't change, in fact, she does, from the audience's
perspective), which connects these shows as much to a realist, psychological
drama as to the heteronarrative of musical theatre, where the heroine's choice
is often to accept her man or not. Individuality and likeability, the liberal humanist bedrock of musical theatre, necessitates that the audience must sympathize with the protagonist's plight and be invested in her journey.

The female principal's first musical number, which each chapter in this book
has referred to or discussed in detail, introduces and defines her character,
who she says she is, and what she wants. In *Caroline, or Change* and *The Color
Purple*, the female principal's first song opens the show. In these cases, then,
her number sets the tone for the entire evening, provides information about
the setting—both place and time—and about musical style, and introduces
characters. In 1943, Rodgers and Hammerstein's *Oklahoma!* achieved noto-
riety because of its remarkable, unusual opening moment: a quiet farm scene,

an old woman churns butter, then, from offstage, a baritone sings of the beautiful day.[16] In contrast to earlier musicals that began with a chorus of dancing girls, *Oklahoma!*'s first moments immediately put the audience in the specific location and time, introduced a leading character in song, evoked the feeling of the everyday world of the show, and set up the story to follow. Soon the convention was set: if a musical didn't open with a scene-setting, mood-conveying, character-defining number, it would begin with a book scene, which also locates the audience immediately in the musical's world. The opening is crucial.

By contrast, the song that takes place near the very end of a musical, called the eleven o'clock number because musicals ended just after 11:00 p.m. when they began at 8:30, functions as the climax of the show.[17] Composed and designed as an emotional tour de force, this number tends to be when the heterosexual couple sings of their finally achieved love for one another or when the leading female principal sings her most expressive song. *Parade* and *In the Heights* have eleven o'clock numbers that are heterosexual romantic duets, and those in *Caroline, or Change* and *The Color Purple* are female solo songs.[18]

Parade

"Playing Princesses, Punishers and Prudes" read the headline of a 1999 *New York Times* feature story about Jewish women characters on television, and how they are often the butt of the shows' jokes. Bebe Neuwirth as Lilith on *Frasier,* Jennifer Aniston as Rachel Green on *Friends*, Fran Drescher on *The Nanny*, and Cynthia Harris as Paul's mother on *Mad about You* embodied stereotypes of Jewish women as "high maintenance," "sexless," "corpulent," "daddy-dependent," and "overbearing," according to a focus-group study of Jewish and non-Jewish respondents sponsored by a commission of Jewish professionals in television and film. The study found that Jewish male characters on television, such as Mark Greene on *E.R.*, Michael Steadman on *thirtysomething*, and Joel Fleishman on *Northern Exposure*, once portrayed as angstridden or as victims of anti-Semitism, no longer "read" as Jewish. But stereotypes of Jewish women remained, and the focus groups characterized Jewish women in movies and on TV as "pushy, controlling, selfish, materialistic, shallow, domineering" and enumerated ways to identify Jewish women: by "their prominent noses, their dark Middle Eastern complexions, and an inclination to be overweight."[19] In *Parade*, Leo is a Jewish male stereotype and Lucille is different in kind.

Parade theatricalizes one of the watershed moments in the history of Jews in the United States, the true story of Leo Frank, a Jewish businessman in Atlanta, Georgia, who in 1913 was found guilty of killing Mary Phagan, a fourteen-year-old white girl who worked in the pencil factory that he managed. Frank's conviction hinged on the testimony of an African American employee, who was the only other suspect in the case. After Frank was convicted of murder on very shaky evidence, the governor of Georgia received countless letters of protest from politicians and business leaders, both Jewish and not, who were certain of Frank's innocence, including the notoriously anti-Semitic Henry Ford. When the governor commuted Frank's death to life imprisonment, Frank was kidnapped by a group of white men and lynched. In response, U.S. northerners publicly expressed their disdain for the backward parochialism of the South and formed the Anti-Defamation League. The South, meanwhile, saw a resurgence of the Ku Klux Klan.[20] Librettist Alfred Uhry, a southerner and a Jew whose family knew the Franks, wrote in a preview article in the *New York Times* that the case forced Atlanta's southern German-Jews out of their comfortable, assimilated lives: "They were a group of lawyers, doctors and merchants proudly and clearly on the rise. . . . The men were making good money and the women were enjoying the benefits. They blended discreetly and successfully into the Southern way of life." He continued, "But the Frank case changed all that. Suddenly, they were just Jews. It was Europe all over again. Their windows were broken and their lives were threatened." He concluded, "Why am I stirring all this up again? I guess I'm trying to reconcile my Southern heart with my Jewish face."[21]

A collaboration among veteran artists Uhry, who wrote the lyrics and the book, director Harold Prince, and then-newcomer composer Jason Robert Brown, *Parade* was greeted with a scathing *New York Times* review by Vincent Canby, who wrote that "'Parade' is without life. It plays as if it were a collection of notes for a show that has yet to be discovered."[22] It ran for only eighty-four performances, but still was nominated for nine Tony Awards and won for Best Book and Best Original Score, perhaps because few new musicals were produced at all that season.[23] The musical was somewhat better received on tour, especially in Atlanta, since the subject resonated for audiences there, and the Mark Taper Forum produced an acclaimed revival for a limited run in 2009.[24]

Presenting the travails of Leo Frank from the day before the girl's death through his trial, imprisonment, and lynching, *Parade* is a book musical that alternates realist scenes with musical numbers comprising three different musical vocabularies that characterize the cultures that collide and occasionally harmonize in its theatrical world: Jews, white Christians, and African

Americans. Brown and Uhry infuse their representation of the South with ambivalence, at once critical of the forces that scapegoat Leo Frank—crooked politics, a rabid Christian right, limitless racism, a bored media, and a mob easily stirred into a frenzy—and also sympathetic to the South, which suffered its own losses of men and of pride. The four African American characters are unapologetically stereotyped and include a stammering laborer, a deferential maid, and the slick, fast-talking Jim Conley, whose guilt is revealed at the end of the show. The quartet sings a number "A Rumblin' and a Rollin'" in which it's clear that they know precisely how the white people operate, but that song does little to expand the audience's understanding of their historical situation or, in the end, to mitigate the musical's unfortunate racism. Leo and his wife Lucille's changing relationship forms the musical's spine according to mid-twentieth-century convention: although they are married from the start, they are opposites, so the musical tracks their growing affection and attachment, contingent on Leo's problematic masculinity and Lucille's coming into her own as a Jewish southern woman.

Parade begins with a young Confederate soldier singing an epistolary love song at once to his girl and to the "old hills of Georgia" (241).[25] In the second verse, as the music swells, an older actor replaces the younger, the time shifts to 1913, and the song expands to a full ensemble number in which the chorus of citizens celebrates Confederate Memorial Day. This is first of three Confederate Memorial Day parades in this cyclically organized show. The thematically based opening ensemble number links *Parade* to other post-mid-1960s "concept" musicals, such as *Cabaret, Fiddler on the Roof,* and *Company,* that are built around a metaphor or idea. The theme here is "home." An opening, theme-setting song type became a convention, evident in later musicals like *Cats,* a megamusical, or the book musical *Wicked. Parade's* form also incorporates numerous songs for supportive characters that provide a documentary feeling.

The perspective of white southerners dominates the musical's lush score and provides its aural unity, primarily through the anthem-like phrase "God bless the sight/Of the old hills of Georgia/The old red hills of home" (242). These characters and the ensemble sing music of the 1910s, which includes marches, ragtime, and hymns.[26] Defiantly nostalgic, the southern Christian whites long for the agrarian, preindustrial, slave-holding past.[27] They imagine African Americans and Jews as different sides of the same problem: the encroachment of the present onto the ways of the past. The near-final image of the play—Leo's body hanging from the big oak tree that arches over the set through the whole production—manifests the metonymy that propels the events of the play: in this particular rendering of the history of the white Christian South, African American men and Jewish men are interchangeable.[28]

Leo's otherness, his difference from everyone and everything in this world, is stressed at every turn in *Parade*, constructed at once through gender, race and ethnicity, class, and region. He sings in his opening number, which directly follows the musical's first romantic and nostalgic anthem of Georgia, about how the South is a "foreign land" to him. He longs to be with "People who look like I do,/And talk like I do,/And think like I do." As "a Yankee with a college education," he finds that even "the Jews are not like Jews" (245–47). Leo's music is light, quick, and spoken as much as sung, in contrast to the rousing march sung by the ensemble. He sings over an unchanging ostinato (the patterned accompaniment to a vocal line), which stresses his rigid, unmoving personality.[29] In the Broadway production, Prince staged Leo weaving his way through the crowd, as if drowning in a mass of humanity that he finds alienating and repugnant. The crowd in the South, as the musical shows, is dangerous, unthinking, even fascistic. Leo soon reveals himself to be too serious a worker (he is in his office doing accounts while the rest of the town is celebrating Confederate Memorial Day); too prissy in his tastes (he needs his coffee before he goes to the police station; he refuses to eat prison food); and not a sufficiently masculine husband (he blushes and changes the topic when Lucille presses him about having children). His Jewishness is noted specifically in only a few instances, including the haunting last line of the murdered girl's mother's hymnlike, country-inflected dirge, "My Child Will Forgive Me": "My Mary will teach me/To open my heart,/And so I forgive you,/Jew" (290). But *Parade* underlines that Leo's Jewishness stands in for all that makes him "other" in the South. Before he is hanged, he sings the words of the "Sh'ma," the most basic, sacred prayer of Judaism, to the melody of "The Old Red Hills of Home." The finale shows that Leo and his legacy are intertwined with the history of the South.

Lucille enters the musical relatively late, after Leo and the ensemble, which embodies and envoices the Christian South, are set in clear opposition. Leo refers to her in the opening number when he sings, "I'm trapped inside this life/And trapped beside a wife/Who would prefer that I'd say,/'Howdy!,' not 'Shalom!'" (247), and then addresses her in his imagination in the last lines of the song: "Well, I'm sorry, Lucille/But I feel what I feel/And this place is surreal,/So how can I call this home?" (247). Even before the audience meets her, they are challenged by Leo's evident frustration with her. Then in their first scene, her southern insiderness is portrayed through careless, white entitlement when she accidentally drops a hair pin on the floor as she is fixing her hair. She doesn't pick it up, since, she says, "Minnie will get it when she cleans up," but, the stage directions state, "*This irritates him. He picks up the hairpin and puts it on the vanity*" (243). Her late entrance and his critical view of her render her eventual dramaturgical and emotional significance surprising.

In Lucille's first song, "What Am I Waiting For?" she narrates the story of their courtship, notes her good fortune to have married him, and yet quietly expresses what she feels as a lack of passionate attachment. Her solo is combined with his song, "Leo at Work," which finds him in his office, figuring numbers and dreaming of their financially secure future. They are portrayed as a stereotypical married couple with two completely different sets of priorities and perspectives, except that they both feel trapped. What they have in common is their mutual disappointment. Lucille's first musical expression encapsulates two conventional song structures—her "I am/I want" number and the couple's "hypothetical love song." *Parade* adapts the conventional pattern of heterosexual romance; typically, a musical presents two newly acquainted principal characters in opposition, but *Parade* presents characters in a troubled marriage and then charts their gradual romantic union. Since the principals sing different melodies within the same chord structures but with opposing preoccupations, musical theatre's conventions tell the audience that they will eventually join. Moreover, the song is a light waltz, suggesting romance in contradiction to the unhappy feelings expressed by the lyrics.

Lucille's opening number introduces a childlike woman, overprotected and spoiled, passed from her mother's house to her husband's, possessing the goods that she thought she wanted, but lonely and sad. She sings to herself that she "married so well, Lucille," futilely trying to persuade herself that material luxuries can satisfy her. She wants to be happy with what she has, an unambitious desire for a musical's female principal. The song conveys little of the character she becomes over the course of the musical, and the fact that it simultaneously introduces their marriage and its discontents underplays her eventual fortitude all the more. But because she fails to convince herself that she wants what she is supposed to want, the number does signal that she wants more but she can't even articulate it yet. In this way, Lucille is pre-desirous, not yet a person.

In *Parade*, Lucille's actions are motivated by Leo's needs. She brings him clothing, food, and books in jail and only halfway through the show begins to act and take matters into her own hands. She explodes in frustration that he treats her as helpless. In her biggest number, "Do It Alone," she gathers her strength and sings, "I could be a quiet little girl/And cook your little meal . . . And bow to your command;/Or, I could start to scream/Across the whole damned South . . ./Until they understand" (308). She adds, "I can be

more . . ./I can bring you home, Leo" (308). After this scene, she is changed
and determined. She uses her feminine wiles to get invited to a party also
attended by the governor and sidles up to him. As they dance, she charms
and then berates him for allowing Leo's sentence, the result of a misman-
aged trial, to stand under his jurisdiction (fig. 5-1). After the governor agrees
to reopen Leo's case, she interviews all of the witnesses again and constructs
a strong defense, which leads to the commutation of his death sentence to
life imprisonment. She saves Leo's life and they both know it; as Mordden
observes, Lucille "rises to greatness from housewifely trifles."[30] In the
meantime, as she gradually falls in love with him over the course of the second act, her motivations shift from wanting to prove that he is an upright
person to needing to save him for herself because she loves him.[31] Her intelligence and energy win him over.

Parade's eleven o'clock number, their love duet, "All the Wasted Time," is a
Broadway standard with swelling strings, soaring harmonies, and brass and
kettle drums that punctuate their passionate kiss and segues into lovemaking at
the end. Again, Lucille maneuvers their privacy in his jail cell by bribing the
guard with a bottle of whisky, which he promptly drinks and falls asleep. In the
song, both Leo and Lucille look back on their relationship with regret for how
they didn't understand one another, singing, "I never knew anything at all" (336).

Figure 5.1 In *Parade* (1998), Lucille (Carolee Carmello) enters the governor's
house, ready to convince him to reconsider Leo's case. Courtesy Photofest.

They have come to appreciate each other by the end of the musical primarily because he has allowed her to help and she has solved his predicament; they have become equals. When he desires her by the end of the musical, after this song, and he "clutches her to him" and "lowers her to the ground" (336), Leo loses the stereotype of the effeminate, asexual Jewish man. He has become properly heterosexualized, which the musical underlines by assigning the last line of the duet to him alone.

As for Lucille, to become a viable mate for Leo, she needs to reject the practices of a stereotypical southern Jewish woman. But the musical nowhere overtly references her Jewishness. Her desire for wealth and a comfortable life stand in for her Jewishness, as she enumerates what she has gained in her first song, "House and a maid," "Everything I was wishin'—/New winter coat;/ Real Ermine collar" (251). She also sings of "Two sets of china," which may indicate that she keeps a kosher home. When she figures out how to get the governor on her side and constructs a viable legal defense, her actions confirm her Jewishness, as the musical implies that a Christian woman would not have the cleverness to pull off such a feat. The final affirmation of her Jewishness, though, is Leo's acceptance of her and desire for her. The musical suggests that the passive acquiescence that she understood as her former place was neither good for her nor true to her and asks how she, like librettist Uhry, will reconcile her Jewishness with her southernness. *Parade*'s eleven o'clock number uses a romantic duet to bring both principals to authentic identities: Leo to heteronormative masculinity and Lucille to intelligent and hardworking Jewish femininity.

For most of *Parade*, Lucille acts on Leo's behalf, but she sings frequently in the musical and the last moment is hers.[32] Although she loses him to a gruesome, anti-Semitic lynching, her own agency has given her a renewed sense of place and belonging in the South: "I'm not leaving home. . . . I'm a Georgia girl. I always will be" (340). The script's stage directions locate Lucille "at home," but in Prince's production, Carolee Carmello as Lucille stands amidst the throng of the parade in an image that ressembles Leo's first crowd scene; she is at once a part of the society and alone. The stage picture, with the crowd moving in slow motion and waving toward the audience, stresses that however she has grown and changed through this experience, the place has not. To the introductory section of the musical's unifying melody, "the old hills of Georgia," that is, the same melody that the old Confederate soldier sings, "Farewell my Lila," in the musical's opening moment, Lucille sings, "Farewell, my Leo—/You're right here beside me" (341). Her last lines, "And you're finally . . ./. . . free" are interrupted by a momentary flashback to Leo's "primal scene" with Mary, who wishes him a happy (Confederate) Memorial Day. The interpolation of this scene into Lucille's last lines serve as a reminder that while Leo's body and soul might be "free," his story will always be contested. After Carmello sings the last note, a snare drum coda accompanies her walking off stage right. She looks at his wedding ring on her finger—that is, the ring that he wore—which he had insisted she receive after his death. In the middle of the last measure, the drum halts, and Lucille suddenly stops and looks up, as if someone called her name, and the crowd freezes. She exits slowly, almost as if she is in another world.

Parade finds hope not in the male protagonist's action but in the future, in a newly empowered southern Jewish wife. Lucille's journey is the most dramatic in the musical, and she has grown though resistance and rebellion. She defies her presumed subservient position and is determined to remake the South and find her place there.[33] This musical uses ethnic difference and outsiderness to allow Lucille to contest conventional, white, Christian femininity. Her growth is marked by the transformation from her first number through the eleven o'clock duet to her solo at the finale.

Caroline, or Change

Around the millennium, when Caroline, or Change opened, artists in other media were engaged in revising the pervasive stereotype of the Mammy figure. Novelist Alice Randall's parody of Gone with the Wind, The Wind Done Gone (2001), for example, which prompted a legal battle with Margaret Mitchell's estate, renders the Mammy sexual and powerful in the household, but doesn't give her a name. She resists the stereotype but fails to thoroughly dismantle it.[34] Collage artist and painter Tina Dunkley, in "Ain't Cha Mamma Yemanja" (1999), imagines who Aunt Jemina might have been in a different country than the United States. Linking her name to the Yoruba goddess of mother-hood, Yemanja, Dunkley portrays the Mammy figure on a mock five dollar bill, surrounded by etchings of African and Caribbean women in similarly styled headscarves.[35] Dunkley's strategy is to connect the Mammy figure with her roots in countries where she is valued and not demeaned. The character of Caroline is an anti-Mammy image, drawn in sharp distinction to the romanti-cized selfless maternal figure in Gone with the Wind and Aunt Jemima pancake mix boxes.

Caroline, or Change, a fictional portrayal that is partly autobiographical for librettist-lyricist Tony Kushner, focuses on an African American maid who works for a Jewish family in Lake Charles, Louisiana, in 1963.[36] The musical charts Caroline's shifting relationships with Noah Gellman, who is the eight-year-old son of her employer, the rest of the Gellman family, her own children, and her best friend, all in the context of the civil rights movement in the southern United States.

Kushner began the libretto as a commission from the San Francisco Opera, and collaborated with George C. Wolfe, who was then the artistic director of the Public Theatre in New York, and had directed Kushner's *Angels in America*. According to Kushner's preface to the published script, Wolfe conceived of the dramatically demanding piece as musical theatre rather than opera and wanted to hire singing actors and not acting opera singers.[37] Kushner wrote the entire script in verse, but when Kushner and Wolfe took the script to Jeanine Tesori, their chosen composer, she turned them down. "It read so beautifully as a script I wasn't sure how music could enhance it," she said.[38] After working with Kushner on another project, though, Tesori signed on. The musical was well received at the Public, but its small scale and serious subject matter meant that it only moved to Broadway because Kushner determinedly raised the funds. As he said, "You work on something for five years, you don't want to see it gone in three months."[39] *Caroline* received excellent reviews and was nominated for six Tonys, but, like *Parade*, could only sustain a short Broadway run of 136 performances. Since then, *Caroline* has been frequently produced and very well received in regional theatres across the country.

Although the characters in *Caroline, or Change* are imaginary, the musical evokes the historical specificity of November and December 1963, including references to the civil rights movement and the assassination of John F. Kennedy. *Caroline*'s action is instigated when Noah's new stepmother, Rose—the best friend of his mother, who recently died of cancer—angry at the child's carelessness in leaving change in his pants pockets, decides that Caroline should keep the coins that she finds when she does the laundry. Her children benefit from the extra money, and Noah, deeply attached to and in awe of Caroline, fantasizes about his influence on her family. The play turns when Noah accidentally leaves a twenty dollar bill—a Chanukah gift from his grandfather—in his pocket, and he demands that Caroline return the money to him. In a wrenching confrontation scene, he sings in a childlike chant over only a steady beating kettle drum, "I HATE YOU!/There's a bomb!/President Johnson has built a bomb/special made to kill all Negroes! . . . Really! For true!/I hope he drops his bomb on you!" and she responds, speaking over trembling drums, "Noah, hell is like this basement,/only hotter than this . . . Hell's so hot it makes flesh fry," then sweetly sings a capella on only a few notes, "Hell is where the Jews go when they die" (104). Caroline doesn't keep the money; she doesn't return to work for several days, and it seems as if she has quit. She does come back at the end, but the musical sustains uncertainty about her future, and her relationship with Noah is permanently altered.[40]

Caroline is almost entirely sung-through, with little spoken dialogue. Some songs follow musical theatre's convention of pausing the action to extend an emotional moment, and others use a recitative structure in which the characters sing their conversations. The Jewish characters, who sing much less than the African American ones, each have a musical theme that suggests their personalities—a childish and sad clarinet for Noah; a quick-paced, bouncy, and slightly grating violin for Rose; a somber saxophone for Noah's grieving father, Stuart. He and Noah often sing the same musical theme.[41] In addition, *Caroline* is peppered with recognizable Jewish prayers and holiday songs. African Americans dominate the musical vocabulary of *Caroline*, though, as Caroline, her children, and her friend Dotty, as well as the anthropomorphized appliances, the Moon, and the Bus, sing the blues, jazz, gospel, bebop, and girl-group harmonies.[42]

The conflict between African American and Jewish characters in *Caroline*, as well as in *Parade*, is overdetermined by both groups' minority status in a white southern culture, which is presented as racist and anti-Semitic in both musicals. By setting these shows in hostile geographical locations, Kushner, Tesori, and Wolfe, like Brown, Uhry, and Prince, create immediate empathy for their otherwise unlikeable protagonists, and also raise the stakes of power between the two disenfranchised groups. In addition, the motif of "change" resonates on multiple levels in the musical: the coins in Noah's pants; the political change afoot, in which Caroline refuses to participate; her inability to change; the various emotional changes taking place in most of the characters' lives. *Caroline* contributes to the historical and performative archive of U.S. black–Jewish relations by theatricalizing the mundane and the everyday.

Caroline, or Change features a complex woman as its single protagonist. This musical deals with the emotional life of a character seldom seen on stage: a middle-aged, poor, African American working mother of four children, including one son stationed in Vietnam, and single after leaving an abusive ex-husband.[43] Caroline is unhappy, trapped, and gruff. She notes that her friend makes different choices, as Caroline sings, "And some folks goes to school at nights,/some folks march for civil rights./I don't./I ain't got the heart,/I can't hardly read" (117).

Caroline's first number, her "I am/I want" song, is embedded in an extended scene that introduces her world in the Gellman household, the appliances that surround her, and Noah, who visits her daily after school. The musical opens with Caroline at work in the basement, humming to herself. In a mournful blues, she sings a capella, "Nothing ever happen underground in Louisiana" (11), after which the instruments sound a tremulous, harsh chord that calls up African American and Creole music. Then, one by one, the lights come up on actors playing the Washing Machine, Dryer, and Radio (three women, Supremes look-alikes). In musically onomatopoeic phrases, the Washing Machine pulsates, the Dryer hums, and the Radio sings, each adding details about Caroline's situation. Soon Noah enters, delighted to share a secret cigarette with her, and leaves (fig. 5-2). Once she has taken the clothes out of the

Figure 5.2 In *Caroline, or Change* (2004), Caroline (Tonya Pinkins) and Noah (Harrison Chad) share a moment in the basement each day. Courtesy Photofest. Copyright Photographer Michal Daniel.

cool, damp Washing Machine and moved them into the hot Dryer, which "the Devil made," Caroline muses about her life, her four kids, her work as a maid for twenty-two years, her crush on Nat King Cole, and her prayers in a pulsing, syncopated, darkly minor and circular melody: "I thought for sure by now I be/better off than this! . . . It Nineteen-Sixty Three and I/wish every afternoon I die./Cook and clean and mind that boy,/doing housework doing laundry" (17). While Caroline's backstory with her violent, alcoholic, unemployed veteran ex-husband who left after she hit him back isn't revealed until later in act 1, the first song expresses her exhausted despair. The mundane drudgery of Caroline's labor, barely offset by a fantasy life of singing appliances, organizes the scene and her work life. When she repeats the first line at the end of the song, the audience understands the irony of her declaration, since so very much does in fact happen underground in this Louisiana home. In truth, as she says, "Cept in this house, . . . At nine-thirteen Saint Anthony Street/in Lake Charles Louisiana:/This house got/a basement" (13).

Caroline's first number reveals how race and gender and class are intertwined in this musical, and it performs the complex dynamics of power. On the one hand, she doesn't get a typical solo number early in the show, which corresponds to her lack of autonomy and agency (not unlike Lucille, who is also denied a character-defining solo, who also can only complain about what she is missing and not express what she desires, and who also lacks agency— but for completely different reasons, since Lucille is expected to occupy a role superior to the African American woman who works for her). So entrenched is Caroline in the necessary mundane details of labor, both emotional and physical, that she can't muster the energy to take up the musical and physical space of a solo number. On the other hand, she is the source of power that brings the appliances to life and brings Noah to the basement. The opening points to the unexplored depths of Caroline's character.

As *Caroline, or Change* proceeds, the musical underlines how, although Caroline is the employee and has no economic or material power, she holds tremendous affective power over the Jews with whom she has contact, as they misread her and project their desires onto her. Noah adores her; his musical motif is a national anthem-like march, "Caroline our maid! . . . Caroline is the President of the United States! . . . Caroline who's stronger than my dad" and a more lyrical, "I like it that you're always mad./And I can tell you like me too./At least I think you do" (14, 46). Caroline allows him to "light her daily cigarette," and she talks to him, saying that "cancer was your momma's test,/ and her death is your test," but she also reminds him that we "weren't never friends" (14, 21, 123).[44] Rose tries to be nice to Caroline, offering her food for her children (to which Caroline answers, "My kids don't like it,/turn they noses up./The smell"), but Rose is also intimidated by Caroline and feels guilty and embarrassed to be her new boss. Still, Rose cannot understand why Caroline is "Miss Crabby Appleton" (19, 78).[45] When Rose tells Caroline that she can keep the money that Stuart, her husband, leaves in his pockets, too, Caroline explodes, "I've got to iron now . . . it cramp in here and there's no air/so please get out/so my arm can swing/with this hot iron/and not hit nobody" (76). These scenes of "small domestic tragedies," as the Dryer character wryly calls them, make up the archive of African American–Jewish relations in the United States as much as the protests of the civil rights movement (79) (fig. 5-3).

Caroline, or Change's eleven o'clock number, "Lot's Wife," was rewritten many, many times for the musical, as Kushner, Tesori, Wolfe, and Tonya Pinkins, who originated the role of Caroline, as well as the designers and dramaturgs, searched for the appropriate music and lyrics for the heroine's climactic expression. Indebted to Jule Styne and Sondheim's tour de force musical soliloquy "Rose's Turn" in *Gypsy*, "Lot's Wife" moves among several subjects, both literal and musical, as the pained and angry character searches to articulate her feelings. Sections shift from dissonant, almost shouted lines of frustration

Figure 5.3 In *Caroline, or Change* (2004), Dotty (Chandra Wilson) goes to night school, and Caroline (Tonya Pinkins) is reluctant to change. Courtesy Photofest. Copyright Photographer Michal Daniel.

accompanied by a single trembling bass line ("my hate rise up, rip my insides out./My madness rise up in a fury so wild and I let myself go" [116]) to jazzy, syncopated visions of hope for other people ("Some folks do all kinds of things and/black folks someday live like kings/and someday sunshine shine all day!" [117]) to even more aurally grating explosions of fury and suppression ("I'm gonna slam that iron/down on my heart/gonna slam that iron/down on my throat/gonna slam that iron/down on my sex" [117]). The number's last section is composed of a sweet, heart-wrenching, gospel-inflected prayer that moves from a first person address to third person and back to first, as Caroline at once struggles to articulate and simultaneously dissociate from her pain. She sings, "Murder me God down in that basement,/murder my dreams so I stop wantin" (118), and then expands the prayer into "Lord set her free," to "set me free./Don't let my sorrow make evil of me" (118–19). The number's apparent lack of musical structure and progress combines with the lyrics' associative route, from "money" to "change" to "hope" to "slam" to "take me away" to "set me free," to enforce the sense that Caroline must make do, moment to moment. Since the musical's opening moments, Caroline's experiences have been more the same than different, and the traumatic fight with Noah merely reveals the tragedy—personal and political, domestic and national—that a careless little white boy has power over her. She must work; she must go back.

But for the audience and for her daughter Emmie, who sings the final "Epilogue" of *Caroline*, there is hope for the next generation. The feisty, smart, articulate, and politicized young woman admits that she participated in an event alluded to earlier in the musical: someone, presumably African American youths, vandalized and beheaded the town's statue of a Confederate soldier. Emmie sings in the musical theme of the Moon, connecting her to natural cycles and the changing of the tides, "I'm the daughter of a maid . . . Nothing can ever make me afraid! . . . For change come fast and change come slow but/everything changes!" (126). Emmie finds power in being the daughter of a maid, while Caroline is used up and exhausted by her role. Like *Parade*, *Caroline, or Change* envoices the future in a woman, though neither of these characters were the musicals' leads, as if they need to move past their protagonists' stories to imagine gender, race, and ethnicity differently in the twenty-first-century United States. *Caroline* envisions a young daughter, an African American woman from the South, as its future, not Noah. The middle-class, assimilated, southern, Jewish, and, the musical more than hints, gay boy is stuck in a world of fantasy, projections, and unmet desires.

In making Emmie's position central at the end as an activist voice of political resistance, one who refuses to be the "good" southern African American girl her mother asks her to be, this musical suggests that the future of the South—or at least of "others" in the South—requires challenging traditional feminine, heterosexual roles. (Look what traditional heterosexuality did for Caroline.) This musical also implies that it might be difficult to unify people who are similarly "othered." Emmie may be able to make it in the South, but Noah (that is, Kushner) may have to leave.

In spite of the strikingly similar image that ends both *Parade* and *Caroline*—a single woman on stage, singing of her bittersweet hope for the future—each musical contributes to the performative archive of race on the U.S. stage in very different ways. Of course, their subjects are different, as is the time period during which each is set. Still, *Parade* performs whiteness as its norm. *Caroline*, in contrast, foregrounds the subject positions of African Americans through the Motown-stylized singing appliances and Caroline's blues-based, highly variegated music. Furthermore, *Caroline* emphasizes and critiques the Jewish characters' dependence on her and locates their music in the old world. Finally, the score of *Caroline, or Change* is seductive and wrenching, with several musical themes woven through, but it eschews conventional song structures that might be extractable from the performance. *Parade*, by contrast, has clearly delineated production numbers, so although the musical criticizes and even condemns the community it represents, it still allows its members to sing together beautifully. The music of *Caroline*, however, creates a fragmented mode, a language that refuses to resolve the tensions among the characters by allowing them to sing together and so denies the audience the pleasure of a rousing, community-affirming finale.[46]

The Color Purple

Based on the 1983 Pulitzer Prize–winning novel by Alice Walker and adapted with her cooperation, with a libretto by Marsha Norman (who won the Pulitzer Prize in 1983 for her play, *'night, Mother*), and directed by Gary Griffin in his Broadway debut, *The Color Purple* originated at the Alliance Theatre in Atlanta in 2004 and opened on Broadway six months later.[47] Oprah Winfrey, as the production's major backer, had her name above the title.

The musical follows Celie's life from childhood, through her unhappy marriage to Mister, her lesbian relationship with singer Shug Avery, and her eventual independence and creation of a business sewing pants for women. The musical also includes the subplot of Sofia, the character Winfrey played in the 1985 film version and for which she won an Oscar for Best Supporting Actress, and Sofia's marriage to Harpo, and Celie's sister's Nettie's life as a teacher in Africa. At the end of the musical, Mister has repented and become a good man; he offers to marry Celie again, but she demurs, "Let's us stay friends."[48]

The gorgeous, sprawling production was well received by critics and audiences alike. It was nominated for eleven Tony Awards, and LaChanze won for Best Actress in a Musical. In addition, *The Color Purple* brought in an audience of 50 percent African Americans through most of its 910-performance run, increasing the attendance of African American audiences on Broadway threefold.[49] Griffin observed an "absolutely celebratory event that happens in the theater every night. . . . People walk in as a group of individuals, and leave as one group."[50]

The musical traces Celie's journey to self-love and acceptance. Unlike *Caroline, or Change*, which places an African American woman in relation to a Jewish family and which limits Caroline's community to her relationship with her friend Dotty and her children, Celie acts entirely within an African American context. Her struggles are about gender; the musical thematizes male and female relationships, power between the sexes, and the importance of female self-knowledge, growth, and empowerment. When Celie curses Mister, he says, "You can't curse me. You poor, you ugly, you black, and you a woman." Librettist Marsha Norman, who is white, said, "Celie is a normal girl who is writing her own *Feminine Mystique*."[51] The women in the musical, from Nettie to Shug to Squeak to Sofia, perform unique modes of self-actualization; none but Celie is ever a victim. *The Color Purple* stresses how Celie's community of women shapes her and allows her to find self-love and independence. Like the previous two musicals discussed in this chapter, *The Color Purple* finds no solutions in traditional heterosexuality for a woman of color, which these musicals' first and last numbers show.

The Color Purple begins with an overture. Heard less frequently in Broadway theatres after the mid-1970s and the abrupt, middle-of-the-action opening moment of *A Chorus Line*, this "song" form allows the audience to settle in and begin to get acquainted with the musical vocabulary of the show. The overture, almost always written by the orchestrator and not the composer, typically moves smoothly from one song fragment to the next. Audience members already familiar with the music can identify a song within the larger musical structure. The overture also delays introducing all of the elements of the performance to the audience. It demands—especially since it's now less common—that the audience sit and listen and not have anything to see or any action to follow.[52] For *The Color Purple*, the overture is played in front of a large scrim with young Celie's scrawled letter to God, which had been visible to the members of the audience as they entered the house. The first few moments of *The Color Purple* rely on older, perhaps even old-fashioned tools of musical theatre. The overture signals to the audience that this will be, formally at least, a traditional Broadway musical.

When the scrim is raised, a huge tree is revealed with two small girls in pastel-colored, ruffled dresses sitting in its branches. Backlit by a rich orange light, which creates the feeling of a warm summer day and gorgeously outlines the branches of the tree, the young sisters play a clapping game and sing in sweet and clear children's voices, as Celie begins, "Hey, sista, whatcha gon do," and Nettie answers, "Goin' down by the river/Gonna play with you." The verse continues: Celie sings, "Papa don't like no screamin' round here," and Nettie calls back, "No lip from da woman when they chug dat beer." They sing the chorus in unison, "Sho nuf sun gon shine/Gonna be grown ladies of da marryin' kind/Sho nuf moon gon rise/Like a huckleberry pie/In da middle of the sky," and they conclude, "Gon be alright/Gon be alright" (113).[53] The song goes by very quickly, likely too quickly for the audience to pick up the ironic lyrics, but it introduces issues that will prove central to the musical: the girls' intense connection as sisters, Celie's childlike engagement with the world, and her well-founded fear of dominant and explosively dangerous men. Although Celie and Nettie sing that they'll grow up to marry—as inevitably as the moon rises in the sky—neither one ends up married. Part of the musical's purpose, like Walker's novel, of course, is to show the different routes these two girls take to unmarried adulthoods. In addition, the brief singsong provides the framework for a melody that becomes a short theme that the soon-to-be-separated sisters use to greet each other when they meet in various stages of their lives. That theme grows into their song of togetherness, "When I Lay Me Down to Sleep," which they sing, still perched in the tree. Celie sings their song when she is miserably caring for Mister and his children to remember her sister's love. Librettist Marsha Norman explained how the musical's creators worked with the image of a bird in a tree for Celie's character: "In the beginning, what we see is the girls in the tree, and they're completely by themselves. . . . By the end . . . everybody has come back to roost in the branches of Celie. . . . She has become the family tree."[54]

The opening scene of *The Color Purple* combines conventions from different periods in musical theatre history. While the overture signals a 1950s book musical, the extended opening sequence of several minutes of music that doesn't stop for applause is more typical of musicals after the 1980s, from *Les Misérables* to *In the Heights*.[55] Then, after the first section, *The Color Purple* moves away from a sung-through format and features a pop and rhythm and blues score of separate songs and a looser, less unified sound. The show's score was the first foray into musical theatre writing for the songwriting team of Brenda Russell (composer of "Get Here"), Allee Willis (whose many hits included "Boogie Wonderland" and the theme from "Friends"), and Stephen Bray (former collaborator with Madonna and co-composer of many of her biggest hits), who arrived at the project with impressive pop music resumés and little theatre experience. In contrast to *Caroline* and especially to *Parade*, most of the songs in *The Color Purple* don't evoke the historical setting of the musical; rather, they chart Celie's emotional journey over four decades and make her profound transformation believable. A few of the character-oriented songs—what might be considered charm songs or throwaway numbers—are more historically specific in their musical styles of ragtime, jazz, or the cakewalk.

Like Lucille in *Parade*, Celie sings her first number of self-expression relatively late, after the play's setting and ensemble characters are introduced. Following the little girls' song, lights come up stage left on four women, a solo singer and the three church women. They begin a gospel song, which provides the frame for the scene that delineates the musical's place, time, and culture, but not specific characters. (This is a very different artistic route than that of *In the Heights*, in which the extended opening section introduces all but one of the principals.) The three women become a Greek chorus of sorts, providing backstory and commenting on the characters and the events in a gossipy, catty, and sometimes accurate way. Later in the musical, when the action moves to Nettie's life as a missionary teacher, the trio is humorously remade as African women gossips. This character pattern figures again in *In the Heights* with the women in the hair salon. In both musicals, a group of shallow women provide comic relief and contrast with the female principal, whose journey is serious and developed. The church women's prayer-song expands to a full group number, with the refrain, "The good lord works in mysterious ways," and a chorus of men and women enter singing in call and response (113–16). Forming a single-file line one behind the other from downstage to upstage, the congregation-cast moves downstage in a line and then each actor peels off stage left, in a parade-like formation.

Although this number is obviously choreographed, the dance here, like the rest of the musical, is performed lightly and feels spontaneous and "natural" to the characters' everyday movement, as is typical for a formally integrated musical. At the end of the line are Celie, now fourteen years old and pregnant, and twelve-year-old Nettie; years have passed and the girls are now half-grown. The church women stand a few feet to the side to comment on Celie's pregnant state and ask, "Who de daddy?" and they cluck that Celie's father raped her and took her first baby from her; this is her second by him. In the next moment, Celie screams with pain from a contraction—the baby is coming. She and Nettie exit "as everyone sings, claps, and shouts louder" (116). The opening sequence uses music, lyrics, and choreography to evoke the musical's setting, to mark the passage of time, and to fill in considerable backstory. The audience knows the story is Celie's but hasn't heard her perspective yet. Appropriately, the opening of *The Color Purple* finds her as an almost passive object in her own world.

Celie's first solo number caps off the first section of the musical. She sings a sweet and simple A-B-A lullaby to her child, "Somebody Gonna Love You," a prayer for a better life that she concludes with the promise, "I'm always gonna love you" (117). Interestingly, this song is the least memorable in the show. While it expresses Celie's true self at that moment, she is barely a person yet. Her music is borrowed and small. The absence of the conventional "I am/I want" song allows the poignancy and uplift of Celie's journey to emerge through the show. Celie's expanding musical vocabulary is in sharp contrast to Caroline's, who grows as a character not at all in her musical. Caroline articulates pathos in her opening scene and throughout the show, each section of her music cast differently based on the events of the moment. Celie, on the other hand, has none of her own music to sing in the beginning of *The Color Purple*.

This choice guarantees the power of her transformation when a much-older Celie sings her eleven o'clock number, "I'm Here." On Broadway, LaChanze, who starred in *Once on This Island* and *Dessa Rose*, added depth to this change by lowering her voice as Celie aged from a teenager to a woman in her fifties. Celie has extricated herself from abusive relationships with men, created a vibrant community, become a maker of pants for women, a financially independent woman, and a lesbian. She is stable and secure. The scene takes place outside of the house of her lover, singer Shug Avery, and the details of the set indicate a level of comfort and sophistication with a small table with an umbrella for shade, sporting Chinese food cartons and a pitcher of lemonade. Shug has just returned from performing on the road, and she tells Celie that she has fallen in love with a nineteen-year-old boy but that she wants to return to Celie after that relationship has run its course.

Audiences' responses to Celie's lesbianism and the onstage kiss between Celie and Shug seemed to range from nonplussed and comfortable to fidgety and anxious to coldly hostile. (This assessment is based on anecdotal evidence [which, although unscientific, is likely accurate] from my observations at the performance I attended, conversations with others who saw it, on-line blogs, and video clips.) The African American community, especially those affiliated with church groups that brought many spectators to see the musical, has a long history of homophobia, which this musical was unable to shake. A review of the production in the African American *New York Amsterdam News*, in fact, completely ignored their romance and wrote, "Shug and Celie end up becoming close friends and looking out for each other."[56] On the other hand, Associated Press theatre critic Michael Kuchwara noted "the musical doesn't shy away from its lesbian subplot."[57]

The song begins with Celie singing lines from their earlier love song, "What About Love?" while Shug speaks, which gives the aural sensation of a reprised duet, but Celie owns the performative power because she sings. (At the performance I attended and from which these notes are drawn, when Shug announced "all I want is 16 months to have my last fling," one woman in the audience warned, "Don't go there!") At the end of this dialogue, "finding her strength," Celie speaks, "No. You know I love you and you still do this? No" (173). She sings tremulously, "I don't need you to love me/I don't need you to love," locating herself at once as object-to-be-loved and as acting subject to love; relationships, she implies, go two ways. At the same time, the set rotates and Shug disappears, seated on a revolve that moves that scene off. Celie begins to enumerate what she's "got" in terms of relationships—sister, children; of material objects—her house, her chair; and of body—her hands, her heart, her eyes, each line growing in strength and conviction. By the end of this verse, Celie, who began singing in tears and despair, seems convinced that she can and will survive and even flourish without Shug (fig. 5-4).

During the musical bridge, Celie crosses upstage, and suddenly, lights come up on a large wisteria vine covered with purple blooms upstage, and Celie sees the flowers, gasps at the sight of such beauty, and moves further upstage (an unfortunate blocking choice that caused the actor to upstage herself at a crucial emotional moment). The song's B section, determined, beat-driven, expansive, and bluesy, explains what she is "gonna" do—"hold my head up," "throw my shoulders back," "look you straight in the eye," "flirt with somebody" (173). In the original Broadway production, LaChanze gradually became physically looser in this section and sang more lines with her arms outstretched. Celie moves from singing about self to singing about action.

The song's third section moves directly into a rock-music-based series of lines, as she sings, "I believe I have inside of me everything I need to live a bountiful life" with heavier drums. These lines continue to develop the tropes of belief and thankfulness. By the end, the accompaniment music pulls back and she sings, "Most of all I'm thankful for loving who I really

Figure 5.4 Celie sings "I'm Beautiful and I'm Here" in her big number of self-expression and assurance. Fantasia in *The Color Purple*. Photo © Paul Kolnik

am/I'm beautiful/And I'm here," the last few lines sung a capella, with shimmery chords punctuating her words of joyful determination. LaChanze's facial expression confirms that Celie has never before thought of herself as beautiful, and that this realization can propel her into the rest of her life. The song ends quietly—in sharp contrast to the more typical, loud female solo number at this point in a musical—as she sings, "I'm beautiful, I'm beautiful, and I'm here" (173), with her arms simply outstretched in front and head facing forward in a confident, calm celebration of self.

The song almost feels like three different numbers, as if Celie is experimenting with a range of musical and linguistic self-expressions. Rather than build, the song shifts modes and moods in each section. The lyrics, while not especially complicated, outline Celie's character and what she would value: "I believe I have inside me, everything I need to live a bountiful life." It is a classic song of self-assertion and self-definition, the eleven o'clock female belting number, as resonant and expansive, if not as complicated, layered, or multifaceted, as "Rose's Turn" in *Gypsy*, or Sally Bowles singing the title song in *Cabaret*, or "Lot's Wife" in *Caroline, or Change*. And like Caroline's number, Celie's is inflected with the blues and the expression of an African American female character, voice, and singing style. In certain ways, though, Celie's eleven o'clock number, in spite of its placement, is an "I am/I want" song. By the end of *The Color Purple*, Celie arrives where most female protagonists begin. The musical is about, in fact, her coming into voice.

In the Heights

In 2006, two years before *In the Heights* opened on Broadway, the television series *Ugly Betty* premiered to wide acclaim on ABC. Adapted from a wildly popular Colombian telenovela, *Ugly Betty*, which ran for five seasons, was a campy and smart dramedy that followed the adventures of educated, ambitious, not-especially-attractive but thoroughly likeable Betty Suarez. The show was remarkable for its representation of an upwardly mobile young Latina and a loving Latino family who supported Betty even when they didn't understand her aspirations. *In the Heights* benefited from the circulation of Latinidad in popular culture by way of *Ugly Betty*, other television series, including *Resurrection Boulevard* (Showtime, 2000) and *American Family* (PBS, 2002), and mainstream films, including *Girlfight* (2000), *Tortilla Soup* (2001), *Real Women Have Curves* (2002, which also starred *Ugly Betty*'s America Ferrera), and *Raising Victor Vargas* (2002).[58]

These cultural products landed in a United States whose demographics were shifting. By 2000, Latinos were the fastest growing "minority" in the United States. That year's census allowed citizens to check off multiple categories of race and almost seven million people did so, including many self-identified Hispanics, an identity that was not listed on the census as a race.[59] Six months after *In the Heights* opened, an article in the *New York Times* reported that "José," which had been the number one Hispanic name for United States–born babies, declined in popularity, as more second generation Latino parents were not choosing "Hispanic" names for their children. The *Times* reported that "a growing proportion of Hispanic people are being raised as Americans from birth," and quoted Jeffrey S. Passel, senior demographer at the Pew Historical Center: "This is the future."[60]

In the Heights reflects these generational shifts. Winner of five Tonys, including Best Musical in 2008, *In the Heights* is the first Broadway musical about a Latina/o community, predominantly Puerto Rican, Dominican, and Cuban, written by Latina/o artists and with an entirely Latina/o cast. While its subject matter and characters are new, its story, themes, structure, and musical theatre conventions are not: *In the Heights* is *West Side Story* meets *Fiddler on the Roof* by way of *Rent*. It resembles *West Side Story* because, in addition to Puerto Rican characters and Latin-inflected music, one of the plots concerns a budding romance between characters from different cultures, which the young woman's father forbids.[61] In addition, *In the Heights*, like *West Side Story*, uses dance as a primary communicative mode, and similarly conveys the sense that the mostly young and emotionally volatile characters most readily express themselves in movement and dance. A father who attempts to control a changing world also appears in *Fiddler*, and like that 1964 musical, this one portrays a community that is changing: governmental anti-Semitism pushes the Jewish families out of Anatevka, and gentrification threatens the Latina/os in Washington Heights. Both musicals, as well as *Rent*, which opened in 1996, also spread a series of stories and plots across a number of characters, thus painting a picture of an entire community rather than of one character or one couple. And like *Rent*, *In the Heights* contains more music than speech, including many recitative scenes, directly communicative "speech," whether in rap or nonrhyming prose set to a musical line. These similarities to older musicals are, of course, partly what it took to get a show produced that features Latina/os. To prove its commercial viability, a twenty-first-century musical must pitch itself as new and as a version of an already successful formula. Composer and lyricist Lin-Manuel Miranda, who began writing the musical as a sophomore at Wesleyan University, cites all of these theatrical influences. *Rent* was the first musical he saw that took place in the present, he said, which allowed him to write a musical about his own life and experiences.[62] In essence, the theme of the musical is "home," which is the final word of the show, sung by the whole company.

In the Heights uses conventions of "golden age" Broadway musicals in a savvy, irresistibly vibrant, Latino-inflected style. In the opening sequence, for example, Usnavi serves as a tour guide, narrating the audience's entry to Washington Heights on a hot July morning. He raps, "Lights up on Washington Heights, up at the break of day/I wake up and I got this little punk I gotta chase away," and the number also introduces all but one of the principals, as Usnavi points out and identifies each character, and each sings an "I want/I am" section.[63] In addition, *In the Heights* begins and ends with an examination and celebration of the community (fig. 5-5). Finally, the scenography of *In the Heights* hearkens back to musicals of the 1950s and early 1960s with its realistically rendered backdrop and saturated colors on the set and lights.

Director Thomas Kail observed that the positive representation of Latina/os on Broadway was so new at the time that the story had to be told in a fairly conventional, even conservative form and structure.[64] The narrative's organization around two heterosexual romances also links it to "golden age" musicals. The first couple is Nina, the intellectual, with Puerto Rican business-owning parents,

Figure 5.5 The residents of Washington Heights sing and dance "good morning" in the opening title song of *In the Heights* (2008). Courtesy Joan Marcus.

and Benny, the Dominican troublemaker-turned-ambitious young man, who works for her parents. Their attraction emerges in their first encounter, although they've known each other since childhood, and finds a series of conflicts, obstacles—most obviously, her father who forbids her to be with him—and misunderstandings, which are resolved by the show's end. A parallel romance between Usnavi and Vanessa functions more humorously, like Rodgers and Hammerstein's secondary romantic couple. Usnavi is brash and friendly to everyone else but shy and awkward around her. She is sexy and ambitious but appreciates his guileless intelligence and sense of responsibility, since he owns a bodega that had been his parents', who are now dead. Still, all four characters and the two couples productively challenge and contemporize those older musical theatre conventions. Nina might be the ingénue, but she is book-smart and articulate; Vanessa stands in for the sexy Latina, but she evades stereotype by her determination to move downtown and by how she shrugs off excessive male attention. In her "I am/I want" song, "It Won't Be Long Now," she sings jauntily, "If I'm in the mood, it will not be with some dude/who is whistling cuz he has nothing to say/or who's honking at me from his Chevrolet." Moreover, Karen Olivo's rendition of Vanessa gave the character both warmth and an edge. Still, the couples' gradual coming together, at once theatrically inevitable and narratively paralleled by the neighborhood's self-assertion, echoes Rodgers and Hammerstein but with a twist: Latina/o characters and a twenty-first-century sensibility about gender.[65]

In the Heights is also self-conscious about that difference, its otherness as a Broadway musical, if more in content than in form. Usnavi's narration and direct address to the audience throughout the show is reminiscent of Mark in *Rent* but also of Tevye in *Fiddler*, the local observer of change, sweetly unself-reflexive. Usnavi, who speaks only in rap, originally played by Miranda him-self, tells the audience a few minutes into the opening number, after he's introduced his Abuela, "She's not really my 'abuela,' but she practically raised me," and "Now, you're prob'ly thinking, 'I'm up shit's creek/I never been north of ninety-sixth street!'" Part of the ideological project of *In the Heights* is, for those who in fact haven't been north of Ninety-sixth Street, a gentle, acces-sible, insistently bilingual introduction to contemporary Latina/o culture in New York. At the same time, the musical does crucial political work for working artists, both by offering jobs to Latina/o performers, many in their first Broad-way show, and better still by offering nonstereotypical roles. As Robin de Jesus, who first played Sonny (Usnavi's cousin), said, "Finally a role where I do not have to carry a gun, I am not in a gang, I am not selling drugs. I'm just a normal human being who happens to be Hispanic and live in this wonderful place called Washington Heights."[66]

Time Magazine called *In the Heights* the first musical of the Obama years, and the musical captures a "national affect" of Latinidad.[67] Writing in the mid-1990s, Suzanne Oboler argues that the label "Latino" was created from outside of the "Latino" or "Hispanic" community and falsely unifies people with vastly different backgrounds, histories, and most importantly, class locations. In *Eth-nic Labels, Latino Lives: Identity and the Politics of (Re)Presentation in the United States*, she stresses what is debilitating about a homogenization of races and ethnicities from Spanish-speaking countries.[68] Still, Miranda chooses to ima-gine a kind of pan-Latino utopia in his Washington Heights, where Cubans, Dominicans, and Puerto Ricans peacefully coexist.[69] The "enemy" is the not-represented but implicitly white gentrifier of the neighborhood. The musical's setting also pays homage to the neighborhood's past, as the sign on Nina's par-ents' business has faded letters in Hebrew and also an Irish name of the busi-ness's previous, then-immigrant owners.

Even as *In the Heights* portrays many characters in the community, and even as Usnavi is the narrator, spokesman, and liaison to the audience, the women occupy key and active roles. The story of Abulela Claudia, Usnavi's surrogate grandmother and the community's matriarch, and her influence on the neigh-borhood's young people, threads through the show. The oldest character, she first appears upstage center in the opening sequence with her characteristically optimistic trademark line, "Paciencia y fe" (Patience and faith). Claudia represents the first generation of immigrants who were brought to the United States by their parents—in her case, from La Vibora, Cuba—as she sings in her big number, appropriately titled, "Paciencia y Fe." By the end of the song, which narrates her story of displacement and readjustment to Nueva York, she reveals that she won $96,000 in the lottery and has decided to leave New York with Usnavi to move to the Dominican Republic. She dies near the end of the show, a convenient dramaturgical move, which leaves Usnavi and Sonny a generous nest egg. Another featured supporting character, Daniela, owns the beauty salon that is the center of the community's gossip. She closes up shop by the end to move her business to the more affordable real estate in the Bronx. Vanessa, Usnavi's paramour and one of Daniela's employees, wants to leave Washington Heights, and she manages to gather the money and find an apartment to move to the West Village by the musical's end. Nina Rosario returns after her first unsuccessful year at Stanford. She is the smart and hard-working Latina who "escapes" the barrio only to find seemingly unmanageable challenges in the culture shock of a privileged, white, private school education. Nina's mother, Camila, played by the indomitable Priscilla Lopez (who created the role of Diana Morales in *A Chorus Line*), sings a key number in which she chastises both Nina and her father for shutting out the family during a time of crisis. Interestingly, all of these women leave the barrio by the end of *In the Heights*, which, while it isn't intended to be a statement about the community's vitality, inadvertently suggests that men will sustain the place and its traditions. At the same time, in contrast to the traditional role of women as "cultural preservers" in ethnic communities, *In the Heights* takes an unconventional stance by "allowing" the women to leave. In this way, this musical, like the other three discussed in this chapter, challenges conventional gender roles.

Because she undergoes the most significant growth and change in the musical, Nina serves as the musical's female principal. Miranda and librettist Hudes adapt and revise musical theatre conventions to portray Nina, intertwining gender and race at every turn. Nina does not appear in the musical's opening, introductory segment that portrays the neighborhood's coffee-driven morning routine. Her absence makes sense narratively because she has just returned from college during the previous night, but also thematically because she is the outsider-insider. Her first number, "Breathe," is the first solo in the musical, and it comes after a brief, sweet book scene with Usnavi and Abuela Claudia, who greet her warmly. Nina's "I am/I want" number takes up a completely different musical language than the first section of *In the Heights*, as if Nina is not of this world. Interlacing Spanish and English in a simple AABA structure and accompanied by a 3/4 time acoustic guitar, the song begins with the Piragua Guy, who sings, "Sigue andando el camino por toda su vida/Respira," and Nina answers on a high, sustained note, "Breathe." The "community" echoes the Piragua Guy, "Y si pierdes mis huellas que dios te bendiga/Respira." Nina sings as if alone, even as the people in the neighborhood know to urge her to "keep going your way, your entire life, [and] and breathe," and "if you lose me [lose my footprints], God bless you."[70] She finds herself effortlessly recognized by the people around her—"this is my street./I smile at the faces/I've known all my life. They/regard me with pride"—yet they don't see all of her, they don't know the truth of her story. Her music is sweet and lilting, without the percussion or syncopation of Usnavi's and the rest of the neighborhood. She recounts her sad story: how, as a child, she climbed the fire escape to look out over the city and to the future elsewhere, how she studied hard, won scholarships, was "the first to go to college," and yet felt out of place and with "so much to hide" at Stanford. As Nina's disappointment in herself and anxious anticipation of delivering the bad news to her parents escalates, the song takes on more of a Broadway sound, weaving together "Latin" and "white" music. In the number's B section, Nina belts the climatic, "How do I tell them why/I'm coming back home,/With my eyes on the horizon." Here Nina complicates what "home" means, since she is back east but already (that is, still) looking out. Her first attempt at an alternative to home didn't work, but even her first song predicts that Nina won't be contained here. Then, she recovers her composure, bracing herself for the encounter and returns to the quiet A section, "Straighten the spine./Smile for the neighbors./Everything's fine./Everything's cool," and the song's last line, "Can I go in there and say/'I know that I'm letting you down'/Just breathe," with the final clear note sustained over a steady guitar.

Like *In the Heights* as a whole, Nina's first song plays with and against Broadway musical theatre conventions. On one hand, it allows Nina to express who she is and to provide the backstory, like other first solos. On the other hand, rather than expressing a grand vision of what she wants in her life, like Fanny Brice in *Funny Girl* or Elphaba in *Wicked*, Nina tentatively and anxiously imagines the few moments of encounter with her parents. While this confrontation has everything to do with her life, of course, in this moment she remains mired in disappointment, unable to imagine a future beyond the admission of failure to live up to their expectations of her.[71] As Mandy Gonzalez, who originated the role of Nina (and who has a Mexican father and a Jewish mother herself), said, "'Breathe' is like every time that I didn't make it, what am I going to tell my parents? . . . I know how it feels to want to be the best and sometimes it just doesn't happen."[72] By placing this song in the position of Nina's "I am/I want" number, the musical stresses the complexity of success for a Puerto Rican girl from the barrio. The "I am/I want" number by definition rests on a privileged form of subjectivity, one not always seen as entangled with the desires of parents and community members. Also, Vanessa's number several scenes later, as a more classic, optimistic, declarative, belting "I am/I want" song, heightens the uniqueness of Nina's.

In addition, Nina performs in the musical style for which she longs, the bolero. In 3/4 time, Nina's song also functions as a kind of corrido, as it recounts the story of a "hero." As theatre scholar David Román observes about the fact that Nuyorican Nina sings in a musical style of Mexican origins (and in a song that deeply expresses her feelings), "The musical idiom might not match the nationalist cultural background of the character but it participates in the pan-Latino cultural politics that characterize the musical."[73] The melody's seductive sweetness contrasts with the despairing words that she sings.[74]

Nina's journey in *In the Heights* requires her to reconcile the comfortable pleasant sound of the bolero with a future "out West" that she has already experienced with difficulty. Nina represents the next generation, whose parents emigrated from Cuba, Puerto Rico, or the Dominican Republic, and who can choose to leave the barrio for a different life. Demographer Passel explains that "the second generation historically has been the generation that becomes American, that integrates."[75] This is the generation of most of the cast of the production, too, including more than a few who had to learn to speak Spanish. As Karen Olivo said, "My parents had a really, really hard time when they came here. They were ostracized and neither of them spoke English. They didn't want me to have to deal with the fact that some people will always look at you like you don't belong."[76]

Each scene in *In the Heights* in which Nina appears presents her on the edge of the community, not quite a part of it anymore, but not gone either, and each scene is awkward for her. Nina and Dominican Benny are soon attracted to one another, and this interethnic romance forces yet another confrontation with her father, who forbids her to be with him. When the Rosarios decide to sell their taxi dispatch business to pay for Nina's tuition—since she lost her scholarship because her grades were poor—Benny loses his job and is furious with Nina, who unintentionally dashed his professional plans. The trajectory of their relationship, while specific to the setting of Washington Heights in the early twenty-first century, follows the conventional musical theatre pattern of a series of obstacles and eventual understanding.

One key scene in their courtship is legitimated by musical theatre conventions rather than historical accuracy. On the fire escape, Nina teaches Benny Spanish in their sweet love song that opens act 2, "Sunrise." As theatre and performance studies scholar Deborah Paredez argues, "It seems highly unlikely, given the immigration patterns of these communities to New York City, that the Puerto Rican Nina would teach the Dominican Benny Spanish," but that the scene plays into memories of *West Side Story*. *In the Heights*, Paredez asserts, "finds a need to invoke this kind of narrative gesture even though it doesn't make narrative sense."[77] The trope of teaching language functions as a performance of intimacy.

In the Heights' eleven o'clock number belongs to Nina and Benny, and, not surprisingly, their duet is immediately preceded by an almost-comic love duet between Usnavi and Vanessa. In the song, Nina and Benny affirm their love for one another, even as Nina will return to Stanford in the fall, and Benny, unemployed, will "try to make my way out West" (fig. 5.6). The song puts a contemporary spin on heterosexual romance, as the bright young woman will complete her education, and the two don't marry but navigate a bicoastal relationship. The short ABAC song, "When the Sun Goes Down," is not their first declaration of love but rather their mutual decision to try to stay together even after she leaves at the end of the summer. The song begins with electric bass and snapping fingers and follows a slow build with the gradual addition of other instruments—guitar, piano—and in the second verse, more piano and drums. Most of the song consists of simple, alternating lines, with one finishing the other's thought, and easy overlapping harmonies, with their voices moving harmonically closer by the end of the song. Benny supports Nina, singing, "Lemme take this moment just to say/You are gonna change the world some day," and they sing together, "And I'll think of you every night at the same time," and then echo and repeat, "When the sun goes down," and the song comes to a quiet end. Even here, the conventional heterosexual closure doesn't happen, although it buttresses the fantasy that it will work out in the end. Nina does not hitch her future to Benny and is planning to ensure her own success.[78]

While the song is perfectly appropriate to the characters in this moment, it sounds like a standard pop-rock love song. Significantly, the song lacks the Latin flavorings of Nina's "Breathe" or the Spanish language of "Sunrise," their earlier love song, which begins with a Spanish lesson for Benny and in which the community chimes in with phrases from Nina's first number. A day later, and refering to sunset rather than sunrise, both Nina and Benny sing in a more conventional "American love song" idiom, performing their integration into the Broadway musical and so into America itself.

Figure 5.6 In *In the Heights* (2008), Nina (Mandy Gonzalez) and Benny (Christopher Jackson) decide to make their relationship work even as she plans to return to college in "When the Sun Goes Down." Courtesy Joan Marcus.

The female characters in twenty-first-century musicals are unique individuals, their identities explicitly formed by gender, race, class, and sexuality, no longer presumptively white, middle-class, or heterosexual when inflected by a Third Wave feminist consciousness. These shows use musical theatre's conventions in a variety of ways and through various musical idioms, but all still rely on the first and last songs as definitive and defining, emotionally, narratively, and characterologically. These numbers track the female principal's journey and encourage the audience's investment, sympathy, and interest.

CHAPTER 6

"Changed for the Better": Queer Conventions in *Wicked* (2003)

In act 1, scene 1 of Rodgers and Hammerstein's *Oklahoma!* (1943), Curly, the cowboy, and Laurey, the farm girl, the musical's principals, sing to one another in alternating verses, "Don't throw bouquets at me/Don't please my folks too much," and "Don't praise my charm too much/Don't look so vain with me." To the characters, the duet is meant to express their incompatibility, as each worries (and sings) that "people will say we're in love" (37).[1] To the audience, though, the song conveys what Curly and Laurey don't yet realize: that they are, of course, already in love. This "hypothetical love song" early in the musical propels the characters through a series of conflicts and misunderstandings that ultimately leads to their marriage. Near the end of *Oklahoma!*, the couple reprises one verse of the song together, and then leads the ensemble into a celebratory rendition of the musical's title song. This kind of duet, in which two characters who are (or who will be) in love deny it or avoid it, or disagree, argue, or claim to hate each other, was, even in 1943, a recognizable, conventional song type in Broadway musical theatre.

Sixty years later, in act 1, scene 1 of Stephen Schwartz and Winnie Holzman's *Wicked*, Elphaba, the smart green-skinned outcast, and Galinda, the popular blond, sing to one another in alternating lines, "What is this feeling so sudden and new?"/"I felt the moment I laid eyes on you"/"My pulse is rushing"/"My head is reeling"/"My face is flushing"; and then in unison, "What is this feeling?" The audience might think the pair is singing a lesbian love song, until they get to the punch line, and it turns out that "this feeling" is "loathing!" (146) (fig. 6-1).[2] Schwartz plays with the audience's expectations in the musical's first duet and renders the song doubly queer: first the song seems to defy conventions of genre because it sounds like an actual love song, and then, to defy conventions of gender because it seems to be a love song between two women in the resolutely heterosexual form of the Broadway musical. When the number turns into a "hate song" like those early "hypothetical" love duets in musicals such as *Carousel* (1945; "If I Loved You") and *Guys and Dolls* (1950; "I'll Know"), *Wicked* signals that it will follow the conventions of mid-twentieth-century musical theatre, but queerly, with two women as the musical's couple. As the penultimate chapter of *Changed for Good*, this one examines a number of conventions previously explored in the book and loops back to the Rodgers and Hammerstein or "golden age" model from chapter 1, with particular emphasis here on the importance of the book (the script, the libretto) and its relation to the musical numbers.

Based on Gregory Maguire's 1995 novel, *Wicked* is both a prequel and sequel to *The Wizard of Oz* that recounts how a precocious, green-skinned girl became the Wicked Witch of the West.[3] The musical, whose marketing blurb says, "So much happened before Dorothy dropped in," follows the unlikely friendship between Elphaba (her name is based on *The Wizard of Oz*'s author, L. Frank Baum), the smart, political outcast, and Galinda, the vapid, popular girl who becomes Glinda the Good Witch. *Wicked* follows Elphaba from birth to boarding school, where she is sent to care for her disabled sister, Nessarose (who will become the Wicked Witch of the East). There, Elphaba is treated cruelly because she is outspoken and green, until Galinda, her unwilling, accidental roommate, befriends her and soon drops the "ga" from her name to show Elphaba how much she has been changed by her new friend. Elphaba distinguishes herself as a gifted student of sorcery and becomes an articulate defender of the Animals (with a capital A), a race of creatures that once were equal to humans but who are now losing their ability to speak. When Elphaba and Glinda, as partners in crime, visit the Wizard of Oz to ask for his help to save the Animals, they find out that he is actually a weak and anxious man who in fact masterminded the anti-Animal plot. Here the two girls take divergent paths. Elphaba rebels against the Wizard, becomes an Animal activist, and is labeled a dangerous enemy of the state. Glinda, though, decides not to join Elphaba as a rebel, and rather pursues a career as a public figure. She also becomes engaged to Fiyero, a pretty boy who first returns her affection and later falls in love with Elphaba, the deeper, smarter, more political girl.

In the second act, the girls find and lose each other several times. Public hysteria around Elphaba's power mounts, and she soldiers on as a political activist and therefore an outsider. By the end of the show, Elphaba martyrs herself as the scapegoat: to allow her friend to follow her own political ambitions, Elphaba gives herself up to become the emblem of wickedness and evil. She makes Glinda promise not to clear her name, and she stages her own death to

Figure 6.1 In *Wicked* (2003), Elphaba (Idina Menzel) and Galinda (Kristin Chenoweth) feel "loathing" in their first duet. Courtesy Joan Marcus.

preserve the community's peace. The audience is aware that she is still alive but Glinda is not, and she secretly mourns her friend. Glinda becomes the governor of Oz, and Elphaba leaves Oz with Fiyero.

Although it opened to mixed reviews in 2003, *Wicked* soon became a blockbuster hit, as noted in the introduction. *USA Today* critic Elysa Gardner called *Wicked* "completely satisfying" and "thoroughly enchanting," but UPI reviewer Frederick Winship called it an "unholy mess of a musical" and "one of the season's most tedious entertainments," and Charles Isherwood in *Variety* found it "cumbersome," "lumbering, overstuffed," and "murky." *New York Times* reviewer Ben Brantley waxed rhapsodic about Kristin Chenoweth and noted that the show is "steeped in talent," but in general described it as "bloated," and a "Technicolorized sermon of a musical."[4] Nevertheless, word of mouth spread quickly, and the show recouped its then-record-breaking $14 million investment in a record-breaking fourteen months. It won three Tony Awards, including Best Actress for Menzel, and its cast album won a Grammy. As of December 2010, it continued to fill 100 percent of its seats at the Gershwin Theatre on Broadway, an unheard-of statistic even for the most popular shows, grossing $2.1 million a week.[5] For the week ending Sunday, November 29, 2009, Wicked became the first show in Broadway history to gross more than $2 million for the week. In addition, by 2010, Wicked played simultaneously to packed houses in five other sit-down productions: open-ended runs in San Francisco, London (which opened starring the original Elphaba, Idina Menzel), Osaka, Sydney, and Oberhausen, plus North American touring companies, whose runs were entirely sold out moments after tickets went on sale.[6]

In some ways, Wicked's massive commercial success in the early twenty-first century comes as no surprise, as it fits the formula of a popular megamusical. With catchy music, clever lyrics, quirky and recognizable characters, huge sets, lavish costumes, and spectacular theatrical effects, such as robotic lighting, smoke, fire, trapdoors, and flying actors, Wicked epitomizes to a certain degree the kind of crowd-pleasing musical theatre that has dominated Broadway since the "British invasion" of the 1980s: a combination of Andrew Lloyd Webber's poperettas (it even makes direct visual reference to Evita, as noted in chapter 4), Disney's extravaganzas, and megamusicals like Les Misérables. In The Megamusical, Jessica Sternfeld describes Wicked as "third generation," exhibiting its predecessors' scale but with a less earnest, more ironic tone and greater musical range.[7] One important difference between Wicked and its megamusical neighbors, which chapter 4 explored, is that this musical is not sung through or "locked down"; to the contrary, actors are encouraged to interpret the characters anew and to make the parts their own.

Wicked's familiar source material also accounts for some of its popularity, as it imagines the backstory of one of America's most well-known and beloved tales, most familiar in the now classic film version with Judy Garland and also used in the 1973 all–African American version, The Wiz, discussed in chapter 3. Wicked self-consciously poaches lines from the movie, for instance, when Nessa asks, "What's in the punch?" Boq answers in the famous rhythm, "Lemons and melons and pears," and Nessa replies, "Oh my!" For her entrance, Glinda, who is made up to look like Billie Burke (the actor who played the Good Witch in the movie), floats down in a steel orb that refers to the bubble in which Glinda enters in the movie. She greets the gathered crowd of the citizens of Oz (and the audience in the theatre) with tongue-in-cheek cleverness, winking straight out front, "It's good to see me, isn't it?" Set details, such as the iconic yellow brick road and the fallen Kansas house with the Wicked Witch of the East's striped stockings and ruby-slippered feet poking out, nod to the movie as well. By the end of *Wicked*, the audience learns how Dorothy's companions became brainless, heartless, and cowardly, and why the ruby slippers matter to the Wicked Witch of the West.

In addition to allowing audiences the nostalgic pleasure of puzzling its intersections with *The Wizard of Oz*, *Wicked* features an all-American tale in which the underdog is different and unique, triumphant to the audience if not in the musical's world, the land of Oz.[8] The musical celebrates the unarguable U.S. values of "freedom" and "independence," and gently keys into early-twenty-first-century critical attitudes about politics. In the spring of 2003, Jessica Lynch was rescued from Iraq, putting a face to women in combat and underlining U.S. troops' vulnerability in a hotly debated war. The Human Genome Project was completed earlier that year; scientists seemed to possess an endless capacity for understanding the human condition. In June 2003, antisodomy laws were declared unconstitutional in *Lawrence v. Texas*, overturning years of discriminatory invasions of privacy in gay men's lives. The former action hero movie star Arnold Schwarzenegger was elected governor of California. These events provide the historical context of *Wicked's* opening.

Moreover, because the brave protagonist is female, *Wicked* converses with the ideology of Third Wave feminism discussed in chapter 5, which values individualism and the imbrications of different identity vectors of gender, race, class, and sexuality. Third Wave feminism also imagines an expansive and flexible range of attachments, investments, and intimacies between women with which Elphaba and Glinda's friendship, trust, and intimacy resonate. The two also fit into an early-twenty-first-century lexicon of "girl power" images, such as strong, independent, supernaturally powerful TV action heroines like Xena, Buffy the Vampire Slayer, Jennifer Garner's character on *Alias*, Joan of Arcadia, or girls' friendship films like *Heathers*, *Mean Girls*, or even *High School Musical*.[9] What Salman Rushdie observes about the movie of *The Wizard of Oz* is true here, too: "The power of men is illusory; the power of women is real."[10]

But *Wicked* does more than portray women as powerful and as friends; it presents the story of a queer romance between Elphaba and Glinda. In this way, *Wicked* makes a fascinating, perhaps surprising, contribution to the feminist musical theatre performance archive. From feminized men to flamboyant women, from doubly entendred lyrics to utopian expressions of emotion, musicals offer interpretive entries for spectators, queer-self-identifying and not, who are willing to see and hear resistantly.[11] What sets *Wicked* apart is that feminism aligns with the musical's "preferred" reading, in accordance with musical theatre's conventions and expectations. In this case, one would need to read *Wicked* "against the grain" to enunciate a straight interpretation. Even the show's logo consists of a drawing of the two witches: Glinda, in profile, white-skinned and wearing a white dress and hat, whispers conspiratorially, in a stereotypical pose for girlfriends, in Elphaba's ear. The latter is dressed in black, her skin bright green. Only Glinda's eyes are visible—she covers her nose and mouth with her hands, while Elphaba's mouth and nose are visible but the hat hides her eyes—as if both women are necessary to make a whole face.[12] This intimate sketch of two girls intensely connected in a bond of trust and communication is the image created and projected by the producers, what they want audiences to immediately associate with the show.

Elphaba and Glinda are constructed as a queer couple in *Wicked*'s theatrical, musical world. Schwartz and Holzman's deployment of well-hewn and well-known conventions of musical theatre guarantees that the women's "romance" succeeds theatrically. *Wicked*'s flashy exterior belies the older scaffold on which the musical itself is built—the formal conventions of mid-twentieth-century musical theatre. *Wicked* has more in common with *The Sound of Music* and *Guys and Dolls* than it does with *The Phantom of the Opera* and *Les Misérables*. *Wicked*'s distinction, then, is in how it uses a very traditional musical theatre formula but infuses its with newly gendered and queered content and relationships that are in large part responsible for its enormous theatrical and financial triumph. *Wicked*'s success proves that popular forms in mainstream venues can bring progressive values to wide audiences.

The tenets established by Rodgers and Hammerstein and their peers in the mid-twentieth century that characterize the formally integrated book musical include a realist narrative (even in a fantasy locale); an articulate and self-reflexive book; some kind of social commentary; and nondiegetic dance numbers. Other conventions include a leading character (especially a woman in Rodgers and Hammerstein) who is both flawed and admirable; a romance whose development forms the spine of the story; and a chorus that embodies the community and its values.

Wicked depends on the audience's recognition—if a subconscious, affective, and experiential recognition—of these particular elements. Although it's unlikely that most spectators consciously detect the degree to which *Wicked* uses a "golden age" book musical format, the musical taps into what Raymond Williams evocatively termed "structures of feeling."[13] From *The Music Man* to *Camelot*, golden age musicals are a part of the collective memory. Audiences "believe" the formation of a couple in musical theatre—if unconsciously—because the romance develops through the musical's conventions that have become part of the U.S. cultural imaginary. Moreover, they "accept" the practice of characters' suddenly breaking into song and dance, a modal shift that the proponents of the integrated musical sought to alleviate.

Wicked exemplifies this conventional duality. Unlike the musicals of Andrew Lloyd Webber such as Phantom of the Opera (examined in chapter 4) or Jonathan Larson's Rent (1996), Wicked is not sung-through, but rather places realist spoken scenes in tension with exuberant musical numbers. While its music, narrative, character, and design cohere, as was typical of formally integrated musicals of the mid-twentieth century, Wicked also relies on the formal and phenomenological distinction between the script and the music—that is, the very architecture that characterizes mid-twentieth-century musical theatre—to harness its emotional power and to do its ideological work. The spoken text tells the political story of an ethically responsible, individual girl who becomes a scapegoat, while the musical numbers emplot the two women as a romantic couple.

According to the conventions of Broadway musical theatre explored throughout this book, the form's structure is thoroughly gendered and the celebration of heterosexual romance is its very purpose. What Virginia Wright Wexman writes about Hollywood films applies to Broadway musicals, too: "Hollywood's emphasis on courtship and romantic love is a function of the movies' place within American—and indeed world—culture as a commercial enterprise. It constitutes a significant cultural practice, the conventions of which are related to the way we live."[14] While the principals in a musical may begin as rivals—Sarah Brown and Sky Masterson in Guys and Dolls; or as enemies—Eliza Doolittle and Henry Higgins in My Fair Lady; or as annoyances to one another—Maria and the Captain in The Sound of Music; or at best, in mutual misunderstanding—Nellie and Emile in South Pacific, their differences of background or temperament signal that they will eventually form a couple. Indeed, the ideological project of musical theatre in the mid-twentieth-century United States was to use the heterosexual couple's journey from enemies to lovers to stand in for the unification of problematic differences in American culture—between the city and the country, between work and leisure, between us and them, between whites and racialized Others.[15]

Wicked works out its ideological struggle by constructing the two women as a romantic couple within the conventions of musical theatre. Like mid-twentieth-century musicals, Wicked "fashions a myth out of the American courtship ritual."[16] Similarly, Wicked uses the women's distinctiveness and their ultimate union to do its liberal ideological work; that is, to value individualism, integrity, and fairness over the desire for fame and fortune at any cost. The women are constructed in opposites: pretty and ugly, popular and outcast, dumb and smart, silly and political, femme and butch, white and "colored." But while in mid-twentieth-century musicals, the difference of gender at once undergirds and overdetermines the couple's differences of culture or personality, in *Wicked*, the two women form a couple of both sameness and difference.

Elphaba's Difference in *Wicked*'s Script

The binary difference of gender forms the key building block of "golden age" musical theatre. Not only are personality differences subsumed into gender, but the architecture of the performance depends on contrasting physicalities of staged and choreographed bodies, and contrasting sounds of male and female voices in harmony. For the musical's structure to hold up, *Wicked* needs to replace gender difference with another unavoidable physical difference between the characters, which it does with skin color.[17] Elphaba's peers ostracize her at first for her physical difference, but we soon see that her real difference is political. Her green skin is a synecdoche for her other differences from Glinda and the other students: she is independent, a free thinker, exceedingly intelligent, unafraid to rebel, politically progressive. She also possesses magic powers and the ability to cast spells. Over and again, the musical stresses how she is unique by using other characters to bracket what she is not. The musical wants the audience to recognize and sympathize with Elphaba.[18]

Two likely readings of Elphaba's green skin and painful fate—that she is a person of color who suffers other people's racism or that she is disabled and discriminated against—are emphatically foreclosed in *Wicked*. In spite of the green color of her skin, then, she is not constructed as a person of color, for that would require linking her to a larger social and sociohistorical group, like the female protagonists in the musicals in chapter 5: *Parade, Caroline, or Change, The Color Purple*, and *In the Heights*. Rather, the Animals stand in for the racialized other, with strong associations with Jewishness in the musical. They are the professors whose ability to speak (literally) is being taken away. In the classroom scene, Dr. Dillamond, who is a goat, queries the class about the meaning of "scapegoat," which anticipates both his and Elphaba's victimization by the citizenry of Oz. When he rotates the blackboard to continue the lesson, someone has scrawled on it, "Animals should be seen and not heard." Dr. Dillamond is so upset that he dismisses the class, but Elphaba stays to share her lunch with him (he eats the paper in which her sandwich is wrapped), and they sing the duet, "Something Bad (Ba-a-a-a-a-d)." Dr. Dillamond tells her about the Animals who are losing their jobs, their power, and their speech, to which Elphaba sings, "It couldn't happen here/In Oz" (147). A later scene shows scientists who look strikingly like Nazis experimenting on and caging Animals. By portraying another character (primarily Dr. Dillamond, but also the group) so definitively marked as Jewish and thus racialized, and by positioning Elphaba as their defender but not a member of that group, the musical certifies that her color is not a race.[19]

The musical also discourages a reading of Elphaba's difference as disability. Her father's and peers' rejection of her is based on apparently understandable disgust and horror; they judge her skin color not simply as different, but as a disfigurement. Their moralizing is supported by the illicit circumstances of Elphaba's conception—her mother's one-night, drug-induced affair (with, it is later revealed, the Wizard)—that Glinda narrates in the first few minutes of the musical. At the same time, the musical presents Elphaba's sister, Nessarose, the wheelchair-bound "tragically beautiful girl." Nessa's existence in the musical puts pressure on Elphaba's meaning from the other side: the green girl is not disabled, just different.[20] Nessa begins as a sweet girl but eventually becomes the bitter and despotic governor of Oz. She is also desperately in love with Boq, a munchkin who loves Glinda, whom Nessa makes her slave-servant-houseboy-boyfriend. When Elphaba uses her magical powers to make her sister walk, Boq tries to leave the newly mobile Nessa, but Elphaba, ever loyal to her sister, turns him into the Tin Man. For a musical like *Wicked* that works overtime to send a politically progressive message, its use of disability as a metaphor for evil is, simply put, an ideological blind spot.[21]

Two potential ways of explaining Elphaba's difference, then, are displaced onto other characters: the Animals' race and Nessa's disability. These gestures are necessary for the musical to show that Elphaba's green skin makes her neither disabled nor of a racial minority; she is solely a unique and special individual, the presumed subject of the audience's identification and attachment. *Wicked*'s producers, not surprisingly, emphatically stress its universality, asserting that Elphaba's "difference" stands in for all difference. As producer Mark Platt is frequently quoted as saying, "We all have a green girl inside of us."

Wicked's Queer Love Story in the Musical Numbers

Wicked's script and spoken, visual, and embodied texts ground its fantasy setting in early twenty-first-century concerns, and represent the female protagonist as a brave individualist. But the key structuring convention in musical theatre is the heterosexual romance plot, which *Wicked*'s musical numbers follow and develop. Mark N. Grant observes the importance of the various components of a musical, "but," he writes, "everything comes back to the music."[22] Those numbers follow a crucial order, as they are functional and construct the plot, not merely serving as decoration or distraction. Composer Stephen Schwartz notes that in *Wicked*, "many of the songs are structured to carry the story of the show."[23]

THE PRINCIPALS

Like many mid-twentieth-century musicals, *Wicked* employs the convention of introducing each principal early in the show in a solo. These songs in musicals instantly define the main characters, at once signaling the two principals' dissimilarity and foreshadowing their union, for example, Curly's "Oh, What a Beautiful Mornin'" and Laurey's "Many a New Day" in *Oklahoma!*, or Higgins's "Why Can't the English?" and Eliza's "Loverly" in *My Fair Lady*. In *Wicked*, Glinda's first number takes place within the show's opening moments: as the Ozians celebrate the death of the Wicked Witch, Glinda floats down in her "bubble." She sings in a high soprano, "Let us be glad/Let us be grateful/Let us rejoicify that Goodness could subdue/The wicked workings of you-know-who" (140). She comes off the last note in a flourish, eyebrows raised, with a slight wink and two fingers gesturing the quotation marks around "you-know-who," in a flagrant imitation of Billie Burke in the movie of *The Wizard of Oz*. The visual and musical cues, and the fact that her song is not a full solo number but rather a brief interlude within a chorus number, mark her as an angel figure who is both (literally) above the community and strongly connected to it. When Glinda sings "rejoicify," the audience hears the first of many malapropisms in the show that foreshadow (and at the same time, since this beginning is actually the end of the plot, confirm) her coming into power. In this world, leaders speak badly.[24] The audience only realizes in retrospect, at the end of the show, that Glinda is only pretending to be happy about Elphaba's death, and that actually she is mourning, covering up their relationship. Unusual for musical theatre, this first number does not accurately reflect Glinda's true character but instead stages a performance of a performance in her role as a public figure. Sung in a significantly higher register than any other song in the show, this song is Glinda's only true soprano number; its unusual tessitura stresses the song's status as public display, as performance.[25]

This song also introduces Glinda's relationship to Elphaba in language that highlights its queerness. Before she departs, an Ozian asks, "Is it true that you knew her?" and Glinda replies, "I did know her. That is, our paths did cross—at school. But you must understand, it was a long time ago and we were both very young." The first few lines that explain her relationship to Elphaba suggest that the relationship was intimate and illicit and play out a double entendre from the beginning.

In contrast, Elphaba, from her first appearance, is what she seems to be. Her opening song, "The Wizard and I," explains her character completely. She begins with, "When I meet the Wizard/Once I prove my worth/And then I meet the Wizard/What I've waited for since—since birth!" She imagines how he will understand her, "With all his Wizard wisdom/By my looks he won't be blinded," and even how he will value her: "He'll say to me:/'I see who you truly are/A girl on whom I can rely!'" (144). Her number is fast and pulsing with a lightly syncopated accompaniment that gives it drive, force, and movement. The song seems to hesitate and then build; the singer conveys the sense of going back, taking a breath, and moving forward again. The notes move up the scale, as Elphaba begins quietly convincing herself of her value and then belts with complete confidence, her final note held long and loud. Elphaba's first song is an "I am/I want" song, a typical form for an early, character-defining song in a book musical. The number builds gradually verse by verse, to become an "I will/I can" song, very much like "I'm the Greatest Star" from *Funny Girl*. Schwartz, in fact, said that he modeled Elphaba on Barbra Streisand as Fanny Brice in *Funny Girl*.[26] The song tells the audience that she is a diva, a visionary, independent, and ambitious—the opposite of Glinda in spirit; and that she is a vulnerable girl, who wants to be pretty and popular and not green—the opposite of Glinda in appearance. While Glinda imitates the film's Good Witch, Elphaba's theme motif, the line "unlimited, my future" contains the exact same sequence of notes as Harold Arlen's line "somewhere over the rainbow." Here Schwartz subtly positions Elphaba as a Dorothy-like heroine.[27] However Glinda and Elphaba are introduced as opposites, they both sing Elphaba's signature phrase in several different songs, which signifies Glinda's (eventual) deep understanding of her friend.

THE FORMATION OF THE COUPLE IN SONG AND DANCE

After the women meet, they sing four duets of various tones and tempos over the course of the show. Because music and dance are the most concentrated and meaningful forms of expression in musical theatre, a duet—the performative force of two people singing together on stage—reveals the shape and tenor of the relationship. As in many mid-twentieth-century musicals, the principals' duets trace, in sequence, the characters' developing romance; thus, it matters how frequently and in what ways characters sing together. In *Carousel*, for example, Julie and Billy sing "If I Loved You." In *Guys and Dolls*, Sky and Sarah sing "I'll Know" and "I've Never Been in Love Before." In *West Side Story*, Maria and Tony sing "Somewhere," "Tonight," and "One Hand, One Heart." As an extraordinary, oft-noted exception, in *South Pacific*, the principals sing no love duets, since Mary Martin refused to sing with the great opera singer Ezio Pinza, as she was intimidated by his voice. Nellie and Emile's attachment is rendered musically in consecutive songs—"Twin Soliloquies"—and reprises. The very need for Martin to explicitly refuse a duet, and Rodgers and Hammerstein's willingness to write another musical version of romance, underlines the importance of the convention of the romantic duet in musical theatre, even by the late 1940s.

In *Wicked*, the number of duets between the principals is unusually high for any romantic couple in a musical. The women's relationship, like those of the couples in mid-twentieth-century musicals, is developed through these songs. Their first duet, "What Is This Feeling?" is acutely aware of and plays on the conventions of earlier musical theatre. A musical's first romantic duet tends to be a song in which the couple tries to express their lack of compatibility, but since they do it by singing a duet—that is, by singing together as one—their performance contradicts the very animosity on which they insist. Songs like "People Will Say We're in Love" from *Oklahoma!* or "If I Loved You" from *Carousel* are love songs in the subjunctive. The lyrics express discord but the characters' singing together unifies them. For *Wicked*, after a verse that sets the scene of the two girls each writing home to family to complain about her roommate, they sing in snappy, alternating lines of crisp eighth notes:

Galinda: What is this feeling
      So sudden and new?
Elphaba: I felt the moment
      I laid eyes on you
Galinda: My pulse is rushing. . .
Elphaba: My head is reeling. . .
Galinda: My face is flushing. . .
Both: What is this feeling?
      Fervid as a flame

Does it have a name?
Yes!
[They continue with the chorus]:
Both: Loathing
Unadulerated loathing. . .
Galinda: For your face. . .
Elphaba: Your voice. . .
Galinda: Your clothing. . .
Both: Let's just say—I loathe it all! (77)

The lyrics describe perfectly the feeling of falling in love, and yet, the refrain turns to their true feeling: "loathing." Although it's not actually a queer love song, the number's energy and the mutual engagement of the women, who sing much of the song in unison, link them passionately and set up the audience to be teased by queer potential throughout the show. The number also underlines how performance moves across time; we figure out what the song is about as it proceeds. Schwartz noted that he wrote this song to function like "Ten Minutes Ago" from Cinderella, which is a musical declaration of love at first sight.[28] In addition, the number is choreographed as "approach and avoidance": the actors move close and then back off; they twirl around each other like magnets. Like many romantic couples in musical theatre, Elphaba and Galinda at once hate each other and are irresistibly drawn to one another.

The next key moment in the women's relationship occurs through dance. In many "golden age" musicals, love is revealed in a big dance scene, as in, for example, Rodgers and Hammerstein's television musical of Cinderella, as well as My Fair Lady, West Side Story, and The Sound of Music. In Wicked, the number is not a lilting waltz, as it is typically in a mid-twentieth-century musical (or a quiet variation of a cha-cha, as in West Side Story), but rather is a pulsing pop song. Fiyero, the nominal male interest in the show, opens the song, but then the chorus (students at Shiz University) and the women take it over. In the musical's previous scene, Galinda has played a nasty joke on Elphaba to emphasize her status among the other girls: she gives Elphaba a black pointy hat and sings that "black is this year's pink" (pink is Galinda's cool, fashionable color, although the show's overall design is more green in hue—Elphaba's color), but the hat is actually an ugly accessory, a gift from her grandmother, which Galinda doesn't want. Since Elphaba has no fashion sense—because she is smart, a stereotype that the musical invokes and then resignifies—she accepts the gift to wear to the dance.

The scene takes place at the Ozdust Ballroom, a disco of sorts where the whole company, except for Elphaba, is dancing. Elphaba arrives late to the party, wearing her version of party clothes—a drab dress and heavy, brown, lace-up boots—and the unstylish hat, and she enters upstage center. All the kids stop dancing, turn to stare, and start to laugh at her. She realizes immediately that she has been duped and quickly removes the hat in embarrassment. But then but she regains her poise and walks slowly downstage center. She stops and deliberately re-places the iconic pointy black hat on her head, adding one more ingredient to her coming-into-focus image as the Wicked Witch of the West. Then, still being watched, she begins to dance slowly with undulating movements, alone in a pool of light, as the chorus fades into the background. Galinda stands downstage right with Fiyero, who says, "Well, she doesn't give a twee what anyone else thinks." Galinda, though, is both guilt-stricken and attracted to Elphaba's bravery, and after a moment, she leaves him to join Elphaba. Galinda asks if she can cut in, a line both funny and sweet, since Elphaba is dancing absolutely alone, and then she imitates Elphaba's movement. The two women dance together, in a writhing movement vocabulary completely unlike the rest of the show's choreography. This moment, the most erotic in the show, looks like the scene in *West Side Story*, when Maria and Tony see each other in the gym and everyone else fades into the background. The women speak their own choreographed language, with Elphaba, the former underdog, leading. As the song returns to the bright, boppy chorus, everyone in the company imitates the choreography of the two women, and their union is celebrated in a dance that extends to the whole community.

OBSTACLES TO THE ROMANCE

Once the women's relationship is established, personal and social conflicts necessarily ensue, since a mid-twentieth-century book musical, while concerning a romantic couple's formation, which the audience readily anticipates, actually represents on stage the obstacles to their relationship. As in the musicals of Rodgers and Hammerstein, their very struggle becomes the musical's content.[29] Like Fanny Brice and Nick Arnstein in *Funny Girl*, Eliza and Henry Higgins in *My Fair Lady*, and Sarah Brown and Sky Masterson in *Guys and Dolls*, Galinda and Elphaba are different in kind. In this theatrical world of schoolgirls, their key difference is their popularity. Once they are friends, Galinda (who renames herself Glinda at the end of this scene) decides that Elphaba is also her project, and she sings the bedroom number, "Popular" (fig. 6-2).

This show-stealing song articulates many of the concerns of girls, and it uses the trope of girls' bedroom makeover scenes common in films and TV shows, as in the movie *Clueless* (1995), for example.[30] Galinda's exuberant arrogance is

Figure 6.2 In *Wicked* (2003), Elphaba (Idina Menzel) allows Galinda (Kristin Chenoweth) to make her "Popular." Courtesy Joan Marcus.

both awkward and sweet, as the number at once announces the elements of popularity and also gently makes fun of them. She does a bumpy jêté and almost trips into a curtsy; she yodels the last syllable of "popular"; she sings multiple internal rhymes, which include "tender heart" and "tends to start," "makeover" and "take over," "succeed" and "lead" and "indeed," "aptitude" and "the way you're viewed" and "very shrewd." To force a rhyme with "instead of dreary who-you-were . . . are," she changes the last syllable of the frequently repeated word, and sings, "Populer. lar." In this way, the song's humor reveals the machinations of the alpha girl and disempowers her, but doesn't dismiss her, since Galinda's interest in her friend is heartfelt and her belief in the power of popularity is genuine, even ingenuous. Moreover, even though the song is technically a solo, in performance it requires Elphaba to be there: the address is crucial; the song features an idea and a response, and Galinda's profound effect on Elphaba (in spite of her desire not to care about being popular, she does) constitutes the number's drama and emotion. When Elphaba leaves embarrassed at the end of the song, the girls are bonded and friends.

The rest of the musical charts the women's connection through songs that divide and unite them. "One Short Day," for example, a jazzy, bright celebration of their visit to the Emerald City, allows them to lead the ensemble in an homage to cosmopolitanism—to the museums, palaces, and dress salons—

and to sing, "It's all green!/I think we've found the place where we belong!" in an overtly queer anthem: "So I'll be back for good someday/To make my life and make my way" (155).

Even in the numbers in *Wicked* that stress their differences, the women interact musically as they sing together. For example, when they go together to meet the Wizard and understand him for the power-wielding hypocrite that he is, Glinda wants to keep quiet about the truth, but Elphaba rebels, as she expresses in her biggest number, the act 1 finale, "Defying Gravity." The song's placement at the end of act 1 reveals how the musical privileges Elphaba's values: her independence, determination, and willingness to anger authority to do the ethical act. The number is reminiscent of "Don't Rain on My Parade" from *Funny Girl*, which contains musical phrases from the earlier "I'm the Greatest Star," as this one includes musical phrases from the earlier "I am/I want" number, "The Wizard and I." However, unlike *Funny Girl*'s song of self-assertion and determination, this song is not only a solo. It begins with Glinda singing phrases from Elphaba's "The Wizard and I" to her, which underlines how well Glinda knows Elphaba's dreams: she sings her music. Then, in the middle part of the song, Elphaba speaks, "Come with me. Think of what we could do . . . together" (161). They sing a proud and brave chorus, "Unlimited/ Together we're unlimited" (161), and it seems as if they may fly off on the broomstick as a team. When Glinda decides not to leave and backs off from the broom that will become Elphaba's signature prop, she continues to sing with Elphaba, in tight harmonies, to the last line of the song. Act 1 ends with Elphaba ascended high above the ensemble, spotlit and with huge, prism-like shafts of light emanating from her limbs, visually isolated but her voice backed by Glinda, who looks up at her admiringly. In these middle scenes, the show certifies how the two women represent not only differences in personality and style but also opposite relationships to power. And yet they perform as a couple.

THE ENDING OF WICKED

By the end of the show, the two women do part ways, but not before they reconcile and sing "For Good," the last new song of *Wicked* (that is, the last song that is not a reprise) that cements their union. In this scene, Elphaba passes her book of spells to Glinda, who, Elphaba insists, must educate herself and learn to speak the mysterious and powerful language of magic. They sing, "Who can say if I've been changed for the better? . . . Because I knew you . . . I have been changed for good" (176). This song, like their other duets, places their voices in the same register, as if the music insists on putting them in the same place. Emotionally and musically, the two are intertwined, as they switch between alto and soprano parts, each taking her turn to sing higher than the other. They share the melody and the harmony, and each woman's voice crosses over the other's. Then they sing the last line in unison, ending together on the same, mid-range note.[31] The actors are placed downstage left, a strong visual position on stage, with the two women standing face to face, close and holding hands, singing to each other. The visual image stresses their complementary differences, as Glinda has blond curls and wears a white sparkling ball gown, while Elphaba, invariably played by a taller actor, is dark, simply attired in a close-fitting but unrevealing black dress, and of course, green-skinned. The women sing to each other with passion, longing, and appreciation, and they end the number with a teary embrace. However Wicked's plot divides the women, the musical continues to present them as unified and as a couple.

In terms of musical theatre's reception, the power of the image, of performance in the moment, carries a much stronger interpretive force than do the mechanisms of plot.[32] As the musical ends, its meaning (its content, the plot), that the women are separated, contradicts its feeling or affective force, that the women are together. The very end of Wicked underlines, again, how the women form the musical's romantic couple when this song comes back, although not in a strict reprise. Rather, a few lines from "For Good" are repeated in the very end of the show, as a tag to the final chorus number, with Elphaba singing "because I knew you" an octave below Glinda in mutually supported melodies:

> Company: Good news! Good news!
> Glinda: Who can say if I've been changed for the better? But—
> Glinda and Elphaba: Because I knew you
> Company: No one mourns the wicked
> Glinda: Because I knew you
> Glinda and Elphaba: I have been changed
> Company: No one mourns the wicked, wicked, wicked!

And here the show ends. Rather than the women finishing the line with "for good," the Company comes in after they sing "changed," which pulls the women's line to a different key, concluding on the same powerful chord that ends the musical's opening ensemble number. This ending conveys the musical's ambivalence and anxiety about its subject and its meaning. Wicked wants to end on a note of harmony and tenderness between the two women, who would sing "for good" and end together on middle C as in the song's first rendition, but instead gives (or, gives up?) the last chord of the show to the dissonance of the community, who sing, "wicked."

The ending of *Wicked* foregrounds how the musical both converses with and revises other conventions of 1950s musicals, and thus reconfigures, or queers, the mid-twentieth-century, Cold War associations of those elements. Many musicals' finales, such as "Oh, What a Beautiful Morning" from *Oklahoma!* or "Seventy-Six Trombones" from *A Music Man* (1957), celebrate the community.[33] Within the world of the musical, *Wicked*'s finale also recognizes the community's centrality when the company sings a reprise of "No One Mourns the Wicked," which was the first song in the show. As the plot comes full circle, though, the community is not idealized, romanticized, or even rendered neutral. Unlike the positive vision of American communities of the Cold War era, the cynical, early-twenty-first-century perspective represents political leaders as evil and weak, and the community as an easily fooled mob. Whether the ensemble plays students at Shiz or citizens of Oz, they follow the charismatic leader (or the popular girl) without question. When the citizens of Oz sing that "the Wicked Witch is dead" joyfully but in a minor key, the audience sees them for the mindless crowd that they are. Like almost all of the musicals of Rodgers and Hammerstein's era, *Wicked*'s finale unifies the community, but, in 2003, with irony and a critical slant.

In contrast to 1950s musicals, in which the principals and the ensemble are in sync, *Wicked*'s ending reveals their lack of correspondence—quite audibly, their lack of harmony. According to the theatrical conventions of mid-twentieth-century musical theatre, the ensemble-affirming finale is either enabled by or incorporates the marriage of the principals. Because the principals stand in for conflicting values within the community, their (heterosexual) union signifies the community's solidarity.[34] *Wicked*'s queer "marriage" is private, only spoken between the women and impossible to be revealed publicly. The principals must permanently separate because the community refuses to tolerate their union. The audience, though, sees how Glinda, while serving as the governor of Oz, mourns what she thinks is Elphaba's death and remains apart from the group. The audience has known throughout the musical that the "wicked witch" is not wicked, and sympathizes with Elphaba and sees the community critically.

The Heterosexual Leading Man

Twentieth-century musicals exhibit contradictory conventions in terms of a male principal. On the one hand, presumptive spectating practices require little musical or textual demonstration of heterosexual romance to render it apparently legible. On the other hand, as Mark Steyn writes, "We still joke about Broadway being boy-meets-girl but, in fact, hardly any musicals are concerned with conventional heterosexual romance."[35] *Wicked* is not very anxious about the pale presence of its male leading character, Fiyero, whose part isn't even quite large enough to consider him a principal. Fiyero enters more than thirty minutes into act 1, well after the two female characters and their relationship have been established. His first scene with Elphaba, his eventual mate, occurs almost an hour into the show. Even the men who have played him know that the character merely exists to foreground the women's strong connection and attachment. Norbert Leo Butz, who originated the role, said that "the real love story is between the two ladies. So, *who is this guy* became the overwhelming question," and actor David Ayers observed that "Fiyero is a vehicle to tell the story of the two women."[36] In *Wicked*, as in *Gypsy*, *Mame*, and *Funny Girl*, as D. A Miller writes, "Every female who enters the star spot is paired with a less brightly lit male figure, ridiculous or pathetic, of whom is it variously demonstrated that *he may not take her place there*."[37]

Musically, Fiyero fails to register as a significant force in *Wicked*. He is introduced as beautiful, stupid, and lazy, as he sings in his character-defining number, "Dancing through life/Skimming the surface/Gliding where turf is smooth/Life's more painless/For the brainless" (147). In addition to foreshadowing his future as the scarecrow, these lyrics associate Fiyero with a "disavowal of labor" typically assigned to women characters and women actors.[38] Fiyero's one solo in the show quickly moves into an ensemble number at the dance and then is taken over by the women in their "mating" dance; that is, Fiyero doesn't even get the stage space to sing a complete song alone. Miller explains (quite humorously) a "general law of the musical":

> This law ordains that, though male and female alike may and indeed must appear on the musical stage, they are not equally welcome there: the female performer will always enjoy the advantage of also being thought to *represent* this stage, as its sign, its celebrant, it essence, and its glory; while the male tends to be suffered on condition that, by the inferiority or subjection of his own talents, he assist the enhancement of hers.[39]

The relationships among Elphaba, Glinda, and Fiyero are variously triangulated, with the women always emerging as the real couple. Fiyero and Glinda meet first and declare themselves "perfect" and "perfect together," which alerts the audience that, according to the conventions of musicals, they're not a perfect match at all. Rather, Elphaba, Fiyero's opposite in temperament and type, is meant to be his mate, since she sees him for more than he is, and he comes to appreciate her uniqueness, too, in much the same way that Glinda does. At different points in the show, Elphaba and Glinda each sing "I'm Not That Girl," and grieve over Fiyero's attraction for the other with sadness more than jealousy. While the song sets up a characterological parallel and underlines how they both like him and both feel badly when he chooses the other girl (a slightly nauseating and conservative male-centered choice in a show that otherwise privileges women and their strength and autonomy), the doubled performance of the song, like the women's duets, links them musically. Fiyero may be the common subject but the women are intimately tied together through song. He is, as in L. Frank Baum's world of Oz, "the straw man."[40]

Although *Wicked*'s plot renders Fiyero and Elphaba lovers and permanent partners, the performance itself continually undermines the power of their relationship, since their romance is barely represented on stage and so not substantiated through musical theatre's conventions of music or dance. Moreover, their one and only duet, "As Long as You're Mine," is a typical pop love song, with unspecific lyrics: "Just for this moment/As long as you're mine/Come be how you want to/And see how bright we shine" (170). The number is staged with the actors mid-center stage, kneeling and then seated on the floor. For any performance, this location and position on stage is a weak one visually. But in a show like *Wicked* that so values height and verticality—Glinda makes her entrance and exit by floating in and out on a bubble; Elphaba's biggest number has her flying up, victorious at the end of act 1; she even comes up and out of the floor at the end of the show—placing the heterosexual couple on the floor diminishes the visual power and so the believability of their importance.

Critics, Audiences, Producers, and the Performative Politics of *Wicked*, or Are Girls Universal?

When the audience applauds wildly after *Wicked*'s final, powerful chord and an instantaneous blackout, what is the target of their appreciation? What is the story that merits the approval of seven-year-old girls, their mothers, and their grandmothers? If *Wicked* quite overtly represents, as I've argued here, a love story between two women, why has there been no commentary on the musical's queerness? A few writers have noted the musicals' feminism, or its less vibrant twin, girl power. Eve Ensler, for example, author of *The Vagina Monologues*, praises *Wicked* as "the story of a complicated relationship between two women, both of whom, in their way, suggest Everywoman."[41]

Wicked makes use of a "both/and" strategy.[42] First, it epitomizes the twenty-first-century megamusical in its production values, which are spectacular, and in its marketing strategy, which is global capitalism. It can be replicated "with unprecedented meticulousness across a greater number of international venues."[43] For audiences familiar with *Phantom* or *Les Miz*, these aspects of *Wicked* seem familiar. Second, it is structured by the conventions of traditional, classic, "golden age" musical theatre and so calls up ideas and feelings about musical theatre thoroughly embedded in the U.S. cultural imaginary and recognizable to anyone who has seen the movie of *The Sound of Music*. Third, *Wicked* uses those conventions—especially its script—to tell a contemporary parable, a liberal story about an individual, power gone awry, and a stupid mob-oriented society. Fourth, *Wicked* uses those same conventions—but especially its music—to represent two women in an intense, primary relationship. Audiences may key into any of these strains. *Wicked* can succeed in meaning multiply because, like the other musicals discussed in this book, it's entertainment, it's popular culture. Richard Dyer writes that "it is precisely on seeming to achieve both these often opposed functions simultaneously"—that is, supporting capitalist patriarchy and opening a space for subordinate groups—that entertainment's "survival largely depends."[44] Musical theatre qualifies as mass culture because its meanings are multiple and because audiences engage with musicals through a range of spectating practices, including cast albums and bootleg and legal video clips on YouTube, as well as the performance itself, as the next chapter demonstrates.

The affective power of *Wicked*—or any musical that succeeds commercially—is what ultimately touches audiences. Miller writes, "The stuff of mass culture (as our first culture) conducts psychic flows with an efficiency that the superior material of no second, later culture ever comes close to rivaling. It is by way of Shane, not Sophocles or Freud, that Oedipus stalks our dreams, just as the Beach Boys have a power of refreshing our memories unknown to Brahms."[45] Many critics' preoccupation with spectacle and marketing causes them to miss that the political punch of this musical regards what happens on stage in relation to musical theatre's formal conventions: two women form a primary relationship and sing and dance together. In other words, the progressive power of the piece is less in the overtly stated politics of the show about government and leadership, and more in the representation and performative power of a pair of women on stage together.[46] Some may see them as friends; some may see them as co-conspirators; some may even see them as competitors. But if one sees them through the conventions of musical theatre on which *Wicked* is built, they look like a queer couple.

In *New Broadways: Theatre across America: Approaching a New Millennium*, Gerald M. Berkowitz writes, "This point is so important: *you have to please the audience*," whether this means giving "an audience what it wanted," or guiding "an audience, carefully and gradually, into wanting what was offered."[47] Still, Susan Bennett argues that "entertainment retail might be driven by its commitment to sell things, but that does not stop its producers from at least imagining that they can achieve an effect we have often reserved for accounts of socially or politically motivated performance—changing the lives of audiences."[48] Rodgers and Hammerstein and their peers knew this, which is why Broadway musicals were both commercially successful and politically influential during and since the Cold War. *Wicked*, by using the conventions of "golden age" musical theatre in the twenty-first century and putting two women in the center to make the biggest hit of the twenty-first century's first decade, might simultaneously please its audience and guide them to want a queer and feminist Broadway musical theatre.

CHAPTER *7*

"It's All About Popular": *Wicked* Divas and Internet Girl Fans

Voice [of the "Diva"] is important, but like the scent of a flower it must be attached to beauty to be complete. And beauty is that undefinable charm and magnetic force which is communicated by the subtlest means from singer to hearer.
—D. MacClean Rawcliffe, "Singers Past and Present: What Is Lacking?"
   The Musical Times, 1931

Close your eyes and listen as their larynxes stretch and vibrate with the pain of being an underdog and the joy of being really loud. Bet you can't tell them apart. For that matter, bet you can't distinguish the heroines of the current Broadway musicals "Wicked," "Little Women" and "Brooklyn" from the average female finalist on "American Idol."
—Ben Brantley, *New York Times*, March 2005

And THEN the guy yells "LOOK ITS GLINDA" and there she was. I cried guys, I cried. I mean we have been doing all of this obsessing and what not. But there she was, as freaking amazing as ever. Megan's voice is SO much more incredible in person. The double emotion of "pretending to be happy but devastated inside" was flawless. That high E at the ending was F-ing incredible. OMG. . . It sounds so freaking effortless. The obsessing was definitely worth it guys.
—BelleOfTheBand, www.witchesofoz.com, April 2006

Near the end of the January 9, 2005, Broadway performance of *Wicked*, Glinda the Good Witch (then played by Jennifer Laura Thompson) floated twenty feet above the stage in her steel orb "bubble," ready to accept her position as the new governor of Oz. Fiyero (Joey McIntyre), now the Scarecrow, knocked on a trap door in the Gershwin Theatre's stage floor to alert Elphaba (Shoshana Bean), the Wicked Witch of the West, who had faked her own death, to come out of hiding. Instead of the trap door opening and Elphaba/Bean's head appearing, though, a different actress, Idina Menzel, walked slowly and gingerly from the wings onto the stage, decked out in a red Adidas warm-up suit and red sneakers. The actor, Menzel, who originated the role of Elphaba when the musical opened in 2003, had been injured during the previous day's performance when the elevator beneath the stage into which she "melts" near the end of the show during her faked death dropped early, and she fell and broke a rib. While few stage injuries are newsworthy, this one got coverage in the New York Times and by the Associated Press in part because Menzel, who had achieved considerable fame in the role, was to have appeared as Elphaba for the last time on that January night.[1]

Those in the audience who had come especially to see Menzel's final performance that evening may not have seen her play Elphaba, but they got what they paid for. As Jesse McKinley wrote in the New York Times, "She wasn't in costume, she wasn't in makeup, and she wasn't even in character." But as soon as Menzel entered from upstage left, the audience went wild. He described a standing ovation "like few you've ever seen: a screaming, squealing, flashbulb-popping explosion that was equal parts ecstatic hello and tearful goodbye." The performance was completely halted by "this outpouring of love," with only a few lines of dialogue and a half-verse of a song remaining in the show.[2] Finally, after much grinning and stammering from the actors, Thompson picked up her cue, "Fellow Ozians," and then shouted, "I love you, Idina Menzel!" The crowd erupted again, but soon Thompson and Menzel continued, spoke their actual lines, and sang the last few phrases of the show together in harmony.[3]

That Menzel's final performance "as" Elphaba was actually as "herself"— dressed in typical urban gear, her dark hair pulled back in a ponytail, her shoulders slouched (perhaps unconsciously guarding her taped ribs)—was at once wholly accidental and entirely appropriate to this musical, this role, this performer, and especially to her ardent fans. Unlike other Broadway shows that might want to preserve the illusory world of the musical, Wicked revels in spilling outside of its frame to frankly acknowledge the passionate girl fans who sustain it. Menzel's appearance proved to her fans that she was okay and that she cared enough to say good-bye in person. It also heightened her value as a star-diva in her very extraordinary ordinariness—in the vulnerability of her previously belting body.[4] Then, when Thompson broke character, she and Menzel demonstrated their affection for one another, making their relationship real and believable, and stressing how, in spite of Elphaba's final departure with Fiyero, the show, as the previous chapter demonstrated, is really about these two women as a couple. At the curtain call, with two Elphabas on stage— one in greenface and Wicked Witch costume and one not—the performance anticipated its future: that the musical as of this writing in summer 2010 continues its run with more, other Elphabas and more Glindas, each of whom gathers a huge fan following.[5] This moment thus encapsulated the three aspects of the diva figure who stars in this chapter: the diva as character; the diva as celebrity; and the girl fan herself as diva. Here I return to Menzel, whose Tony Award–winning performance opened this book.

Wicked's astonishing commercial success, discussed in the previous chapter, means that it must attract a wide range of spectators. Anyone with some knowledge of the show is aware of its cult status among tween (preadolescent) and teenage girls.[6] In June 2005, less than two years after its Broadway opening, for example, a *Los Angeles Times* journalist noted that the only way you could not know about the musical *Wicked* would be if you "haven't been following Broadway or living with adolescent" girls.[7] A month later, *New York Times* critic Jason Zinoman wrote disparagingly that *Wicked*'s "popularity among teenage girls borders on the religious."[8] On the evening of Menzel's last scheduled performance, Jesse McKinley noted the crowds of girls waiting outside the theatre to see if she would perform despite the accident. As one high-school-age, aspiring actress said, "I had to be here. I wanted to say goodbye to Idina."[9] Every local review of the first touring production, including those in the *Washington Post*, the *Pittsburgh Post-Gazette*, the *Boston Globe*, the *Atlanta Journal-Constitution*, and the *Cleveland Plain Dealer*, commented on the scores of girls—typically described, in time-honored pejorative tradition as "screaming"—in the audience.

When *Wicked* opened in October 2003, critics who did not like the show used girls' fandom to justify their own negative appraisal, arguing that girls, who could not distinguish between good and bad theatre, were the obvious intended audience for the silly show. Then, by fall 2005, when the musical's success was ensured, journalists began to credit the producers with the foresight to target girls as an impressionable fan base who would seed a much larger audience. A year later, in 2006, with the musical's popularity still growing, coverage attempted to establish that in fact girls were actually inconsequential to *Wicked*'s success. The critics, who then claimed to appreciate the show, and the producers stressed the musical's "universal appeal" and disavowed any notable relevance to girls' lives. In all these characterizations of girl fans, they are portrayed as cultural dupes, their tastes fickle, easy, and undiscriminating, and their presence and loyalty ultimately irrelevant.

The media's representation of girls as poor judges of culture, especially popular music, goes back at least to the mid-twentieth century, when middle-class youth as a generation emerged as an identifiable audience segment with disposable income that producers could target. In the early 1960s, for example, photographs of and quotations from the Beatles' female fans, whose display of erotic energy transgressed boundaries of appropriate femininity at the time, allowed journalists to write them off as hysterical and immature.[10] In the mid-to-late 1990s, music critics portrayed fans of the teenybopper group the Backstreet Boys as silly and weak.[11] Historicizing the devaluation of girls' tastes shows how categories of cultural worth are highly gendered, thereby contesting the media's negative, demeaning characterizations of girls as easily fooled, as unreliable, as possessing bad and fickle taste.[12]

When girl fans of *Wicked* expressed themselves, though, they appeared as anything but cultural dupes.[13] This chapter considers Internet fandom from 2004 to 2006, a period during which *Wicked* played on Broadway and in Chicago and was on its first round of a national tour; that is, when the audience was still relatively limited. This period predates *Wicked*'s extraordinary global visibility and its expansive Internet presence. This case study examines a circumscribed time period, and its subjects are enthusiastic "early adopters."

On the many fan websites for *Wicked*, including www.wickedonbroadway. net, www.witchesofoz.com, www.musicals.net, and www.verdigris.com,[14] self-identified girls between the ages of twelve and twenty dominate the discussions.[15] However critics might disregard (or regard with condescension) girls' tastes, *Wicked* fans clearly feel empowered by the musical and by their relationship to it.[16] As active, perceptive spectators, they debate interpretations of moments in the show and analyze performances of different actors in minute (admittedly sometimes excruciating) detail.[17] As fans whose interests extend outside of the three-hour performance frame, they share strategies for getting an actor's autograph and post pictures from their trips to New York.[18] Finally, as aspiring performers themselves, they solicit advice for an audition number and describe their dreams of performing on Broadway. Girls' distinctly homosocial fandom extends well beyond spectatorship, as they create their own performances—songs, poems, stories, and artwork on fan websites, at *Wicked* singing contests, and even in *Wicked* yoga classes. These fan practices coalesce around the icon of the diva.

Girls' attraction to *Wicked* has everything to do with the musical's representation of divas—both the characters and the actors—and that these divas are fundamentally nonnormative and nonheterosexual; that is, queer. In this chapter, I turn my attention to reception and fandom, specifically around the figure of the diva. This chapter explores girls' attention to *Wicked* as articulated on fan websites in order to examine what girl audiences *do* with the musical, and more specifically, what they do with the musical's divas. By taking girls seriously as participants in culture, I aim to revalue their fandom and to demonstrate the pleasurable productiveness of queer divas on the Broadway musical stage.

A word about method, which is unique to this chapter: Fan cultures of the twenty-first century, perhaps especially youth fan cultures, are easily accessible on websites, fansites, home pages, Facebook, Twitter, and Web-based discussion boards. The plethora of sites for fans' self-expressions are valuable sources to understand reception, but such handy and plentiful (read: overwhelming) material begs analysis.[19] Although exploring fan websites cannot unlock the complex mystery of musical theatre reception, it can reveal some clear patterns of use, engagement, and utterances of feeling. As sociologist Valerie Hey writes, "[D]espite their individual mode (in the form of feelings, subjectivities, emotions, memories)," everyday knowledges are "intimately related to dominant and systematic features of social life."[20] Girls who post on fansites perform their spectatorship and their fandom. Rather than proving something scientific about *Wicked*'s fans, each example works like a newspaper review: at once idiosyncratic and yet typical and revealing of its moment. Also, these examples focus only on selected topics of Web discussion that deal with identification and affiliation with the musical, which only constituted a tiny fraction of girls' conversations about *Wicked* on the Web from 2004 to 2006.

The Stage, the Cast Album, the Bootleg Video: The *Wicked* Diva as Character and Actor

The diva character is a mainstay of musical theatre. From Mama Rose (*Gypsy*) to Dolly Levi (*Hello, Dolly!*), from Fanny Brice (*Funny Girl*) to Sally Bowles (*Cabaret*), the strong, unique woman with a powerful voice, whom this book has examined, appears regularly on the Broadway stage. "Larger-than-life," divas are "imposing, spectacular women stars."[21] According to John Clum in *Something for the Boys*, "Feminine assertiveness and survival are hallmarks of a diva."[22] Describing performers like Barbra Streisand and Liza Minnelli, Clum writes that their "toughness comes out of performance, which is often a triumph over personal limitations or disaster."[23] For Clum and other scholars of musical theatre and opera, the diva, the extraordinary woman, often emerges from the conjunction of an "ugly" exterior and a beautiful, powerful voice—an accurate appraisal of *Wicked*'s Elphaba. Brantley sees Elphaba as "a Broadway archetype: the unprepossessing, unlikely creature transformed into a powerhouse whenever she sings."[24] As *Wicked*'s producer Mark Platt said, "[I]n a stage musical, you can turn to your audience and sing to them exactly what you're feeling."[25] The diva is exuberantly self-expressive.

The diva's excessive, performative display of self refutes the limits of femininity even as her voice and body are insistently female. She exhibits "transgressive excess," as Susan Leonardi and Rebecca Pope put it. In *The Diva's Mouth*, their feminist, lesbian study of literary representations of divas, Leonardi and Pope stress how the diva is not only a powerful singer and a striking presence but, more than that, "she has a loud voice in the public world," and yet "she is presented as intensely feminine." As they assert, "Divahood is ever a gender disorder."[26] In *Wicked*, both Elphaba and Glinda trouble presumptions of hetero-femininity. While Glinda performs the quintessential alpha girl who flips her hair, flirts with boys, and values popularity above all else, the character is so over the top that she sustains a critique of those behaviors even as she plays them out. Moreover, in *Wicked*'s second act, Glinda's values shift and she learns the importance of loyal and close female friendship, while she also becomes, as a single woman, a public leader.

Wicked reinvents the Broadway diva for the twenty-first century and for twenty-first-century girl fans. While drawing on well-established conventions of musical theatre that I discussed in the previous chapter, the show injects a contemporary sensibility that transforms the typical Broadway diva from a larger-than-life force to an everyday girl. By presenting an ordinary personality in an extraordinary singer, *Wicked* invites young female spectators' identifications and attachments. Glinda and Elphaba experience the typical challenges of adolescence—of identity formation, of social acceptance, of success, of loneliness, of loyalty and the challenges of friendship—all issues to which girls readily relate.[27] Yet it is the practice of performance that truly confers divadom in *Wicked*. Each character sings and the actor who plays her sings. Whatever the situation in the musical itself, the performer transcends that place through singing. Whatever the problems of the character's life, the performer makes the character into a heroine. Audiences assimilate these layers of performance at once; this is the pleasure of musical theatre. Girl fans' discussions of *Wicked*'s divas demonstrate the ease with which they move among analyzing these characters, relating to them, and performing the diva themselves.

INTERPRETING THE EVERYDAY DIVA

Girl fans first approach the diva through interpreting her character.[28] They see how Glinda performs the diva who always plays to her audience—from the awestruck citizens of Oz to her giggly entourage of school chum fans to the crowd that cheers her brash imitation of Evita (as one girl fan complains knowingly, "Why does no one ever get the Megan [the actor, Megan Hilty]/Evita pose; I think it's hysterical").[29] In the Jerry Herman (Dolly Levi, Mame) tradition, she is a cheerful meddler.[30] Her solos are funny and character oriented.

Even as fans observe Glinda's sparkly gown, blond curls, and her frequent, hilarious malapropisms, they read her as an everyday girl, and they judge her accordingly. On one thread, for example, they look closely at her troubling self-centeredness. Is she wicked? they ask. ElphieatShiz replies, "Glinda is kind of Wicked at the beginning when she's thinking of herself."[31] Another fan complicates the discussion by asking, "[I]s Wickedness really the same as selfishness or vainness or shallowness?"[32] The discussion expands: "I think Galinda is the Wicked one. Wicked is not the same as evil. Galinda's a little b*tch."[33] Finally, ChancetoFly quotes the libretto:

> The whole point of the show is essentially what Glinda says in the beginning, about people being born Wicked, or having Wickedness thrust upon them. Elphie, for all her good intentions, made some mistakes that contributed to the propoganda that she was, in fact, evil. On the other hand, the "good" characters, like Glinda, have evil in them as well.

She concludes that "for however good we may profess to be, we are ALL Wicked."[34] On this thread, fans parse out details of characterization, interpret the musical's meaning, and think through a range of bad behaviors that are relevant to their lives. Through their debate, the girls build on each other's comments, cementing an intellectual and ethical community.

While Glinda embodies the diva's excesses (all the while parodied), Elphaba typifies Broadway's traditional diva: she is the dark, alto outsider who sings the musical's well-known belting numbers, "The Wizard and I" and "Defying Gravity."[35] She breaks the rules and is condemned for her strength and determination. Unlike many earlier diva musicals, though, in which the protagonist ends up alone at the end—*Funny Girl*, for example, and *Sweet Charity* and *Cabaret*, which were explored in chapter 2—Elphaba gets the man (although this plot point is much less significant than the fact that she and Glinda still love each other at the end). Her awkward outward "difference," her green skin, signifies her internal difference, her sensitivity, awareness, intelligence, and both render her sympathetic to almost all girl fans. As one writes, "[S]he's trying so hard to act like she's a strong person, even though deep down inside she wants to be like everyone else more than anything."[36]

In one discussion of Elphaba, fans debate key elements of her character through a discussion of the meaning of her cry at the end of "Defying

Gravity"—the belting number that ends act 1 with Elphaba flying over the crowd in a prism-like shaft of light, broomstick in her hand. As they analyze possible readings of this intensely emotional, diva-like sound, they point out what they see as her essential traits. "I think it's Elphaba's way of saying, 'I'm not afraid,'" Emeraldgreen writes.[37] Another suggests, "I always thought of it as part of her laugh," adding, "I also agree that it can be a symbol/sound of rage."[38] DareToDefy writes that she thought it meant, "I'm in the moment, and it's awesome."[39] Pianist391 compares different performers' versions of the cry: "Each actor so far has had a different interpretation," from "a fierce yell of frustration" to "a more determined Elphaba, like yelling 'bring it on!'" and finally, "a more a regretful but still determined feeling like 'things will never be the same' sort of thing."[40] This is the moment in the show when Elphaba asserts her independence and cements her public identity as "wicked." As girls interpret the cry's meanings, they inevitably think through the emotional and social implications of such independence and anticipate Elphaba's social ostracism. At the same time, they notice and admire each actor's performance choices as choices, assigning the actor agency and independence. In this moment, the diva as character and diva as actor collide, as girl fans project self-possession onto Elphaba/actor as she sings the last notes of act 1.

Because fans interpret characters through the lens of contemporary assumptions about acting, psychology, and interiority—even in musical theatre—they value the diva who, like them, grows and changes, and they appreciate the actor who can represent that change realistically and convincingly. Threads that address these issues typically ask what is unique about a specific actor's performance, and most sites feature at least one thread for every woman who has played the leads. One fan praises Julia Murney as Elphaba: "i love how she uses this almost kiddy voice in act 1 and then act two she brings out her real voice her real deep real gut of a voice."[41] Eileeno671 adds, "She shows a great difference between the younger, nicer Elphaba and the older, angrier Elphaba."[42] On an emotional level, girls are sensitive to the difference between youth and adulthood. On a performance level, they readily perceive the actor's labor in making the transition legible in performance. Another explains, "When [Julia] is on stage working her magic, she's not only acting her role as Elphaba, but playing her role as a storyteller, revealing Elphaba's life story."[43] This fan astutely notes the metanarrative of the musical, and the difference between the actor's different modes of performance: becoming a character versus foregrounding a role that comments on that character.

On a similar thread, fans describe Kendra Kassebaum's portrayal of Glinda, praising the actor while providing details of what girls think this diva should be. One explains, "She's incredibly hilarious and gives the young Galinda just the right amount of humor, but then in act II she completely turns around and makes Glinda warm and touching."[44] Wicked4Ever observes, "I love the way Kendra plays up the perkiness, bratiness, even the innocence of Galinda in act one. [T]he whole of the 'Popular' scene reminded me of early Carol Burnett, in that she was also very physical with her comedy. She did an amazing job of showing Glinda's growth in act two, making her more mature and venerable."[45] Fans notice the specific components of a performance: the actor's comic skill. They are also invested in Glinda's aging process, in her transformation to a more likeable character, which is an extremely important attribute to them.

IDENTIFYING WITH THE EVERYDAY DIVA

Despite the fact that *Wicked* takes place in a fantasy world and that the characters are witches, girl fans relate to the characters as if they are real people in their worlds.[46] The question "Which character in *Wicked* is most like you?" is one of the busiest threads on every fansite. Girls in a life stage of intense identity formation embrace the opportunity to explain themselves through their conscious identification with a character. In *Star Gazing*, her study of female fans of 1940s and 1950s women film stars, Jackie Stacey identifies four increasingly intense stages of fan attachment: emotional affinity ("a loose attachment to the star"), imitation (using stars as role models for appearance or behavior), projection ("processes whereby the audiences' identities become bound up" with those of the stars outside of the performance context), and identification ("intense pleasure of taking on the identity of the star" while watching the performance).[47] Girl fans of *Wicked* negotiate all these levels of connection, except the first (if they are fans participating on a website, they already have more than a "loose attachment"). These young fans use the diva to navigate daily life, to understand themselves better, and to feel confident in themselves. As Stacey writes, "The match or mismatch between self and ideal is constantly reassessed by female spectators."[48]

Not surprisingly, most girls identify with Elphaba, naming similarities to themselves such as being a good student, a bookworm, insecure, sarcastic, realistic, outspoken, fatalistic, dorky, being an outsider, not being pretty, and into animal rights and social rights. As lizziemae7 explains, "I feel I am a lot like Elphaba, especially in her lyric, 'this weird quirk I've tried to suppress or hide is a talent that could help me meet the Wizard.' I have always felt like there was so much of me that was hidden and tucked away, for fear of being too much."[49] At the same time, these girls are well aware that identifying with the character who has a hard time also aligns them with the quintessential diva, the singer of big, belting songs of self-determination and self-celebration.

A number of girls say that they are like Glinda, pointing out how she is popular, perky, bubbly, clueless, bouncy, and girlie, likes pink, is conscious of hair and clothes, wants to help people, and is, of course, blond. Because Glinda might not be taken seriously, many of the girls who claim to be like her also explain her character more complexly. One explains that "she wants popularity, power, to be loved. But then she isn't as happy as she thought she would be once she does get all those things. Unfortunately, she figures it out too late and the damage has already been done so she is left to carry on alone, which ultimately makes her one of the show's more tragic characters."[50] Another, galinda724, writes that Glinda "puts on a bright face every day, goes out and acts happy, when inside shes hurt, and confused, and crying, and yes—misunderstood, people think she's snobbish, but really thats just the only way she knows, and thats a lot like me too."[51] Girls are trying to balance social pressures and emotional desires, to find a place for themselves. They are acutely aware of their appearance in the world, sensitive to imagining how others perceive them. Pam Gilbert and Sandra Taylor write about soap opera viewing that "girls' real life and fantasy worlds merge and allow them to rehearse conflicts and problems which they experience in their lives."[52] Glinda becomes a model against which to measure themselves.

DOUBLE DIVAS, OR THE QUEER DIVA COUPLE IN *WICKED*

Wicked is structured like a queer 1950s Rodgers and Hammerstein musical, as the previous chapter demonstrated. It follows many narratological and musical conventions of the "golden age" musical but places two women as the central couple. Like the heterosexual couples of mid-twentieth-century musicals, Glinda and Elphaba begin as enemies and competitors, opposites in voice and temperament. Constructed as a butch-femme couple, they eventually merge vocally through the show's numerous duets. By the end, they express their love for one another and promise eternal commitment in "For Good," as they sing, "Who can say if I've been changed for the better? Because I knew you, I have been changed for good." In this duet, they cross voice parts: Glinda sings alto, Elphaba sings soprano, and they finish the song together on middle C. *Wicked*'s very project is double divadom.

In addition to presenting a queer, feminist musical, *Wicked* confounds the typical representation of the diva as singular by valuing both women and their choices, and by using their relationship to structure the narrative. Neither witch is punished, so the musical also differs from many representations on film and TV of girls, in which the alpha girl gets her comeuppance.[53] Here, they both get something that they want—but, importantly, not everything.

These double divas offer several important entrees for girl fans. First, they allow girls to identify with both Elphaba and Glinda, selecting aspects of two very different characters and two very different actors who play them. For example, many girls claim to be like Elphaba, but with "G(a)linda moments." And many say they are a "mix"of both Elphaba and Glinda; as one writes, "I'm very outgoing and perky. Also very comical. Also, when I hear Galinda talk and see her faces, I'm reminded so much of myself. But I'm also like Elphie because, I care about the world and human rights. And I'm VERY sarcastic and sometimes a bit awkward."[54] Wickedelphie1121 explains, "im more elphie because im really into school and people sometimes dont understand me and come too quick to judge. but im a galinda because im really perky and i love girlie things like pink and shopping and makeovers and all that kind of stuff so i'd have to say im a mix!"[55] Girls' self-assessments touch on issues of appearance, preferences, relationships, and how they see themselves in the world. The presence of two divas encourages girls to imagine a complex, even contradictory subjectivity. In addition, girl fans frequently note how they see themselves and their best friends in the two divas. Like Elphaba, one girl explains, "I'm shy, a bit dorky. And, as I'm sure many people have said before, I have a friend who is popular, perky, outgoing, and she has just recently dyed her hair blonde, so I call her Galinda."[56]

In addition to enabling a complex identification, the double diva narrative values and makes public the story of lasting love between women. With their ups and downs, breakups and reconciliations, each woman defines herself in relation to the other, and they are together—emotionally if not physically—at the end. This structure mirrors that of heterosexual couples in most Broadway musicals as well as real-life friendships between adolescent girls. On a thread that asks about favorite moments in the show, many examples were scenes in which Elphaba and Glinda express affection for each other. One notes "the beginning, when the Ozians are singing 'No one mourns the Wicked,' etc. and Glinda's up on her bubble, she looks like she wants to bawl her eyes out."[57] Elphie likes the school dance scene "when Ga goes to do the Elphie dance with El." In that moment, Galinda knows that she behaved badly toward Elphaba, and she leaves Fiyero to join Elphaba's solo dance. Their modern pas-de-deux is intimate and erotic. "Love it!" she concludes.[58]

Other fans make explicit connections between what they experience during the performance of the women's relationship and how they translate it to their lives; for example: "The last moment that G(a)linda and Elphie share together in FG ['For Good'], my best friend and I were holding each other, tears streaming down our cheeks. The thought of separating is too painful to think about."[59] One explains how the song "For Good" "really rung true to my own experience of parting ways with a friend. The whole idea of a relationship where you must be pulled apart not being a wasted relationship was very clear, and very true. I was shaking. I tried to absorb as much of the actual song as I could, but they pushed me to focus inwardly. It's such a strong, heart-breaking song."[60] The representation of the divas' friendship and its intensity is important to girl fans, and they apply both the message and the affective power of "For Good"—the women's love duet near the end of the show—to their lives. The rare theatrical representation of a close friendship between women, rendered more powerful through music, supports girls' relationships with one another.

The Stage Door: The *Wicked* Diva as Celebrity-Person

Musical theatre relies on a broad, open, face-front performance style, so spectators are always aware that performers are performing. The musical theatre diva, then, is a relational construct whose success depends on both performance and reception; she is both created and sustained through interaction with the audience. Performance is built into divaness, as is the spectator's emotional labor; girl fans are necessary for the diva to be a diva.

The diva is both an on- and offstage phenomenon; she is both the character and the self. On each fansite, girls express admiration for their idol, and virtually every comment on the discussion boards is an intense expression of affection. "[T]here is in fact a long tradition of 'sapphic' diva-worship in the world of opera," Terry Castle observes, "a history of female-to-female 'fan' attachments [that are] intense, fanatical, and sentimental."[61] Similarly, Jackie Stacey's female subjects share "an intense, often homoerotic bond between idol and worshipper."[62] *Wicked* fans are passionately invested in specific performers. They refer to performers by their first names, as if they are all close friends. On a thread about Eden Espinosa, for example, AnaElphieLove writes, "Is this where I get to rant about how much i am IN LOVE WITH EDEN??? Because I tend to do that a lot. Eden will you please come live with me and sing me to sleep every night with the unfinished lullaby? Because that would be amazing."[63] Fansites become spaces that encourage such outpourings of adoration. In a culture in which heterosexualization so dominates a young woman's world, a space that permits homoerotic expression is radical and important, both personally and politically. *Wicked* validates girl fans' attachments to women performers as a legible emotional and social force (whatever the girl fans' present or future sexuality or sexual identification).[64]

The stage door meeting is the ultimate encounter of passion regularly expressed on fansites for each performer. When fans recount their experiences of seeing *Wicked*, their stories are always punctuated by an attempt to see the performers, talk to them, and get their autographs and photos.[65] The stage door meeting has several functions for *Wicked* fans. First, it caps off detailed accounts ("reviews") that they post of the performance attended. While each spectator writes pages and pages that recount and judge every song and scene of the performance, dissect the performances of actors, and measure her experience against her expectations or against other productions of the show, the stage door scene is the required and expected ending. Extending the performance frame after the curtain falls—the cool down, as performance studies scholar and director Richard Schechner would call it—is not really an extension at all.[66] It proves that the spectator was there and saw the diva in the flesh and had access to her. Fans post photos to the site; one girl even provided a link to a four-minute video clip of her stage door meeting.

The stage door meeting ensures that the diva on stage is indeed a diva in life; that is, for *Wicked* girl fans, she is a really nice girl who is also a star. The important markers of "sincerity or authenticity"—requisite star qualities that Richard Dyer notes—are, for *Wicked*'s divas, that she is "cute," "funny," "sweet," and "nice."[67] She accepts gifts and tokens of affections graciously; she enthusiastically engages in conversation; she sincerely asks if the girl wants to be an actress; she gives hugs; she takes pictures. As writteninveggies tells it: "I'm really shy, and I have never stage-doored but Kendra was extremely sweet, and friendly (even though I was probably being really crazy and annoying)."[68] Another writes about Eden: "I told her that it was an amazing show and that she is my favorite beyond favorite Elphie! She was really sweet and nice! And she had her adorable Yorkie dog with her! The dog is also in the pic I got with her."[69]

Finally, the stage door meeting reaffirms publicly the fan's knowledge of the diva, of her performance quirks, of her personality, of her plans to continue with the show or to move on. The girl's status as an "amateur-expert,"[70] which precedes and exceeds this one performance, gives her cultural capital among fans and presumes intimacy with the diva. On one thread, for example, fans argued about Megan Hilty's rumored shyness. In another instance, BelleOfTheBand writes of her stage door experience:

> Also waiting there was this loser who wanted to prove that he knew everything about *Wicked*. So he was talking to these two bimbo girls about how Steph was the first Elphaba, and Kristen taught Ellen DeGeneres to sing "opera" and all this other crap that I TOTALLY KNEW. Oh yes, he was also under the impression that Steph was STILL ON TOUR. *Shakes head* Oy vey I was just sitting there laughing at him under my breath.[71]

This post, one of the more outwardly aggressive on the sites, is also one of the few that mentions a boy. Here the girl positions herself as a good fan, against what she sees as his fake and often wrong knowledge and his inappropriately boastful behavior. She also places herself in opposition to "bimbo" girls—presumably not smart girls, not like her or real, knowing *Wicked* fans. She conveys a proprietary desire to own fandom of *Wicked*, and her exclamation, "Oy vey" links her to Jewishness so resonant with Broadway's divas from Barbra Streisand to Menzel and the other Jewish Elphabas. In contrast, on another thread, one fan asked what others would do if they arrived at the theatre to find Britney Spears playing Elphaba, and everyone answered, scoffing, that they would return their tickets. *Wicked* fans value their own categories of cultural capital, which excludes pop music and pop divas.

A Girl's Life: The *Wicked* Diva as Transformational

The divas of *Wicked* are clear and obvious role models for girl fans and especially for girl performers. Girls' use of *Wicked* extends beyond their spectatorship and analysis of the musical, beyond their adoration of the stars and effort to write to them or meet them at the stage door, to constructing themselves and performing themselves as divas. Jackie Stacey calls this kind of social practice the "transformation of the self," which, for her subjects, included changing their hair or gestures to imitate the style of their idol as well as reenacting scenarios from movies with their friends.[72] Although some *Wicked* fans strive to imitate the divas (one noted after she bought her pink "Popular" T-shirt at the Ozdust Boutique, "Now I'm just like Megan!"), more typically *Wicked*'s divas provide ways for girls to negotiate their own theatrical and personal identities.

While all spectatorship of musical theatre is kinesthetic and active—as song and dance encourage all audiences to tap their toes and hum along—for the young, self-declared musical theatre performers who are the majority of *Wicked*'s online fans, the show is quite literally a script for life. One fansite's monikers of each user includes username, age, gender, and "currently perform-ing in," "currently rehearsing for," and "dream roles." Threads proliferate on which girls engage in lengthy discussions of vocal range, debate about which songs to use for an audition, and share stories of performing songs from *Wicked* for family or at school, often singing duets with their friends. They brag about their school choirs, complain about the musicals performed at their schools where there are not enough big roles for girls and too many parts for too few boys, and frequently observe that they are different from other girls because of their love for *Wicked* and for musical theatre.

Girls identify with the pleasure and power and satisfaction of performing: an ugly, weird, smart, green-faced girl and her blond, perky, surprisingly sensi-tive friend take up center stage and sing and sing. Girl fan performers identify according to the songs they want to sing and the kind of diva they desire to be. Many girls talk about being inspired by the show; for example, "My dream is to work in the theatre, and now with my new role model (Shoshana Bean) I just may be able to pursue my dream. *Wicked* has changed my life in so many ways."[73] Another writes, "When Elphie sung her last note in DG and the stage & house went completely black, there was a moment of silence; my heart skipped a beat, my breath was caught in my chest and my eyes teared up. It was the most incredible feeling in my life. I knew from that moment on that this was what I wanted to do for the rest of my life."[74] Their longing for the diva captures both identification and desire; it is an intensely homoerotic affect that is expressed not as about *having* her but about *being* her. More precisely, girls fall in love with performers not because they want to be them *in toto* but because they want to be them *performing*.

While *Wicked* supports some girls' desire to perform, for others, it actually provides them with the material for their acts.[75] Mary Celeste Kearney, in *Girls Make Media*, argues that girls have too long been seen solely as consumers rather than producers of culture. Girl fans of *Wicked* may begin as spectators (although, of course, they are never passive consumers), but they soon become creators, producers, and artists themselves. One explains, "I enjoy singing and lip-synching to her [Elphaba's] music as an expressive outlet for frustrations of the day and it feels as if it could come from me as a person." She then broadens her ideas to musical theatre more generally. She says she can express "things I don't think I can express to friends or family, and instead, I can act out on stage for people to look inside my soul and maybe see me through my character, as awful as they can be. It's honesty within a character and myself."[76] This girl takes on the song as her own; singing becomes an empowering emotional out-let, both revealing and concealing what she sees as her true self.

As much as girl performers use *Wicked*'s solos to perform as divas alone, they also perform the duets, using the music as a performative and emotional tie to their friends. *Wicked* offers them many choices, since four of the show's musical numbers are female duets—an unusually high number for any romantic couple in a musical, as I noted in chapter 6. Performing a duet moves identification into action, since a girl needs her friend to sing with her in harmony for the song to work. On one post, a girl explains that she and her friend are rehearsing to perform "For Good" at a coffeehouse. She recounts the lyrics, then says, "I can honestly tell you that is how I feel about my best friend. I think the song is rather truthful about the fact that there are people in your life who make you who you are and who change the course of your life."[77] Another says, "To this very day, we still role play as if she's G(a)linda and I'm Elphaba."[78] When girls find themselves and their friends in the divas, and when they perform the duets, the enactment becomes a performative act, the saying-singing is the doing, the thing done. The relationship grows through its practice. The girls also serve as each other's audience. In the singing of duets, as Terry Castle writes, each character-actor gives "voice to her pleasure, to reveal herself on stage, without shame or self-censoring, as a *fan* of other women."[79] Through song, *Wicked* encourages friendship, loyalty, and love between girls. These discussions and real world activities suggest that attending *Wicked* as a spectator is both the effect of and the cause of grander participation in musical theatre culture. Fandom leads to a new performance.

After *Wicked*: Musicals and Girls

In *The Diva's Mouth*, Leonardi and Pope's description of the diva sounds remarkably like that of an adolescent girl. They observe that "divahood is immature, potentially regressive, merely a stage on the way to wifehood."[80] Like divas, teens are passionate, tempermental, demanding; they are both masculine and feminine. And the teen, like the diva, is in process.[81] Judith Halberstam argues that this life stage should be valued, that "preadult, preidentitarian girl roles offer a set of opportunities for theorizing gender, sexuality, race, and social rebellion precisely because they occupy the space of the 'not-yet,' the not fully realized." Moreover, she asserts, girlhood, adolescence, and teenness should not be seen "as stages to pass through but preidentities to carry forward, inhabit and sustain."[82] By the same token, not all teens will grow up to be wives, nor should they.

When *Wicked* brings divas and teens together, they perform a certain queerness by valuing the power of the girl singer, the harmony of female duets, and the love between girl friends. *Wicked's* girl fans legitimate homosocial attachments, create community, and validate each other's expressions of vulnerability. Girls' active fandom and their insightful use of musical theatre should urge critics, scholars, and fellow spectators to take their tastes seriously and to value that space of girl bonding as a queer social practice, not merely a stage to be gotten through, which only exists to lead up to heteronormative adulthood. Girls' writings on the Web adhere culturally; the Web becomes a public-private place for their thoughts and feelings, interpretations and affiliations, expectations and desires, experiences and fantasies. As Anita Harris writes, "The web is simultaneously there and not there. This capacity to be present and absent, public and private, reflects the position of young women today as both too visible and not visible enough."[83] Moreover, when girls shriek and applaud the appearance of the injured Idina Menzel on her final night, or when they wait outside the stage door for Kristin Chenoweth's autograph, they model how to be a musical theatre spectator. By creating an intense relationship with the divas in the performance and with their peers, girls and their responses to and uses of *Wicked* offer hope for the energetic continuation of musical theatre in U.S. culture.

Epilogue: "Changed for Good"

A feminist history of the Broadway musical is one that continues to be written and rewritten by artists, spectators, critics, and scholars, as every new show opens and as every old show is revived. It's a history that takes place on Broadway, of course, and also in theatres across the country eight times a week, in rehearsal halls, workshops, and during the annual New York Musical Theatre Festival, where new musicals are presented in typically barebones formats and may be discovered, as happened with *Avenue Q* (2003) and *[title of show]* (2008).[1] It's a history that takes place, as well, in high schools and colleges, community centers and summer camps.[2] As Lin-Manuel Miranda rapped on the closing night of *In the Heights* on January 9, 2011, "Somewhere chillin' in some outer theater lobby/Some little high school is gonna be playin' Usnavi," and, of course, high school girls will play Nina and Vanessa, too.[3] Each future production of *In the Heights* will hearken back to 2008, to when Mandy Gonzalez as Nina sang a plaintive "Breathe," and Karen Olivo as Vanessa sang an effervescent "It Won't Be Long Now." Ghosts of the actors haunt every performance of the numbers, their voices preserved on the cast album whose first listening provides an initiation for so many fans.

At the end of the first decade of the twenty-first century, it's tempting to turn to the multiple, ever-increasing modes of communication that both buttress and undermine live theatre's force, to wonder how the now almost primitive medium of television, and smart phones that instantly capture and disseminate video, audio, and photographs via Twitter and Facebook affect artistic work, production concerns, and spectating practices.[4] Indeed, as the previous chapter demonstrated, young female fans' engagement with *Wicked* (and of course, other musicals) depended on their access to musical theatre via YouTube and Internet fansites. If Broadway musicals in the 1950s found a mass audience that bought original cast albums and watched stars on the Ed Sullivan Show and Edward R. Murrow's *Person to Person*, today's spectators download cast albums (or individual songs) on iTunes and watch a plethora of TV shows that converse with the musicals, from contest shows like *American Idol* and *Dancing with the Stars*, to reality shows in which actors compete to be cast in stage revivals of *Grease* and *The Sound of Music*,[5] to series dramas that reference Broadway musicals, such as *Friday Night Lights*, *Ugly Betty*, and *Modern Family*. Fox TV's hit series *Glee* quotes the Broadway musical in its tone and style, its weekly guest stars like Idina Menzel and Jonathan Groff, and most fundamentally in its validation, valorization, and celebration of the desire to sing, dance, and bring a musical theatre number to life.

In "The Glee Generation," a 2010 feature story in the *New York Times*, David Kamp observes that "something weird and profound has happened" since the Disney channel aired *High School Musical*.[6] Kamp muses about *Glee*'s surprising popularity and widespread influence—what some commentators call "The Glee Effect"[7]—and attests, "We're raising a generation of Broadway Babies."[8] Noting the hoards of young people who saw Broadway musicals during the 2010 season—including *American Idiot*, with music by rock group Green Day, and the revival of *Hair*—Kamp says that what's different now is that being a musical theatre nerd is cool and socially acceptable. Applications to attend Stagedoor Manor, the musical theatre camp that Lea Michele, who plays *Glee*'s diva, Rachel (and who starred in *Spring Awakening* on Broadway), attended, have risen exponentially. Kamp contrasts new spectators with "the passive, bused-in tourist young people of yore who went to see *The Phantom of the Opera* or *A Chorus Line* simply because it was what one did when visiting New York."[9]

Kamp is right that *Glee* and *American Idiot* attract new musical theatre spectators, but in truth, young fans have always been passionate about what's playing, and fandom is intimately related to whichever Broadway season corresponds to one's coming of age. I will never forget seeing *A Chorus Line* (seven times); my younger sister and her friends wanted to be Annie; my graduate students are *Les Miz* fanatics; and current undergrads know *Wicked* upside down and backward. Moreover, Broadway musical theatre—as a place, as a myth, as a site of performance, as a street of glitter and glitz, billboards and lights and all that jazz—continues to represent the apotheosis of performance for the spectator and fan and the highest aspiration for the triple threat performer. However fans engage with TV and online media, the Broadway musical—the show itself—retains a real live and a real life worth.

For its part, the Broadway musical—on stage in New York City—must contend with the highbrow force of the *New York Times* (commentators and reviewers both), the middlebrow influx of tourist audiences, and the lowbrow intertext of Fox TV. Like all of the musicals discussed in this book, every show converses with its historical context; every show is built from the elements of the form—music, lyrics, script, staging, dance, and design—and on the conventions of the genre that arrange those essentials. Ever striving to reach audiences, to win a good review from the *Times*, and now, to get good buzz on Broadway.com, artists play with these conventions in new ways, find new musical styles and forms, new choreographic vocabularies, and new uses of design and technology to tell new stories and develop new characters, all in dialogue with conventional performance architecture. Every show aims for artistic excellence, critical acclaim, and commercial success.

Long-running musicals complicate how musicals speak to and from their context. The long gestation and development process of a new show means that cultural and social history is threaded through a musical, looped into each choice that resonates anew with each revision and with each new playing. *Wicked*'s intertexts have changed since its first 2001 reading, from the first breath of the show that somehow anticipated the girl-power movement that followed, to its remarkable staying power, which over time has sustained the very feminist perspective that it first tapped into. When musicals run for years, as hits now do, culture and society change around them. New audiences come to the show with changing horizons of expectations, influenced by musical theatre gossip and by daily events, trends, tastes, and fads, as well as by their identities and spectating-interpretive habits.

This book has surveyed musicals from the 1950s to the present, exploring a few shows from each decade in relation to salient issues around gender, each chapter focusing on one convention of the form. While much has changed for women since the 1950s, and while much has changed on Broadway, the conventions of the musical remain. *Changed for Good* understands the musical as a dramatic form—it looks at characters and representations, at what each woman means in the context of the narrative, in relation to other characters, and in terms of the ideological work of the musical as a whole. But it also finds each character and each actor in the theatre. And in many cases, through music and dance and staging and scenography, what happens in the performance contradicts what happens in the dramatic text.

A feminist history of the Broadway musical is an argument and a story, but it's also a method and a perspective. In this way, I hope this book will serve as a jumping off point for future projects that query how gender and genre remain intertwined, how history, culture, and performance stay everbraided. A feminist history needs to keep asking how gender and genre sing a duet. This final section offers a brief sampling of several twenty-first century musicals, gesturing toward an ongoing feminist history of the musical, and suggesting what's changed and what hasn't—for good.

Spring Awakening (2006) reoriented musical theatre's conventions with brazenly anti-integrated, rock-based musical numbers, capitalizing on the powerful, postmodern contrast between a rock-concert aesthetic with the band on stage and a huge chalkboard scrawled with the song titles set upstage, and the nineteenth-century German Lutheran setting of the play on which it is based.[10] Each song is a character's interior monologue, and Duncan Sheik's intense, energetically pulsing score, Steven Sater's ultracontemporary lyrics, Bill T. Jones's abstract, geometric, stamp-filled choreography, and Michael Mayer's clever, economical directing perfectly express teenage angst in a repressive society. *Spring Awakening* won eight Tony Awards, including Best Musical.

The musical's seductive, engaging formal inventiveness is undercut by its conservative presentation of gender roles, which the 1891 Frank Wedekind play (banned in its day) as its source material fails to excuse. Both of the featured girls in the musical, Wendla and Ilse, are identified primarily through their sexuality: Wendla knows so little about sex that, vulnerable to a handsome and smart boy's charms, she unknowingly gets pregnant and later dies during a botched abortion. Ilse is sexually abused—as are other girls in the show—and has found her way to an artists' colony, a place outside of society. She sings the lead in the musical's final, direct-address anthem to life, "The Song of Purple Summer" (recalling *Rent*'s "Seasons of Love"), but remains marginal to the lives that the musical explores. In the end, *Spring Awakening* is an energetically masculine musical, homosocially arranged and homoerotically charged. While it explores masculinity in complex, fascinating ways and is exceptionally entertaining, it relegates women to the sidelines.[11]

American Idiot, also directed by Michael Mayer, with music by Green Day, lyrics by Green Day's lead singer, Billie Joe Armstrong, and co-written by Armstrong and Mayer, roared onto Broadway in 2010, attracting a young, hip audience that knew the music and other adventurous spectators who appreciated a rock album translated into theatre. Like *Spring Awakening*, *American Idiot* hoped to attract young theatergoers, and it succeeded. The show is visually splendid, extravagantly designed by Christine Jones and Kevin Adams (set and lights, respectively, and both won Tony Awards), with a wall of television screens insistently commenting on the action through iconic images and slogans. A few pieces of furniture are rolled in to represent living rooms, bedrooms, a hospital, a hotel, or public meeting places. A tall working staircase on wheels (that is, the kind of unit used to hang theatre lights) is propelled around the stage, transporting actors from openings in the wall to a platform upstage and down again. The design pays homage to *Rent*'s rock-concert-like metal scaffold but replaces the earlier musical's spare brick wall backdrop with a vibrant, even overstimulating array of constantly moving pictures and words.

American Idiot, in the tradition of megamusicals like Webber and Rice's *Jesus Christ Superstar* (1971), *Evita* (1979), and The Who's *Tommy* (1993), was based on an album, Green Day's raucous 2004 attack on suburbia. *American Idiot* follows the adventures of three young men—best friends—who try to make their way after high school. Disgusted and disaffected, they reject their roots, and each takes a different path: one marries his pregnant girlfriend and stays put; one enlists in the military and is sent to Iraq; and Johnny, the central character, goes to New York City to pursue his dream of being a rock star. The actors are the band in the show and the supporting cast also plays instruments, dances in choreographer Steven Hoggett's angry, viscerally grounded style, and portray the other friends, roommates, and strangers they encounter in their lives.

Although the three young men wallow predictably in postadolescent angst, the show's intense energy, much rougher than *Spring Awakening*'s, and its fantastic music and design, are electrifying. Somewhat disturbing, though, is the utter disregard of women in the musical and the lack of critical commentary on the subject. Only one of the women in *American Idiot* even has a name, much less a coherent story line, and all are painfully stereotypical. Heather is the named girlfriend who entraps Will, then eventually leaves him, gets a rock star boyfriend, and in the end, gives him the baby; Whatshername—as she is called—is Johnny's sex and drugs partner (played by the spectacular Rebecca Naomi Jones); and Extraordinary Girl takes care of Tunny after he is injured in the war. Jones gets to sing the lead on "21 Guns," the loveliest song in the show, which expands to a powerful ensemble anthem, and the three women sing a few lines of gorgeous, wrenching harmony, too. But the musical just doesn't care about them. In an article that revisited the show when Armstrong joined the cast in January 2011, Ben Brantley rhapsodized that *American Idiot* is "a potent fable about growing up in a distracted and disappointed America, and how finding yourself can often involve losing yourself, at least for a little while, through the time-honored time killers of sex, drugs and rock 'n' roll."[12] Brantley finds the ensemble "full of the exultation, abandon and frustration of being young,"[13] and to be sure, the women in the cast of *American Idiot* are as committed and as galvanizing performers as the men. But how can a show be said to capture the essence of a generation with no female perspective whatsoever?

Spring Awakening and *American Idiot* (and Monty Python's *Spamalot* [2005]) overtly appeal to male audiences and especially to young men. The Broadway musical has always been nervous about its affiliations with femininity and never more than when costs are stratospheric and every seat needs to be filled. Attracting (straight?) men to Broadway musicals is a badge of pride, just as the owner of the Stagedoor Manor bragged that recent applications from boys have increased dramatically. While I certainly don't begrudge more men seeing Broadway musicals—I value the health and artistic activity of the form above all—I worry about the masculinization of the Broadway musical. *Spring Awakening* and *American Idiot* take us two steps forward and one step back.

Women on the Verge of a Nervous Breakdown (2010) also follows characters who are lost, aimless, and misguided, but the story is outrageous, the style is farce, the music is Latin-inflected Broadway, and the actors are Broadway musical luminaries Sherie Rene Scott, Patti LuPone, Laura Benanti, and Brian Stokes Mitchell. Based on the Pedro Almodóvar film, with music and lyrics by David Yazbek and book by Jeffrey Lane, directed by Bartlett Sher, choreographed by Christopher Gattelli, and with fantastic projections by Sven Ortel, the musical is all about women. Each character is so vibrant that it plays like an ensemble piece. Yazbek said, "It's been a challenge and a delight to write for female characters in this piece, to find their voices."[14] The women sing but they also scream, throw things, ride motorcycles, set a bed on fire, and are suspended at the end of act 1 on trapeze-like swings. While Mitchell's character, Iván, controls the many women who love him and who are on the verge of nervous breakdowns because of him, he is more narratively than performatively significant. *Women on the Verge* is the epitome of a musical that victimizes women in the narrative and celebrates them on stage. John Schaefer, author and host of Soundcheck on WNYC radio, commented that a "rich mother lode of song exists in which a woman tells of her abandonment and woe."[15]

Pepa, the putative protagonist (played by Scott with her typical laid-back, eyebrow-raised ease), is the eye of storm, so she does little besides pine for the unfaithful cad. LuPone plays Lucia, his first wife recently released from a mental hospital, with great verve. But Laura Benanti as Candela, Pepa's friend who is sleeping with and harboring a drug dealer, steals the show with a hilariously mincing walk, exaggerated facial expressions, and perfect comic timing. The actors chew the scenery in a show that isn't a love story at all. The women bond in an absurdist way but none gets (or wants) Iván in the end. Schaefer observes "the strong feminist aesthetic behind so much of Almodóvar's work. Pepa comes to her senses and realizes that Iván is not worth the trouble and sets off to live her own life."[16] LuPone said that the show "strikes a chord with women."[17]

These three musicals are just a glance at recent or current offerings. The wonder of Broadway is that so many shows can all play at the same time in the same neighborhood. Then, they leave the neighborhood and travel across the country, are performed on tour and in repertory theatres, in schools and colleges, community theatres and summer camps, churches and Jewish Community Centers by professional actors, amateurs, and students. These musicals, and all of the ones discussed in this book, form an ever-expanding archive of performance possibilities. Because musicals can be revived and revivified, they offer a living archive, a living, breathing, singing, and dancing archive. And because women are often so central, active, and vocal, a future for feminist musical theatre is certain.

To revisit the title of this book and the echoes (melodies, harmonies, and reverbs) of "changed for good": Permanent change, major change, improvement. The exchange of value, of worth, of meaning, of effect. What's good? What's better? Girls and women empowered over the decades, on Broadway and in U.S. society. And musical theatre's conversation with change. As Nona Hendryx famously sang in her 1983 hit, "Transformation": for women, "Change is the only constant."

Elphaba and Glinda sing, "Because I knew you," affirming their friendship, their interdependency and trust, their knowledge that they change each other. In the performance of the song, they also show that musical theatre is relational, between and among performers, artists, and technicians, and mostly between the performers and the audience.[18] That's been a constant that one experiences each time at the theatre: by going, the spectator is changed for good.

NOTES

Introduction

1. Qtd. in David Cote, *Wicked: The Grimmerie* (New York: Hyperion, 2005). Although *Wicked*'s libretto is unpublished, *The Grimmerie* contains the songs' lyrics and bits of dialogue. Other lines and performance details are quoted from the performance, which I saw many times.

2. Although musical theatre is among the oldest, most popular, and most recognizably "American" forms of U.S. culture, the academic field of musical theatre studies is relatively new. Only in the past ten years or so have scholars begun to analyze musical theatre as a serious art form. *Changed for Good* is only the second book on musicals from an explicitly feminist perspective, the first being my study *A Problem Like Maria: Gender and Sexuality in the American Musical* (Ann Arbor: University of Michigan Press, 2002).

    The earliest books published in musical theatre studies (aside from hagiographies, biographies, coffee table tomes, and encyclopedic surveys), such as Gerald Mast's *Can't Help Singin': The American Musical on Stage and Screen* (Woodstock, NY: Overlook Press, 1987), Joseph P. Swain's *The Broadway Musical: A Critical and Musical Survey* (Lanham, MD: Scarecrow Press, 1990, rev. 2002), Geoffrey Block's *Enchanted Evenings: The Broadway Musical from* Show Boat *to Sondheim and Lloyd Webber* (New York: Oxford University Press, 1997, rev. 2009), and the essays collected in *Approaches to the American Musical,* ed. Robert Lawson-Peebles (Exeter: University of Exeter Press, 1996) and the *Cambridge Companion to the Musical,* ed. William A. Everett and Paul R. Laird (Cambridge: Cambridge University Press, 2002), delineate histories of the form. These texts, whether they study one musical per chapter or offer shorter readings of a number of shows, follow the musical's development chronologically, and feature the composers and lyricists as the primary creative artists. These scholars also privilege the formally integrated musical as the apotheosis of the form, but they trace an important formal, historical trajectory and offer incisive readings of numerous musicals.

    Later studies take a more polemical perspective on the now-apocryphal teleology of how musical theatre rose with Rodgers and Hammerstein, climaxed with either *Guys and Dolls, West Side Story,* or anything by Stephen Sondheim, and fell with Disney and

Lloyd Webber. Mark Steyn's *Broadway Babies Say Goodnight: Musicals Then and Now* (New York: Routledge, 2000) and Mark N. Grant's *The Rise and Fall of the Broadway Musical* (Boston: Northeastern University Press, 2004)—the titles say it all—map out a progress-and-demise narrative. Nonetheless, Steyn offers valuable analyses of specific musicals, and Grant ably historicizes sound design and orchestration, set design, and choreography. Still, whether these books proffer a purportedly value-free history of the form or argue that musicals died when Oscar Hammerstein II died, they neglect to account for gender, for the predominance of conventions as structuring elements of musicals, and, except for Grant, for the contribution of theatre artists other than the composer and lyricist.

Other accounts emphasize musicals in their historical context. Some books, such as the series of decade-organized studies by Ethan Mordden, John Bush Jones's *Our Musicals, Ourselves: A Social History of the American Musical Theatre* (Hanover, NH: University Press of New England, 2003), and David Walsh and Len Platt's *Musical Theater and American Culture* (Westport, CT: Praeger, 2003) use a traditional theatre history approach, making connections between the ideas expressed in each show and the time in which they opened. A chatty survey of musicals after 1977 is Barry Singer's *Ever After: The Last Years of Musical Theater and Beyond* (New York: Applause Theatre and Cinema Books, 2004). Elizabeth L. Wollman's *The Theater Will Rock: A History of the Rock Musical, from* Hair *to* Hedwig (Ann Arbor: University of Michigan Press, 2006) and Jessica Sternfeld's *The Megamusical* (Bloomington: Indiana University Press, 2006) (which is more musicological than performance-oriented in its analysis) focus on subgenres within musical theatre that flourished during specific historical periods. Admirably, many of these scholars, plus Steven Adler's *On Broadway: Art and Commerce on the Great White Way* (Carbondale: Southern Illinois University Press, 2004), Susan Bennett on tourism ("Theatre/Tourism," *Theatre Journal* 57 [2005]: 407–28), Jonathan Burston on the labor of actors in megamusicals ("Spectacle, Synergy and Megamusicals"), David Román on commercial theatre (*Performance in America: Contemporary U.S. Culture and the Performing Arts* [Durham, NC: Duke University Press, 2005]), and David Savran on the musical as middlebrow culture ("Middlebrow Anxiety," *A Queer Sort of Materialism: Recontextualizing American Theater* [Ann Arbor: University of Michigan Press, 2003], 3–55), refuse to apologize for musical theatre's commercial aspirations, and they value audiences' affection for the form.

Identity-oriented studies of musicals are extremely important, too. D. A. Miller's *Place for Us: Essay on the Broadway Musical* (Cambridge, MA: Harvard University Press, 1998), John M. Clum's *Something for the Boys: Musical Theater and Gay Culture* (New York: St. Martin's Press, 1999), and chapters by Alexander Doty, Richard Dyer, David Román, and Michael Schiavi argue for the relevance of musicals to the lives of gay men. Alberto Sandoval-Sánchez's *José, Can You See?: Latinos On and Off Broadway* (Madison: University of Wisconsin Press, 1999), Allen L. Woll's *Black Musical Theatre: From* Coontown *to* Dreamgirls (Baton Rouge: Louisiana State University Press, 1989), Stephen J. Whitfield's *In Search of American Jewish Culture* (Hanover, NH: University Press of New England, 2001), Henry Bial's *Acting Jewish: Negotiating Ethnicity on the American Stage and Screen* (Ann Arbor: University of Michigan Press, 2005), and Andrea Most's *Making Americans: Jews and the Broadway Musical* (Cambridge, MA: Harvard University Press, 2004) foreground musical theatre in the formation of

Latino, African American, or Jewish American identities. While each of these authors situates the musical from the perspective of gender, race, or ethnicity and models excellent analytical methods, none deals with women exclusively, and none finds the building blocks of musicals as a genre utterly inextricable from those identities, as I do.

The analysis of genre that is central to this project finds common cause with scholarship in ancillary fields of literary, cultural, film, and television studies, including for example, Rick Altman's *The American Film Musical* (Bloomington: Indiana University Press, 1988) and his edited *Genre, the Musical: A Reader* (London: Routledge, 1981), Jane Feuer's *The Hollywood Musical* (Bloomington: Indiana University Press, 1993), Linda Williams's work on melodrama and race, John Frow's *Genre* (London: Routledge, 2006), Janet Staiger's recent project on film genres and affect, and Richard Dyer's "Entertainment and Utopia" (*Only Entertainment* [New York: Routledge, 1992]), which categorizes film genres according to their affective and emotional power as well as their ideological work. These scholars provide helpful models, terms, and theories, but because my object of study is performance, which is ephemeral, I necessarily develop different methods of analysis.

This book's most direct influences are Raymond Knapp's two-volume study, *The American Musical and the Performance of National/Personal Identity* (Princeton, NJ: Princeton University Press, 2005/2006), and Scott McMillin's *The Musical as Drama* (Princeton, NJ: Princeton University Press, 2006). Knapp's books are excellently wide-ranging in their subject matter and offer a number of important thematic inroads, especially from a musicological perspective. Knapp's intentionally broad orientation allows him to reference the importance of gender in many musicals. From a different view, McMillin's is the first book to address musicals' formal and aesthetic conventions across time, but he explicates the parts of a musical as nonideological. This book opens a politicized, historicized conversation with Knapp's and McMillin's books to interrogate musical theatre's conventions and how they work from a feminist perspective.

Finally, this book leans on Bruce Kirle's *Unfinished Show Business: Broadway Musicals as Works-in-Process* (Carbondale: Southern Illinois University Press, 2005), which troubles the very idea of an "original production" by demonstrating how the exigencies of production overdetermine what we inaccurately call without qualifiers "the production of a musical." Kirle's book serves a constant reminder of musical theatre's shifting place in history. Susan McClary's *Conventional Wisdom: The Content of Musical Form* (Berkeley: University of California Press, 2001) theorizes the politics of musical conventions over time and in relation to hegemonic assumptions about music and also speaks directly to *Changed for Good*.

3. McClary, *Conventional Wisdom*, 6.

4. Carol de Giere, *Defying Gravity: The Creative Career of Stephen Schwartz from Godspell to Wicked* (Milwaukee: Applause, 2008), 368. For a description of the creation of the number, see 341–42.

5. On musical theatre as commercial enterprise, see Adler, *On Broadway*; Bennett, "Theatre/Tourism"; Savran, "Middlebrow Anxiety"; Savran, "Toward a Historiography of the Popular," *Theatre Survey* 45.2 (2004): 211–17; and Elizabeth Wollman, "The Economic Development of the 'New' Times Square and Its Impact on the Broadway Musical," *American Music* 20.4 (2002): 445–65.

6. In point of fact, in the twenty-first century, a musical can run if the corporation makes a profit. As Jonathan Burston explains, Disney, for example, can make enough money from toys and DVDs to subsidize its Broadway musicals, thus maintaining visibility on Broadway and in the world of live theatre, even if the theatre isn't full. See Jonathan Burston, "Recombinant Broadway," *Continuum: Journal of Media and Cultural Studies* 23.2 (2009): 159–69.

7. See Adler, *On Broadway.*

8. Ben Brantley, "There's Trouble in Emerald City," *New York Times*, October 31, 2003, p. E1.

9. Julie A. Noonan writes, "Vocal quality or timbre is a composite of the characteristics that help distinguish one voice from another. Through a perceptual process, a listener associates a sound with a source referent" (86). See Julie A. Noonan, "Popular Voices: Amplification, Rock Music and Vocal Quality in *Grease*," *Studies in Musical Theatre* 3.2 (2009): 185–200.

10. Richard Rodgers and Oscar Hammerstein II, *Oklahoma!* (New York: Applause Theatre and Cinema Books, 2010).

11. Fred Ebb, Bob Fosse, and John Kander, *Chicago: A Musical Vaudeville* (New York: Samuel French, 1976).

12. Carolyn Abbate, "Opera; or, the Envoicing of Women," *Musicology and Difference: Gender and Sexuality in Music Scholarship*, ed. Ruth A. Solie (Berkeley: University of California Press, 1993), 254.

13. Sally Banes, *Dancing Women: Female Bodies on Stage* (New York: Routledge, 1998), 9.

14. Banes, *Dancing Women*, 10.

15. Lehman Engel and Howard Kissel, *Words with Music: Creating the Broadway Musical Libretto*, (1971) rev. ed. (New York: Applause, 2006), 113.

16. Most musical theatre histories begin by tracing the form's antecedents in operetta, vaudeville, minstrelsy, and burlesque. See, for example, Knapp, *National Identity.*

    The labeling of "the golden age musical," as well as the "integration" narrative, are ubiquitous in musical theater historiography, even as some scholarship strives to refute these historiographical, formalist assumptions. Still, most scholars see Jerome Kern, Hammerstein, or the team of Rodgers and Hammerstein as the key players in the form's development. See, e.g., Block, *Enchanted Evenings*, 19–23; Grant, *The Rise and Fall of the Broadway Musical*, 30–34; Jones, *Our Musicals, Ourselves*, 123–60; Larry Stempel, "The Musical Play Expands," *American Music* 10 (1992): 136–69; and Thomas L. Riis and Ann Sears with William A. Everett, "The Successors of Rodgers and Hammerstein from the 1940s to the 1960s," *The Cambridge Companion to the Musical*, 137–66. Here, "golden age" signifies a set of conventions, not a value judgment.

17. Alan Jay Lerner and Frederick Loewe, *My Fair Lady* (New York: Signet, 1980).

18. Kern and Hammerstein's *Show Boat* (1927) could be the first formally integrated musical, as Mark Grant, in *The Rise and Fall of the Broadway Musical*, observes: "Kern's melodies—attractive enough to soar yet earthbound enough to be effectively sung on lyric—once tethered to dramatically logical scripts, helped invent the modern book musical" (31). In this book, I use the terms "book musical," "golden age musical," and "mid-twentieth-century musical" interchangeably. The formal quality of integration also became tied to musical theatre's aspirations to be high art and to espouse progressive social messages.

19. See Tim Carter, *Oklahoma! The Making of an American Musical* (New Haven, CT: Yale University Press, 2007).

20. Leonard Bernstein, *The Joy of Music* (New York: Simon and Schuster, 1959), 164.

21. See Bruce McConachie, *American Theater in the Culture of the Cold War: Producing and Contesting Containment, 1947–1962* (Iowa City: University of Iowa Press, 2003).

22. Margaret M. Knapp, "Integration of Elements as a Viable Standard for Judging Musical Theatre," *Journal of American Culture* 1.1 (1978): 114, 112, 115.

23. Greg Kotis and Mark Hollmann, *Urinetown: The Musical* (New York: Faber and Faber, 2003). Directed by John Rando. Also see Anne Beggs, "'For Urinetown is your town ...': The Fringes of Broadway," *Theatre Journal* 62 (2010): 41–56.

24. See Laurie A. Finke and Susan Aronstein, "Got Grail? Monty Python and the Broadway Stage," *Theatre Survey* 48 (2007): 289–311.

25. These distinctions of mode don't apply to the sung-through musical, of course, which uses different theatrical tools to make meaning.

26. Knapp, *National Identity*, 12–13.

27. Miller, *Place for Us*, 3, 57.

28. McMillin, *The Musical as Drama*.

29. This book doesn't deal with female artistic creators of the musical. See Bud Coleman and Judith Sebesta, eds., *Women in American Musical Theatre: Essays on Composers, Lyricists, Librettists, Arrangers, Choreographers, Designers, Directors, Producers and Performance Artists* (Jefferson, NC: McFarland, 2008).

30. See Burston, "Recombinant Broadway"; Wollman, "Economic Development of the 'New' Times Square."

31. Brooks Atkinson, *Broadway* (New York: Macmillan, 1970), 444.

32. Jones, *Our Musicals*, 3.

33. Gerald M. Berkowitz, *New Broadways: Theatre across America 1950–1980* (Totowa, NJ: Rowman and Littlefield, 1982), 167.

34. See http://www.playbill.com/celebritybuzz/article/82428-Broadway-Rush-Lottery-and-Standing-Room-Only-Policies (accessed August 16, 2010).

35. Adler, *On Broadway*, 161.

36. On tourist audiences, see Bennett, "Theater/Tourism."

37. See Kirle, *Unfinished Show Business*.

38. "Behind the Mask: The Story of *The Phantom of the Opera*," dir. Jamie Crichton, Really Useful Films, 2005.

39. See Stephen Banfield, "Bit by Bit: Stephen Banfield Finds Five Ways of Looking at Musicals," *Musical Times*, April 1994, 220–23.

40. Atkinson, *Broadway*, 444.

41. Roland Barthes calls the materiality of song "the grain of the voice," capturing the sense of sung music's tactility. He writes that the grain is imparted in the "very specific space (genre) in which *a language encounters a voice*" (269). Roland Barthes, "The Grain of the Voice," *The Responsibility of Forms: Critical Essays on Music, Art, and Representation*, trans. Richard Howard (New York: Hill and Wang, 1985), 269.

42. Joseph P. Swain, for example, uses the published piano and vocal score as his primary evidence in *The Broadway Musical*. Kirle uses a range of materials and finds it "puzzling" that a scholar would rely solely on any notion of "text" (7).

43. Banfield, "Bit by Bit." Also see Stacy Wolf, "In Defense of Pleasure: Musical Theatre History in the Liberal Arts [A Manifesto]," *Theatre Topics* 17.1 (March 2007): 51–60.

44. John Mowitt, "The Sound of Music in the Era of Reproducibility," *Music and Society: The Politics of Composition, Performance, and Reception*, ed. Richard Leppert

and Susan McClary (New York: Cambridge University Press, 1987), 175. McMillin talks about this aspect of musical repetition, too. See *The Musical as Drama*.

45. See Christopher Small, *Musicking: The Meanings of Performing and Listening* (Hanover, NH: University Press of New England, 1998), 152. Some composers had limited musical training or couldn't play the piano. Irving Berlin famously composed every song in F#. Sondheim, on the other hand, studied with the avant garde composer Milton Babbitt.

46. Grant, *Rise and Fall*, 47.

47. See, for example, Swain, *Broadway Musical*; and McMillin, *Musical as Drama*.

48. Arthur Laurents, Leonard Bernstein, and Stephen Sondheim, *West Side Story: A Musical* (New York: Bantam Doubleday Dell, 1965). Directed and choreographed by Jerome Robbins.

49. See Stephen Sondheim, *Finishing the Hat* (New York: Alfred A. Knopf, 2010).

50. James Bueller, "Music of *Oklahoma!*," lecture, University of Texas at Austin, January 30, 2007. Also see Andrea Most, "'You've Got to Be Carefully Taught': The Politics of Race in Rodgers and Hammerstein's *South Pacific*," *Theatre Journal* 52 (2000): 307–37.

51. Qtd. in William B. Turner, *A Genealogy of Queer Theory* (Philadelphia: Temple University Press, 2000), 135. For gay male studies of the musical, see Clum, *Something for the Boys*; Miller, *Place for Us*; and Alexander Doty, *Making Things Perfectly Queer: Interpreting Mass Culture* (Minneapolis: University of Minnesota Press, 1993).

52. Key sources on women's history and the history of feminism include Ginette Castro, *American Feminism: A Contemporary History*, trans. Elizabeth Loverde-Bagwell (New York: New York University Press, 1990); Deborah G. Felder, *A Century of Women: The Most Influential Events in Twentieth-Century Women's History* (Secaucus, NJ: Carol Publishing Group, 1999); Sara M. Evans, *Born for Liberty: A History of Women in America* (New York: Macmillan, 1989); Susan Douglas, *Where the Girls Are: Growing Up Female with the Mass Media* (New York: Random House, 1994); Jane Gerhard, *Desiring Revolution: Second-Wave Feminism and the Rewriting of American Sexual Thoughts 1920 to 1982* (New York: Columbia University Press, 2001); Ruth Rosen, *The World Split Open: How the Modern Women's Movement Changed America* (New York: Viking, 2000); and William Chafe, *The Unfinished Journey: America since World War II* (New York: Oxford University Press, 1986).

53. Judith Butler, "Performative Acts and Gender Constitution," *Theatre Journal* 40.4 (1988): 519–31.

54. McClary, *Conventional Wisdom*, 9.

55. McClary, *Conventional Wisdom*, 5.

56. To be clear, I'm not arguing for a one-to-one correspondence between musicals and historical context, but musical theatre's commercial drive makes those connections necessary.

57. This book does not work with the source material of musicals (Runyon's stories for *Guys and Dolls*, Gregory Maguire's novel for *Wicked*) and does not compare non-musical adaptations to this version. I am concerned with the time of the original production and how representation and elements of the genre were significant in that period. In this sense, for example, *Cabaret* matters as a cultural product of the mid-1960s and not 1920s Germany.

58. Interestingly and surprisingly, musical theatre negotiated gender, sexuality, and power in ways that were virtually unseen in the explicitly political works of groups

that sought to transform society in other ways—to eradicate racism, to get the United States out of the war in Vietnam, or to change oppressive labor conditions of migrant farm workers. As the writings by and about the women who participated in radical theatre groups as well as those in the Student Nonviolent Coordinating Committee (SNCC) and other political organizations of the Left declare, misogyny flourished there in both rhetoric and practice. Although it would be exaggerating to suggest that Broadway musical theatre enabled the feminist theatres of the 1970s, Broadway musicals in this decade—from *Camelot* to *Cabaret,* from *Funny Girl* to *Fiddler on the Roof,* from *Mame* to *Hello Dolly!*—do reveal a sensitivity toward gender and a curiosity about sexuality that is not evident in more directly political performances. See Stacy Wolf, "'Something Better Than This': *Sweet Charity* and the Feminist Utopia of Broadway Musicals," *Modern Drama* 47.2 (Summer 2004): 309–32.

59. Sondheim created many musicals in the 1970s and 1980s, of course, and a focus on his oeuvre would produce a differently inflected feminist history.

Chapter 1

1. Shaw's *Pygmalion* as the source material in fact provided the plot and characters, but Alan Jay Lerner and Frederick Loewe adapted it to the conventions of 1950s book musicals. What seems an inevitably perfect adaptation was the result of extraordinary labor and talent and probably genius. Rodgers and Hammerstein famously turned down the project, saying that they couldn't figure out how to musicalize Shaw's play.

2. Alan Jay Lerner and Frederick Loewe, *My Fair Lady* (New York: Signet, 1980).

3. Shaw wrote the sequel in response to Gabriel Pascal's 1939 movie version of *Pygmalion,* in which Eliza and Higgins are together at the end. The film was partly the basis for *My Fair Lady.*

4. Wayne Koestenbaum, "Queering the Pitch: A Posy of Definitions and Impersonations," *Queering the Pitch: The New Gay and Lesbian Musicology,* ed. Philip Brett, Elizabeth Wood, and Gary C. Thomas (New York: Routledge, 1994), 1.

5. Qtd. in William H. Chafe, *The Unfinished Journey: America since World War II* (New York: Oxford University Press, 1986), 84.

6. Chafe, *The Unfinished Journey,* 85.

7. Stephanie Coontz, *The Way We Never Were: American Families and the Nostalgia Trap* (New York: Basic Books, 1992), 33.

8. Chafe, *The Unfinished Journey,* 108.

9. George Lipsitz, *Time Passages: Collective Memory and American Popular Culture* (Minneapolis: University of Minnesota Press, 1990), 44.

10. Lipsitz, *Time Passages,* 39–42.

11. Andi Zeisler, *Feminism and Pop Culture* (Berkeley: Seal Press, 2008), 37.

12. See John D'Emilio, *Sexual Politics, Sexual Communities: The Making of a Homosexual Minority in the United States, 1940–1970* (Chicago: University of Chicago Press, 1983).

13. Walter Kerr, "Fresh, Vigorous, Stubborn 'Gypsy,'" *New York Herald Tribune,* May 31, 1959, p. 1.

14. On the history of the cast album, see George Reddick, "Cast Album," *Oxford Handbook of the American Musical,* ed. Raymond Knapp, Mitchell Morris, and Stacy Wolf (New York: Oxford University Press, 2011). On gay male fandom and the cast

album, see Wayne Koestenbaum, "The Shut-in Fan: Opera at Home," *The Queen's Throat: Opera, Homosexuality, and the Mystery of Desire* (New York: Random House, 1993), 46–83; and Michael R. Schiavi, "Opening Ancestral Windows: Post-Stonewall Men and Musical Theatre," *New England Theatre Journal* 13 (2002): 77–98.

15. See http://www.museum.tv/eotvsection.php?entrycode=edsullivans (accessed August 15, 2010).

16. See Tim Carter, *Oklahoma! The Making of an American Musical* (New Haven, CT: Yale University Press, 2007), who demonstrates that much of the language in the press about *Oklahoma!* and its remarkable new form was disseminated by the marketing materials and press releases of the Theatre Guild—that is, the producers provided the language and the critical lens through which audiences experienced the musical.

17. See Rick Altman, *The American Film Musical* (Bloomington: Indiana University Press, 1987).

18. Joseph P. Swain, *The Broadway Musical: A Critical and Musical Survey*, 2nd ed. (Lanham, MD: Scarecrow, 2002), 165–66. Also see Raymond Knapp, *The American Musical and the Performance of Personal Identity* (Princeton, NJ: Princeton University Press, 2006), 264.

19. Scott McMillin, *The Musical as Drama* (Princeton, NJ: Princeton University Press, 2006), 8.

20. Suzanne G. Cusick, "On a Lesbian Relationship with Music: A Serious Effort Not to Think Straight," Brett, Wood, and Thomas, *Queering the Pitch*, 73.

21. Joke Dame, "Unveiled Voices: Sexual Difference and the Castrato," Brett, Wood, and Thomas, *Queering the Pitch*, 149.

22. Dame, "Unveiled Voices," 150, 151.

23. Stephen M. Barber and David L. Clark, "Queer Moments: The Performative Temporalities of Eve Kosofsky Sedgwick," *Regarding Sedgwick: Essays on Queer Culture and Critical Theory*, ed. Stephen M. Barber and David L. Clark (New York: Routledge, 2002), 8.

24. See Jill Dolan, *Utopia in Performance: Finding Hope at the Theater* (Ann Arbor: University of Michigan Press, 2005).

25. Barber and Clark, "Queer Moments," 2.

26. See Peter W. Ferran, "The Threepenny Songs, Cabaret, and the Lyrical Gestus," *Theater* 30.3 (2000): 4–21.

27. Mark N. Grant, *The Rise and Fall of the Broadway Musical* (Boston: Northeastern University Press, 2004), 27.

28. *Guys and Dolls* is frequently explored by musical theater scholars, although few discuss "Marry the Man Today" in detail, as I do here. On the musical's creation, analysis, and reception, see, for example, Ethan Mordden, *Coming Up Roses: The Broadway Musical in the 1950s* (New York: Oxford University Press, 1998), 29–36; Keith Garebian, *The Making of Guys and Dolls* (Oakville, ON, Canada: Mosaic Press, 2002); Raymond Knapp, *The American Musical and the Formation of National Identity* (Princeton, NJ: Princeton University Press, 2005), 134–44; Thomas L. Riis, *Frank Loesser* (New Haven, CT: Yale University Press, 2008), 74–116; and Geoffrey Block, *Enchanted Evenings: The Broadway Musical from Show Boat to Sondheim and Lloyd Webber*, 2nd ed. (New York: Oxford University Press, 2009), 233–47.

29. Brooks Atkinson, *Broadway* (New York: Macmillan, 1970), 348.

30. Mordden, *Coming Up Roses*, 30.
31. Block, *Enchanted Evenings*, 236.
32. Lyrics transcribed from Frank Loesser, "Adelaide's Lament," *Guys and Dolls,* original cast recording, Decca, 1950.
33. Qtd. in Mordden, *Coming Up Roses*, 33. No extant script has been published.
34. Knapp, *National Identity*, 139.
35. Mordden, *Coming Up Roses*, 9.
36. Knapp, *National Identity*, 139.
37. Mordden, *Coming Up Roses*, 30.
38. Lyrics transcribed from Frank Loesser, "Marry the Man Today," *Guys and Dolls,* original cast recording, Decca, 1950.
39. Block, *Enchanted Evenings*, 247.
40. Terry Castle, *The Apparitional Lesbian: Female Homosexuality and Modern Culture* (New York: Columbia University Press, 1993), 235.
41. Mordden, *Coming Up Roses*, 33.
42. Grove Music Online (accessed July 3, 2010).
43. Mordden, *Coming Up Roses*, 33.
44. For a reading of *Wonderful Town*, see Gerald Mast, *Can't Help Singin': The American Musical on Stage and Screen* (Woodstock, NY: Overlook, 1987), 299.
45. Betty Comden, Adolph Green, and Leonard Bernstein, *Wonderful Town: The New York Musicals of Comden and Green* (New York: Applause, 1997), 85–188. Book by Joseph Fields and Jerome Chodorov, original direction by George Abbott.
46. Arthur Laurents, Stephen Sondheim, and Jule Styne, *Gypsy: A Musical* (New York: Theatre Communications Group, 1989).
47. Lyrics transcribed from Richard Rodgers and Oscar Hammerstein II, "The Stepsisters' Lament," *Cinderella*, teleplay, dir. Ralph Nelson, 1957.
48. Lyrics transcribed from Richard Rodgers and Lorenz Hart, "Take Him," *Pal Joey*, Columbia Records, 1940.
49. See Carol Oja, "*West Side Story* and *The Music Man*: Whiteness, Immigration, and Race in the U.S. During the Late 1950s," *Studies in Musical Theatre* 3.1 (2009): 13–30.
50. Arthur Laurents, Leonard Bernstein, and Stephen Sondheim, *West Side Story: A Musical* (New York: Bantam Doubleday Dell, 1965). Directed and choreographed by Jerome Robbins.
51. For critiques of *West Side Story*'s racial politics, see, e.g., Frances Negrón-Muntaner, "Feeling Pretty: *West Side Story* and Puerto Rican Identity Discourses," *Social Text* 63 (2000): 83–106; and Alberto Sandoval-Sánchez, "A Puerto Rican Reading of the America of *West Side Story*," *José, Can You See? Latinos On and Off Broadway* (Madison: University of Wisconsin Press, 1999), 62–82. For a critical response that persuasively recuperates the show, especially on the stardom of Chita Rivera, see David Román, "Comment—*Theatre Journals*," *Theatre Journal* 54 (2002): 325–37.
52. Many critics have analyzed this song and its importance in the show. See, e.g., Keith Garebian, *The Making of "West Side Story"* (Buffalo, NY: Mosaic, 2000), 103–4; Knapp, *National Identity*, 213–15; and Swain, *Broadway Musical*, 3–6, 257–59.
53. Block, *Enchanted Evenings*, 300.
54. Wilfrid Mellers, "The Narrative and Thematic Significance of Music in *West Side Story*," *Readings on West Side Story*, ed. Mary E. Williams (San Diego: Greenhaven

Press, 2001), 75. In a fairly technical reading of the music in *West Side Story*, Mellers explains the key changes in this song: "'Deathly' B flat minor" to "blessed G major to innocent A major, then to the sacral G flat major," and "finally lifting again to G major" (74–75).

55. Richard Rodgers and Oscar Hammerstein II, *The Sound of Music* (New York: Applause Theatre & Cinema Books, 2010). Book by Howard Lindsay and Russel Crouse.

56. Lyrics transcribed from Richard Rodgers and Oscar Hammerstein, *Cinderella*, teleplay, dir. Richard Nelson, 1957.

Chapter 2

1. From http://www.now.org/issues/economic/factsheet.html (accessed August 15, 2010).

2. Todd Gitlin, *The Sixties: Years of Hope, Days of Rage* (New York: Bantam Books, 1987), 14–15.

3. Hilary Radner, "Introduction: Queering the Girl," *Swinging Single: Representing Sexuality in the 1960s*, ed. Hilary Radner and Moya Luckett (Minneapolis: University of Minnesota Press, 1999), 5. By the 1960s, the 1950s assumption that women were pure and valuable only as virgins or as married women no longer held sway.

4. See Beth Bailey, "Sexual Revolution(s)," *The Sixties: From Memory to History*, ed. David Farber (Chapel Hill: University of North Carolina Press, 1994), 235–62; David Allyn, *Make Love Not War: The Sexual Revolution: An Unfettered History* (New York: Little, Brown, 2000); Alice Echols, "Nothing Distant about It: Women's Liberation and Sixties Radicalism," Farber, *The Sixties*, 149–74; and John Heidenry, *What Wild Ecstasy: The Rise and Fall of the Sexual Revolution* (New York: Simon and Schuster, 1997).

5. Bailey, "Sexual Revolution(s)," 244.

6. Allyn, *Make Love*, 21. On the "flight from manhood," see Barbara Ehrenreich, Deirdre English, and Anne McLeer, *The Hearts of Men: American Dreams and the Flight from Commitment* (New York: Anchor Books, 1987).

7. Brooks Atkinson, *Broadway* (New York: Macmillan, 1970), 448.

8. William Goldman, *The Season: A Candid Look at Broadway*, 3rd ed. (New York: Limelight Editions, 1998), 379.

9. Qtd. in Keith Garebian, *The Making of Cabaret* (Buffalo, NY: Mosaic Press, 1999), 136.

10. Carol Ilson, *Harold Prince: From* Pajama Game *to* Phantom of the Opera *and Beyond* (New York: Hal Leonard, 1992); and Gerald Bordman, *American Musical Theater: A Chronicle*, 3rd ed. (New York: Oxford University Press, 2001), 672.

11. On the history of musical theatre and its "demise" in the 1960s, see, for example, Gerald Mast, *Can't Help Singin': The American Musical on Stage and Screen* (Woodstock, NY: Overlook Press, 1987), 290–347.

12. Garebian, *Making of Cabaret*, 19.

13. Garebian, *Making of Cabaret*, 19.

14. Garebian, *Making of Cabaret*, 19.

15. Goldman, *The Season*, 165. Also see William J. Baumol and William G. Bowen, *Performing Arts: The Economic Dilemma* (New York: Twentieth Century Fund, 1966).

16. Although *Billboard*'s top one hundred singles tracked changing musical tastes, LPs of cast albums for Broadway musicals and musical film soundtracks held sway well into the mid-1960s. On the list of top-selling stereo LPs for the week ending January 13, 1963, for example, *West Side Story* was number one. *Oliver!* was number four on the charts before the musical even opened in New York.

17. Altman analyzes film musicals but the same holds true for mid-1960s Broadway musicals. Rick Altman, *The American Film Musical* (Bloomington: Indiana University Press, 1987), 268.

18. Moya Luckett, "Sensuous Women and Single Girls: Reclaiming the Female Body on 1960s Television," Radner and Luckett, *Swinging Single: Representing Sexuality in the 1960s*, 278.

19. Radner, "Introduction," 10.

20. Jane and Michael Stern, *Sixties People* (New York: Alfred A. Knopf, 1990), 9.

21. Radner, "Introduction," 10.

22. Radner, "Introduction," 10.

23. Radner, "Introduction," 16–17. See also Allyn, *Make Love Not War*. (Although on *That Girl*, Ann Marie dated but did not sleep with Don Hollinger, her boyfriend.)

24. Radner, "Introduction," 10.

25. Radner, "Introduction," 10.

26. These characters, of course, are not racially specific. Debbie Allen played *Sweet Charity* in 1986. Thanks to David Savran for reminding me of that production.

27. Eric Wilson, "Naomi Sims, a Pioneering Cover Girl, Is Dead at 61," *New York Times*, August 4, 2009, p. A21.

28. John Bush Jones, *Our Musicals, Ourselves: A Social History of the American Musical Theatre* (Hanover, NH: Brandeis University Press, 2003), 203–5.

29. Luckett, "Sensuous Women," 280.

30. On the history of dance in musical theatre, see Liza Gennaro, "Evolution of Dance in the Golden Age of the American 'Book Musical,'" *Oxford Handbook of the American Musical*, ed. Raymond Knapp, Mitchell Morris, and Stacy Wolf (New York: Oxford University Press, 2011); and Robert Emmet Long, *Broadway, The Golden Years: Jerome Robbins and the Great Choreographer-Directors, 1940 to the Present* (New York: Continuum, 2002).

31. Martin Gottfried, *All His Jazz: The Life and Death of Bob Fosse* (New York: Da Capo Press, 1990), 178.

32. Neil Simon, Cy Coleman, and Dorothy Fields, *Sweet Charity* (New York: Random House, 1966).

33. The movements, said the movie's screenplay writer, Peter Stone, were "based on his wife's form." Qtd. in Gottfried, *All His Jazz*, 192.

34. David Ewen, *The New Complete Book of the American Musical Theater* (New York: Holt, Rinehart and Winston, 1970), 518.

35. Glenn Litton, "Musical Comedy in America: From *The King and I* to *Sweeney Todd*," *Musical Comedy in America* (New York: Theatre Arts, 1981), 291.

36. David Van Leer, "What Lola Got: Cultural Carelessness and Minority Convergence," *The Queening of America: Gay Culture in Straight Society* (New York: Routledge, 1995), 162.

37. Van Leer, "What Lola Got," 161.

38. On the music, see Litton, *Musical Comedy*, 291; and Mark Steyn, *Broadway Babies Say Goodnight: Musicals Then and Now* (New York: Routledge, 1999), 232. On Coleman, see Ewen, *New Complete Book*, 634–35.

39. On Fields, see Ewen, *New Complete Book*, 648–49; and Charlotte Greenspan, *Pick Yourself Up: Dorothy Fields and the American Musical* (New York: Oxford University Press, 2010).

40. Litton, *Musical Comedy*, 291.

41. For details on the musical's production, see, for example, Ewen, *New Complete Book*, 517–19; Gottfried, *All His Jazz*, 176–99; and Litton, *Musical Comedy*, 291. The 1969 film version, also directed by Fosse, starred Shirley MacLaine, as Universal Studios insisted on a big-name movie star for the role.

42. *Sweet Charity*'s opening in January 1966 came less than two years after the Kitty Genovese murder. She was a woman living in Queens, New York, whose murder got national attention because no witnesses—and there were more than thirty who heard her screams—helped her. The event prompted investigation into the psychological phenomenon of the "bystander effect." Although comedic in *Sweet Charity*, this scene resonates with the nightmare of an apathetic, standoffish public and very well might have piqued New Yorkers' not-so-distant memory of the event, which took place in March 1964. Thanks to Aaron Schloff for pointing this out to me.

43. Qtd. in Gottfried, *All His Jazz*, 178.

44. Steyn, *Broadway Babies*, 232.

45. Ann Cvetkovich, "White Boots and Combat Boots: My Life as a Lesbian Go-Go Dancer," *Dancing Desires: Choreographing Sexualities On and Off the Stage*, ed. Jane C. Desmond (Madison: University of Wisconsin Press, 2001), 339.

46. In a differently nuanced reading, Richard Dyer notes that this number is contrived, not spontaneous, since Charity finds real emotional attachment only with women and at work, not in love or romance. See Richard Dyer, "*Sweet Charity*," *Only Entertainment* (New York: Routledge, 1992), 64.

47. Charity's desire to be with "somebody" anticipates Robert's announcement that he wants "someone" by the end of *Company* (1970).

48. Qtd. in Radner, "Introduction," 12.

49. Like the term "integrated musical," the term "concept musical" has its adherents and its detractors. John Bush Jones, for example, prefers the term "fragmented musical." See Jones, *Our Musicals*, 270–73.

50. The 1972 film and 1998 revival make the male protagonist's bisexuality explicit.

51. While the original production—the subject of this chapter—contributed significantly to a transformation of the Broadway musical, both the 1972 film version, directed by Bob Fosse, and the 1998 revival, codirected by Sam Mendes and Rob Marshall and choreographed by Marshall, added to *Cabaret*'s relevance in later decades. Fosse, in spite of his failed directing effort in the film version of *Sweet Charity*, lobbied hard to make *Cabaret* on film, and the result was almost unanimously applauded. Unlike the former film, which mimicked the stage version, *Cabaret* was entirely reconceived, with characters from Isherwood's stories added, all nondiegetic songs removed, and quick intercuts inserted between realist scenes and the cabaret performative commentary. Liza Minnelli played an American Sally Bowles; Joel Grey revived his role as the Emcee. The Isherwood character was renamed Brian Roberts, made bisexual and British, and played by Michael York. After the movie opened, *Cabaret* and the character of Sally Bowles became fully identified with Liza Minnelli, and the title song was one of her signature numbers. Sam Mendes reimagined the show again, setting it in Studio 54, with the theatre audience seated at small tables and thoroughly involved as spectators of the cabaret. Songs from the 1966 production that had been cut for the

film, especially the songs of Fräulein Schneider and Herr Schultz, were reinserted. The aesthetic was heroin-chic, with emaciated, dark-eyed Kit Kat girls and a Sally Bowles not flamboyant like Minnelli but more like a lost child, as she was created by Natasha Richardson. The fact that many strong performers, from Brooke Shields to Ally Sheedy, circulated through the role of Sally during *Cabaret*'s run of more than 2,300 performances and just as many well-known actors followed Alan Cumming as the Emcee underlined how, by the late 1990s, musicals functioned more as detailed conceptual productions than as star vehicles. See James Leve, *Kander and Ebb* (New Haven, CT: Yale University Press, 2009), 35–76.

52. Lotte Lenya, Kurt Weill's widow, who starred in *The Threepenny Opera*, played Fräulein Schneider, and she garnered rave reviews.

53. Ewen, *New Complete Book*, 62.

54. Walter Kerr, "The Theater: 'Cabaret' Opens at the Broadhurst," *New York Times*, November 21, 1966, p. 62; and Walter Kerr, "Today's Musicals: Green Around the Girls?" *New York Times*, December 4, 1966, p. X5+.

55. Joe Masteroff, John Kander, and Fred Ebb, *Cabaret*, (New York: Random House, 1967).

56. Qtd. in Bruce Weber, "Jill Haworth, Original Sally in 'Cabaret,' Dies at 65," *New York Times*, January 5, 2011, p. A21.

57. Qtd. in Weber, "Jill Haworth," p. A21.

58. This number was replaced in the film version with the much more assertive and aggressive "Mein Herr."

59. Before *Cabaret*, Field choreographed *Café Crown* (1964), and after *Cabaret*, he choreographed *Zorba* (1968), and he won a Tony for his direction and choreography of *Applause* (1970), the musical version of *All about Eve*, with music by Charles Strouse and lyrics by Lee Adams, a team that also wrote *Bye Bye Birdie* (1960). Field also directed a revival of *On the Town* in 1971.

60. Qtd. in Svetlana McLee Grody and Dorothy Daniels Lister, *Conversations with Choreographers* (Portsmouth, NH: Heinemann, 1996), 82–83.

61. From http://www.youtube.com/watch?v=N5U9CehM3tQ (accessed August 20, 2009). There is a clip of Haworth performing in the 1967 Tony awards, and while it captures her appearance and energy, it reveals little of Field's choreography.

62. See Jerry Herman, *Showtime: A Memoir*, with Marilyn Stasio (New York: Donald I. Fine Books, 1996); and Stephen Citron, *Jerry Herman: A Poet of the Showtune* (New Haven, CT: Yale University Press, 2004). In 2010, Herman was awarded a Kennedy Center Honor.

63. John Anthony Gilvey, *Before the Parade Passes By: Gower Champion and the Glorious American Musical* (New York: St. Martin's Press, 2005), 116. Herman was among the first musical theatre artists to come out as gay and to talk about being Jewish. *Milk and Honey* was the first musical to represent Jews as Jews on the very-Jewish-but-repressed Broadway musical stage. Herman later wrote *La Cage aux Folles* (1983), the first musical to represent gay men and drag queens.

64. Michael Stewart wrote the libretto and Oliver Smith designed the set, Freddy Wittop the historical costumes, and Jean Rosenthal the lights.

65. Thorton Wilder, preface to *The Matchmaker, Three Plays* (New York: Harper and Row, 1957).

66. Michael Stewart and Jerry Herman, *Hello, Dolly!* (New York: Drama Book Specialists, 1964).

67. In an unfortunate but not surprising twist in the 1960s plot device, Dolly pretends that a fat Ernestina is actually Mrs. Molloy whom Vandergelder intends to marry. Of course he can't, and the fat woman's body becomes the butt of the joke and a plot device that turns Vandergelder toward Dolly (75–76).

68. David Payne-Carter, *Gower Champion: Dance and the American Musical*, ed. Brooks McNamara and Steve Nelson (Westport, CT: Greenwood Press, 1999), 93.

69. I observed the choreography on clips from *Words and Music by Jerry Herman*, dir. Amber Edwards, PBS Home Video/NJN Television, 2007.

70. Payne-Carter, *Gower Champion*, 93.

71. Payne-Carter, *Gower Champion*, 91. Because of his experience working at MGM, Champion enjoyed using props in his staging and choreography.

72. Payne-Carter, *Gower Champion*, 87–89.

73. Payne-Carter, *Gower Champion*, 84.

74. Payne-Carter, *Gower Champion*, 89.

75. For an account of the Merrick-Bailey production, see Allen Woll, *Black Musical Theatre: From* Coontown *to* Dreamgirls (New York: Da Capo Press, 1989), 224–28.

76. Woll, *Black Musical Theatre*, 224–28.

77. Jesse H. Walker, "'Hello, Dolly!' Is Now 'Hello, Pearlie'!" *New York Amsterdam News*, November 18, 1967, p. 20.

78. Jackie Robinson, "Home Plate: 'Hello, Dolly!' Something Else," *New York Amsterdam News*, March 9, 1968, p. 17.

79. Jerome Lawrence, Robert E. Lee, and Jerry Herman, *Mame* (New York: Random House, 1967), v–vi.

80. See Martin Gottfried, *Balancing Act: The Authorized Biography of Angela Lansbury* (Boston: Little Brown, 1999); and Rob Edelman and Audrey E. Kupferberg, *Angela Lansbury: A Life on Stage and Screen* (Secaucus, NJ: Carol, 1996).

81. Lawrence, Lee, and Herman, *Mame*, v–vi.

82. *Words and Music by Jerry Herman.*

83. White also choreographed film versions of *Bye Bye Birdie* and *Oliver!* and she worked extensively with Michael Kidd. She earned eight Tony nominations including *The Music Man*, *Bye Bye Birdie*, and *Mame*, but she never won a Tony. Although there is no Academy Award for choreography, White was honored with an Honorary Oscar in 1969 for her work on *Oliver!*, and the opening sequence with the boys in the orphanage was especially noted. "Obituaries: Onna White," *Variety*, April 18–April 24, 2005, p. 44. Her obituary also noted that she when she started working on *Oliver!*, she reread Dickens.

84. Steven Suskin, "On the Record: Dolly, Oliver, and Tevye Remastered," *Playbill*, June 29, 2003, http://www.playbill.com/features/article/80387-ON-THE-RECORD-Dolly-Oliver-and-Tevye-Remastered/all (accessed June 12, 2010).

85. Howard Taubman, "Theater: 'Oliver Twist' as a Musical," *New York Times*, January 8, 1963, p. 5.

86. "Oliver Twist Sings for His Supper," *New York Times*, December 9, 1962, p. 141, https://libserv7.princeton.edu:82/pul/nph-pul2.cgi/000000A/http/proquest.umi.com/pqdweb=3findex=3d11&did=3d90890467&SrchMode=3d2&sid=3d1&Fmt=3d10&VInst=3dPROD&VType=3dPQD&RQT=3d309&VName=3dHNP&TS=3d1245411417&;clientId=3d17210">https://libserv7.princeton.edu:82/pul/nph-pul2.cgi/000000A/http/proquest.umi.com/pqdweb=3findex=3d11&did=3d90890467&SrchMode=3d2&sid=3d1&Fmt=3d10&VInst=3dPROD&VType=3dPQD&RQT=3d309&VName=3dHNP&TS=3d1245411417&;clientId=3d17210 (accessed June 22, 2009).

87. Taubman, "Theater: 'Oliver Twist' as a Musical," 5.

88. See Howard Kissel, *David Merrick, The Abominable Showman: The Unauthorized Biography* (New York: Applause, 2000), 247–51, 256–59. In addition to discussing Merrick's meticulous work on *Oliver!*, Kissel describes Merrick's long-running feud with reviewer Walter Kerr and his futile attempt to bar Kerr from the production. Kissel notes that the ad for *Oliver!*'s cast album featured not the poster art for the show but a profile of producer Merrick (248).

89. "Oliver Twist Sings for His Supper," 141.

90. Taubman, "Theater: 'Oliver Twist' as a Musical," 5.

91. Tabuman, "Theater: 'Oliver Twist' as a Musical," 5.

92. Taubman, "Theater: 'Oliver Twist' as a Musical," 5.

93. *Oliver!*, script typed and reproduced by L.G. Quinney Ltd London, Donmar Productions, n.d. (first production: New York Imperial Theatre, January 6, 1963). Billy Rose Theatre Collection, New York Public Library, hereafter cited as NYPL. No page numbers on script.

94. Kissel, *David Merrick*, 248.

95. Charles Sinclair, "'Oliver' Fine and Geared to LP Sales," *Billboard*, January 19, 1963, p. 16.

96. Dale Wasserman, Joe Darion, Mitch Leigh, *Man of La Mancha: A Musical Play* (New York, Random House, 1966), vii–viii. Also see Raymond Knapp, *The American Musical and the Performance of Personal Identity* (Princeton, NJ: Princeton University Press, 2006), 180–88; Alberto Sandoval-Sánchez, "Cervantes Takes Some Detours to End Up on Broadway: Re-imagining *Don Quijote* in *Man of La Mancha*," *Cervantes and/on/in the New World*, ed. Julio Vélez-Sainz and Nieves Romero-Díaz (Newark, DE: Juan de la Cuesta, 2007), 179–212; and Mary S. Gossy, "Aldonza as Butch: Narrative and the Play of Gender in *Don Quijote*," *¿Entiendes? Queer Readings, Hispanic Writings*, ed. Emilie L. Bergmann and Paul Julian Smith (Durham, NC: Duke University Press, 1995), 17–28.

97. Wasserman, *Man of La Mancha*, viii.

98. Wasserman, *Man of La Mancha*, viii.

99. Harold Taubman, "Theater: Don Quixote, Singing Knight," *New York Times*, November 23, 1965, p. 52.

100. Atkinson, *Broadway*, 448.

101. See Donnalee Dox, "Constructions of Rape: Two American Musicals," *Frontiers: A Journal of Women Studies* 17. 3 (1996): 210–38.

102. Taubman, "Theater: Don Quixote, Singing Knight," 52.

Chapter 3

1. Michael Bennett, Marvin Hamlisch, and Edward Kleban, *A Chorus Line: The Book of the Musical* (New York: Applause Books, 1995). Book by James Kirkwood and Nicholas Dante. Conceived, choreographed, and directed by Michael Bennett.

2. Bruce J. Schulman, *The Seventies: The Great Shift in American Culture, Society, and Politics* (Cambridge, MA: DaCapo Press, 2001), xi. Also see Beth Bailey and David Farber, eds., *America in the 70s* (Lawrence: University Press of Kansas, 2004); and Peter Carroll, *It Seemed Like Nothing Happened: America in the 1970s* (New Brunswick, NJ: Rutgers University Press, 1990).

3. Julia Sheeres, "Review of *When the White House Was Ours*, by Porter Shreve," *New York Times Book Review*, November 2, 2008, p. 19.

4. Sheeres, "Review," 19.
5. See, for example Bonnie J. Dow, *Prime-Time Feminism: Television, Media Culture, and the Women's Movement since 1970* (Philadelphia: University of Pennsylvania Press, 1996).
6. Qtd. in Ruth Rosen, *The World Split Open: How the Modern Women's Movement Changed America* (New York: Viking, 2000), 284.
7. Tom Wolfe, *Mauve Gloves and Madmen, Clutter and Vine, and Other Stories, Sketches, and Essays* (New York: Farrar, Straus, and Giroux, 1976), 143.
8. Deborah G. Felder, *A Century of Women: The Most Influential Events in Twentieth-Century Women's History* (Secaucus, NJ: Carol, 1999), ix–x.
9. See Ginette Castro, *American Feminism: A Contemporary History*, trans. Elizabeth Loverde-Bagwell (New York: New York University Press, 1990). In 1986, Barbara Ehrenreich, Elizabeth Hess, and Gloria Jacobs wrote that they'd noticed a backlash against feminism beginning in the 1970s: "It was the fear of liberation that helped motivate the antifeminist backlash that began in the 1970s" (200). *Re-Making Love: The Feminization of Sex* (New York: Anchor Press, 1986).
10. Estelle B. Freedman, *No Turning Back: The History of Feminism and the Future of Women* (New York: Ballantine Books, 2002), 313.
11. Andi Zeisler, *Feminism and Pop Culture* (Berkeley, CA: Seal Press, 2008), 81.
12. Thomas Frank, *The Conquest of Cool: Business Culture, Counterculture, and the Rise of Hip Consumerism* (Chicago: University of Chicago Press, 1997), 152–56.
13. Qtd. in Frank, *The Conquest of Cool*, 155.
14. From a larger conceptual vantage point, Scott McMillin discusses what he calls "the ensemble effect" in musicals, by which he means the musical, dramatic, and theatrical tug toward group expression that exists in all musicals but in some more than others. See *The Musical as Drama* (Princeton, NJ: Princeton University Press, 2006).
15. Interestingly, all of these songs refer to a moment in time.
16. Alan Jay Lerner and Frederick Loewe, *My Fair Lady* (New York: Signet, 1980).
17. On directing ensembles or choruses in schools, see Joe Deer, "Directing the Chorus," *Teaching Theatre* 9.4 (2008): 4–11.
18. George Furth and Stephen Sondheim, *Company: A Musical Comedy* (New York: Theatre Communications Group, 1996; lyrics copyright 1971). All quotes from this version of the script.
19. Gerald Bordman, *American Musical Theater: A Chronicle*, 3rd ed. (New York: Oxford University Press, 2001), 723.
20. I've relied on the cast album from the original Broadway production and the 2006 revival, as well as an archival copy of the 1970 version, which I viewed at the Theatre on Film Library at the NYPL on March 11, 2009, and the DVD recording of the revival. I've noted key differences between the versions when they're relevant.
21. Amy Henderson and Dwight Blocker Bowers, *Red, Hot, and Blue: A Smithsonian Salute to the American Musical* (Washington, DC: Smithsonian Institution Press, 1996), 230.
22. The collaborators had a famously difficult time with the last song, and "Being Alive" was Sondheim's fourth attempt at the last song in the show. Three others were written and rejected, two that Bobby sang to Amy and one that was, it was decided, too dark and pessimistic.
23. See David Frum, *How We Got Here: The 70's: The Decade That Brought You Modern Life—For Better or Worse* (New York: Basic Books, 2000), 189–213.

24. See Stacy Wolf, "Keeping *Company* with Sondheim's Women," *Oxford Handbook of Sondheim Studies*, ed. Robert Gordon (New York: Oxford University Press, forthcoming).

25. Rosen, *World Split Open*, 263.

26. On *Godspell*'s production history, see Carol de Giere, *Defying Gravity: The Creative Career of Stephen Schwartz from* Godspell *to* Wicked (Milwaukee: Applause, 2008), 43–66.

27. From http://www.spolin.com/violabio.html (accessed August 9, 2010).

28. John Bush Jones, *Our Musicals, Ourselves: A Social History of the American Musical Theatre* (Hanover, NH: Brandeis University Press, 2003), 282–83; and Elizabeth L. Wollman, *The Theater Will Rock: A History of the Rock Musical from* Hair *to* Hedwig (Ann Arbor: University of Michigan Press, 2006), 94.

29. Of course, interested and well-financed producers could revive the show at any time.

30. Stephen Schwartz, *Godspell*, script notes and revisions by Stephen Schwartz, 1999, i (Schwartz's note on pp. i–v). Also, "Author's Note to the Director," *Godspell*, conceived and originally directed by John-Michael Tebelak, music and new lyrics by Stephen Schwartz, originally produced on the New York stage by Edgar Lansbury, Stuart Duncan, and Joseph Beruh (New York: Music Theatre International, 1971).

31. Schwartz, script notes, ii.

32. Performance notes are from the 1973 Promenade Theatre production, which I viewed at the Theatre on Film Library at the NYPL on March 1, 2009.

33. And it did; "Day by Day" hit number thirteen on the *Billboard* pop singles chart.

34. From http://www.musicalschwartz.com/godspell-notes-from-directors1.htm (accessed April 7, 2009).

35. See http://www.stephenschwartz.com/faq/#q10. Schwartz's comment is in response to a question: "Do we have to dress like hippies in our production of GODSPELL?" Schwartz replies: "No, you do not. The characters in GODSPELL were never supposed to be hippies. They were supposed to be putting on 'clown' garb to follow the example of the Jesus character as was conceived by GODSPELL's originator, John-Michael Tebelak, according to the 'Christ as clown' theory, propounded by Harvey Cox of the Harvard Divinity School (among others). Mr. Cox wrote a book called *Feast of Fools* that goes into detail about this. The chapter that is most relevant to GODSPELL is called 'Christ the Harlequin.' Because the show was originally produced in the hippie era, and because the director of the GODSPELL movie somewhat misinterpreted the characters as hippie-esque, that misunderstanding has come to haunt the show a bit" (accessed August 15, 2009).

36. Exceptions are "Learn Your Lessons Well," "All for the Best," and "Alas for You." One might argue that these are the least engaging songs in the show.

37. As an M.A. student at the University of Virginia, I directed first-year students in *Godspell* and cast African American women as Jesus and John/Judas. The casting only enhanced the message of the musical, I think.

38. Schwartz, script notes, iii.

39. Depending on the theatre architecture, different productions may or may not use environmental staging. The script has many suggestions for moments when the cast might or should go into the audience or engage it directly.

40. I use the term "black" rather than the currently preferred "African American," since that was the terminology of the time. *The Wiz* is consistently described as a black *Wizard of Oz*.

41. See Allen Woll, *Black Musical Theatre: From* Coontown *to* Dreamgirls (New York: Da Capo Press, 1989), 263–66. Producer Ken Harper's papers are housed at the Schomberg Center for Research in Black Culture and there is a Ken Harper file at the Billy Rose Theatre Collection, both NYPL. *The Wiz* was revived on Broadway in 1984 for thirteen performances and by City Center Encores! in summer 2009; see http://www.broadwaymusicalhome.com/shows/wiz.htm (accessed September 11, 2009).

42. Ken Harper file, Billy Rose Theatre Collection, NYPL.

43. Michael Veny, "It Will Kidnap Your Imagination," *New York Amsterdam News*, January 18, 1975, p. D 12.

44. Jones, *Our Musicals*, 224.

45. James P. Murray, "Black Producers May Dominate," *New York Amsterdam News*, August 10, 1974, p. D12. Also see James P. Murray, "Blacks Invade Broadway in a Big Way . . . With Soul Cheers and Society Boos," *New York Amsterdam News*, January 18, 1975, p. D10.

46. Clive Barnes, "Stage: 'The Wiz' (of Oz)," *New York Times*, January 6, 1975, p. 32.

47. Walter Kerr, "'The Wiz' Misses," *New York Times*, January 12, 1975, p. D5.

48. "Special Editorial—Part II: Now, It's the Drama Critics," *New York Amsterdam News*, January 11, 1975, p. D3.

49. Mel Tapley, "The Flame of Extraordinary Talents," *New York Amsterdam News*, January 18, 1975, p. D12.

50. Jessica Harris, "Another View: 'The Wiz' Is Great," *New York Amsterdam News*, January 25, 1975, p. 44.

51. In 2010, producers labored to attract a black audience for the Tony Award–winning *Memphis* by reaching out to church groups and targeting black women in focus groups. Based on the response of focus groups, the producers even changed the tagline on the poster from "The Birth of Rock 'n' Roll" to "His Vision, Her Voice. The Birth of Rock 'n' Roll." Patrick Healy, "Broadway Is Seeing Benefits of Building Its Black Audience," *New York Times*, June 28, 2010, pp. A1, A3.

52. "Theatre Notes," *New York Amsterdam News*, January 11, 1975, p. D8.

53. Thomas S. Hischak, *Through the Screen Door: What Happened to the Broadway Musical When It Went to Hollywood* (Lanham, MD: Scarecrow Press, 2004), 140.

54. *The Wiz*, book by William F. Brown, music and lyrics by Charlie Smalls (New York: Samuel French, Inc., 1974, 1979 [rev]).

55. In a personal interview, Encores! director Thomas Kail remarked on the incredible, multigenerational enthusiasm for the revival among African American audiences.

56. John Lahr, "Toeing the Line: 'A Chorus Line' Is Back on Broadway," *New Yorker*, October 16, 2006, http://www.newyorker.com/archive/2006/10/16/061016crth_theatre (accessed July 6, 2010).

57. From http://tigerweekly.com/article/04-16-2008/8238 (accessed September 11, 2009).

58. From http://www.achorusline.com/achorusline_history.php (accessed September 11, 2009).

59. Ken Mandelbaum, A Chorus Line *and the Musicals of Michael Bennett* (New York: St. Martin's Press, 1989). Also see http://www.thestar.com/entertainment/Theatre/article/523483 (accessed September 11, 2009). There has been extensive litigation over the enormous and unexpected profits of *A Chorus Line*, particularly from the participants in the workshops whose stories were used but who were not cast as actors.

60. Rosen, *The World Split Open*, 196–97.

61. Rosen, *The World Split Open*, 197.

62. Rosen, *The World Split Open*, 197.

63. Donna McKechnie, *Time Steps: My Musical Comedy Life*, with Greg Lawrence (New York: Simon and Schuster, 2006), 108.

64. Common knowledge holds that Cassie was modeled on McKechnie and the relationship between Zach and Cassie echoed that of Bennett and McKechnie, who were briefly married, but in *Time Steps*, McKechnie confirms that some of Cassie's history is hers but that the Zach-Cassie relationship was modeled on Bennett's stormy relationship with a man. *A Chorus Line* predates McKechnie's and Bennett's marriage. See *Time Steps*, 108.

65. McKechnie, *Time Steps*, 107.

66. McKechnie, *Time Steps*, 116–17.

67. McKechnie, *Time Steps*, 119.

68. McKechnie, *Time Steps*, 127.

69. See Alberto Sandoval-Sánchez, "Not Such a 'One, Singular Sensation' for U.S. Puerto Rican Crossovers," *José, Can You See? Latinos On and Off Broadway* (Madison: University of Wisconsin Press, 1999), 83–102; and Stacy Wolf, "Gender and Sexuality," *Oxford Handbook of the American Musical*, ed. Raymond Knapp, Mitchell Morris, and Stacy Wolf (New York: Oxford University Press, 2011).

70. See Elizabeth L. Wollman, *Hard Times: The Adult Musical in New York City in the 1970s* (New York: Oxford University Press, forthcoming.).

Chapter 4

1. The original studio cast recording of *Evita* with Colm Wilkinson and Julie Covington was released in 1976, the original London cast recording with David Essex and Elaine Paige was released in 1978, and the original Broadway cast recording with Mandy Patinkin and Patti LuPone was released in 1979. The show opened in London on June 21, 1978. The show opened in New York on September 25, 1979.

2. Although this practice became commonplace at this time, in previous decades London cast albums, such as *Oliver!*'s (1960), were often released before the Broadway production opened. The idea of the cast album as a souvenir, to create consumer demand to see the show, or as a separate commodity originated with the first cast albums in the 1940s.

3. Qtd. in Foster Hirsch, *Harold Prince and the American Musical Theatre*, expanded ed. (New York: Applause Theatre Books, 1989), 159.

4. Andrew Lloyd Webber and Tim Rice, *Evita, the Legend of Eva Perón (1919–1952)* (New York: Drama Book Specialists, 1978). No page numbers in the text.

5. Qtd. in James García, "Stage Performers and Film Actors," *Encyclopedia of Latin Popular Culture*, ed. Cordelia Candelaria, Peter J. García, and Artruo J. Aldama (Westport, CT: Greenwood, 2004), 804.

6. Julie A. Noonan notes that the role of Evita requires a singer with "specialized skills singing in both rock and musical theatre styles" (198). See Noonan, "Popular Voices: Amplification, Rock Music and Vocal Quality in *Grease*," *Studies in Musical Theatre* 3.2 (2009): 185–200.

7. Raymond Knapp, *The American Musical and the Performance of Personal Identity* (Princeton, NJ: Princeton University Press, 2006), 348.

8. For scholarly analyses of megamusicals, see Jonathan Burston, *The Megamusical: New Forms and Relations in Global Cultural Production* (diss., University of London, 1998), which was the first critical scholarly study of the megamusical. Also see related publications: Jonathan Burston, "Theatre Space as Virtual Place: Audio Technology, the Reconfigured Singing Body and the Megamusical," *Popular Music* 17.2 (1998): 205–18; Jonathan Burston, "Spectacle, Synergy and Megamusicals: The Global-Industrialisation of Live-Theatrical Production," *Media Organisations in Society*, ed. James Curran (London: Arnold, 2000), 69–81; and Jonathan Burston, "Enter, Stage Right: Neoconservatism, English Canada, and the Megamusical," *Soundings* 5 (Winter 1997): 179–90. Also see Jessica Sternfeld, *The Megamusical* (Bloomington: Indiana University Press, 2006); David Walsh and Len Platt, "Modernity, Globalization, and the Megamusical," *Musical Theater and American Culture* (Westport, CT: Praeger, 2003), 157–71.

   On *Les Misérables*, see Margaret Vermette, *The Musical World of Boublil and Schönberg* (New York: Applause Books, 2006); Edward Behr, *Les Misérables: History in the Making* (London: Jonathan Cape, 1989); Joseph P. Swain, "The Epic as Musical," *The Broadway Musical: A Critical and Musical Survey*, 2nd ed. (Lanham, MD: Scarecrow, 2002), 385–408; Scott Miller, "Les Misérables," *From Assassins to West Side Story: The Director's Guide to Musical Theatre* (Portsmouth, NH: Heinemann, 1996), 165–75; and William A. Everett, "From French to European to Global: The Saga of Schönberg and Boublil's *Les Misérables*," *European Culture in a Changing World: Between Nationalism and Globalism*, ed. Daniel Meyer-Dinkgräfe (New York: Cambridge University Press, 2004), 229–36.

   On Webber, see Michael Walsh, *Andrew Lloyd Webber: His Life and Works: A Critical Biography* (New York: Harry N. Abrams, 1997); Michael Coveney, *Cats on a Chandelier: The Andrew Lloyd Webber Story* (London: Hutchinson, 1999); and John Snelson, *Andrew Lloyd Webber* (New Haven, CT: Yale University Press, 2004).

9. On the 1980s, see Graham Thompson, *American Culture in the 1980s* (Edinburgh: Edinburgh University Press, 2007); and Bob Batchelor and Scott Stoddart, *The 1980s* (Westport, CT: Greenwood, 2007).

10. For an analysis of the transatlantic development of the megamusical, see Jonathan Burston, "Recombinant Broadway," *Continuum: Journal of Media and Cultural Studies* 23.2 (2009): 159–69. Burston asserts that "Broadway's own globalization tale is traceable to the 1980s" (161).

11. Michael Omi and Howard Winant, *Racial Formation in the United States: From the 1960s to the 1990s*, 2nd ed. (New York: Routledge, 1994), 125.

12. Omi and Winant, *Racial Formation*, 125.

13. Omi and Winant, *Racial Formation*, 134.

14. Omi and Winant, *Racial Formation*, 134.

15. Omi and Winant, *Racial Formation*, 134.

16. Ruth Rosen, *The World Split Open: How the Modern Women's Movement Changed America* (New York: Viking, 2000), xxvii.

17. Sara M. Evans, *Born for Liberty: A History of Women in America* (New York: Free Press, 1989), 308.

18. Susan Bolotin, "Views from the Postfeminist Generation," *New York Times Magazine*, October 17, 1982, pp. 29+. For a broader contextualization of postfeminim, see Astrid Henry, *Not My Mother's Sister: Generational Conflict and Third-Wave*

Feminism (Bloomington: Indiana University Press, 2004). Christine Stansell also demonstrates how feminists lost traction in Washington once Reagan took office and the ERA was defeated in 1982 (343). See Stansell, *The Feminist Promise, 1792 to the Present* (New York: Modern Library, 2010).

19. Rosen, *The World Split Open*, xxxviii.
20. Thompson, *American Culture in the 1980s*, 32.
21. Susan Faludi, *Backlash: The Undeclared War against American Women* (New York: Anchor Books, 1991).
22. Faludi, "Dressing the Dolls: The Fashion Backlash," *Backlash*, 181–21.
23. Andi Zeisler, *Feminism and Pop Culture* (Berkeley, CA: Seal Press, 2008), 15.
24. Zeisler, *Feminism and Pop Culture*, 13.
25. Ginia Bellafante, "Television: A Series That Shows Its Age," *New York Times*, August 21, 2009, p. C1.
26. Zeisler, *Feminism and Pop Culture*, 90.
27. Zeisler, *Feminism and Pop Culture*, 94–95.
28. Stansell, *The Feminist Promise*, 349.
29. See Thompson, *American Culture in the 1980s*, 129–31.
30. On acting practices of the 1950s and the dominance of psychologically based Method acting, see, for example, Bruce McConachie, *American Theater in the Culture of the Cold War: Producing and Contesting Containment, 1947–1962* (Iowa City: University of Iowa Press, 2003).
31. See Douglas Martin, "Tharon Musser, 84, Stage Lighting Designer," *New York Times*, April 21, 2009, p. B10; and http://www.usitt.org/sightlines/archive/v49/n06/stories/TharonMusser.html (accessed January 10, 2011).
32. Qtd. in *Broadway: The American Musical*, dir. Michael Kantor, 2004.
33. From http://www.pbs.org/wnet/broadway/musicals/cats.html (accessed July 23, 2009).
34. Qtd. in Gerald Bordman, *American Musical Theater: A Chronicle*, 3rd ed. (New York: Oxford University Press, 2001), 770.
35. Bordman, *American Musical Theater*, 770.
36. From http://www.pbs.org/wnet/broadway/musicals/cats.html (accessed July 23, 2009).
37. See Burston, "Recombinant Broadway." Disney, of course, was a major player in this transformation of theatrical practices and global merchandising starting in the mid-1990s.
38. Thompson, *American Culture in the 1980s*, 148.
39. Qtd. in Ed Behr, "The 'Middlebrow' Maestro of Megahits," *Newsweek*, October 2, 1989, p. 68.
40. "The Theater Boom," *American Decades*, ed. Judith S. Baughman, Victor Bondi, Richard Layman, Tandy McConnell, and Vincent Tompkins, vol. 9: *1980–1989* (Detroit: Gale, 2001) (*Gale Virtual Reference Library*, accessed March 4, 2008).
41. Richard Isackes, personal e-mail, April 17, 2009.
42. "The Theater Boom" (accessed March 4, 2008).
43. From http://www.pbs.org/wnet/broadway/musicals/cats.html (accessed July 23, 2009).
44. Burston, "Recombinant Broadway," 163.
45. Christopher Baugh, *Theatre, Performance, and Technology: The Development of Scenography in the Twentieth Century* (New York: Palgrave Macmillan, 2005), 212.

46. Mel Gussow, "Revisiting Eight Musicals with New Casts," *New York Times*, April 14, 1989, p. C1.

47. Burston, "Theatre Space as Virtual Place," 208. Also see Mark N. Grant, *The Rise and Fall of the Broadway Musical* (Boston: Northeastern University Press, 2004).

48. Mark Steyn, *Broadway Babies Say Goodnight: Musicals Then and Now* (New York: Routledge, 1999), 279.

49. Steyn, *Broadway Babies Say Goodnight*, 278.

50. Geoffrey Block, *Enchanted Evenings: The Broadway Musical from Show Boat to Sondheim and Webber*, 2nd ed. (New York: Oxford University Press, 2009), 394–95.

51. Vermette, *The Musical World*, 41.

52. Baugh, *Theatre, Performance, and Technology*, 207.

53. Miranda Lundskaer-Nielsen argues that *Les Miz* directors Trevor Nunn and John Caird emerge from a British tradition of classic, text-focused drama. She discusses how rehearsals for *Les Miz* were character-driven and collaborative and made frequent use of improvisation, so they should be seen not in relation to other U.S. musicals but to, for example, the RSC production of *Nicholas Nickleby*. See Lundskaer-Nielsen, *Directors and the New Musical Drama: British and American Musical Theatre in the 1980s and 90s* (New York: Palgrave Macmillan, 2008). She sees Harold Prince, especially in *Cabaret*, as the exception to typical directors of Broadway fare and, moreover, the originator and precursor to this subgenre of productions. Overall, her project is to reframe the critical conversation around megamusicals to place them in a more positive light.

54. Frank Rich, "Stage: 'Misérables,' Musical Version Opens on Broadway," *New York Times*, March 13, 1987, p. C1.

55. Qtd. in Bordman, *American Musical Theater*, 781.

56. Bordman, *American Musical Theater*, 781.

57. Jeremy Gerard, "Already, 'Miserables' Is a Box-Office Marvel," *New York Times*, January 17, 1987, p. 11.

58. Bordman, *American Musical Theater*, 281.

59. See Holley Dawn Replogle, "Crossover and Spectacle in American Operetta and the Megamusical," diss., University of California, Los Angeles, 2009, 115–16. Illustration in Behr, *Les Misérables*, 147.

60. Qtd. on *20/20*, which featured a piece on *Les Miz* before it opened on Broadway, http://www.youtube.com/watch?v=ZoPhfa1n5vc&feature=related (accessed July 20, 2009).

61. Vermette, *The Musical World*, 130.

62. Vermette, *The Musical World*, 125.

63. Bordman, *American Musical Theater*, 781.

64. Rich, "Misérables," C3.

65. *Les Miz* exhibits a lively homosocial/homoerotic energy between various pairs of men. The chase narrative, one of the main plotlines of the musical, pits the noble Jean Valjean against the scoundrel Javert. Locked in a struggle to the death and symbolizing good and bad, lightness and dark, generosity and anger, Valjean and Javert sing many of the same melodies and join for several duets. Much of the first part of the musical charts their relationship. Later, Marius and Enjolras sing together in "Red and Black," a song in which each expresses his desire—Marius for his love, the then-unnamed Cosette, and Enjolras for his politics, which, as he says, are no longer child's play. Both sets of men form a queer couple.

66. Vermette, *The Musical World*, 141.
67. Rich, "Misérables," C1.
68. Block, *Enchanted Evenings*, 270–75.
69. Vermette, *The Musical World*, 72.
70. David Ronney, "'Les Miz' Heads Back to Broadway Barricades," *Variety*, November 13–19, 2006, p. 56.
71. My observations about *Les Miz* are taken from having seen the musical several times on Broadway, on tape at the NYPL (Theatre on Film Library), and on various YouTube clips. Consistent with Mackintosh's intentions, there are virtually no variations across productions.
72. Vermette, *The Musical World*, 133.
73. Vermette, *The Musical World*, 120.
74. Vermette, *The Musical World*, 130.
75. Vermette, *The Musical World*, 70.
76. Vermette, *The Musical World*, 73.
77. Vermette, *The Musical World*, 68.
78. Vermette, *The Musical World*, 72.
79. Vermette, *The Musical World*, 120.
80. Vermette, *The Musical World*, 47.
81. Vermette, *The Musical World*, 73.
82. For an excellent reading of this number, see Replogle, "Crossover and Spectacle," 108–12.
83. Walsh, *Andrew Lloyd Webber*, 206.
84. Frank Rich, "Stage: 'Phantom of the Opera,'" *New York Times*, January 27, 1988, p. C19.
85. Qtd. in Carol Ilson, *Harold Prince: A Director's Journey* (New York: Limelight Editions, 2000), 355.
86. From http://www.thephantomoftheopera.com/the_show/facts_and_figures.php (accessed January 2, 2011).
87. Ilson, *Harold Prince*, 353.
88. Ilson, *Harold Prince*, 354.
89. Coveney, *Cats on a Chandelier*, 132.
90. Ilson, *Harold Prince*, 349.
91. Rich, "Stage: 'Phantom of the Opera,'" C19. "The drapes are another technical marvel, in that they sail, leap, drop and fly in the many changes of scene," writes Ilson, *Harold Prince*, 355.
92. Hirsch, *Harold Prince*, 166.
93. Hirsch, *Harold Prince*, 166.
94. Ilson explains how this stage trick "is commanded by the most advanced computer and back-up system ever used in a theatre" (354).
95. Rich, "Stage: 'Phantom of the Opera,'" C19.
96. Rich, "Stage: 'Phantom of the Opera,'" C19.
97. Coveney, *Cats on a Chandelier*, 136.
98. Snelson, *Andrew Lloyd Webber*, 88.
99. Coveney, *Cats on a Chandelier*, 137.
100. Christine is drawn in opposition to the few other women in the musical: Carlotta, the badly behaved temperamental, not-very-talented diva; Mme Giry, who knows the Phantom's backstory and is reasonably respectful of his wishes throughout; Meg, the ordinary

dancer who doesn't have a Phantom obsessed with her. It's important that Christine is none of these things: a diva, a smart if masculinized woman, an ordinary girl.

101. My observations are taken from having seen *Phantom* on Broadway and national tour numerous times.

102. Although the musical itself makes this argument, countless fans protest that Christine made a bad choice by marrying the conventional rich guy rather than the passionate artist.

103. Walsh and Platt and Snelson argue that the Phantom's score is modernist and experimental and the music of Webber—the music with which Christine aligns herself and that she chooses for her future—is conservative. It's not simply Christine's characterization that is conventional and conservative but also where the musical lands aesthetically. See Walsh and Platt, "Modernity"; and Snelson, *Andrew Lloyd Webber*.

104. To be sure, in many places, Christine sings frequently on stage alone or without scenic adornments. These sections tend to isolate her from the diegesis, not unlike *Les Miz*'s placement of its women.

105. Rich, "Stage: 'Phantom of the Opera,'" C19.

106. Coveney, *Cats on a Chandelier*, 131–32.

107. Snelson, *Andrew Lloyd Webber*, 99–101.

108. See Snelson, *Andrew Lloyd Webber*, 101. Mordden describes this number as "raucous disco" (78) and writes, "But pop opera is not a pop version of opera. It's an opera version of pop: building opera's intensity out of vernacular musical idiom" (82). Ethan Mordden, *The Happiest Corpse I've Ever Seen: The Last Twenty-Five Years of the Broadway Musical* (New York: Palgrave Macmillan, 2004).

109. Ilson, *Harold Prince*, 349. When she awakes, she sings the melody of "a collector's piece indeed/every detail exactly as she said," the musical theme used when someone is trying to grasp something out of reach—when Christine is trying to remember what happened when the Phantom brought her down to his place: "I remember there was a mist . . . swirling mist upon a vast, glassy lake" (Snelson, *Andrew Lloyd Webber*, 89).

110. Coveney, *Cats on a Chandelier*, 132.

111. See Snelson, *Andrew Lloyd Webber*, 87; Vermette, *The Musical World*, 120.

112. Burston, "Recombinant Broadway," 161. Also see David Lister, "The Cloning of Andrew Lloyd Webber," *Independent* (London), February 11, 1995, p. 25.

113. Baugh, *Theatre, Performance, and Technology*, 209.

114. Burston, "Recombinant Broadway," 161–62.

115. See Susan B. Russell, "The Performance of Discipline on Broadway," *Studies in Musical Theatre* 1.1 (2007): 97–108.

116. Burston, "Recombinant Broadway," 162.

117. Russell, "The Performance of Discipline," 106.

118. Ronney, "'Les Miz' Heads Back," 56.

Chapter 5

1. Steinem is not identified in any way, so the viewer must be able to recognize her.

2. From http://colorpurple.com/color_purple_sights_and_sounds.php (accessed August 9, 2010).

3. Unlike the other chapters in this book, this one surveys musicals across a longer span because the production process became so attenuated by the late twentieth century. On the long development process and its effects on musical theatre history, see Stacy Wolf, "Broadway Musical as Political Conversant," *Patriotic Dissent: Theatre after 9–11*, ed. Jenny Spencer (New York: Routledge, forthcoming).

4. Leslie Heywood and Jennifer Drake, introduction to *Third Wave Agenda: Being Feminist, Doing Feminism* (Minneapolis: University of Minnestoa Press, 1997), 7.

5. Yvonne Tasker and Diane Negra, introduction to *Interrogating Postfeminism: Gender and the Politics of Popular Culture* (Durham, NC: Duke University Press, 2007), 2.

6. Although in common parlance, a Jewish woman is not typically referred to as a "woman of color," Jewishness in musical theatre functions as a characterological marker like race or ethnicity. I refer to Lucille in *Parade* as a woman of color because so few women whose Jewishness has been marked have been represented in Broadway musicals, so her ethnicity is notable. Given that countless Jewish men have been among musical theatre's most prolific and successful creators, this absence might be surprising.

7. Walter Benn Michaels, *The Trouble with Diversity: How We Learned to Love Identity and Ignore Inequality* (New York: Henry Holt, 2006), 172.

8. Michaels, *The Trouble with Diversity*, 116.

9. Michaels, *The Trouble with Diversity*, 56–58.

10. David S. Mason, *The End of the American Century* (New York: Rowman & Littlefield, 2009), 90–91.

11. Paul Gilroy, *Against Race: Imagining Political Culture beyond the Color Line* (Cambridge, MA: Harvard University Press, 2000), 21–22.

12. Gilroy, *Against Race*, 16–17.

13. "*In the Heights*: Chasing Broadway Dreams," *Great Performances*, dir. Paul Bozymowski, PBS, 2009.

14. On the changing economics of Broadway, see Elizabeth L. Wollman, "The Economic Development of the 'New' Times Square and Its Impact on the Broadway Musical," *American Music* 20.4 (2002): 445–65. On tourist audiences, see Susan Bennett, "Theatre/Tourism," *Theatre Journal* 57 (2005): 407–28. From the 1990s, the flow of theatre making shifted: the old model was that the show began on Broadway and then moved onto national and international tours, but under the new model, more shows began in regional or not-for-profit theatres and then moved to Broadway. Producers' awareness that a show really makes its money on tour underpinned many decisions so that Broadway success mattered less than regional interest. Critics for the *New York Times* became less influential. Aesthetically, virtually all post-1990 musicals have an electronic, back-beat, rock-based sound, and all actors wear body mics.

15. Dean J. Franco, *Ethnic American Literature: Comparing Chicano, Jewish, and African American Writing* (Charlottesville: University of Virginia Press, 2006). The status of Jewishness as a race, ethnicity, or culture complicates this comparative approach, too. In *The Price of Whiteness*, Eric Goldstein notes that while Jews have generally been positioned as white since World War II, their sense of difference, even racial difference, has supported a sense of distinctiveness that has been important, even if it is difficult to locate its source. Eric Goldstein, *The Price of Whiteness: Jews, Race, and American Identity* (Princeton, NJ: Princeton University Press, 2006), 7.

16. On the history of *Oklahoma!* and the producers' self-generated praise and publicity, see Tim Carter, *Oklahoma! The Making of an American Musical* (New Haven, CT: Yale University Press, 2007).

17. According to Otis L. Guernsey, curtain times were moved back from 8:30 to 7:30 in 1971 to encourage suburbanites to have a quick dinner and stay in the city to see a show. *Curtain Times: The New York Theater: 1965–1986* (New York: Hal Leonard, 1987), 201.

18. In an article surveying the 2008 cast albums following the Tony Awards, Stephen Holden compared revivals and new musicals and observed that the new musicals, which included *Next to Normal, 9-to-5*, and *Billy Elliot* eschewed an eleven o'clock number. The revival albums were *Hair, West Side Story*, and *Guys and Dolls*. Stephen Holden, "Broadway Musicals Sing a Different Tune," *New York Times*, June 19, 2009, p. C4.

19. Joseph Hanania, "Playing Princesses, Punishers and Prudes," *New York Times*, March 7, 1999, pp. 35, 38.

20. There has been much written about the Leo Frank case and its aftermath, as well as numerous songs, plays, novels, and film versions. Most people believe that Frank was innocent. See, for example, Leonard Dinnerstein, *The Leo Frank Case* (New York: Columbia University Press, 1968), and Albert S. Lindemann, *The Jew Accused: Three Anti-Semitic Affairs (Dreyfus, Beilis, Frank), 1894–1915* (New York: Cambridge University Press, 1991), 194–272. The richest and most provocative analysis (which also accounts for other scholarship) is Jeffrey Melnick, *Black-Jewish Relations on Trial: Leo Frank and Jim Conley in the New South* (Jackson: University Press of Mississippi, 2000). Melnick brackets the question of Frank's innocence and instead teases out the social forces that allowed the majority of northerners to believe his innocence and southerners to find him guilty.

21. Alfred Uhry, "A Sorry Chapter, a Source for Song," *New York Times*, December 13, 1998, p. AR7. Lucille, then, is the character who navigates Uhry's own ethnic struggle.

22. Vincent Canby, "Pedigree Versus Play: The Mystery of 'Parade,'" *New York Times*, December 27, 1998, p. AR5.

23. Brown notes that the show got Tony nominations only because it was such a weak season with only four new musicals: *Parade, Footloose, The Civil War*, and *Fosse*. Jackson R. Bryer and Richard A. Davison, eds., *The Art of the American Musical: Conversations with the Creators* (New Brunswick, NJ: Rutgers University Press, 2005), 45.

24. On Brown's assessment of the more successful out of town reception of the show, see Bryer and Davison, *The Art of the American Musical*, 46–47.

25. Jason Robert Brown and Alfred Uhry, *Parade, The New American Musical*, ed. Wiley Hausam (New York: Theatre Communications Group, 2003), 229–351. Co-conceived by Harold Prince, original New York production directed by Harold Prince.

26. See Kenneth J. Bindas, ed., *America's Musical Pulse: Popular Music in Twentieth-Century Society* (Westport, CT: Prager, 1992).

27. The fact of child labor, a key issue in the case, gets only passing mention in the musical. *Parade* wants to blame the irrational and hysterical South for Leo's false conviction, but as historians note, this anti-industrial sentiment was conflated with anti-Semitism. Leo is associated with industrialization because of both his factory supervisor job and his northern origins. The musical portrays Leo as a gentle middle manager, eliding the brutal facts of child labor and industrialization

in the early twentieth century. For Leo to hold up as a victim in this show, he needs to be flawed but not an oppressor.

28. In the plot as in the historical case, Leo's conviction hinges on Joe's testifying that Leo seduced women and girls in his office. The white southern imagination finds African American and Jewish men both wrongly sexual.

29. Donald Whittaker, "Subversive Aspects of Musical Theatre," diss., Louisiana State University, 2002, 134. Also, Leo sings this same musical theme in his testimony, "It's Hard to Speak My Heart," the last verse of which is set against a reprise of "The Old Hills of Georgia."

30. Ethan Mordden, *The Happiest Corpse I've Ever Seen: The Last Twenty-Five Years of the Broadway Musical* (New York: Palgrave Macmillan, 2004), 277.

31. Thanks to Margaret White for pointing this out to me.

32. Mordden points out that she is the only character in the show to have "an evening's worth of music." *Happiest Corpse*, 277.

33. In some ways, when Lucille becomes the active figure in the show, she resembles some Rodgers and Hammerstein heroines like Nellie Forbush, Maria Von Trapp, or Anna in *The King and I*.

34. Kimberly Wallace-Saunders, *Mammy: A Century of Race, Gender, and Southern Memory* (Ann Arbor: University of Michigan Press, 2008), 136–39.

35. Wallace-Saunders, *Mammy*, 143–44.

36. On the relations between Africans Americans and Jews in the 1960s, see Cheryl Lynn Greenberg, *Troubling the Waters: Black-Jewish Relations in the American Century* (Princeton, NJ: Princeton University Press, 2006); Eric J. Sundquist, *Strangers in the Land: Blacks, Jews, Post-Holocaust America* (Cambridge, MA: Harvard University Press, 2005); and Cornel West and Jack Salzman, eds., *Struggles in the Promised Land: Toward a History of Black-Jewish Relations in the United States* (New York: Oxford University Press, 1997). On Jewish identity in the U.S. South, see Richard L. Rubenstein, "The Rabbis Visit Birmingham," *The Jewish 1960s*, ed. Michael E. Staub (Waltham, MA: Brandeis University Press, 2004), 23–30; and Seth Forman, "The Unbearable Whiteness of Being Jewish: Desegregation in the South and the Crisis of Jewish Liberalism," *American Jewish History* 85.2 (1997): 121–42.

37. Tony Kushner and Jeanine Tesori, *Caroline, or Change* (New York: Theatre Communications Group, 2004), xi–xii.

38. "Production: *Caroline, or Change*," *Working in the Theatre*, video podcast, http://americantheatrewing.org/wit/detail/caroline_or_change_04_04 (accessed March 15, 2009).

39. "Wrestling with Angels: Playwright Tony Kushner," dir. Freida Lee Mock, American Film Foundation/Sanders and Mock Productions, 2006.

40. Andrea Levine observes that "Noah's and Caroline's invectives diverge in significant ways. First, Noah is no longer calling Caroline the 'President,' but instead uses the name of the real President who assumed power after JFK's assassination. He summons a world in which federal authority will work on his behalf. His outraged imagination conjures the specter of a bomb that will target 'Negroes'; it is as if his fight with Caroline reveals the genuine power each holds in relation to the executive branch and national politics. Caroline, by contrast, never mentions the state, but instead moves from the lived reality of her labor in the Gellmans' basement to the realm of the Christian G-d. Noah appeals to the force and authority of the nation for his hateful tirade; Caroline, on the other hand, doesn't imagine that the 'President'

is on her side, so she must hope that G-d is." Andrea Levine, "Embodying Jewishness at the Millennium," unpublished ms., 27.

41. The Jewish characters do sing but not much and not beautifully. Also, it's interesting that Stuart is a musician but Noah is in some ways entirely unmusical. All of his music is borrowed. Noah's mother died (that music died), and Rose really can't sing at all. Also, while Stuart is a jazz musician—a style with African American roots—he mostly plays klezmer in the show.

42. On the blues and the South, see James Smethurst, "How I Got to Memphis: the Blues and the Study of American Culture," *American Popular Music*, ed. Rachel Rubin and Jeffrey Melnick (Amherst: University of Massachusetts Press, 2001), 47–64. Also see Jeffrey Melnick, "Tin Pan Alley and the Black-Jewish Nation," Rubin and Melnick, *American Popular Music*, 29–46; and Josh Kun, "The Yiddish Are Coming," *Audiotopia: Music, Race, America* (Berkeley: University of California Press, 2005), 48–85.

43. As Bruce Kirle observes, many musicals of the late twentieth century feature unlikable singular protagonists, including Mama Rose in *Gypsy*, Sweeney Todd, and the whole cast of *Assassins*. See Bruce Kirle, *Unfinished Show Business: Broadway Musicals as Works-in-Process* (Carbondale: Southern Illinois University Press, 2005).

44. In a discussion about the production on the American Theatre Wing's podcast, *Working in the Theatre*, Kushner noted that many Jewish and white audience members identified so keenly with Noah that they missed the musical's sharp criticism of that relationship. See http://www.americantheatrewing.org/seminars/detail/caroline_or_change_04_04/ (accessed May 27, 2007).

45. In some ways, Rose is a parallel figure to Leo in *Parade*; she is the New Yorker, the outsider who misses home. And like Leo, Rose does not sing much—or in her case, sing well—again, musical theatre's technique for devaluing a character's perspective.

46. More than a few commentators found *Parade* and *Caroline, or Change* inappropriately serious and difficult for the genre. Perhaps it's not coincidental that they prominently feature Jewish characters and are utterly unsentimental about racism and anti-Semitism.

47. Griffin, associate director of the Chicago Shakespeare Festival, had extensive directing experience, including *Saved* at Playwrights Horizons, *The New Moon* for Encores!, and *Pacific Overtures* at the Donmar Warehouse in London.

48. Script quotations and observations are taken from the performance I attended on March 28, 2006.

49. It opened on December 1, 2005, and closed on February 24, 2008.

50. Qtd. in Lise Funderburg, *The Color Purple: A Memory Book of the Broadway Musical* (New York: Carroll & Graf, 2006), 174.

51. Qtd. in Funderberg, *Color Purple: Memory Book*, 22.

52. Perhaps the fact that the audience talked through the entire overture of the performance that I saw suggests that audiences no longer know the purpose of the music and don't understand the performance's proper start until the curtain is raised and the lights come up on stage.

53. Qtd. in Funderberg, *Color Purple: Memory Book*. Song lyrics are reproduced in this book and are noted parenthetically.

54. Qtd. in Funderberg, *Color Purple: Memory Book*, 22.

55. This convention began much earlier, with Gilbert and Sullivan's *Mikado*. Thanks to Ray Knapp for pointing this out to me.

56. Linda Armstrong, "The Color Purple Has Regal Opening on Broadway," *New York Amsterdam News*, December 8–14, 2005, p. 21.

57. Michael Kuchwara, "Oprah Winfrey's 'The Color Purple' Debuts at NYC's Broadway Theatre," *Fort Lauderdale Westside Gazette*, December 8–14, 2005, p. 2B. Also, Kuchwara was among the few reviewers who criticized the exoticized representation of Africa in the "long tribal dance segment."

58. Deborah Paredez, "All about My (Absent) Mother: Young Latina Aspirations in *Real Women Have Curves* and *Ugly Betty*," unpublished ms. Paredez's article examines the trope of the absent mother in popular culture narratives of Latina aspirations and argues that such absence signifies postfeminist cultural and political anxieties about the increasing presence of ambitious, educated, financially independent Latinas whose bodies cannot be only sexualized. Nina in *In the Heights* definitely qualifies as an aspiring Latina, but her mother plays a key and supportive role in her life.

59. On Latino history, see Juan Gonzalez, *Harvest of Empire: A History of Latinos in America* (New York: Viking, 2000). On Latino cultures, see, e.g., Juan Flores, *From Bomba to Hip-Hop: Puerto Rican Culture and Latino Identity* (New York: Columbia University Press, 2000); Frances Negrón-Muntaner, *Boricua Pop: Puerto Ricans and the Latinization of American Culture* (New York: New York University Press, 2004); and Suzanne Oboler, *Ethnic Labels, Latino Lives: Identity and the Politics of (Re)Presentation in the United States* (Minneapolis: University of Minnesota Press, 1995).

60. Sam Roberts, "What's in a Name? For Hispanics, a Generational Shift," *New York Times*, May 29, 2009, p. A16.

61. For an extended analysis of similarities between *In the Heights* and *West Side Story*, see Deborah Paredez, "'Queer for Uncle Sam': Anita's Diva Turn in *West Side Story*," unpublished ms. On Latina/o critiques of *West Side Story*, see, for example, Frances Négron-Muntaner, "Feeling Pretty: *West Side Story* and Puerto Rican Identity Discourses," *Social Text* 18.2 (2000): 83–106. Also see Alberto Sandoval-Sánchez, *José, Can You See? Latinos On and Off Broadway* (Madison: University of Wisconsin Press, 1999).

62. "*In the Heights*: Chasing Broadway Dreams," *Great Performances*, dir. Paul Bozymowski, PBS, 2009. Also see interviews with Miranda, http://www.youtube.com/watch?v=YKzhS96KdtY and http://www.youtube.com/watch?v=_WJ1y1MyC8s&;feature=related (accessed May 20, 2009).

63. *In the Heights*, music and lyrics by Lin-Manuel Miranda, book by Quiara Alegría Hudes, conceived by Lin-Manuel Miranda, directed by Thomas Kail, choreographed by Andy Blankenbuehler, music direction by Alex Lacamoire. Libretto including lyrics contained in cast album. No page numbers. Performance notes are from online clips and from the March 5, 2008, performance.

64. Thomas Kail, personal interview, July 21, 2009.

65. Perhaps not surprisingly, there is nothing gay to be found anywhere in the show.

66. Qtd. in "Chasing Broadway Dreams."

67. Richard Zoglin, "Life After *Rent*," *Time*, February 29, 2008, http://www.time.com/time/magazine/article/0,9171,1718572,00.html (accessed August 15, 2010). On "national affect" and Latinidad, see Ramón H. Rivera-Servera, "Exhibiting Voice/Narrating Migration: Performance-based Curatorial Practice in ¡Azúcar! The Life and Music of Celia Cruz," *Text and Performance Quarterly* 29.2 (2009): 131–48.

68. Oboler, *Ethnic Labels, Latino Lives.*
69. See Paredez, "'Queer For Uncle Sam.'"
70. Thanks to Joshua Wolf for translation help.
71. One might read Nina's failure as an expression of a larger cultural anxiety about Latina aspirations. See Paredez, "All about My (Absent) Mother."
72. Qtd. in "Chasing Broadway Dreams."
73. David Román, personal e-mail, June 17, 2009.
74. Thomas Kail explained that Nina doesn't sing a specific song form, but she does sing an older style of music and is linked to the older generation in the musical. He talked about how Nina is struggling between worlds and trying to take the positive aspects of her tradition to make a new life. Interview.
75. Qtd. in Roberts, "What's in a Name?," p. A16.
76. Qtd. in "Chasing Broadway Dreams."
77. Deborah Paredez, personal e-mail, January 31, 2010.
78. Kail pointed out that it's Benny who needs to expand at this point and be willing to move west to be with Nina. In the younger generation, conventional power roles between genders have changed. Interview.

Chapter 6

1. Richard Rodgers and Oscar Hammerstein II, *Oklahoma! Six Plays by Rodgers and Hammerstein* (New York: Random House, 1953).
2. Qtd. in David Cote, *Wicked: The Grimmerie* (New York: Hyperion, 2005). *The Grimmerie* contains the songs' lyrics and bits of dialogue. Other lines are quoted from the performance. Also see Carol de Giere, *Defying Gravity: The Creative Career of Stephen Schwartz from* Godspell *to* Wicked (Milwaukee: Applause, 2008), 271–434.
3. *Wicked*'s music and lyrics were written by Stephen Schwartz (*Godspell*; *Pippin*). The libretto was written by Winnie Holzman, the creator of the short-lived but critically acclaimed television series *My So-Called Life*, with Claire Danes, which, like *Wicked*, was a sensation among adolescent girls. It was directed by Joe Mantello, with musical staging by Wayne Cilento. The original cast featured Kristin Chenoweth as Glinda, Idina Menzel as Elphaba, and Broadway veteran Joel Grey as the Wizard. *Wicked* was nominated for eleven Drama Desk Awards and ten Tony Awards.

   On Holzman's career and fans' support of her work, see Jane Feuer, "The Lack of Influence of *thirtysomething*," *The Contemporary Television Series*, ed. Michael Hammond and Lucy Mazdon (Edinburgh: Edinburgh University Press, 2005), 27–36.

   Many fans of the novel find the musical vapid and apolitical. Certainly, the musical downplays the novel's sharp critique of power and reframes the narrative to focus on the women's relationship, which occupies a small part of the original. The changes wrought to the novel call attention to the musical version's reliance on formal conventions of musical theatre in its form—that of a developing love story.
4. Elysa Gardner, "Something 'Wicked' Comes to Broadway," *USA Today*, October 31, 2003, p. 9E; Frederick M. Winship, "Broadway's 'Wicked' Is an Odd Oz Offshoot," *United Press International*, November 17, 2003; Charles Isherwood, "More Bothered Than Bewitched by 'Wicked,'" *Variety*, November 3, 2003, p. 30. Isherwood

goes on: "*Wicked* is stridently earnest one minute, self-mocking the next, a fantastical allegory about the perils of fascism in one scene, a Nickelodeon special about the importance of inner beauty in another." Ben Brantley, "There's Trouble in Emerald City," *New York Times*, October 31, 2003, p. E1.

5. From http://www2.broadwayworld.com/grossesshow.cfm?show=Wicked&year=2010 (accessed January 3, 2011).

6. From http://www.wickedthemusical.com/page.php# (accessed August 15, 2010). In addition, its cast album hit platinum by selling over a million copies, and bootlegged video clips on YouTube get thousands of hits a day. The musical's audience now extends well beyond those who have seen it in the theatre.

7. Jessica Sternfeld, *The Megamusical* (Bloomington: Indiana University Press, 2006), 348–50. Sternfeld's is the first full-length, musicologically oriented study of the megamusical. Also see Barry Singer, *Ever After: The Last Years of Musical Theatre and Beyond* (New York: Applause, 2004). He completed his book before *Wicked* opened but it fits into his categorization of megamusicals.

Other musical theatre scholars consider *Wicked* as a megamusical but critically, with ever-expanding international markets, endlessly replaceable actors, and a superficial message. Raymond Knapp, for example, in *The American Musical and the Performance of Personal Identity* (Princeton, NJ: Princeton University Press, 2006), primarily faults "the way the show compromises its starkly original source material," which is an accurate assessment (351).

8. On the persistent themes of "idealism and inspiration," see Knapp, *The American Musical and the Performance of Personal Identity*, 164–204.

9. By featuring a young woman as the protagonist, *Wicked* also responds to the many musicals discussed in this book from the 1950s to the mid-1960s, in which the protagonist was a woman. Elphaba hearkens back to the independent, smart, strong-willed belting women of earlier musical theatre who also sing from a softer side: Ruth in *Wonderful Town*, Anita in *West Side Story*, Fanny Brice in *Funny Girl*, Sally Bowles in *Cabaret*, the title divas in *Hello, Dolly!* and *Mame*, Mama Rose in *Gypsy*. She also resonates with some of the feisty, forthright women in the musicals of Rodgers and Hammerstein: Nellie in *South Pacific*, Anna in the *King and I*, Carrie in *Carousel*, and Maria in *The Sound of Music*.

10. Salman Rushdie, *The Wizard of Oz* (London: British Film Institute, 1992), 42. There are many fascinating connections and contradictions among Baum's novels, which presented unusually progressive gender politics and could easily be read as queer, the various stage versions of the Oz stories, the film, and *Wicked*. For a comparison of the earlier (pre-*Wicked*) versions, see Mark Evan Swartz, *Oz before the Rainbow: L. Frank Baum's* The Wonderful Wizard of Oz *on Stage and Screen to 1939* (Baltimore: Johns Hopkins University Press), 2000.

11. Scholars of musical theatre and film and also gay-lesbian-queer studies—including John Clum, Alexander Doty, Bruce Kirle, D. A. Miller, David Román, Michael Schiavi, and me—have addressed the multiple ways in which musicals signify queerly. See, for example John M. Clum, *Something for the Boys: Musical Theater and Gay Culture* (New York: St. Martin's, 1999); Alexander Doty, *Making Things Perfectly Queer: Interpreting Mass Culture* (Minneapolis: University of Minnesota Press, 1993); Bruce Kirle, *Unfinished Show Business: Broadway Musicals as Works-in-Progress* (Carbondale: Southern Illinois University Press, 2005); D. A. Miller,

Place for Us: Essay on the Broadway Musical (Cambridge, MA: Harvard University Press, 1998); David Román, *Performance in America: Contemporary U.S. Culture and the Performing Arts* (Durham, NC: Duke University Press, 2005); Michael R. Schiavi, "Opening Ancestral Windows: Post Stonewall Men and Musical Theatre," *New England Theatre Journal* 13 (2002): 77–98; and Stacy Wolf, *A Problem Like Maria: Gender and Sexuality in the American Musical* (Ann Arbor: University of Michigan Press, 2002).

12. Importantly, I am not arguing that Elphaba and Glinda are lesbians, but rather that the musical represents them as a queer couple.

13. Raymond Williams, *Marxism and Literature* (Oxford: Oxford University Press, 1977). Also see Susan McClary, *Conventional Wisdom: The Content of Musical Form* (Berkeley: University of California Press, 2000).

14. Virginia Wright Wexman, *Creating the Couple: Love, Marriage, and Hollywood Performance* (Princeton, NJ: Princeton University Press, 1993), 4.

15. See, for example, Rick Altman, *The American Film Musical* (Bloomington: Indiana University Press, 1987); and Richard Dyer, "The Sound of Music," *Movie* 23 (Winter 1976–77): 39–49.

16. Altman, *The American Film Musical*, 27.

17. In a now-classic article, Teresa De Lauretis argues that different skin color in two women characters in film positions them as a lesbian couple. See "Film and the Visible," *How Do I Look? Queer Film and Video*, ed. Bad Object-Choices (Seattle: Bay Press, 1991), 223–63.

18. See Michelle Boyd, "Alto on a Broomstick: Voicing the Witch in the Musical *Wicked*," *American Music* 28.1 (Spring 2010): 97–118.

19. In spite of the musical's effort to distance Elphaba from the Animals, to many spectators, she looks, acts, and seems Jewish, and many women who have played Elphaba are Jewish.

20. Nessa emerges as what David Van Leer calls an "unintended Other." David Van Leer, *The Queening of America* (New York: Routledge, 1995), 157–201.

21. On the politics of representations of disability, see, for example, Robert McRuer, *Crip Theory: Cultural Signs of Queerness and Disability* (New York: New York University Press, 2006); Rosemarie Garland Thomson, "Narratives of Deviance and Delight: Staring at Julia Pastrana, the 'Extraordinary Lady,'" *Beyond the Binary: Reconstructing Cultural Identity in a Multicultural Context*, ed. Timothy B. Powell (New Brunswick, NJ: Rutgers University Press, 1999), 81–104; and Carrie Sandahl, "Ahhh Freak out! Metaphors of Disability and Femaleness in Performance," *Theatre Topics* 9.1 (1999): 11–30.

22. Mark N. Grant, *The Rise and Fall of the Broadway Musical* (Boston: Northeastern University Press, 2004), 7.

23. Stephen Schwartz, "Note from the Composer," *Wicked Piano/Vocal Selections* (Milwaukee: Hal Leonard, 2004), 9.

24. Elphaba, in contrast, uses proper grammar, when she sings in "The Wizard and I," "a girl on whom I can rely." Thanks to Korey Rothman for pointing this out to me.

25. On the typical sincerity of a character's first number, see Lehman Engel, *Words with Music: The Broadway Musical Libretto*, 2nd ed. (New York: Schirmer Books, 1981). All of Glinda's solos as a public figure are sung in a higher range than her other numbers, emphasizing how her political role is a performance.

26. Marilyn Stasio, "Every Witch Way But Loose," *Variety*, April 26, 2004–May 6, 2004.

27. Thanks to Holley Replogle for pointing this out to me.

28. Qtd. in Cote, *The Grimmerie*, 77. Many of Schwartz's comments about his process indicate that he is entirely aware that the structure is based on a typical mid-twentieth-century book musical.

29. Joseph P. Swain, *The Broadway Musical: A Critical and Musical Survey*, 2nd ed. (Lanham, MD: Scarecrow Press, 2002), 165–66. Swain attributes the audience's anticipation of heterosexual romantic closure to "tradition."

30. See Mary Celeste Kearney, "Productive Spaces: Girls' Bedrooms as Sites of Cultural Production," unpublished ms., 2006.

31. On the cast album they finish on C#. In the published vocal selections, the last note is a middle C. Either way, it is a comfortable, middle, solid note to sing.

32. See Andrea Most, "'You've Got to Be Carefully Taught': The Politics of Race in Rodgers and Hammerstein's *South Pacific*," *Theatre Journal* 52 (2000): 307–37.

33. See Jane Feuer, *The Hollywood Musical* (Bloomington: Indiana University Press, 1993); and Scott McMillin, *The Musical as Drama* (Princeton, NJ: Princeton University Press, 2006), 78–101.

34. On the heterosexual couple and the nuclear family as the symbol of the community in the Cold War United States, see, for example, Elaine Tyler May, *Homeward Bound: American Families in the Cold War Era* (New York: Basic Books, 1988). For the significance of the metaphor of containment as embodied by the couple and the family, see Bruce McConachie, *American Theater in the Culture of the Cold War: Producing and Contesting Containment, 1947–1962* (Iowa City: University of Iowa Press, 2003).

35. Mark Steyn, *Broadway Babies Say Goodnight: Musicals Then and Now* (New York: Routledge, 1999), 200.

36. Cote, *The Grimmerie*, 46.

37. Miller, *Place for Us*, 73.

38. Wexman, *Creating the Couple*, 143.

39. Miller, *Place for Us*, 71.

40. Thanks to Ray Knapp for pointing this out to me.

41. Quoted in Bruce Weber, "The Wicked Young Witches," *New York Times*, October 26 2003, section 2, p. 5.

42. Anne Beggs proposes a similar dynamic with *Urinetown*. *Urinetown* opened just after 9/11, which Beggs doesn't note in her article and which no doubt influenced the musical's initial reception. Arguing that "the radical can be sustained within the mainstream" (43), Beggs demonstrates that the "thoroughly commercial product" of *Urinetown* can "reveal truly transgressive potential" (46). As a parallel to my argument in this chapter, Beggs asserts that *Urinetown*'s use and reuse of musical theatre's conventions, especially the refusal to offer a happy ending, is foundational to its political work. See Anne Beggs, "'For Urinetown is your town . . .': The Fringes of Broadway," *Theatre Journal* 62 (2010): 41–56.

43. Jonathan Burston, "The Megamusical: New Forms and Relations in Global Production," qtd. in David Walsh and Len Platt, "Modernity, Globalization, and the Megamusical," *Musical Theater and American Culture* (Westport, CT: Praeger, 2003), 157.

44. Richard Dyer, "Entertainment and Utopia," *Only Entertainment* (New York: Routledge, 1992), 18.

45. Miller, *Place for Us*, 68.
46. See Sally Banes, *Dancing Women: Female Bodies on Stage* (New York: Routledge, 1998); and Carolyn Abbate, *Unsung Voices: Opera and Musical Narrative in the Nineteenth Century* (Princeton, NJ: Princeton University Press, 1991).
47. Gerald M. Berkowitz, *New Broadways: Theatre across America, Approaching a New Millennium*, rev. ed. (New York: Applause, 1997), 235.
48. Susan Bennett, "Theatre/Tourism," *Theatre Journal* 57 (2005): 422.

Chapter 7

On fan's posts, I have only corrected punctuation and spelling for readability but have kept as much capitalization and other emotive typography as possible to try to retain the sense of the post. Aliases appear as they were on the fansites.

1. All of this changed in December 2010, when Julie Taymor and Bono's *Spiderman* received constant coverage of its cast's numerous injuries during its extended preview period.
2. Jesse McKinley, "For a Fallen Witch, an Uplifting Farewell," *New York Times*, January 10, 2005, p. B1.
3. This event was discussed in detail on www.witchesofoz.com, one of the many fansites for *Wicked*. One fan complained that if she had paid $100 for a ticket, she would not have appreciated the actors' breaking their characters during the performance or a new Elphaba playing the last few minutes of the show in street clothes. This comment was roundly criticized by one spectator who had been there and by many more who'd seen a clip of the event circulating on the Internet on a bootleg video. Other fans of *Wicked* emphasized that "everybody" in the audience appreciated the public acknowledgment of Menzel's last appearance and that "everybody" knew that she had been injured during the performance the day before. On the fansite, insider knowledge matters.
4. See Richard Dyer, *Heavenly Bodies: Film Stars and Society* (London: Macmillan, 1986), 13. Also see Barry King, "Articulating Stardom," *Star Texts*, ed. Jeremy G. Butler (Detroit: Wayne State University Press, 1991), 125–54.
5. Brantley argues that the leads of *Wicked* are "eminently replaceable" and perhaps so, but, as this chapter shows, girl fans ably distinguish performance choices and character interpretations among different actors. Ben Brantley, "How Broadway Lost Its Voice to 'American Idol,'" *New York Times*, March 27, 2005, Section 2, p. 9. On how musicals are "open" and change with different casts, see Bruce Kirle, *Unfinished Show Business: Broadway Musicals as Works-in-Progress* (Carbondale: Southern Illinois University Press, 2006).
6. While *Wicked* needs an enormous number of spectators for such massive success, its audience is decidedly gendered. A casual glance at the audience of any given performance confirms that *Wicked*'s audiences are predominantly women and girls, many of whom attend in groups. A 2005 study found that 63 percent of Broadway's audience were women, and that the average Broadway theatregoer was a fifty-two-year-old white woman (Michael Kuchwara, "Broadway Musicals Tapping into the Ticket-buying of Young Women," http://archive.seacoastonline.com/2005news/02202005/accent/65698.htm [accessed August 7, 2010]). Statistics are from the League of American Theatres and Producers. A Broadway musical's success, then, depends in no

small part on the tastes of women. This is not a new phenomenon; even before statistics demonstrated a female majority in the Broadway audience, the image of the 1950s businessman being forced to see a Broadway musical with his wife occupied a key place in the cultural imagination.

On *Wicked* from the creators' perspective, see Carol de Giere, *Defying Gravity: The Creative Career of Stephen Schwartz from* Godspell *to* Wicked (Milwaukee: Applause), 2008, 271–434.

7. James C. Taylor, "Theatre Review: A '*Wicked*' Remix of Oz," *Los Angeles Times,* June 24, 2005, p. E1.

8. Jason Zinoman, "A Pair of New Witches, Still in Search of the Right Spell," *New York Times,* July 15, 2005, p. E2.

9. McKinley, "For a Fallen Witch," p. B1.

10. Barbara Ehrenreich, Elizabeth Hess, and Gloria Jacobs, "Beatlemania: Girls Just Want to Have Fun," *The Adoring Audience: Fan Culture and Popular Media,* ed. Lisa A. Lewis (New York: Routledge, 1992), 84–106.

11. Gayle Wald, "'I Want It That Way': Teenybopper Music and the Girling of Boy Bands," *Genders* 35 (2002). http://www.genders.org/g35/g35_wald.html (accessed January 3, 2011).

12. On the history of female fans of popular culture, see Lisa A. Lewis, *Gender Politics and MTV: Voicing the Difference* (Philadelphia: Temple University Press, 1990); Georganne Scheiner, *Signifying Female Adolescence: Film Representations and Fans, 1920–1950* (Westport, CT: Praeger, 2000); and Jennifer Fisher, "Experiences and Relationships," *"Nutcracker" Nation: How an Old World Ballet Became a Christmas Tradition in the New World* (New Haven, CT: Yale University Press, 2003), 132–70.

13. Needless to say, "girls," as they appear in this essay, are extremely privileged. If they have seen *Wicked,* someone paid upward of $50 (and more likely, $100) for a ticket for them. If they traveled to see the show, then even more dollars were spent. Girls who participate on the fansites that I cite had access to computers and the knowledge to participate in fansites in 2004–2006. The concerns of adolescent "girls" about which I generalize in this chapter, then, are, of course, overdetermined by class.

14. Between 2004 and 2006, there was another pseudo-fansite that was linked to the musical's own website, www.wickedthemusical.com. At first it seemed to demonstrate the producers' savvy in reaching potential audience members where they live and in capitalizing on spectators' practices by providing a space to express fandom and simultaneously prominently featuring easy links to purchasing tickets, T-shirts, and other souvenirs. On closer examination, though, it wasn't a true fansite. There were fan letters and accolades posted, but a spectator had to send an e-mail to the producers, who decided which letters to post (or who created these fan posts themselves).

15. On girls and the web, see Sharon Mazzarella, ed., *Girl Wide Web: Girls, the Internet, and the Negotiation of Identity* (New York: Peter Lang, 2005); and Rhiannon Bury, *Cyberspaces of Their Own: Female Fandoms Online* (New York: Peter Lang, 2005).

16. On fandom as an active practice, see Cheryl Harris and Alison Alexander, eds., *Theorizing Fandom: Fans, Subculture and Identity* (Cresskill, NJ: Hampton Press, 1998); and Lisa A. Lewis, ed., *The Adoring Audience* (New York: Routledge, 1997).

17. In her lecture "Children, Youth, the Internet, and the Production of Culture," Susannah Stern stressed the value of girls' parsing out the details of a given performance, which hones analytical skills (University of Texas at Austin, April 26, 2006). See also Susannah Stern, "Virtually Speaking: Girls' Self-Disclosure on the WWW," *Women's Studies in Communication* 25.2 (2002): 223–53.

18. When I started this research in fall 2005, fans either had seen the show or owned the cast album. Discussions tended toward accolades, advice for getting tickets, and comparisons of the book and the musical. Between 2005 and 2006, many more people saw *Wicked* all over the country, and many saw it multiple times with different casts. As I perused websites, I was amazed at girls' abilities to analyze moments in the production in rich detail. It took me a while to realize that bootleg clips from a number of productions began circulating on Google and YouTube in 2006, and that girls could watch *Wicked* at home every day. In this way, even girls who hadn't seen the show live could participate in discussions about an actor's performance choices or interpretations. Interestingly, when a girl saw the show live, she still tended to be overwhelmed. While I am pleased that many girls have access to *Wicked* in some form, and no doubt this allows a certain degree of democratization of fandom, I also think that live performance matters. For a history of different modes of spectatorship, see Richard Butsch, *The Making of American Audiences, From Stage to Television, 1750–1990* (New York: Cambridge University Press, 2000).

19. See Matt Hills, *Fan Cultures* (New York: Routledge, 2002). Also, while girls might be lying online about their ages or their affection for the musical or that they are girls and not boys, I'm taking their self-disclosures at face value. While each post is unique, none is unusual in its observations or expressions of attachment, thus trends are observable.

20. Valerie Hey, *The Company She Keeps: An Ethnography of Girls' Friendships* (Philadelphia: Open University Press, 1997), 3.

21. Mark Steyn, *Broadway Babies Say Goodnight: Musicals Then and Now* (New York: Routledge, 1999), 243; and Alexander Doty, *Making Things Perfectly Queer: Interpreting Mass Culture* (Minneapolis: University of Minnesota Press, 1993), 6. Steyn asks, cynically, "How can you have larger-than-life characters with smaller-than-life actresses?" (243).

22. John M. Clum, *Something for the Boys: Musical Theater and Gay Culture* (New York: St. Martin's Press, 1999), 137.

23. Clum, *Something for the Boys*, 137.

24. Brantley, "How Broadway Lost Its Voice," 9.

25. Rohan Preston, "Musical Has a '*Wicked*' Case of Success," *Minneapolis Star Tribune*, July 9, 2006, p. F1.

26. Susan J. Leonardi and Rebecca A. Pope, *The Diva's Mouth: Body, Voice, Prima Donna Politics* (New Brunswick, NJ: Rutgers University Press, 1996), 163, 21, 57, 57.

27. The field of girl studies is growing, as "adolescents" are no longer defined only as boys. Ethnographic studies of girls, friendships, and identity formation include Pam Gilbert and Sandra Taylor, *Fashioning the Feminine: Girls, Popular Culture and Schooling* (North Sydney: Allen and Unwin, 1991); Vivienne Griffiths, *Adolescent Girls and Their Friends: A Feminist Ethnography* (Brookfield, VT: Ashgate, 1995); Lorraine Delia Kenny, *Daughters of Suburbia: Growing Up White, Middle Class, and Female*

(New Brunswick, NJ: Rutgers University Press, 2000); and Hey, *Company She Keeps*. It's important that *Wicked* does not simply present a "girlpower" narrative but embeds more contradictory female characters in a story of lasting friendship. On "girlpower," see Anita Harris, *Future Girl: Young Women in the Twenty-First Century* (New York: Routledge, 2004). Also see Catherine Driscoll, *Girls: Feminine Adolescence in Popular Culture and Cultural Theory* (New York: Columbia University Press, 2002).

28. The girl fans never use the term "diva," but they readily note the characteristics that qualify both protagonists as such. On the diva, also see Wayne Kostenbaum, *The Queen's Throat: Opera, Homosexuality, and the Mystery of Desire* (New York: Random House, 1993).

29. Posting by ChenoAsGlinda, October 31, 2005, http://www.witchesofoz.com/forums/viewtopic.php?t=318. Fans frequently reveal their knowledge about theatre and musicals through references like this one. Other posts ask for explanations of theatre terms, such as the meaning of the "green room." In general, much teaching takes place on the fansites.

30. Jason Mann, "Defying the Diva: Breaking through Queer and Feminist Models for the Musical Theater Heroine in *Wicked*: The Musical," unpublished ms., Northwestern University, March 15, 2004.

31. Posting by ElphieatShiz, February 28, 2004, http://verdigris.proboards19.com/index.cgi?board=general&action=display&thread=1078003861&;page=1.

32. Posting by Elphie, March 2, 2004, http://verdigris.proboards19.com/index.cgi?board=general&action=display&thread=1078003861&;page=1.

33. Posting by gypsy, March 2, 2004, http://verdigris.proboards19.com/index.cgi?board=general&action=display&thread=1078003861&;page=1.

34. Posting by ChancetoFly, March 2, 2004, http://verdigris.proboards19.com/index.cgi?board=general&action=display&thread=1078003861&;page=1.

35. These songs echo the two character-defining and defending songs in *Funny Girl*, "I'm the Greatest Star" and "Don't Rain on My Parade." In each pair, the second song contains musical phrases of the earlier one.

36. Posting by Valjean_Jean24601, June 12, 2006, http://www.musicals.net/forums/viewtopic.php?t=49555&;sid=c4c1cc7066022f32e4163b6f8b8db8ed.

37. Posting by Emeraldgreen, July 4, 2006, http://www.witchesofoz.com/forums/viewtopic.php?t=11577.

38. Posting by Green.bubbles, July 5, 2006, http://www.witchesofoz.com/forums/viewtopic.php?t=11577.

39. Posting by DareToDefy, July 5, 2006, http://www.witchesofoz.com/forums/viewtopic.php?t=11577.

40. Posting by pianist391, July 5, 2006, http://www.witchesofoz.com/forums/viewtopic.php?t=11577.

41. Posting by Guest, July 9, 2006, http://www.witchesofoz.com/forums/viewtopic.php?t=11767.

42. Posting by Eileeno671, July 10, 2006, http://www.witchesofoz.com/forums/viewtopic.php?t=11767.

43. Posting by Krimz, July 10, 2006, http://www.witchesofoz.com/forums/viewtopic.php?t=11767.

44. Posting by Pseudomaunt, July 11, 2006, http://www.witchesofoz.com/forums/viewtopic.php?t=11771.

45. Posting by Wicked4Ever, July 13, 2006, http://www.witchesofoz.com/forums/viewtopic.php?t=11771.

46. In *Star Gazing,* Jackie Stacey finds that "the recognition of a potential self in the fictionalized situation" is operating (129), but I think this practice happens less with *Wicked,* since the situations are in a fantasy world. Rather, girls extrapolate the emotional substance of the situation and then imagine themselves in the (emotional, relational, performative) scene. Jackie Stacey, *Star Gazing: Hollywood Cinema and Female Spectatorship* (New York: Routledge, 1994).

47. Stacey bases her schema on the work of Andrew Tudor (*Star Gazing,* 136). Although her fans are adults who articulate their fandom through somewhat distanced memories, Stacey's book introduces a number of helpful paradigms through which to consider female fans of women. Analyzing the comments of her fans and how they describe their fandom, she delineates the practices of devotion, worship, adoration, transcendence, aspiration and inspiration, pretending, resembling, imitating, and copying (126–75).

48. Stacey, *Star Gazing,* 128.

49. Posting by lizziemae7, April 30, 2006, http://verdigris.proboards19.com/index.cgi?board=general&action=display&thread=108609691.

50. Posting by DramaRobin 2002, May 1, 2006, http://www.musicals.net/forums/viewtopic.php?t=48550.

51. Posting by galinda724, June 19, 2004, http://verdigris.proboards19.com/index.cgi?board=general&action=display&thread=1086096940.

52. Gilbert and Taylor, *Fashioning the Feminine,* 69.

53. In some contemporary representations of strong women, however, the protagonist does have friends or a community or a cohort. See for example, Sherrie A. Inness, "Introduction: 'Boxing Gloves and Bustiers': New Images of Tough Women," *Action Chicks: New Images of Tough Women in Popular Culture* (New York: Palgrave, 2004), 1–15; and Eric Freeman, "Television, Horror and Everyday Life in *Buffy the Vampire Slayer,*" *The Contemporary Television Series,* ed. Michael Hammond and Lucy Mazdon (Edinburgh: Edinburgh University Press, 2005), 158–80.

54. Posting by dramaqueen25, June 1, 2004, http://verdigris.proboards19.com/index.cgi?board=general&action=display&;thread=1086096940.

55. Posting by Wickedelphie1121, January 21, 2005, http://verdigris.proboards19.com/index.cgi?board=general&action=display&;thread=1086096940.

56. Posting by theatreangel, December 10, 2004, http://verdigris.proboards19.com/index.cgi?board=general&action=display&;thread=1086096940.

57. Posting by Nancy, May 2, 2004, http://verdigris.proboards19.com/index.cgi?board=general&action=display&;thread=1078602508.

58. Posting by Elphie, May 11, 2004, http://verdigris.proboards19.com/index.cgi?board=general&action=display&;thread=1078602508.

59. Posting by DefyingGravlty, January 30, 2005, http://verdigris.proboards19.com/index.cgi?board=general&action=display&;thread=1078602508.

60. Posting by writteninveggies, 17-5-2006, http://unexamined-life.com/forum/viewthread.php?fid=9&tid=1043&;action=printable.

61. Terry Castle, *The Apparitional Lesbian: Female Homosexuality and Modern Culture* (New York: Columbia University Press, 1993), 202.

62. Stacey, *Star Gazing*, 145.

63. Posting by AnaElphieLove, April 12, 2006, http://www.witchesofoz.com/forums/viewtopic.php?t=7353.

64. As Mary Kearney writes, "Considerable feminist research has shown that around the age of twelve, and often earlier, girls are encouraged by a variety of individuals and social institutions to privilege the traditional practices of femininity over all other activities available to them. Moreover, studies show that female youth of this age are encouraged to identify as heterosexual beings and to position procreation and the attraction of male attention as the primary goals of their adult lives" (5). Mary Celeste Kearney, *Girls Make Media* (New York: Routledge, 2006).

65. In addition, these stories are often contextualized within the story of a girl's trip to New York City. Susan Bennett argues that theatre scholars need to attend to the tourist audience to truly understand contemporary commercial theatre. See Susan Bennett, "Theatre/Tourism," *Theatre Journal* 57 (2005): 407–25.

66. Richard Schechner, *Performance Theory* (New York: Routledge, 2003), 118.

67. Dyer, *Heavenly Bodies*, 11.

68. Posting by writteninveggies, May 17, 2006, http://unexamined-life.com/forum/viewthread.php?fid=9&tid=1043&;action=printable.

69. Posting by BelleOfTheBand, April 16, 2006, http://www.witchesofoz.com/forums/viewtopic.php?t=7641.

70. Stacey, *Star Gazing*, 69.

71. Posting by BelleOfTheBand, April 16, 2006, http://www.witchesofoz.com/forums/viewtopic.php?t=7641.

72. Stacey, *Star Gazing*, 159–70.

73. Posting by zonny88, April 15, 2005, http://theater2.nytimes.com/rnr/theater/rnr_read.html?id=1077011420441&fid=.f5616f6&sort=newest&;oref=login.

74. Posting by DefyingGrav1ty, January 30, 2005, http://verdigris.proboards19.com/index.cgi?board=general&action=display&;thread=1078602508.

75. The show's producers took advantage of fans' desire to perform by organizing singing contests, called "*Wicked* Day," where the winners got free tickets to the show. However empowering the use of *Wicked* is for girl fans, it certainly in no way critiques the workings of capitalism, or even how girls' subjectivities are commodified by way of their fandom. See Maurya Wickstrom, *Performing Consumers: Global Capitalism and Its Theatrical Seductions* (New York: Routledge, 2006).

76. Posting by RemedialSweetSap, April 29, 2006, http://www.musicals.net/forums/viewtopic.php?t=48550.

77. Posting by DramaRobin 2002, April 17, 2006, http://www.musicals.net/forums/viewtopic.php?t=48294.

78. Posting by DefyingGrav1ty, January 30, 2005, http://verdigris.proboards19.com/index.cgi?board=general&action=display&;thread=1078602508.

79. Castle, *Apparitional Lesbian*, 235. Italics in original.

80. Leonardi and Pope, *The Diva's Mouth*, 185.

81. To historicize: In 1916, according to Shelley Stamp, *McClure's* magazine advised treating the "infatuation" of a "stagestruck girl" with "'tender tolerance,' since it was a passing phase that 'amounted only to a disease which every girl had in the course of evolution, like croup or the measles'" (37). Shelley Stamp, *Movie-Struck Girls:*

Women and Motion Picture Culture after the Nickelodeon (Princeton, NJ: Princeton University Press, 2000). For other historical studies of girls, see Kelly Shrum, *Some Wore Bobby Sox: The Emergence of Teenage Girls' Culture, 1920–1945* (New York: Palgrave Macmillan, 2004); and Sherrie A. Inness, ed., *Delinquents and Debutantes: Twentieth-Century American Girls' Cultures* (New York: New York University Press, 1998).

82. Judith Halberstam, *In a Queer Time and Place: Transgender Bodies, Subcultural Lives* (New York: New York University Press, 2005), 177, 179.

83. Harris, *Future Girl*, 162.

Epilogue

1. See http://www.nymf.org/ (accessed January 16, 2011).

2. See, for example, Mickey Rapkin, *Theater Geek: The Real Life Drama of a Summer at Stagedoor Manor, the Famous Performing Arts Camp* (New York: Free Press, 2010).

3. Qtd. in http://artsbeat.blogs.nytimes.com/2011/01/10/stritch-and-miranda-get-last-laughs-at-finales-of-night-music-and-in-the-heights/ (accessed January 14, 2011).

4. Rapkin points out that new media put even more pressure on young actors who are trying to "break in" because their performances are instantly available on YouTube. See Rapkin, *Theater Geek*, 168–70.

5. In December 2010, Andrew Lloyd Webber announced plans for a new revival/re-visal of *The Wizard of Oz*, having cast Dorothy and the Wizard via reality television. Dave Itzkoff, "ArtsBeat Blog: The Man Behind the Curtain: Lloyd Webber Plans Changes to 'Wizard of Oz,'" *New York Times*, December 28, 2010, p. C3.

6. David Kamp, "The Glee Generation," *New York Times*, June 13, 2010, p. ST2. Also see Frank Rich, "Two Weddings, a Divorce and 'Glee,'" *New York Times*, June 13, 2010, p. WK10.

7. See, for example, http://jazztimes.com/articles/26514-the-glee-effect (accessed January 17, 2011).

8. Kamp, "The Glee Generation," p. ST2.

9. Kamp, "The Glee Generation," p. ST2.

10. With music by Duncan Sheik, book and lyrics by Steven Sater, directed by Michael Mayer, and choreographed by Bill T. Jones, *Spring Awakening* won eight Tony Awards (2007), including Best Musical. It opened on December 10, 2006, ran on Broadway for 859 performances, and was on national tour (as of 2011).

11. Like *Wicked*, *Spring Awakening* triangulates its three main characters. If Elphaba and Glinda form the main couple in *Wicked*, with Fiyero offering a heterosexual diversion, Melchior and Moritz are the emotional team in *Spring Awakening*. And yet, because Melchior and Wendla's love/sex scene and touching duet takes place at the end of act 1, this musical conveys its heterosexual purpose a bit more forcibly than does *Wicked*.

12. Ben Brantley, "'Idiot' Welcomes Back a Bad Influence," *New York Times*, January 10, 2011, p. C7.

13. Brantley, "'Idiot' Welcomes Back a Bad Influence," p. C7.

14. David Yazbek, "Music Notes: Q & A with David Yazbek," *Lincoln Center Theater Review* 53, Fall 2010, p. 22.

15. John Schaefer, "Women on the Verge of Song," *Lincoln Center Theater Review* 53 (Fall 2010): 8.

16. Schaefer, "Women on the Verge of Song," 10.

17. Qtd. in Stuart Miller, "Back to Broadway (with a *Breakdown*)," *Playbill*, December 2010, p.10.

18. See Jill Dolan, *Utopia in Performance: Finding Hope at the Theater* (Ann Arbor: University of Michigan Press, 2005).

SELECTED BIBLIOGRAPHY

Abbate, Carolyn. "Opera; or, the Envoicing of Women." *Musicology and Difference: Gender and Sexuality in Music Scholarship*. Ed. Ruth A. Solie. Berkeley: University of California Press, 1993. 225–58.

Abbate, Carolyn. *Unsung Voices: Opera and Musical Narrative in the Nineteenth Century*. Princeton, NJ: Princeton University Press, 1991.

Adler, Steven. *On Broadway: Art and Commerce on the Great White Way*. Carbondale: Southern Illinois University Press, 2004.

Altman, Rick. *The American Film Musical*. Bloomington: Indiana University Press, 1987.

Banes, Sally. *Dancing Women: Female Bodies on Stage*. New York: Routledge, 1998.

Banfield, Stephen. "Bit by Bit: Stephen Banfield Finds Five Ways of Looking at Musicals." *Musical Times* (April 1994): 220–23.

Banfield, Stephen. *Sondheim's Broadway Musicals*. Ann Arbor: University of Michigan Press, 1993.

Baugh, Christopher. *Theatre, Performance, and Technology: The Development of Scenography in the Twentieth Century*. New York: Palgrave Macmillan, 2005.

Bennett, Susan. "Theatre/Tourism." *Theatre Journal* 57 (2005): 407–28.

Bennett, Susan. *Theatre Audiences*. New York: Routledge, 1990.

Berkowitz, Gerald M. *New Broadways: Theatre across America, Approaching a New Millennium*. Rev. ed. New York: Applause, 1997.

Block, Geoffrey. *Enchanted Evenings: The Broadway Musical from* Show Boat *to Sondheim and Lloyd Webber*. 2nd ed. New York: Oxford University Press, 2009.

Bourdieu, Pierre. *Distinction: A Social Critique of the Judgment of Taste*. Trans. Richard Nice. Cambridge, MA: Harvard University Press, 1984.

Brett, Philip, Elizabeth Wood, and Gary C. Thomas, eds. *Queering the Pitch: The New Gay and Lesbian Musicology*. New York: Routledge, 1994.

Burston, Jonathan. "Enter, Stage Right: Neoconservatism, English Canada, and the Megamusical." *Soundings* 5 (Winter 1997): 179–90.

Burston, Jonathan. *The Megamusical: New Forms and Relations in Global Cultural Production*. Diss., University of London, 1998.

Burston, Jonathan. "Recombinant Broadway." *Continuum: Journal of Media and Cultural Studies* 23.2 (2009): 159–69.

Burston, Jonathan. "Spectacle, Synergy and Megamusicals: The Global-Industrialisation of Live-Theatrical Production." *Media Organisations in Society.* Ed. James Curran. London: Arnold, 2000. 69–81.

Burston, Jonathan. "Theatre Space as Virtual Place: Audio Technology, the Reconfigured Singing Body and the Megamusical." *Popular Music* 17.2 (1998): 205–18.

Castro, Ginette. *American Feminism: A Contemporary History.* Trans. Elizabeth Loverde-Bagwell. New York: New York University Press, 1990.

Chafe, William. *The Unfinished Journey: America since World War II.* New York: Oxford University Press, 1986.

Clum, John M. *Something for the Boys: Musical Theater and Gay Culture.* New York: St. Martin's Press, 1999.

Coleman, Bud, and Judith Sebesta, eds. *Women in American Musical Theatre: Essays on Composers, Lyricists, Librettists, Arrangers, Choreographers, Designers, Directors, Producers and Performance Artists.* Jefferson, NC: McFarland, 2008.

Delameter, Jerome. *Dance in the Hollywood Musical.* Ann Arbor: UMI Research Press, 1981.

Dolan, Jill. *Utopia in Performance: Finding Hope at the Theater.* Ann Arbor: University of Michigan Press, 2005.

Doty, Alexander. *Making Things Perfectly Queer: Interpreting Mass Culture.* Minneapolis: University of Minnesota Press, 1993.

Douglas, Susan J. *Where the Girls Are: Growing Up Female with the Mass Media.* New York: Random House, 1994.

Dyer, Richard. *Heavenly Bodies: Film Stars and Society.* London: Macmillan, 1986.

Dyer, Richard. *The Matter of Images: Essays on Representations.* New York: Routledge, 1993.

Dyer, Richard. *Only Entertainment.* New York: Routledge, 1992.

Engel, Lehman, and Howard Kissel. *Words with Music: Creating the Broadway Musical Libretto.* (Engel 1972) Rev. ed. New York: Applause, 2006.

Evans, Sara M. *Born for Liberty: A History of Women in America.* New York: Macmillan, 1989.

Ewen, David. *The New Complete Book of the American Musical Theater.* New York: Holt, Rinehart and Winston, 1970.

Felder, Deborah G. *A Century of Women: The Most Influential Events in Twentieth-Century Women's History.* Secaucus, NJ: Carol, 1999.

Frith, Simon. *Taking Popular Music Seriously: Selected Essays.* Burlington, VT: Ashgate, 2007.

Gerhard, Jane. *Desiring Revolution: Second-Wave Feminism and the Rewriting of American Sexual Thoughts, 1920 to 1982.* New York: Columbia University Press, 2001.

Goldman, William. *The Season: A Candid Look at Broadway.* 3rd ed. New York: Limelight Editions, 1998.

Grant, Mark N. *The Rise and Fall of the Broadway Musical.* Boston: Northeastern University Press, 2004.

Guernsey, Otis L. *Curtain Times: The New York Theater: 1965–1986.* New York: Hal Leonard, 1987.

Hirsch, Foster. *Harold Prince and the American Musical Theatre.* New York: Applause, 1989.

Jones, John Bush. *Our Musicals, Ourselves: A Social History of the American Musical Theatre.* Hanover, NH: Brandeis University Press, 2003.

Kirle, Bruce. *Unfinished Show Business: Broadway Musicals as Works-in-Progress.* Carbondale: Southern Illinois University Press, 2005.

Kislan, Richard, *Hoofing on Broadway: A History of Show Dancing.* New York: Prentice Hall, 1987.

Knapp, Raymond. *The American Musical and the Formation of National Identity.* Princeton, NJ: Princeton University Press, 2005.

Knapp, Raymond. *The American Musical and the Performance of Personal Identity.* Princeton: Princeton University Press, 2006.

Knapp, Raymond, Mitchell Morris, and Stacy Wolf, eds. *Oxford Handbook of the American Musical.* New York: Oxford University Press, 2011.

Lawson-Peebles, Robert, ed. *Approaches to the American Musical.* Exeter: Exeter University Press, 1996.

Litton, Glenn. "Musical Comedy in America: From *The King and I* to *Sweeney Todd.*" *Musical Comedy in America.* New York: Theatre Arts, 1981. 205–348.

Lundskaer-Nielsen, Miranda. *Directors and the New Musical Drama: British and American Musical Theater in the 1980s and 90s.* New York: Palgrave Macmillan, 2008.

Malone, Jacqui. *Steppin' on the Blues: The Visible Rhythms of African American Dance.* Urbana: University of Illinois Press, 1996.

Mast, Gerald. *Can't Help Singin': The American Musical on Stage and Screen.* Woodstock, NY: Overlook, 1987.

McClary, Susan. *Conventional Wisdom: The Content of Musical Form.* Berkeley: University of California Press, 2000.

McClary, Susan. *Feminine Endings: Music, Gender, and Sexuality.* Minneapolis: University of Minnesota Press, 1991.

McConachie, Bruce. *American Theater in the Culture of the Cold War: Producing and Contesting Containment, 1947–1962.* Iowa City: University of Iowa Press, 2003.

McMillin, Scott. *The Musical as Drama.* Princeton, NJ: Princeton University Press, 2006.

Miller, D. A. *Place for Us: Essay on the Broadway Musical.* Cambridge, MA: Harvard University Press, 1998.

Miller, Scott. *From Assassins to West Side Story: The Director's Guide to Musical Theatre.* Portsmouth, NH: Heinemann, 1996.

Miller, Simon. "Towards a Hermeneutics of Music." *The Last Post: Music after Modernism.* Ed. Simon Miller. New York: Manchester University Press, 1993, 5–26.

Mordden, Ethan. *Beautiful Mornin': The Broadway Musical in the 1940s.* New York: Oxford University Press, 1999.

Mordden, Ethan. *Better Foot Forward.* New York: Grossman, 1976.

Mordden, Ethan. *Broadway Babies: The People Who Made the American Musical.* New York: Oxford University Press, 1983.

Mordden, Ethan. *Coming Up Roses: The Broadway Musical in the 1950s.* New York: Oxford University Press, 1998.

Mordden, Ethan. *The Happiest Corpse I've Ever Seen: The Last Twenty-Five Years of the Broadway Musical.* New York: Palgrave Macmillan, 2004.

Mordden, Ethan. *Open a New Window: The Broadway Musical in the 1960s.* New York: Palgrave, 2001.

Most, Andrea. *Making Americans: Jews and the Broadway Musical.* Cambridge, MA: Harvard University Press, 2004.

Most, Andrea. "'We Know We Belong to the Land': The Theatricality of Assimilation in Rodgers and Hammerstein's *Oklahoma!*" *PMLA* 113.1 (1998): 77–89.

Most, Andrea. "'You've Got to Be Carefully Taught': The Politics of Race in Rodgers and Hammerstein's *South Pacific*." *Theatre Journal* 52 (2000): 307–37.

Román, David. *Performance in America: Contemporary U.S. Culture and the Performing Arts.* Durham, NC: Duke University Press, 2005.

Rosen, Ruth. *The World Split Open: How the Modern Women's Movement Changed America.* New York: Viking, 2000.

Sandoval-Sánchez, Alberto. *José, Can You See? Latinos On and Off Broadway.* Madison: University of Wisconsin Press, 1999.

Savran, David. "Middlebrow Anxiety." *A Queer Sort of Materialism: Recontextualizing American Theater.* Ann Arbor: University of Michigan Press, 2003. 3–55.

Savran, David. "Toward a Historiography of the Popular." *Theatre Survey* 45.2 (2004): 211–17.

Show Business: The Road to Broadway. Dir. Dori Bernstein. DVD. Regent, Liberation, Dramatic Forces, 2007.

Singer, Barry. *Ever After: The Last Years of Musical Theatre and Beyond.* New York: Applause, 2004.

Stacey, Jackie. *Star Gazing: Hollywood Cinema and Female Spectatorship.* New York: Routledge, 1994.

Sternfeld, Jessica. *The Megamusical.* Bloomington: Indiana University Press, 2006.

Steyn, Mark. *Broadway Babies Say Goodnight: Musicals Then and Now.* New York: Routledge, 1999.

Swain, Joseph P. *The Broadway Musical: A Critical and Musical Survey.* 2nd ed. Lanham, MD: Scarecrow, 2002.

Walsh, David, and Len Platt. *Musical Theater and American Culture.* Westport, CT: Praeger, 2003.

Wolf, Stacy. "The 2003–2004 Season and Broadway Musical Theatre as a Political Conversant." *Patriotic Dissent: Staging Political Protest since 9/11.* Ed. Jenny Spencer. New York: Routledge, forthcoming.

Wolf, Stacy. "Gender and Sexuality in Musical Theatre." *Oxford Handbook of the American Musical.* Ed. Raymond Knapp, Mitchell Morris, and Stacy Wolf. Oxford University Press, 2011.

Wolf, Stacy. "In Defense of Pleasure: Musical Theatre History in the Liberal Arts [A Manifesto]." *Theatre Topics* 17.1 (2007): 51–60.

Wolf, Stacy. "Keeping *Company* with Sondheim's Women." *Oxford Handbook of Sondheim Studies.* Ed. Robert Gordon. New York: Oxford University Press, forthcoming.

Wolf, Stacy. *A Problem Like Maria: Gender and Sexuality in the American Musical.* Ann Arbor: University of Michigan Press, 2002.

Woll, Allen. *Black Musical Theatre: From* Coontown *to* Dreamgirls. New York: Da Capo Press, 1989.

Wollman, Elizabeth L. "The Economic Development of the 'New' Times Square and Its Impact on the Broadway Musical." *American Music* 20.4 (2002): 445–65.

Wollman, Elizabeth L. *The Theater Will Rock: A History of the Rock Musical from* Hair *to* Hedwig. Ann Arbor: University of Michigan Press, 2006.

INDEX